ALCOHOL
AND
DRUG ABUSE
HANDBOOK

ALCOHOL
AND
DRUG ABUSE
HANDBOOK

Co–edited by

ROLAND E. HERRINGTON, M.D.

GEORGE R. JACOBSON, Ph.D.

DAVID G. BENZER, D.O.

with 15 contributors

WARREN H. GREEN, INC.
St. Louis, Missouri, U.S.A.

Published by

WARREN H. GREEN, INC.
8356 Olive Boulevard
St. Louis, Missouri 63132, U.S.A.

© 1987 by **WARREN H. GREEN, INC.**

ISBN No. 0-87527-274-6

Third printing, 1990

Printed in the United States of America

This book is dedicated to all health professionals who make possible a true multidisciplinary treatment of the diseases of chemical dependency and related disorders.

About the Authors

Ashok R. Bedi, M.D., is currently Associate Clinical Professor, Department of Psychiatry and Mental Health Sciences, Medical College of Wisconsin; Attending Psychiatrist, and Clinical Director, Milwaukee Psychiatric Hospital; and Psychiatric Consultant, Chemical Dependency Division, Milwaukee Psychiatric Hospital. He is a Diplomate in Psychiatry (American Board of Psychiatry and Neurology), and Psychological Medicine (Royal College of Physicians and Surgeons, UK), and a Member of the Royal College of Psychiatrists (UK). His principal publications are on alcoholism, depression, and other aspects of psychiatry.

David G. Benzer, D.O., is currently Medical Director, McBride Center for the Impaired Professional, Milwaukee Psychiatric Hospital; Attending Addictionologist, Alcohol and Drug Treatment Center, St. Michael Hospital; and Consulting Physician in Addictive Diseases at three Milwaukee–area hospitals. He is certified in alcoholism and drug dependence by the California Society for Treatment of Alcoholism and Other Drug Dependencies. His publications, presentations, and teaching/supervision responsibilities have consistently focused on the diagnosis and treatment of substance use disorders.

Donald E. Busboom, B.A., M.Div., is Director of the Pastoral Care Department at De Paul Rehabilitation Hospital. He has also been Consulting Chaplain at three affiliated alcoholism treatment facilities, and for ten years was Senior Pastor at Gloria Dei Lutheran Church in Minneapolis, Minnesota. His clinical experience includes conducting therapy groups for outpatients and couples, and his teaching/supervision responsibilities include the training of clergy and alcohol and drug abuse counselors.

Paul Cushman, Jr., M.D., is currently an Associate Professor in the Departments of Medicine, Pharmacology and Toxicology, and Psychiatry, Medical College of Virginia; and Director of the Alcohol and Drug Dependency Treatment Program, McGuire

Veterans Administration Medical Center, Richmond, Virginia. Previously he was an Associate Professor in the Departments of Medicine, Pharmacology, and Psychiatry, Medical College of Wisconsin; and Assistant Professor of Medicine, Columbia University. He is a Fellow of the American College of Physicians, and the American Society of Clinical Pharmacology and Therapeutics, received a Career Teacher Award from the National Institute on Alcohol Abuse and Alcoholism and the National Institute on Mental Health, and has authored more than 100 publicatons on endocrinology, pharmacology, and substance use disorders.

Mark E. Daley, B.S., M.S.N., is currently the Chief Operating Officer of the Wisconsin Health Organization, a health maintenance organization. In the past he has been President of Health Plus, a health maintenance organization; Vice President for Program Development at St. Anthony Hospital; Director of Satellite Operations and Contract Services for De Paul Rehabilitation Hospital; Director of the substance abuse/chemical dependency programs at St. Alphonsus Hospital; and Director of Nursing at De Paul Rehabilitation Hospital.

James A. Halikas, M.D., is currently Professor of Psychiatry, and Director of Residency Training in Psychiatry, University of Minnesota Medical School, and Co-Director of the University Chemical Dependency Treatment Program. Previously, he was Director of Research and Education in Chemical Dependency, Milwaukee County Mental Health Complex; Director of the Wisconsin Alcoholism and Drug Abuse Research Institute; Associate Professor, Department of Psychiatry and Mental Health Sciences, and Director of the Division of Alcoholism and Chemical Dependency, Medical College of Wisconsin. He is Board-certified in psychiatry (American Board of Psychiatry and Neurology), is a Fellow of the American Psychiatric Association, held a Career Teacher Award from the Nationsl Institute on Mental Health in alcoholism and drug abuse, and has co-authored approximately four dozen publications on various aspects of substance use disorders.

Roland E. Herrington, M.D., is currently Director of the Division of Chemical Dependency, and Director of the McBride Center for the Impaired Professional, at Milwaukee Psychiatric Hospital; Assistant Clinical Professor in the Department of Psychiatry and Mental Health Sciences, Medical College of Wisconsin; and Chairman of the Wisconsin State Medical Society's Committee on Alcoholism and Other Drug Abuse. In addition, he is Vice-Chairman of the Milwaukee County Medical Society's Impaired Physician Committee; Midwest Regional Director of the American Medical Society on Alcoholism and Other Drug Dependencies; and a member of the Board of Directors of the American Academy of Addictionology. He is certified by the California Society for the Treatment of Alcoholism and Other Drug Dependencies. In the past, Dr. Herrington was Medical Director of the Kettle Moraine Treatment Center; Director of the Milwaukee County Mental Health Complex Alcoholism Treatment Unit; and Medical Director, and Corporate Medical Director, of De Paul Rehabilitation Hospital. Dr. Herrington's recent publications and lectures have focused on the treatment of impaired physicians and other professionals.

George R. Jacobson, Ph.D., is currently the Director of Research, Medical Education, and Counselor Training Programs, at De Paul Rehabilitation Hospital; Associate Professor of Psychiatry, and Director of the Alcoholism and Chemical Dependency Division, Department of Psychiatry and Mental Health Sciences, Medical College of Wisconsin; Clinical Associate Professor, Department of Psychology, University of Wisconsin-Milwaukee; and Director of the Wisconsin Center for the Study of Addictive Disorders. He previously taught at Rush-Presbyterian-St. Luke's Medical Center (Chicago, Illinois), and was a psychologist at Chicago's Alcoholism Treatment Center. He has written and/or edited approximately 50 articles, chapters, monographs, and books on various aspects of substance use disorders and other topics in mental health and human behavior, and is a Wisconsin-licensed psychologist, maintaining a part-time private practice in the Milwaukee area.

Jess Johnson, PA-C, is a Physician Assistant at De Paul Rehabilitation Hospital. He is certified in Wisconsin, and is a member of the Wisconsin Academy of Physician Assistants. Earlier in his career he was a line corpsman and hospital corpsman with the U.S. Marines in Vietnam. Currently his major clinical interests are child and adolescent substance abusers, and the use of CT scans in diagnosing organic brain disorders among adult alcoholics.

Robert F. Lipo, M.D., is currently the Chief Executive Officer and Director of Laboratories of Chem-Bio Corporation, a regional laboratory. He is certified in Anatomic and Clinical Pathology by the American Board of Pathology. He is a Fellow of the College of American Pathologists and the American Society of Clinical Pathologists. He is a Clinical Assistant Professor of Pathology, Medical College of Wisconsin; and Associate Clinical Professor, School of Allied Health, University of Wisconsin–Milwaukee.

A. Bela Maroti, B.A., M.B.A., is the founder (1958) and President of De Paul Rehabilitation Hospital, and co–founder and Chairman of the Wisconsin Alcohol and Drug Abuse Research Institute. He was also co–founder and first President of Family Health Plan, Inc.; Chairman of the Board, Madison Family Institute — De Paul Health Systems, Inc.; and a member of the Board of Directors, Behavioral Health Systens, Inc. He has also served on the Board of Directors and chaired a variety of committees of the Alcohol and Drug Abuse Problems Association of North America, American College of Addiction Treatment Administrators, International Council on Alcohol and the Addictions, National Association of Rehabilitation Facilities, and the Hospital Council of Greater Milwaukee. He has been an advisor to the State of Wisconsin Department of Health and Social Services, is currently a member of the Wisconsin Citizens Council on Alcoholism and Drug abuse, and has written and spoken on various aspects of health care planning, finance, and administration.

Mary Nold-Klett, PA-C, is currently a Physician Assistant employed by Herbert C. White, D.O., Medical Director of the Alcoholism Treatment Program at Elmbrook Memorial Hospital, Brookfield, Wisconsin. Previously she worked at De Paul Rehabilitation Hospital in Milwaukee as a Physician Assistant. She is certified by the National Commission on the Certification of Physician Assistants, licensed by the State of Wisconsin, and a member of the Wisconsin Academy of Physician Assistants.

Alan A. Wartenberg, M.D., is currently the Medical Coordinator of the Alcohol Dependency Treatment Program at the Veterans Administration Medical Center, Providence, Rhode Island; and a core faculty member of the Brown University Center for Alcohol Studies. He is certified by the American Board of Internal Medicine. Earlier he was Assistant Medical Director, and Director of Medical Education, at De Paul Rehabilitation Hospital; a faculty member in the Departments of Medicine and Preventive Medicine, at the Medical College of Wisconsin; and a staff member of four Milwaukee-area hospitals. He held a Career Teacher Grant from the National Institute on Drug Abuse, and his teaching, speaking, and research and clinical publications have focused primarily on medical aspects of substance use disorders.

Ronald A. Weller, M.D., is currently Professor of Psychiatry, and Director of Psychiatric Education and Training, Ohio State University Hospitals, Columbus, Ohio. Earlier, he was Associate Professor of Psychiatry, and Director of the Psychiatric Emergency Services, University of Kansas Medical Center; Supervising Psychiatrist at the Malcolm Bliss Mental Health Center, St. Louis, Missouri; and Director of the Marijuana Research Project, Department of Psychiatry, Washington University School of Medicine, in St. Louis. He is Board-certified in psychiatry (American Board of Psychiatry and Neurology), and has authored four dozen or so publications on substance abuse and other facets of psychiatry.

Rita M. Wisniewski, B.A., is now the Coordinator of Family Services at De Paul Rehabilitation Hospital. She is also a Certified Alcoholism Counselor, and is a candidate for the MSW degree at the University of Wisconsin-Milwaukee. In the past she has been the Coordinator of Inservice Training, and a Family Therapist, also at De Paul. Her publications, and many of her community activities, focus on the family in health and illness.

Introduction

Authoritative estimates provided by the U.S. government and other sources consistently indicate that during the past decade problems associated with alcohol and other drug abuse have continued to escalate until, today, it is generally acknowledged that these problems represent one of the major threats to the health, welfare, and economy of the country. It now seems that alcohol and other drug abuse, and the myriad personal and social complications associated with it, has pervaded all strata of society and all aspects of life in the U.S.

Consider, for example, that between 9–12 million individuals are directly affected — i.e., they are alcoholics or drug abusers — and that each individual usually affects at least four other persons in some negative, unhealthy, or destructive manner. One out of every three people participating in a recent national survey reported that alcohol or other drugs had caused problems in his or her family. At least 15% of all hospital patients on any given day are being treated for one or more problems or complications that are the direct and/or indirect effects of alcohol or other drugs.

Relatedly, traffic accidents — the single greatest cause of death for people under the age of 35 — were responsible for 49,000 deaths and 150,000 cases of permanent disability in the last year for which we have complete data, and 50% of those were directly attributable to alcohol or some other drugs. During that same year, it was reported that 50% of all the murders in the U.S. involved alcohol or some other drug (i.e., either the murderer, the victim, or both were intoxicated); 80% of those who attempted suicide had been drinking at the time (the suicide rate among alcoholics is approximately 600% greater than among the general population); alcoholics have a life expectancy that is approximately 12 years shorter than that of nonalcoholics; the death rate from accidental falls is 500% higher for alcoholics than for nonalcoholics, and death in fires is 1,000% greater for alcoholics than for the general population as a whole. The incidence of rape, incest, spouse-abuse, child-abuse, and other forms of family violence is higher among alcoholic families. More recently we have learned that alcohol is the single greatest cause of preventable birth defects, and that the sharing of needles among drug abusers is one of the major routes of contagion for AIDS (Acquired Immune Deficiency Syndrome).

Economically, the costs of medical care for alcohol- and other drug-related illnesses and injuries now exceeds $7 billion per year, and another $7 billion is added to the bill for traffic accidents, fires, crimes, and related costs. Absenteeism and lost productivity is calculated to cost the country another $37 billion annually. We are amazed when we see that the total costs associated with alcohol and other drug abuse represent 25% of our current annual national debt! (On the other hand, we are equally amazed by official government estimates that 10% of the drinking population consumes 50% of the alcoholic beverages sold in the U.S.; and that agencies of government collect $17 million *per day* in taxes on alcohol!)

We hope by means of these brief introductory remarks we have conveyed to the reader some sense of the magnitude and diversity of the problems associated with the use and abuse of intoxicating, mood-altering and mind-altering substances. It is indeed that very magnitude and diversity of problems, that sense of being overwhelmed at times, and confused at others, but often hopeful and optimistic as well, that led us to write, organize, and edit this book in the manner we did.

It is our belief, and it has been our consistent experience, that no single health care discipline has been or will be able to fully understand and explain all of the causes, appearances, ramifications, and implications of alcoholism and other drug abuse problems. Consequently, we are convinced that no single health care discipline can effectively treat alcoholism and other drug abuse problems in isolation. While it is generally agreed that alcoholism, for example, is best understood and dealt with in terms of a disease model, it is also generally agreed that a broader definition of disease, beyond its traditional medical connotations, is implied when we speak of such disorders. Hence, it is our conviction, which is reflected in the plan and content of this book, that alcoholism and other drug use disorders should be conceptualized, approached, and treated as *biopsychosocial phenomena.* Thus, our emphasis is on a multidisciplinary team approach to the treatment of all substance use and abuse disorders.

This frame of reference is reflected in the diversity of our selection of authors, and in the range of health care professions to which we have addressed this book. Chapters have been written by physicians — including specialists in addictive disorders, family practice, internal medicine, psychiatry, pathology, and endocrinology — and physicians' assistants, a psychologist, a social worker, a nurse, a family therapist, an alcoholism counselor, health care administrators, and a clergyman. These authors represent a mixture of clinicians, researchers, and administrators; moreover, several of our authors are successfully continuing their own personal recoveries and remain active participants in Alcoholics Anonymous, Narcotics Anonymous, and other self-help groups. The professionals (and students) for whom this book was written include physicians, physicians' assistants, nurses, psychologists, social workers, alcoholism and other drug counselors, dieticians and nutritionists, members of the clery, occupational and activity therapists, rehabilitation counselors and therapists, paramedics, hospital and clinic directors and administrators, community health care planners, and other health care professionals and allied health scientists and support personnel.

Our frame of reference also reflects changes and trends in the planning, organizing, funding, and delivery of health care services in the U.S. Rarely these days does one encounter health care professionals working in isolation. Instead, we are witnessing an unprecedented growth of HMOs (health maintenance organizations), PPOs (preferred provider organizations), EAPs (employee assistance programs), and other associations of health care professionals who are forming a variety of groups to bring better and more cost-effective treatment to more people. It is our position, obviously, that the integration of diverse health care practitioners will help to ensure the multidisciplinary team approach that we consider essential to the most effective and efficient treatment of all substance use disorders.

Another recent and current development, which substantiates and validates our perception of the field and our purpose in writing this book, involves the need for advanced and specialized training. Obviously those of us who have been actively providing health care services to alcoholics and other drug abusers and their families, and teaching others to do so also, have been acutely aware of the need for relevant education, training, and perhaps credentialing and/or certification in a number of allied health professions. During the past 15 or so years, we have seen the Joint Commission on Accreditation of Hospitals (JCAH), the Commission on Accreditation of Rehabilitation Facilities (CARF),

and other accrediting bodies formulating and modifying the standards for delivery of specialized services to substance use disorder
patients. Similarly, during the same period of time we have witnessed the establishment of a National Institute on Alcohol Abuse
and Alcoholism (NIAAA) and a National Institute on Drug Abuse
(NIDA) at the federal government level. At the same time, very
strong voluntary organizations have developed, on a state and
national level, to successfully press for the examination and
credentialing or certification of professional counselors specifically
trained to work with substance abuse patients and their families.
We applaud these efforts, of course, and are especially pleased to
note the emergence of similar developments among other health
care professions. On the West coast, physicians are currently being
certified by the California Society for the Treatment of Alcoholism
and Other Drug Dependencies, and in 1986, for the first time on a
national basis, the American Medical Society on Alcoholism and
Other Drug Dependencies (AMSAODD), will begin administering
specialty-certification examinations to physicians in addictive
diseases. Within the American Psychological Association (APA)
there is a Society of Psychologists in Addictive Behaviors (SPAB);
and a nation-wide effort on a state-by-state basis to certify
alcohol and drug abuse counselors has been underway for a
number of years. These signs of increasing professionalization and
specialization certainly indicate the continuing and growing awareness among health care providers.

Such developments have fueled our optimism and encouraged
us to produce this book. More importantly, however, is the sense
of hopefulness engendered by the observation that as more qualified, well-trained health care personnel bring their various skills
and knowledge to bear on the treatment of alcoholism and other
durg abuse, the greater the opportunity for recovery among our,
and your, patients. Ultimately, that's what this book is all about.

Consequently, this volume approaches the problems of substance use disorders in a manner that is primarily pragmatic rather
than theoretic. Our operating assumption is that our readers
already possess — or can readily obtain elsewhere — fundamental
knowledge about theoretic issues, current controversies, historic
principles, and so on. We have chosen, therefore, a more empirical
and practical approach more appropriate to a handbook for
students and practicing professionals whose needs are determined

by the exigencies of the emergency room, the inpatient unit, the outpatient clinic, the family in crisis, the client in need of advice and information, or the individual or community in need of specialized services.

Finally, a note about the vocabulary used in this book. Generally, all authors of this volume have adhered to the conventions established by the American Psychiatric Association in their *Diagnostic and Statistical Manual of Mental Disorders, Third Edition (DSM-III*, for short). Thus, for example, *substance use disorder* is a new generic term for what used to be commonly called *alcoholism, drug addiction*, and all related disorders. Neither of these common terms appear in official nomenclature; instead *alcohol abuse* and *alcohol dependence* have now replaced the former term. Although it is still acceptable to use the term *alcoholic* to refer to the person, *alcoholism* is no longer used to refer to the disorder(s). Similarly, instead of the generic notion of drug addiction we now refer to *abuse* and *dependence*, with only the latter denoting addiction or physical tolerance, physical dependence, and/or physical withdrawal. Some of our authors use the term *drug abuse* in a generic manner to refer to alcoholism (i.e., alcohol abuse), which is certainly appropriate, given that alcohol is indeed a drug. On the other hand, our authors tend to avoid the generic use of the term *drug addiction* in most cases, since some drugs with a high potential for abuse seem to have little or no potential for addiction, e.g., marijuana. Although this new language may seem somewhat awkward at first, it encourages clearer communication of meaning and greater specificity of diagnosis.

In closing, we are very pleased to acknowledge the special assistance of Ms. Marion Batchelor and Ms. Pat Johnson. It is hardly descriptive of their contributions to refer to these two persons as our respective secretaries; of course they transcribed many hours of our tape-recorded dictation and typed hundreds of pages of manuscript. But they were also our alarm clocks and our calendars, our translaters, our agents and promoters, our mediators, monitors, motivators, and memories. When our energies flagged and our schedules lagged, they had their ways of restoring our interest and attention. Our greatest sense of gratitude, however, is reserved for Mr. Warren H. Green. His unquestioning patience and his unceasing perserverance in the face of innumerable delays and obstacles are truly objects of our respect, admiration, and thanks.

Roland E. Herrington, M.D.
George R. Jacobson, Ph.D.
David G. Benzer, D.O.

Milwaukee, Wisconsin
February 16, 1986

Contents

ALCOHOL
AND
DRUG ABUSE
HANDBOOK

PART 1

SYMPTOMS
AND CONSEQUENCES

Chapter 1

Cannabis Use and Abuse

Ronald Weller, M.D. and James Halikas, M.D.

OVERVIEW

The authors introduce their chapter with a brief history of hemp cultivation around the world over the past four-thousand years, and the uses of its major psychotropic derivative, marijuana. Special attention is paid to the social, cultural, commercial, and legal customs surrounding marijuana use in America, and the changes in patterns of use that have emerged in the past twenty years.

A significant portion of the chapter is then spent in describing the psychoactive properties of the cannabinoids, and the biologic mechanisms of absorption, metabolism, and excretion. The bulk of the chapter describes in detail the positive and negative effects of cannabinoid use on many aspects of psychological and physiological functioning. Particular emphasis is given to the little-known but dramatic major adverse effects, with concrete recommendations to health professionals who may have to treat persons who present with these syndromes.

Growing public concern over chronic marijuana abuse is addressed in a subsequent section which deals with this increasingly important problem. A section on prevention also addresses itself to important social, medical, legal, and educational problems.

A summary and references conclude the chapter.

INTRODUCTION

Marijuana is a word of Spanish/Mexican origin commonly used to denote the hemp plant, *Cannabis sativa*. Although originally used to refer to the dried stems and flowering tops which produced psychoactive effects when ingested, at times it has been used to refer to any psychoactive preparation derived from the plant or to the plant itself. Recently the term cannabis has partially replaced use of the term marijuana. In this chapter the terms will be used interchangeably to denote the plant or its psychoactive preparations.

The cannabis plant has been able to adapt to a broad range of climatic and soil conditions and is grown worldwide. It has been cultivated by man for two basic reasons. The plant produces long, strong fibers used to make rope, and produces a substance which has mind-altering effects when smoked or eaten. Specific strains have been bred to increase the amount of the psychoactive substance or the quality and strength of the fibers, respectively. In general, strains which produce good fiber do not contain high quantities of psychoactive material. At one point, the plant was classified as two different species — *Cannabis americana* (low psychoactive properties) and *Cannabis indica* (high psychoactive properties). Now both are considered one species, *Cannabis sativa.*

Marijuana has been used by mankind as an intoxicant throughout recorded history. Writings from China contain references to it as early as 2000 B.C., as do the early writings of India, Assyria, Persia, and Greece. It is also mentioned in more familiar writings such as the Old Testament and *The Arabian Nights* (1). Its psychoactive properties were well-recognized in the Middle Ages and Renaissance. Soon after discovery and exploration of the New World began, the hemp plant was introduced there. It was probably first brought by the Spanish in the mid-1500s in South America, but may have been present even earlier. The Pilgrims did not have it when they landed at Plymouth Rock, but Virginia settlers were cultivating plants for fiber as early as 1611.

The hemp plant was widely cultivated in the American colonies as a cash crop, and some colonies imposed penalties for not growing it. However, its importance as a crop began to decline after the Civil War. Today, evidence of this early hemp cultivation can still be seen, as the decendants of once cultivated plants now grow wild. Since these plants derived from strains grown primarily for fiber, their psychoactive properties are not great.

In addition to its fiber, hemp was valued for its "medicinal" properties. Patent medicines which were once popular and widely distributed frequently contained marijauna, sometimes in combination with alcohol. It was listed in the *United States Pharmacopia* as Extractum Cannabis from 1850-1942 and was recommended for neuralgia, gout, rheumatism, tetanus, hydrophobia, cholera, convulsions, chorea, hysteria, depression, delirium tremens, insanity, and internal hemorrhage (1). No less an authority than Sir William Osler, first Chairman of the Medicine Department at Johns Hopkins University Medical School and considered the father of modern internal medicine, advocated marijuana as the most effective treatment of migraine headaches. Several pharmaceutical companies marketed over-the-counter extracts, and special marijuana cigarettes were available for the treatment of asthma.

Marijuana was also used as a recreational drug during this period, and its use became glamorized in books and popular magazines. However, recreational use was an isolated phenomenon and occurred primarily among groups of artists and musicians, certain immigrant populations, and a few subcultures in society. It never gained widespread appeal at that time, and its use was ignored by authorities until 1937, when the passage of the Marijuana Tax Act effectively made marijuana an illegal drug. This, coupled with the concurrent passage of state laws prohibiting the use and sale of marijuana, led to a marked drop in marijuana use. This increased regulation came about after the repeal of Prohibition when the government became concerned about controlling use of other drugs. However, very few people were actually arrested for marijuana-related offenses, because use remained relatively infrequent and isolated.

In the mid to late 1960s, marijuana use rose dramatically in virtually every subgroup of society. The sharpest increase was among young people, particularly the 18-25 year age range. In 1979, 68% of all young adults in this age group had tried marijuana, and 35% were currently using the drug. This pattern represented increases from 48% and 35%, respectively, in 1972. Among adults over 26, use increased from 2.5% in 1972 to 6% in 1979. Adolescents and children have shown increased usage patterns. Eight percent of all 12-15 year olds have tried marijuana. The percentage of adolescents between 12 and 17 who currently use marijuana jumped from 7% in 1972 to 17% in 1979. Finally, among some youth, use has become frequent, with 10% of all high school seniors using marijuana (2).

Explanations for this sharp increase were many, and ranged from boredom, to rebellion against society, to a protest against the then-current Vietnam War. Regardless of the causes, increased use led to a tremendous rise in the number of marijuana-related arrests, and generated controversy over the social policy towards marijuana. Much of this controversy still persists, with some groups advocating strict enforcement and strengthening of anti-marijuana laws, and others advocating decriminalization and/or legalization of marijuana.

Increased public awareness led to a desire for more information about the drug, resulting in increased research involving marijuana. Information has been gathered from animal studies, as well as human research. Despite many obstacles to marijuana research (e.g., its illegality, biochemical complexity, and unusual method of ingestion), much has been learned about its acute and chronic effects.

PSYCHOACTIVE PROPERTIES OF MARIJUANA

The psychoactive substance produced by the marijuana or hemp plant is delta-9-tetrahydrocannabinol (Δ-9-THC). Over 430 different organic compounds have been isolated from this plant; of these, at least 61 are cannabinoids and unique to this species (2). Chemically, THC is a cannabinoid. Although cannabinoids other than THC have psychoactive properties, they are present in such small amounts they contribute little to the overall mind-altering effect of marijuana.

There are several different ways in which the psychoactive materials in the Cannabis plant can be harvested and prepared for consumption. The most common preparation, usually called marijuana (tea, reefer, pot, grass, etc.) is the dried flowering tops of the Cannabis plant. Marijuana from plants grown in the United States has a low THC content while that from strains from other countries specifically grown for their psychoactive ingredients has a high THC content. Nicknames such as Colombian, Acapulco Gold, and Panama Red, have been used to denote this more potent marijuana. In recent years the amount of THC in marijuana used in this country has gradually increased. Marijuana now has a THC content of 2% or more (2). As more potent marijuana becomes available there may be an increase in observed effects.

The Cannabis plant secretes a resinous substance from the tops and stems of the plant. When scraped off the plant this resin is called hashish (hash). It is more potent than marijuana, and contains up to 12% THC. A more potent preparation, called hashish oil, is made when the active ingredients of hashish are extracted into an oil. It contains up to 60% THC. Recently, THC has been sold on the street as pure active ingredient. However, the cost of producing pure THC makes it unlikely that it is really contained in these preparations.

ABSORPTION, METABOLISM, AND EXCRETION

Marijuana is usually smoked. The THC is readily absorbed across membranes in the lung, and is transported directly to the heart via the pulmonary vessels. It then passes to the arterial system and is pumped throughout the body and to the brain. Because it does not pass through the liver (the major site of metabolism for THC) when smoked, it achieves a relatively greater effect than other drugs which are ingested orally and pass through the liver prior to circulation throughout the body. THC is not soluble in water and is transported through the blood stream tightly bound to protein. Because it is very soluble in fat, organs with a high fat content, such as the brain, readily absorb the drug. When marijuana is smoked, THC reaches the brain in a matter of seconds, and the onset of effects is very rapid. Effects usually last 2-3 hours but may persist up to 6 hours. After this time period, intoxication effects quickly disappear.

Metabolism of the drug occurs primarily in the liver, and consists mainly of hydroxylation. The major metabolite of THC is 11-hydroxy-delta-9-tetrahydrocannabinol, which is also psychoactive, and is believed to be even more potent than THC. Metabolites are primarily excreted in the bile. However, some are reabsorbed in the intestine and reenter the body (3). What contribution this entero-hepatic circulation of the drug makes to the psychoactive effects of the drug is not clear. Some metabolites appear in the urine, but in small amounts. The concentration of metabolites in the urine does not correlate well with the blood level.

PHYSIOLOGIC AND PSYCHOLOGIC EFFECTS

Systematic studies have documented the effects of marijuana on different body functions. Acutely, marijuana caused an increase in pulse rate and a drop in standing blood pressure. The conjunctiva became injected (bloodshot eyes). There was slight pupillary constriction, and a sharp decrease in intraocular pressure. The electroencephalogram (EEG) showed some characteristic changes, such as a decrease in the amount and frequency of alpha waves, and a decrease in REM (Rapid Eye Movement; that stage of sleep in which dreaming occurs) sleep time. There was decreased flow of saliva, increased body temperature, and decreased skin temperature. In addition, lethargy, slow speech, pallor, sagging of eyelids, nystagmus, and ataxia were all observed during intoxication (4).

Being high, in general, refers to the pleasant or euphoric effects that occur as a result of marijuana use. In a study conducted by the author (JAH), 100 regular users of marijuana were interviewed regarding effects they experienced (5). Over 105 acute intoxication and postintoxication effects were studied. The most common desirable effects subjectively reported included a high, exhilerated feeling; relaxation; peaceful feeling; keener sound sense; heightened sexual feelings; increased sexual arousal; more talkativeness; a floating sensation; more self-confidence; and increased alertness. These are presumably the effects that prompt continuing use of marijuana. Users also reported the common occurrence of such undesirable effects as increased hunger and thirst; dry mouth and throat; alteration of time sense; laughing and giggling; drowsiness; red eyes; and poor concentration. Other undesirable effects reported much less frequently included despondency, derealization, aggressive feelings, crying, hearing voices, suicidal thoughts, and unreasonable fears. However, marijuana use persisted in spite of the occurrence of these adverse effects.

Aftereffects occurring immediately postintoxication have also been studied (5). Commonly reported desirable aftereffects included a feeling of calm, relaxation, a clear mind, and awakening refreshed. Undesirable aftereffects were less common, but included awakening tired, having a foggy mind, feeling restless, anxious, and craving more of the drug. Since aftereffects occur when the amount of drug remaining in the body is very low, how much is physiologic and how much is psychologic, is unclear.

In addition to acute effects, smoking marijuana has some effects that are chronic in nature. Physiologic changes occur not as a result of the psychoactive ingredients, but result from other properties of marijuana and how it is used. These effects occur in organs such as lungs and heart. Marijuana smoke has more "tar" than cigarette smoke. More particulate matter is retained in the lungs from inhaled marijuana smoke than tobacco smoke (2). Because marijuana leads to decreased activity of alevolar macrophages (cells that normally clean such debris from the lungs), chronic use may impair the lungs' defense mechanisms. Worsening of pulmonary function has been noted after 6-8 weeks of smoking marijuana, and obstructive airway disease may develop. Precancerous cellular changes have also been noted in the lungs of chronic users, as well as increased frequency of laryngitis, pharyngitis, bronchitis, asthma-like symptoms, cough, hoarseness, and dry throat (2).

Marijuana smoking also has been found to effect the cardiovascular system. During intoxication the heart rate accelerates up to 160 beats per minute, and there is an orthostatic fall in blood pressure (2). In animals, increased oxygen demand by the myocardium is coupled with decreased delivery of oxygen, leading to an oxygen deficit in the heart. This could theoretically result in angina, and possibly a myocardial infarction (heart attack) in predisposed individuals (2).

In addition, neurological function and higher mental activities can be affected. Marijuana has been reported to impair judgment of time and distance. A slowing of reflexes has been reported during low levels of intoxication, but in more toxic states, hyperreflexia has been seen (2). Although the exact mechanism has not been specified, marijuana use appears to disrupt short-term memory and interfere with learning. Initial studies (2) indicated actual structural changes — atrophy — in brain tissue attributable to chronic use of the drug, although later research using more advanced methods, failed to confirm those findings. Moreover, such impairments in mental functions have not yet been proven to be directly related to morphologic changes. Further research is needed to clarify these particular drug effects.

MAJOR ADVERSE EFFECTS

Up to this point, discussion has focused on the relatively common acute and chronic effects of cannabis use (most often the smoking of marijuana cigarettes). Neither the subjectively and objectively perceived positive effects, nor the usually mild and/or transient negative consequences, are likely to bring users to the attention of allied health professionals (AHP). Of course, there are some circumstances in which cannabinoid users may be indirectly referred to AHPs, such as following a drug-related arrest, or when respiratory diseases require medical attention, or if parents or school authorities suspect that drugs are implicated in behavioral problems or learning disabilities. It is far more likely, however, that some major or dramatic behavioral changes are likely to require intervention and treatment involving AHPs. Several syndromes are identifiable.

One such dramatic consequence of marijuana use is the *panic-anxiety reaction.* Most signs and symptoms of this reaction are distortions or exaggerations of the common but usually mild effects of marijuana including anxiety and fearfulness which then progresses to the point of incapacitating anxiety and panic. Reactions may also consist of other psychological symptoms as apprehensiveness, paranoid thoughts, depersonalization feelings, misperceptions, emotional lability, and groundless fears, such as losing one's mind. The physiologic symptoms of anxiety may also be present: tachycardia, dizziness, hyperactivity, tightening of the chest, smothering sensation, and trembling. Many of these symptoms may have begun as part of the usual pattern of marijuana intoxication. Complete or partial insight into the causes and circumstances may be present, though at times this can be overwhelmed by the panic and fear. Orientation and memory remain intact. This reaction is basically self-limited, lasting from several minutes to several hours, paralleling the duration of marijuana intoxication.

The panic-anxiety reaction is most commonly seen in novice users who are unprepared for the effects of marijuana intoxication. It can also be seen in experienced users who take an unexpectedly potent or high dose of the drug and attain effects beyond their expectations. Also, preexisting psychological difficulties may play a contributing role in this syndrome. Because this reaction is self-limited, treatment should generally be conservative: continued reassurance to the individual that the effects will pass, and placing the patient in a familiar, nonthreatening environment with minimal stimulation, are both helpful. The incidence of this reaction is not known, but its occurrence may decrease as marijuana use becomes more widespread and people are more familiar with its effects.

A more serious reaction is the marijuana- or hashish-induced *acute brain syndrome*, a toxic delirium caused by the ingestion of very large amounts of the drug. The reaction has been classified under a variety of names including *toxic psychosis, marijuana psychosis, hemp psychosis, acute psychotic reaction*, and *acute schizophrenic decompensation* secondary to marijuana. Charac-

teristic features parallel those of other acute organic brain syndromes and include impaired mentation, clouding of consciousness, impaired reality testing, rambling verbalization, fluctuating
sensorium, memory impairment, disorientation, poor concentration, and illusions. Onset occurs suddenly following ingestion of
marijuana or hashish, and may be concurrent with more common
acute drug effects. Symptoms generally subside within 24-48
hours but may persist longer. Psychotic features such as hallucinations and delusions are typical. Extreme restlessness is common.
After recovery there is residual memory loss for part or all of the
episode. Incidence of this syndrome is also unknown, but is
believed to be rare in the United States, where marijuana has a
relatively low THC content. Most reports of this syndrome have
come from countries where more-potent marijuana is used.
However, if the THC content of marijuana available in this
country continues to rise, there may be increased incidence of this
reaction.

General principles of treatment are similar to those for other
forms of acute organic brain syndrome. If symptoms are severe,
hospitalization for a brief time may be indicated. Generally, the
disorder is self-limited, and treatment should be primarily supportive. The patient should be in a safe, secure environment and may
require constant reassurance for some time. Additional ingestion
of marijuana must be avoided and other medications should be
held to a minimum. However, if the patient's behavior becomes
unmanageable, treatment with tranquilizers may be necessary.
After the acute symptoms have cleared, psychiatric evaluation is
indicated in order to rule out further pathology. Counseling
should be provided concerning the nature of the acute episode to
prevent recurrence. In some patients, outpatient follow-up and
treatment may be indicated.

A so-called *amotivation syndrome* is considered by some to
be another adverse serious consequence of cannabis use (6). This
syndrome is somewhat controversial, and not all experts agree that
it exists. Nevertheless, it has been observed that some individuals
who have chronically used marijuana gradually begin to lose motivation, becoming apathetic and unconcenred over the future. As
a result, they may drop out of school or quit their jobs, spending
most of their time smoking marijuana. They do not engage in any
productive activity. When marijuana use stops, the syndrome disappears, and drive and motivation return. Treatment of this proposed syndrome consists principally, then, of getting the indivi-

dual to stop marijuana use. On the other hand, this still questionable syndrome may represent an episode of depression in an individual who uses marijuana and has no causal relationship with marijuana use. There have been some reports that antidepressants may be helpful. If this syndrome is suspected, a complete psychiatric history and evaluation are indicated to rule out other pathology.

TOLERANCE, WITHDRAWAL, AND FLASHBACKS

Both tolerance and withdrawal symptoms have been identified as occurring with prolonged THC ingestion. When human subjects were given larges doses (over 200 mg daily) of the THC in sesame oil on a fixed dosage schedule, tolerance developed to the following acute effects in 10 days: euphoria, tachycardia, decrease in salivary flow, decrease in skin temperature, increase in body temperature, decrease in intraocular pressure, EEG changes, sleep changes, orthostatic hypotension, nystagmus, and behavior changes. These common effects of marijuana intoxication decreased in frequency or intensity when THC was ingested on a regular basis.

When subjects were abruptly withdrawn from the THC, they developed a characteristic withdrawal syndrome. Symptoms were relatively mild and may have been a rebound to effects for which tolerance had developed. Symptoms of withdrawal were quickly reversed by the administration of THC. Typical withdrawal symptoms were irritability, restlessness, decreased appetite, sleep disturbance, sweating, tremor, nausea and vomiting, and diarrhea. These symptoms lasted less than 96 hours, were not life-threatening, and only produced mild discomfort for the subjects (4).

Flashbacks = the spontaneous recurrence of feelings or perceptual states originally experienced during drug intoxication, but now occurring when the individual is not taking the drug — have been reported with marijuana use (7), but flashbacks have not been well-studied and their existence is questionable. A variety of marijuana flashbacks have been reported by marijuana users who had previous experience with hallucinogenic drugs such as LSD, mescaline, and peyote. Some report that, while using marijuana, they have a recurrence of an effect that they have experienced with hallucinogens, but not with marijuana. Unfortunately, there has been little systematic research in this area. Although there is no specific treatment for flashbacks, the individual should be reassured and encouraged to discontinue drug use as this may aggravate or prolong the flashback.

ABUSE

An |abuse syndrome| can develop in which individuals are unable to control their consumption of marijuana, analogous to alcoholics being unable to control their use of alcohol. In the marijuana abuser a variety of problems can result from cannabis use, just as the alcoholic exhibits multiple problems resulting from his or her use of alcohol. Since many have come to use marijuana as a social intoxicant in a fashion similar to alcohol, the incidence of abuse may increase. Relaxed legal constraints against its use could also facilitate the appearance of abusers. Such abusers have been recently identified and studied.

Using the criteria for alcoholism developed at Washington University Medical School for use in psychiatric research as a model (8), criteria for marijuana abuse were developed (9). Seventeen potential problems resulting from cannabis use were divided into four basic groups: 1 psychological and physiologic effects, 2 problems controlling use, 3 personal–social problems resulting from use, and 4 adverse opinions of the individual or others concerning the individual's marijuana use. If an individual had symptoms in all four of these groups, he or she was classified as a definite abuser. Individuals with symptoms in three groups were probable abusers.

When 97 chronic marijuana users were evaluated, nine individuals were classified as abusers. They averaged 5.6 different problems resulting from marijuana use, while the remaining 88 non-abusers averaged less than one problem. Abusers began using the drug at an earlier age, used it more frequently, and used greater amounts than non-abusers. Overall, abusers seemed to be doing less well than non-abusers (9). Some of the problems, such as increased incidence of fighting and traffic violations are of particular interest to society since they affect others as well as the abuser.

Because this syndrome has only recently been identified, definitive treatment regimens have not yet been developed. In general, treatment should parallel that of the alcohol abuser. That is, the patient should be encouraged to cease marijuana use. Insight into the adverse effects marijuana is having on the patient's life should be developed. Patients should be evaluated for other psychiatric problems and be treated as indicated. They should also be screened for the possibility of other substance abuse. Counseling the patient and family is also indicated. As with alcoholism, a total treatment program may be necessary to effectively manage the patient.   ⌐ *definition?*

MARIJUANA USE AND PSYCHIATRIC PROBLEMS

Besides the syndromes discussed above, there is little evidence to support the theory that marijuana use can cause *de novo* psychiatric illness. That is, marijuana use does not precipitate or cause psychiatric illness such as schizophrenia or neuroses. There is evidence that individuals who use marijuana and have psychiatric problems, had developed these problems prior to the onset of their marijuana use (10).

Patients with schizophrenia may be at a particular risk for developing adverse psychiatric symptoms from marijuana use. Schizophrenics who were doing well and used marijuana relapsed, and those who were symptomatic (psychotic) had marked worsening of symptoms (11). Individuals with a variety of other psychiatric problems have also shown problems when they used marijuana. In general, patients with psychiatric problems, particularly schizophrenia, should be discouraged from using marijuana.

PREVENTION

The dramatic increase in marijuana use among the young, especially school-age children, is of particular concern. There is evidence that marijuana use may lead to impairment of the ability to learn, an amotivational syndrome, or other problems affecting the educational process. This possibility, coupled with the concern that young children may not have the maturity, experience, or knowledge to make intelligent decisions regarding drug use, leads many authorities to advocate concerted efforts to discourage marijuana use among youth.

It has been difficult to translate this desire to discourage marijuana use in the young into some type of effective preventive program. In the past, the cornerstone of prevention consisted of presenting drug use in an unsavory light. Information about drug use or its consequences was calculated to scare the individual into not using drugs. Although effective in some individuals, as marijuana became more available it became apparent to young people that some of the information given to them about the drug was not true. This generalized to the assumption that none of the information given was true. Thus, scare tactics regarding marijuana have become largely ineffective.

As more accurate information about marijuana and its acute and chronic effects has become available as a result of research, there have been attempts to prevent use by presenting accurate information to potential users, on the assumption that, if the individual has the information he or she will choose not to use the drug. Apparently, this overly simplistic approach has not worked particularly well.

Preventing drug abuse has never been easy. There are no clear guidelines that will ensure success. New and innovative approaches will be needed if there is to be hope of developing effective preventive programs. Current approaches include deemphasizing the drug, and concentrating on the personality and environment of the potential abuser. Providing activities for young people that will be alternatives to drugs has also been advocated. Such programs should cut across all aspects of the individual's life and not focus on a single issue such as drug use.

Perhaps use and experimentation in the young can not be prevented, but if such use can be minimized and delayed, the adverse consequences of precocious marijuana or other drug use can be lessened. Certainly further work in the epidemiology of marijuana use needs to be undertaken. As more information becomes available, it will be possible to evaluate the etiology of precocious drug use and misuse, and more effective preventive strategies can be developed. The effectiveness of current preventive strategies can also be better evaluated.

SUMMARY

Marijuana is a drug that has been used by mankind for thousands of years. In the United States, hemp plants, the source of marijuana, were extensively grown for their fiber for many years. Now they grow wild over most of the country. Although widely used in the 1800s and early 1900s as a patent medicine, marijuana use for recreational purposes was not particularly frequent and occurred in only isolated subgroups of the population until recently. In the past 15 years there has been a dramatic increase in marijuana use in all segments of society, especially the young, and most frequently in the 18–25 age group. Probably over 50 million Americans have tried marijuana, and millions consider themselves regular users. This marked increase in use has occurred despite strong laws against use. However, there has been a recent trend toward reduced penalties for use and possession, and less rigorous enforcement of laws that are still in effect. With this more permissive attitude, it is likely marijuana use will continue to increase.

Because of increased public awareness of marijuana use there has been more research which has answered some but not all of the questions about cannabis. Marijuana intoxication or "high" continues to be perceived as a pleasant experience by most users. However, adverse effects do occur with marijuana use, which has persisted in spite of these adverse effects. In addition, tolerance to some effects has been described and a characteristic withdrawal syndrome has been reported. Panic reaction, toxic delerium, and abuse syndrome similar to alcohol abuse (alcoholism) have been described.

There is evidence that marijuana smoking may have deleterious effects on several systems in the body, including the cardiovascular and pulmonary systems. The eventual consequences of chronic, or long-term use in the individual and on the society in which he or she resides, remain largely unknown.

With increased marijuana use and more-potent marijuana now available, the effects of marijuana use will probably become more apparent. Information is still incomplete and much work remains to be done. Research is needed to provide information about the consequences of marijuana use to marijuana users and potential users. With increased knowledge, informed decisions about marijuana may be made by the individual and society.

To date, attempts to discourage or prevent marijuana use have not been particularly successful. Innovative approaches and additional research are needed to develop effective approaches to this problem.

REFERENCES

1. Brecher, E.M.: *Licit and Illicit Drugs.* Boston, Massachusetts: Little, Brown, and Company, 1972.

2. Petersen, R.C. (Ed): *Marijuana Research Findings: 1980.* Rockville, Maryland: National Institute on Drug Abuse. Research Monograph 31, 1980.

3. Braude, M.C. and Szara, S. (Eds): *Pharmacology of Marijuana,* 2 volumes. New York: Raven Press, 1974.

4. Jones, R.T.; Benowitz, N. and Bachman, J.: Clinical studies of cannabis tolerance and dependence. In: *Annals of New York Academy of Science,* Dornbush, R.L.; Freedman, A.M. and Fink, M.D. (Eds), *282:*221-240, 1976.

5. Halikas, J.A.; Goodwin, D.W. and Guze, S.B.: Marijuana effects: A survey of regular users. *Journal of the American Medical Association, 217:* 692-694, 1971.

6. Halikas, J.A.: Marijuana use and psychiatric illness. In: *Marijuana: Effects on Human Behavior,* Miller, L.L. (Ed). New York: Academic Press, 1974.

7. Keeler, M.H.; Reifler, C.B. and Liptzin, M.B.: Spontaneous recurrence of marijuana effect. *Canadian Psychiatric Association Journal, 16:* 181-182, 1971.

8. Feighner, J.P.; Robins, E.; Guze, S.B., *et al.*: Diagnostic criteria for use in psychiatric research. *Archives of General Psychiatry, 26:*57-63, 1972.

9. Weller, R.A. and Halikas, J.A.: Objective criteria for the diagnosis of marijuana abuse. *Journal of Nervous and Mental Disease, 160:*98-103, 1980.

10. Halikas, J.A.; Goodwin, D.W. and Guze, S.B.: Marijuana use and psychiatric illness. *Archives of General Psychiatry, 27:*162-165, 1972.

11. Trefferet, D.A.: Marijuana use in schizophrenia: A clear hazard. *American Journal of Psychiatry, 135:*1212-1215, 1978.

Chapter 2

The Opiates and Opiate Abuse

Alan Wartenberg, M.D.

OVERVIEW

In a well-researched and clearly written chapter the author provides the essence of what all allied health practitioners will need to know about the use and abuse of opiates. He begins with an excellent section on the clinical pharmacology of opiates, including the natural, the synthetic, and the endogenous (those produced by the body) compounds. Dr. Wartenberg then proceeds to an explanation of the pain-reducing, mood-altering, and other effects of such compounds. A well-informed discussion of tolerance and withdrawal phenomena, and implications of those problems for treatment, concludes that section.

Next, the author provides useful information on patterns of incidence and prevalence which describe the current epidemiology of opiate abuse and dependency. He focuses primarily on three important groups of identified users: people he calls street addicts, who are likely to be somehow involved with illegal substances, criminal activities, or law enforcement agencies; iatrogenic users, whose opiate abuse is related to physician-prescribed medications; and physicians and other health professionals themselves, among whom the probability of opiate addiction far exceeds that of the general public.

A subsequent section on etiologies provides a brief look at current thought and data regarding possible causes of drug abuse. In this discussion of etiology the author clearly supports the value of a biopsychosocial approach to causes.

That biopsychosocial approach is shown to be immediately applicable to effective treatment, which Dr. Wartenberg then addresses in the next section. He deals with diagnosis — a necessary first step — and treatment as they relate to problems of body, mind, and environment in full interaction. Methods of detoxification are specified, current (and sometimes controversial) approaches to inpatient and outpatient treatment are examined, and the needs of special target groups are identified within the context of different treatment philosophies and practices. What are the characteristics of a Therapeutic Community; how are their typical treatment practices likely to impact on affluent white males; should street addicts be considered for outpatient detoxification; and a variety of other general and specific issues are addressed.

Recommendations for future directions in research, particularly regarding improved prevention activities, are followed by a summary and references.

INTRODUCTION

To many, the term *drug abuse* is synonymous with that of illicit use of opiates. The image of the "street junkie" with a plastic bag of white powder, a candle, spoon, and syringe has become part of our folklore. Some estimates indicate that such opiate abusers may number up to 750,000, and the criminal activity associated with opiate use may cost society more than $30 billion yearly (2). In addition, the annual medical costs of hospitalization for associated acute and chronic conditions may reach an additional $15 billion (12). The societal cost of treatment, such as methadone maintenance, therapeutic communities, inpatient psychiatric, or other hospital–based care, and a variety of out–patient programs, can be estimated at under $1billion per year (12).

There are also an unknown number of abusers of licit opiates. Business executives with low back pain, housewives with chronic headache, and elderly patients with arthritis are among those who may become dependent on prescribed opiate analgesics. A surprising number of health professionals (physicians, nurses, dentists, pharmacists, and others) who have ready access to opiates also become addicted. In all these groups — the street users, the iatrogenic patient–abusers, and the health professional abuser — opiate abuse exacts an enormous toll of physical, emotional, and spiritual suffering. As in other forms of substance abuse, this price is paid not only by the addict, but by its "ripple" effect, on their families, friends, and society in general.

Abusers of opiates may require an extensive array of professional services in the course of diagnosis, treatment, and recovery.

Police officers, attorneys, and court officials may represent the "front line." Diversion programs for drug abusers have become common mechanisms to provide offenders with the opportunity for treatment rather than incarceration. Health care professionals, including but not limited to social workers, psychologists, physicians, counselors, nurses, restorative therapists, and vocational counselors all may play an important role in facilitating recovery. It is, therefore, essential that all helping professionals develop an understanding of opiate abuse.

To facilitate that understanding, a biopsychosocial model of etiology and treatment is used throughout this chapter. Of course, the clinical pharmacology of opiates — their chemistry, actions, mechanisms of production of tolerance and withdrawal, and their toxic effects — is viewed primarily from the perspective of biology, but certain psychological and social factors may interact in this context. On the other hand, the epidemiology of use and misuse — the incidence and prevalence patterns among populations at risk, and the social, cultural, and ethnic factors involved — places relatively more emphasis on psychological and social variables, but biological factors are still at work. In viewing the individual factors, such as those invoked in the various theories of the development of opiate abuse, or in attempts to define the so-called addictive personality, biological and social factors may temporarily appear to be less important. In discussing methods of control — governmental and other societal efforts to prevent and reduce use, maintenance programs, and treatment and outcome — social factors may be temporarily ascendant. Overall, however, because of the complex ways in which body, behavior, and environment reciprocally interact and mutually influence one another, the biopsychosocial model is best able to facilitate our understanding of all aspects of opiate use and abuse.

CLINICAL PHARMACOLOGY

Chemistry

Opiates are a class of natural or synthetic derivatives of the opium poppy, *Papaver Somniferum*. The seed capsules of this plant contain a juice which, when dried, forms a dark brown gummy mass: opium. Opium contains two major classes of alkaloids: the benzylisoquinolines and the phenanthrenes. The latter includes morphine, codeine, and thebaine, which together constitute about 10% of the total weight of impure opium. The pharmacologic effects of opium are largely due to its major constituent, morphine.

Opium was widely utilized for many centuries as a powder or elixir (laudanum, paregoric), but the modern history of the drug began with the extraction and purification of morphine (after Morpheus, the Greek god of sleep) by Friedrich Setürner in 1803. Codeine, or methylmorphine, was isolated shortly thereafter and found to be more effective orally. Further chemical modifications have led to discovery or development of a number of drugs, some of which have more-specific properties, such as activity as cough suppressants or antidiarrheal agents, and less liability of dependence. Others are more potent than morphine, but are similar in actions and ability to produce addiction: hydromorphone (Dilaudid®), levorphanol (Levo-Dromoran®), oxycodone (Percodan®), and others. The most important of these is diacetylmorphine, or heroin, developed by German chemists at the turn of the century, again in an attempt to find a narcotic analgesic with less addictive potential than morphine.

In addition, a variety of entirely synthetic compounds which possess morphine-like activity but do not have the phenanthrene nucleus, have been developed. These include the pure opiate agonists, meperidine (Demerol®), methadone, and propoxyphene (Darvon®); and mixed agonist-antagonists, pentazocine (Talwin®), butorphanol (Stadol®), nalbuphine (Nubain®). A pure antagonist, naloxone (Narcan®) is also available, which will reverse all opiate activity without any evident agonist activity of its own. An orally effective antagonist, naltrexone, has recently been released.

The exciting discovery of natural opiate-like substances (endorphins, enkephalins) produced by the body has led to greater understanding of the mechanism of action of this class of compounds (see the following section). Because these chemicals, as well as the purely synthetic drugs, do not share the chemical structure of morphine and codeine, it has been suggested that the term *opioid* be used to describe all substances with morphine-like activity. For purposes of clarity and common usage, the term *opiate* will continue to be used in this chapter.

The Role of Endogenous Opiates. A more complete understanding of the actions of opiates should start with a discussion of the natural, or endogenous (produced within), opiate-like substances. For some time, researchers in this field had postulated that cellular receptors for opiate action might have some natural function. Intensive efforts were rewarded with the discovery in 1975 of an extract of bovine pituitary glands which possessed opiate activity (13). This proved to be a polypeptide composed of 31 amino acids (β-endorphin), which was part of a larger polypeptide which also possessed adrenal gland-stimulating activity (adrenocorticotrophic hormone, ACTH) and the ability to stimulate pigment-forming cells (melanocytes) in skin and elsewhere (beta-melanocyte stimulating hormone, BMSH). The larger parent polypeptide has been termed *proopiomelanocortin* to describe its multiple activities, and is also known as β-lipotropin.

While β endorphin possessed opiate activity, it was subsequently determined that smaller fractions of the molecule, the enkephalins, were responsible for the major opiate actions. These are five amino acid chains, of which two forms are biologically important: methionine (or met-) enkephalin and leucine (leu-) enkephalin. These substances have all the known effects of opiates and occupy the same receptor sites as do exogenous opiate drugs.

The natural functions of β-endorphin and the enkephalins are incompletely understood. They are widely distributed within the central nervous system (CNS), including the pituitary gland, and seem to be present in highest concentrations in those areas which involve pain perception and responses, as well as in areas of the limbic system, an older part of the brain which is involved with emotional responses. Stimulation of these areas produces sedation and analgesic effects, which can also be duplicated by microinjection of enkephalins and other opiates. One area, the *locus coeruleus*, located in the roof of the hindbrain, appears to be important in modulating anxiety, fear, and panic states. Stimulation of this area produces a panic state in animals which can be abolished by treatment with either endogenous or exogenous opiates. In addition, there are complex interactions between opiate-like neurotransmitters and other CNS neurotransmitters (norepinephrine, serotonin, dopamine). These interactions are beyond the scope of this chapter, but offer opportunities to understand many of the behavioral effects of psychotropic drugs, and may potentially play a role in treatment of drug abuse.

Actions

Analgesia. The major indication for the medicinal use of opiates, and the impetus behind their development for clinical use, is the relief of pain afforded by these compounds. This property has been known for millenia, and physicians from ancient to modern times have extolled their analgesic effects. Although the mechanism of this analgesia is complex, it appears most likely to be a result of the decrease in activity of afferent (incoming or ascending) nerve impulses within the spinal cord and higher CNS centers, so that there is a decreased perception of pain. In addition, the tranquilizing and sedating effects (see Mood Altering Effects) of opiates may alter both the perception of pain and the host response to pain.

The naturally occurring opiates all are effective analgesics; most of the semi-synthetic and synthetic analogues possess analgesic property as well, as do the enkephalins. They have important differences in potency, and in their ability to alter mood, which in turn effect the quality of analgesia. In general, equipotent doses of opiates produce equal analgesic effects. The liability for psychic or physical dependence on these drugs depends both on the analgesic properties and on their effects on mood.

Mood Altering Effects. Users of intravenous opiates, particularly heroin, describe the initial sensation after injection as *the rush.* It occurs within seconds, rarely lasts more than several minutes, is described as an intense euphoria, and seems to represent the most desired response habitual users of opiates seek. It decreases in intensity after 2-5 minutes, and is replaced by a sedated state with marked reduction in anxiety. Tolerance to the rush effect, and to some extent the tranquilizing/sedating effects, develops quickly with habitual use, and, therefore, increasingly higher doses are required to attain *the high* (see Tolerance and Withdrawal).

Other opiates vary greatly in their ability to alter mood, and the psychoactive effect also varies with the route of administration. Orally administered heroin produces no rush, but will produce sedation if given in adequate dosage. Intranasal insufflation (snorting), or intramuscular or subcutaneous injection (popping), produces an intermediate effect. Hydromorphone (Dilaudid®) and oxycodone (Percodan® and others), when injected intravenously, produce effects which heroin addicts describe as a qualitatively similar rush. Meperidine (Demerol®) and morphine taken intravenously produce an intense high, but one which heroin habitués find mildly unpleasant or dysphoric. Subjects for whom these latter compounds are the predominant drugs of abuse, however, find the sensation pleasurable. The mixed agonist–antagonists, in general, produce dysphoric effects, but nonetheless have their devotees.

One particular combination, pentazocine (Talwin®) and the antihistamine, pyribenzamine (PBZ®) has become a popular feature of the opiate abuse scene in the Midwest. When injected intravenously *Ts and Blues*, as they are known, produce a rush similar to that of heroin. In some hospital emergency departments, Ts and Blues overdose is more frequently seen than overdose with other opiates, especially where the quality of street heroin is poor.

It should be noted that there appear to be subtypes of opiate receptors which serve different functions. Therefore, a mixed agonist–antagonist can activate analgesic receptors while antagonizing or blocking other receptors. Subjects who are not habituated to opiates experience analgesia and sedation with pentazocine; those addicted to agonist opiates (e.g., morphine, heroin, methadone) may develop dysphoria and marked withdrawal symptoms when given pentazocine or other mixed agonist–antagonist drugs.

Other CNS Effects. When used in therapeutic doses, opiates have minimal measurable central effects other than sedation. However, in higher dosages, when used in combination with other CNS depressants (e.g., alcohol, barbiturates), and even occasionally in usual doses in older or debilitated individuals (especially when chronic lung disease is present) these agents cause a significant depression of respiratory centers. Both the depth and frequency of respiration decrease and may lead to respiratory failure, permanent brain damage from lack of oxygen, and death. Actions on the cardiac and circulatory centers may also occur, but are mostly secondary to the decrease in oxygen supply. It is important to note that while tolerance to the mood–altering and analgesic effects may develop quickly, tolerance to respiratory depressant effects does not. Therefore, the most common cause of opiate overdose is the deliberate escalation of dose to produce the rush. The introduction of a higher quality heroin into an area also invariably results in an increase in overdose cases and deaths in that vicinity.

When opiates are used as a medical analgesic, respiratory depression is rarely seen. The central arousal produced by painful stimuli appears to antagonize the depressant effects of opiates, and larger doses may be safely used. When the painful stimuli are reduced, however, the danger of respiratory depression again exists. Therefore, doses of opiates should be carefully monitored and changed as the clinical situation warrants.

Opiates produce nausea and vomiting by stimulating the chemoreceptor trigger zone (CTZ) in the hindbrain. A chemical cousin, *apomorphine*, has been used in the past to induce vomiting in those who have ingested overdoses of toxic substances. A central effect of cough suppression, or antitussive action, is also prominent with most opiates. Codeine is most commonly used for this purpose, but does have abuse potential. A synthetic non-narcotic analogue of morphine, *dextromethorphan*, has antitussive activity without analgesic or addictive properties, although it may cause CNS depression in very large doses.

Miscellaneous Effects. Opiates cause constriction of the pupil (miosis), and this action is of importance in recognizing opiate overdose. Constipation is a well-known side effect, resulting from decreased activity of the stomach and intestinal tract, as well as increased absorption of water and salt from the gut. This effect was recognized in antiquity, and opiates are useful in the treatment of certain diarrheal states. Congeners with antidiarrheal activity and little abuse potential, such as diphenoxylate (Lomotil®) and loperamide (Imodium®) are available for clinical use.

Smooth muscle effects also occur, including relaxation of vascular smooth muscle, causing blood to pool in the legs and a mild decrease in blood pressure in the upright posture. Blood vessels in the skin dilate and flushing may be prominent, and itching and increased sweating may also occur. Hormonal effects also occur, but most are of uncertain clinical importance. With initial use an increase in pituitary secretion of adrenal-stimulating factors occurs, resulting in high levels of adrenal steroids (cortisol). After chronic use, the ability of the body to respond to stress by increasing cortisol production and secretion is blocked, and this effect may impair the individual's resistance in stressful settings, such as injury, surgery, or infection. There is reduction also of pituitary secretion of gonadotropins, hormones which stimulate the ovaries and testes to produce sex hormones, with a consequent reduction of libido, potency, and fertility. The ducts of the pancreas and gall bladder may develop spasm after opiate use, which occasionally can cause clinically significant pancreatitis and gall bladder attacks. Opiates can prolong labor, although the mechanism is uncertain, and may result in respiratory depression in the newborn. Although in usual dosage opiates reduce breathlessness, in a susceptible individual they may provoke an asthmatic attack.

Idiosyncratic reactions may also occur, including excitation, panic states, and toxic delirium. Frequent reports of heroin-induced accumulation of fluid in the lungs (noncardiac pulmonary edema) have appeared in the literature (4, 24) and appear to be relatively specific for heroin. An inflammatory condition of the kidneys (heroin nephropathy) has also occurred in many patients, and appears to be due to abnormal immune responses. Intravenous opiates (and other drugs) appear to play some role in the development of the newly described acquired immunodeficiency syndrome (AIDS), a condition marked by unusual infections and malignancies in previously healthy persons, particularly among male homosexuals. Pentazocine (Talwin®) may elevate blood pressure to dangerous levels, and both pentazocine and propoxyphene (Darvon®) may cause grand mal seizures. Liver disease, including acute and chronic hepatitis, as well as cirrhosis, may also complicate intravenous opiate abuse.

It is important to consider that abusers of street drugs are using impure and contaminated products, which may contain a variety of inert, active, and infected ingredients which, when used intravenously, intramuscularly, or subcutaneously, increase the risk of serious toxic reactions (seizures), as well as local and systemic infections (skin abscess, hepatitis, endocarditis, and pneumonia). With intranasal use, destruction of the nasal septum may occur. If an artery is entered deliberately or inadvertantly, intravenous injection may result in loss of a limb. Cases of injection into the carotid artery, causing strokes, have been described, as well as a variety of neurological syndromes having an allergic or toxic etiology (25). Street heroin is invariably "cut" or mixed with some other substance, and the fillers have ranged from milk sugar to strychnine and rat poison. The health professional dealing with the complications of opiate and other drug abuse should be mindful that "what you see" is not necessarily "what you get."

There are important adverse medical effects which, while not part of the opiates' pharmacology, are a direct consequence of their use. Mental clouding may result in injury from falls or vehicular and other accidents. The criminal lifestyle which may envelop the abuser is often associated with injury, or death from homicide, and depression over the consequences of abuse may lead to suicide. Malnutrition, vitamin deficiencies, and the effects of alcohol and other drugs used add to the burden of disease.

Tolerance and Withdrawal

Opiates, like alcohol and other sedative-hypnotic drugs, produce tolerance to their pharmacological effects with chronic use, and an abstinence syndrome, or withdrawal, after their use is decreased or discontinued. Tolerance to some opiate effects can be discerned in animal systems, and even single-nerve preparations, after the second exposure to the drug. With the development of tolerance, larger doses are required to produce the same physiological effect on the user, and a constant dose will have decreasing effects. As was noted above, tolerance to some effects (rush, analgesia) develops more rapidly than tolerance to others (sedation, respiratory depression), probably due to differences in the opiate receptor subtypes.

In practical terms, the development of tolerance requires users to constantly escalate dosage, and eventually may expose them to the risks of impaired consciousness, aspiration pneumonia, respiratory depression, and accidental death from overdose. In the user of medicinal opiates for legitimate pain (e.g., terminal cancer and postoperative patients), significant tolerance to analgesic effects rarely develops. In the chronic pain patient, however, dosage escalation, with or without the physician's knowledge, is common. In the street junkie, the cost of the habit increases, often leading to criminal activity and desperate acts to maintain the high, or to avoid the withdrawal syndrome. In the medicinal opiate user, requests for frequent refills, repeatedly lost or misplaced prescriptions or pills, escalation to parenteral opiates, and obtaining prescriptions from multiple physicians, often are signs of increasing tolerance. It is not unusual to see street drug users turn to doctors' offices when the supply on the street is low. Prescriptions for imaginatively feigned painful illnesses (especially kidney stones and gall-bladder attacks) are obtained from unsuspecting physicians, or shots of meperidine from naive emergency department personnel. Prescription blanks and drug samples are also regularly stolen from physicians' offices, and pharmacy burglaries and robberies are also common. Conversely, chronic pain patients and others addicted to medicinal opiates may turn to street sources if their regular resources are no longer available. In some cases, such as sickle cell disease patients, it becomes impossible to separate the symptoms of their underlying disease from that of narcotic withdrawal, and addiction to narcotics in these patients is as common as it is unnecessary (see Treatment).

A mild or partial abstinence syndrome may develop when, after even a few days of regular opiate use, the drug is suddenly discontinued. The full-blown syndrome, however, usually requires months of continuous usage and evidence of developing tolerance. The symptoms and signs of withdrawal represent hyperactivity of the autonomic nervous system, as well as considerable psychomotor agitation. Drug-craving and intense drug-seeking behavior are the *sine qua non* of a significant withdrawal episode. Anxiety, insomnia, and anorexia are common and, in severe cases, delirium may occur. Diffuse pain — in muscles, bones, joints, back, and abdomen — are often the most troublesome symptoms.

Examination of the patient reveals the agitated state: sweating, piloerection (the gooseflesh of "cold turkey"), running nose and eyes, and dilated pupils are evident. The pulse and blood pressure are increased, as are respiratory rate and depth. A fine tremor may be present. Sleep is disturbed ("yen" sleep from which easy arousal occurs frequently) and spontaneous ejaculation in men, and orgasms in women, may occur. Convulsions, a regular feature of alcohol and sedative-hypnotic withdrawal, and conspicuously absent in the opiate abstinence syndrome. Should they occur, a multiple drug withdrawal or underlying epilepsy should be suspected.

In general, the shorter-acting opiates (e.g., heroin, meperidine, morphine, hydromorphone) produce withdrawal symptoms within hours of the last use (depending on the severity of the addiction), which peak at 12-24 hours, and generally subside within 72 hours. Longer-acting opiates (methadone) produce a withdrawal syndrome which may not begin for 48-72 hours after last use, may plateau in intensity over days to weeks, and may last for 2-4 weeks. Even after subsidence of major symptoms, a state of full well-being may not return for months, and subtle biological alterations can be detected for more than a year. Some opiates (codeine, propoxyphene) produce minimal abstinence symptoms; the mixed agonist-antagonists (e.g., pentazocine) cause highly variable withdrawal manifestations, with few symptoms in some patients and severe symptoms in others. Different opiates within the same group may also differ in the intensity of their withdrawal syndromes, but the usual signs and symptoms generally hold for the most commonly abused opiates.

The mechanisms by which tolerance and withdrawal occur are speculative, but most theories involve the concept of *counter-*

adaptation. When normal nerve pathways are blocked by opiates, the body tries to achieve a new balance, or homeostasis, either by creating new neural pathways, or by diminishing the number and affinity of the specific receptors for opiates. In time, homeostasis is achieved and the organism will function normally or near-normally despite the presence of chronically elevated opiate levels. The body may also develop mechanisms to increase the degradation and excretion of the drug. Thus, tolerance to drug effects develops. When the drug is suddenly removed, both the new pathways and those neural routes previously blocked by opiates are then available, and a generalized increase in nervous activity occurs. Since this increased action causes distinctly unpleasant sensations, the tolerant individual seeks to restore "normality" by using opiates. This hypothesis represents one explanation for drug-craving and drug-seeking behavior. In some sense, many opiate addicts, long since tolerant to the rush effects, are seeking only not to feel bad, rather than to feel good.

EPIDEMIOLOGY

There appear to be three subtypes of opiate abusers, and the demographics, risk factors, and pathogenesis differ for these groups. The differences also have therapeutic implications which will be discussed later. The drug effects (e.g., tolerance, withdrawal, drug-seeking and toxic effects) may be eventually very similar in individuals in all three groups.

The Street Addict

Estimates of the number of abusers of street opiates range from 500,000 to more than one million, most of whom are in larger urban centers (12, 17). Approximately 60,000 are in methadone maintenance programs, with a similar number enrolled in drug-free programs. There are, in addition, at least 100,000 opiate addicts in prison (17). While the preeminent drug remains heroin, virtually all synthetic and semisynthetic opiates and mixed agonist-antagonists (Talwin®, Stadol®, and others) are abused by this population. For some, one particular opiate may be the drug of choice; others will use whatever is available, including other sedative-hypnotics, such as alcohol. Some may use opiates as part of a polydrug abuse pattern.

The prevalence of opiate abuse increased three- to four-fold from 1967 to 1978, largely due to changes in demographics. In the 1950s and 1960s most opiate abusers were blacks and Hispanics from lower socioeconomic backgrounds, while the late 1960s and 1970s saw a marked increase in abuse by whites, and also increases among higher black and Hispanic socioeconomic groups. While the proportion of black and Hispanic abusers is higher than the proportion among whites, it is estimated that the bulk of opiate abusers are currently white.

Little useful information is available concerning other demographic variables. Women are under-represented, comprising only 15-20% of treated addicts. Certain groups with traditionally low prevalence of substance abusers, such as Jews and Italians, have recently witnessed an increase in their groups' representation among treated addicts. Other groups with high prevalence of alcoholism — Native Americans and Irish — do not appear to be as well represented. Asian-Americans, despite a cultural history of opium use, are markedly underrepresented in treatment statistics.

While it is clear that lower socioeconomic groups with less family income and education have higher rates of prevalence, this is by no means a universal factor. Among blacks, incidence of lifetime heroin use increases with both household income and education. In addition, there has been an alarming increase in use by middle-class and affluent adolescents and young adults of all racial groups.

The Licit Opiate Abuser

Patients with chronic pain syndromes constitute another substantial group at risk for opiate abuse (1, 26). Although precise data are not available, it is likely that there is a substantial number of opiate-dependent individuals among the more than 20 million Americans for whom these drugs are prescribed. In most cases, the short-term prescription of opiate analgesics for self-limiting pain constitutes no threat to the individual, but there are others for whom dependence becomes a consuming factor in their lives. The most common syndromes are those of back pain, abdominal pain, and headache. Most sufferers are women, who outnumber men by a 4:1 ratio. They often have had very extensive medical evaluations, which have either failed to reveal a biogenic source of the pain or show abnormalities that are inadequate to explain the duration or severity of the pain. There may have been multiple surgical and medical interventions which have failed to bring relief. In addition, patients with chronic pain secondary to clearcut organic lesions, such as sickle cell disease or osteomyelitis, may also be in this high risk group.

There is usually ample evidence of physical and psychological disturbances which antedate the development of the pain syndrome (see Etiologies). Family history is usually positive for multiple illnesses, and there is often a history of frequent childhood illness and time lost from school, work, or other responsibilities. The patient is most frequently unwilling to accept anything other than a physical explanation for the pain, and goes from doctor to doctor, and from one medical center to another. It is quite common for the patient to manifest considerable mistrust and hostility for the medical profession, and "horror stories" of their "mistreatment" are not unusual.

During the course of the pain syndrome, the development of psychological and physical dependence on narcotics and other drugs (sedative-hypnotics and tranquilizers) is an all-too-common event. Physicians, who may be well-meaning, will often prescribe an unending supply of medications. Attempts by the physician to discontinue medication may be met by "pain crises," hysterical symptoms, or by the patient's transferring care to another physician. Use of several physicians by one patient, without the knowledge of the doctors, is extremely common.

There is little epidemiological data about the licit opiate abuser other than the marked predominance of females. It is more common in middle-class and more affluent groups, and whites predominate. Information about ethnic group representation is not available. The patients tend to be in their fourth or fifth decade at the time of treatment, but reports range from adolescence well into later life.

Health Professionals

A special group of licit-drug abusers are members of the health professions. Physicians, nurses, and pharmacists constitute most reported cases, but dentists, nurses aides, and other professionals are also affected. Several published series of the results of treatment of addicted health professionals are now available. It is estimated that 15% of all physicians will develop a substance abuse problem during their lifetimes, and that one-third of those will abuse opiates (7, 8, 9, 14, 16, 19), a prevalence of more than fifteen times that of the general population. Data concerning other health professionals are not available.

Among most health professionals who become abusers, the use of opiates and other drugs begins in a "medicinal" manner, with the self-prescribing and administration of a drug to overcome a physical problem. The injection of Demerol® or Sublimaze® (an ultra short-acting narcotic favored by anesthesiologist-abusers) to produce sedation or sleep after a particularly trying day is a common example. The use tends to progress and escalate, although periods of abstinence may also occur. Eventually a pattern of regular use is established, and physical dependence develops.

At the time of an established pattern of drug use, there may be little in the way of visible signs of opiate abuse. Most physician-addicts are conscientious and hard-working, and are most frequently well-thought of in their professions. Anecdotal information suggests the same is true of other addicted health professionals as well. However, with time a breakdown in efficiency is seen and personality changes and erratic behavior become apparent. Depending upon the innate resources of the individual professional, and the knowledgeability about drug abuse of those around him or her, the addiction may progress for considerable lengths of time before being detected. Eventually, family breakdown, loss of professional associations with colleagues and hospitals, license revocation or suspension, and legal action (including imprisonment) may occur. Psychiatric intervention and hospitalization are not uncommon, but rarely lead to benefit unless the drug problem is recognized and treated. Suicide or death from drug-associated illness are sometimes the ultimate consequences.

Most physicians, dentists, and pharmacists involved with opiate abuse have been men; addicted nurses have been predominately women. These observations probably reflect the prevailing gender prevalences of the professionals, but may also suggest sociobiological differences in men and women. The average age at entry into treatment has been decreasing since earlier reports (7, 8, 9, 14), and established drug abuse in residency training is not unusual. However, most reports (7, 8, 16, 19) indicate that nurses and physicians entering treatment are in their 40s and have spent more than 10 years in professional practice. Among MDs, anesthesiologists, general practitioners, psychiatrists, obstetricians-gynecologists, and internists are over-represented in the treated populations. In addition, most are married, have children, and have been financially successful.

ETIOLOGIES

The cause of substance abuse remains elusive, but it is appropriate to consider a biopsychosocial model for development of drug abuse and dependency. It is also clear that the three subgroups — the street addict, the licit drug abuser, and the health professional — may have very different etiologies for their abuse. However, there are generic factors which may operate in all abusers, and these are discussed first.

Biological Factors

Both the intrinsic addictiveness of a drug and host factors must be considered. Opiates all produce tolerance and abstinence syndromes, and in adequate doses over time will promote drug-seeking behavior in certain animal models. However, if this were the dominant factor in producing opiate-abusing behavior, then we could expect a greater incidence of iatrogenically produced addicts than is the case. In fact, iatrogenic addiction to opiates without abuse-related antecedents is a distinct rarity. During the conflict in Southeast Asia, a large proportion of American GIs were using high grade heroin on a regular basis, yet the anticipated epidemic of addicted servicemen returning to the U.S. never materialized. Most were detoxified with or without medical intervention and subsequently have not appeared to resume opiate use.

There are clear heredofamilial patterns for other forms of drug abuse, especially alcoholism. In addition, biological markers for depression have been reported to be increased in the first-order relatives of cocaine abusers. To date, similar patterns of markers have not been associated with opiate abuse, and attempts to demonstrate a preexisting deficiency of endogenous opiates have not shown consistent or clear-cut results.

Psychological Factors

Many attempts have been made to define the *addictive personality*, but all studies suffer from lack of appropriate controls, and the intrinsic inability to separate cause from effect. Studies (11, 20) of detoxified opiate addicts have revealed patterns of characterological disorders (psychopathy and sociopathy) and elevations on psychoneurotic scales as well. However, other studies (10, 21) on groups of institutionalized alcoholics and juvenile delinquents showed similar results. Numerous authors (15, 18) have pointed to abnormal psychodynamics in opiate abusers, including increased need states, archaic ego defenses, and inability to relate closely to the parent of the same sex. Again, these are all traits found frequently in other psychiatric populations, although clustering of certain personality traits may occur in the opiate abuser. Instruments to detect these clusters are not currently of major diagnostic, prognostic, or therapeutic use in the general clinical setting, although they may be of use in epidemiological surveys or in selected high-risk populations.

In addition, there is an increased prevalence of certain psychiatric problems (e.g., major affective disorders) and character disorders (e.g., antisocial personality, borderline personality) among populations of drug abusers. Conversely, there is an increased prevalence of drug abuse among psychiatric populations. In general, however, there is little evidence to support the concept that opiate abuse is secondary to underlying personality problems in most abusers, although it certainly may be a response to these problems. It is important to allow sufficient time after detoxification before attempting a psychiatric diagnosis by either clinical interview or neuropsychological testing.

Social Factors

There is an increased prevalence of opiate abuse among populations of urban adolescents of minority background, low socioeconomic status, broken households (especially absent fathers) and minimal education or job skills. The despair of an economically and culturally impoverished life may be associated with maladaptive coping mechanisms, such as criminal and other antisocial behavior, sexual promiscuity, and drug abuse. Appropriate adult role models, especially the same-sex parent, are often absent. Adults present in the household may themselves be drug abusers or alcoholics, and may subject the child and adolescent to physical, verbal, or sexual abuse, including neglect.

As noted previously, there has been an increase in the prevalence of opiate abuse in populations previously rarely affected. The acceptance of cocaine as a socially acceptable drug among more affluent groups may expose users to dealers in heroin, and may undermine resistance to the use of heroin. The counterculture phenomenon of the late 1960s and early 1970s also played a role in promotion of many forms of drug abuse among the middle and upper classes, and to some extent may have reduced the stigma of opiate abuse.

While it is clear that ethnic and cultural background is important in the development of alcoholism, this does not appear to be as much an influence in opiate abuse. However, among acculturated and assimilated members of ethnic groups who have lost their strong cultural identity and lifestyle, one is more likely to see drug abuse. Where cultural and family ties remain strong, drug abuse is less common. Social factors relating to licit drug abusers and health professionals are less well understood.

Finally, periods of social unrest and turmoil lead to increased drug abuse. The years following our major wars, significant economic downturns, and the nuclear age have all seen increases in drug abuse. A generalized sense of despair, anomie, and hopelessness has been increasingly described by adolescent drug abusers of affluent background. Both the poor and the wealthy may feel a lack of cohesion with societal mores and goals, and this disconnection may manifest itself in antisocial behaviors, including opiate abuse.

MANAGEMENT

Diagnosis

The successful management of opiate abusers depends initially on accurate diagnosis. The criteria for opiate use and dependency disorders are enumerated in the *Diagnostic and Statistical Manual (DSM-III)* (3), of the American Psychiatric Association (see Appendix 1). Briefly the diagnosis of abuse requires 1) duration of abuse of more than one month, 2) a pathological pattern of use, and 3) social impairment as a result of drug use. The addition of tolerance and abstinence syndrome confirms opiate dependency. The use of objective and verifiable criteria is essential, but one must appreciate that opiate abuse occurs as one point on a continuum of opiate use, and that observation over time may be needed in individual cases.

Street Addicts. Detection of street drug abusers only occasionally presents a problem. Many street addicts are referred to health professionals by courts, parole and probation officers, or may be self-referred to methadone programs. Diversion programs such as TASC (Treatment Alternatives to Street Crime) have served to channel into drug treatment those offenders whose crimes were generally drug-related and did not involve violence or personal injury. Opiate abusers may also come to medical attention after accidental overdose, infections, or toxic complications of drug use, or after evaluation for an unrelated problem when needle "tracks" or other stigmata are noted. Some addicts present to doctors' offices or emergency wards with stories suggestive of an acute painful illness such as a kidney stone in an attempt to obtain opiates. They may be quite knowledgeable in describing symptoms, and may place blood in their urine surreptitiously to add credence to the history. A high index of suspicion, careful examination for needle marks, and the use of urine drug screens will assist in making the proper diagnosis in these cases.

Licit Drug Abusers. The abuser of licit drugs presents a more challenging problem. However, the presence of poorly localized and nondescript pain, without a clear organic etiology, in a patient who is extremely demanding of pain medication, is typical of this group. They may ask very specifically for a certain drug, dosage, and route of administration. A long history of chronic or recurrent pain requiring narcotic analgesics or tranquilizers, multiple negative medical evaluations, in a patient with personality disorders apparent on cursory examination, all suggest the diagnosis. It is wise in such patients to be certain that a careful and thorough medical evaluation has been done by a competent physician, and that all reasonable diagnostic tests have been carried out. This degree of certainty requires careful review of all records, and history and physical examination, but repetition of previously negative diagnostic studies should be avoided. Multiple extensive testing may tend to reinforce "sick" behavior and drug-seeking. If the medical evaluation is unrevealing, a psychiatric interview and psychological testing are warranted.

The Health Professional Abuser. This group may present the greatest challenge to diagnosis. Most abusers in this group have high levels of personality integration, significant personal and financial resources, and avoid health hazards associated with drug abuse. They most commonly limit their use initially to situations where detection is unlikely. Gradually, as use increases, changes in personality, lifestyle, and professional abilities may be noted by those close to them. The diagnosis of drug abuse may finally come to light after drugs are stolen or prescriptions forged, or after the professional is discovered in an impaired state. Even after confrontation with irrefutable evidence there may be considerable denial, rationalization, or minimization of the problem by the abuser. Since health professionals are a group at considerable risk for opiate abuse, changes in behavior, lability of mood, and deterioration in performance should be viewed in this group with a high index of suspicion. Diagnosis is not difficult once the behavior has been noted, but may be greatly delayed because of enabling behavior of the family, other physicians, or hospital administrators. There has been, until recently, a collegial conspiracy of silence regarding health professional abusers, but this has been breaking down to some extent. Medical, nursing, dental, and pharmacy societies, groups of professionals' spouses, and licensing boards have all taken an active role in educating their members and the public about impaired professionals, and in many cases are active in case-finding and referral for treatment, as well as monitoring identified members' progress.

Confrontation

Once the diagnosis is suspected or confirmed, the individual must be confronted. This confrontation rarely needs to be dramatic, and should never be judgmental or condemnatory. An explanation of the clinical evidence should be provided, and the likely diagnosis should be given to the individual. However, it may be wise to avoid perjorative terms such as "drug addict" initially, and instead refer to a "problem related to drugs." In the street addict, such confrontation is usually straightforward and may be unnecessary, since most addicts are self-identified. Those who are attempting to conceal the diagnosis to obtain drugs will frequently leave hospital or office against medical advice when confronted. The same outcome may ensue in the licit abuser and the impaired professional, but can generally be avoided. It is usually best for the licit abuser to be confronted by the primary care physician rather than by a consultant or subspecialist. It is extremely important not to minimize the patient's pain or disability initially, but rather to explain that it is out of proportion to the physical findings. A discussion of psychogenic pain and depression should make clear that the pain is *not* "in their heads." Patients are far more likely to accept psychiatric or psychological diagnostic and therapeutic invervention if done as part of a multidisciplinary evaluation. It should be explained that physical evaluation of symptoms will continue, and that the patient's complaints will be taken seriously. However, this does not mean that extensive diagnostic evaluations should be automatically initiated for new or old complaints. Physical complaints must be considered within the entire clinical context. If the patient refuses the recommended evaluation or treatment, it should be made clear that further prescription of controlled substances would not then be warranted. This recommendation should be stated in the chart, and may be also sometime communicated to consulting or referring physicians involved in the case (although one must be careful to maintain confidentiality when appropriate).

The confrontation of the impaired professional is best done by specially trained personnel. State and local medical, nursing, and other societies, and hospital administrations often have established special committees to intervene in these cases. Many drug treatment centers have crisis intervention counselors who may be very useful in this setting. Several medical societies have offered special training for physician–interveners, and these individuals have been used to investigate allegations and confront the individuals involved. The ability of organized groups to function in a non-adversarial or advocacy role has helped increase their effectiveness. Frequently, however, the threat of dismissal, loss of licensure, or exposure to other criminal or civil legal sanctions sometimes may be necessary both to underscore the seriousness of the situation and effect an entry into evaluation and treatment.

TREATMENT

General Principles

When a patient is identified as an abuser of opiates and accepts treatment, the initial step should be an extensive medical evaluation by a physician with expertise in this area. If detoxification is planned, it should be done in a setting where the staff are experienced in the assessment and management of the detoxification process. Multiple medical problems — nutritional, infectious, toxic, trauma-related, and others — need to be identified and treated. A complete psychosocial evaluation should be undertaken, including history of drug use, family history, education, vocational skills, financial situation, emotional resources, interpersonal skills, and other relevant information. The medical and psychosocial evaluation allow an accurate assessment of client needs so that appropriate treatment resources can be mobilized.

The treatment site should offer both a multidisciplinary and interdisciplinary approach to treatment. The degree of impair-

ment in the opiate abuser is often high, and a variety of helping
professionals may be required to promote recovery: physicians
(general medical, psychiatric, and other consultants), nurses,
psychologists, counselors, family therapists, physical and occupational therapists, vocational rehabilitation counselors, and others
may be called upon. These professionals must work together as a
team, with each adding their special talents.

The optimal choice of a treatment facility should be made
taking many factors into account. The individual needs of the
patient, whether street addict, licit drug abuser, or impaired professional, are the major factors to be considered. However, the
availability of certain facilities in a given area, financial resources
available, the patient's general and mental health status, direction
from the courts, and family pressures, all may influence the kind
of treatment facility that is recommended. If detoxification is
needed, inpatient or residential treatment is desirable, although
with certain well-motivated patients supervised outpatient detoxification may be practicable. For patients who are without significant personal resources, lack of supportive home settings,
are in very high-stress employment or school settings, inpatient
structured programs are necessary to initiate and promote a
drug-free lifestyle. Those with significant health problems,
multiple substance abuse, and concomitant psychiatric disorders,
are also best treated in an inpatient setting. Outpatient or day-
hospital programs must exercise care in selection of patients
who have positive prognostic factors. The fundamental requirement of a drug treatment program is abstinence from use of
mood-altering drugs. Outpatient programs may invite the viola-
tion of this rule unless they are properly structured. A pattern of
drug use while in outpatient treatment should prompt urgent consideration of transfer to an inpatient program. Except in cases
where treatment is court-ordered, the ultimate factor determining
mode and setting of treatment is its acceptability to the drug
abuser and the referring health professional. Every effort should
be made to offer the patient treatment options that are appropriate in the judgment of the health professional, rather than only
offering treatment that the abuser is likely to accept. If the recommendation is declined, continued contact with the client and his
or her family or significant others is still warranted. Persistent but
patient counseling efforts to provide education about drug effects
and, above all, a caring and nonjudgmental attitude, may motivate
the drug abuser over time to accept treatment. Those close to the

patient should also be counseled, and referral to self-help groups (Families Anonymous, Alanon, or others; see Chapter 14) may start them on their own road to recovery. Formal family therapy may be useful for parents, spouses, children, and others even when the drug abuser refuses treatment. Such involvement by significant others should always be actively encouraged, and may provide indirect benefit by decreasing enabling behavior (see Chapter 13).

It must be understood that denial is often an integral part of the illness of drug abuse. The drug abuser will often try to choose the mode of treatment that is least likely to be effective. If such treatment is initiated and there is lack of recovery or frequent and serious relapses occur, efforts must again be resumed to persuade entry into more appropriate programs rather than a reflexive repetition of failed programs. Relapse is a common occurrence, and may sometimes be a therapeutic experience. However, a pattern of persistent drug use makes meaningful recovery difficult if not impossible, and the patient's diagnosis, course, and treatment plan should be reviewed by the entire therapy team. Occasionally a remediable cause of recidivism can be found and addressed, such as a learning disability, an undiagnosed psychiatric disorder, or a destructive influence in the home (such as an alcoholic or drug-abusing spouse).

Finally, the concept of recovery must be understood. While abstinence should be the ultimate goal, absolute abstinence occurs only in a minority of patients. The chances of an abstinent lifestyle may be greater for those who can accept the philosophy of Narcotics Anonymous and Alcoholics Anonymous, and who maintain involvement with these groups. For those who do not maintain absolute abstinence, either because of relapses, or with regular or irregular "controlled" use of drugs or alcohol, there is still an excellent chance for improvement. Data are available through the Drug Abuse Reporting Program (DARP) which indicate that the major forms of treatment for street addicts (Drug-Free, Therapeutic Community, Methadone Maintenance) lead to a highly or moderately favorable outcome in almost 55% of cases (23). An additional 30% had outcomes which, while described as moderately unfavorable, were actually an improvement over preadmission status (23). Approximately 15% showed no improvement or deteriorated (23). For those patients treated only by detoxification or intake interview, the percentage of favorable outcomes was significantly lower. Treatment outcome was defined by degree of opiate, non-opiate and alcohol use, employment, ciminality, and return to treatment. Thus, a significant lessening of compulsive use and social impairment was seen in treated patients. While reliable data concerning recovery in licit drug users are not available, impaired professionals do exceptionally well in treatment, with 75-85% returning to the practice of their profession (7, 8, 9). The conclusions based on treatment data must be tempered by an awareness of confounding variables in patient selection, duration of treatment, differences in programs under the same heading, and the unverifiability of some self-reported information. Nevertheless, the evidence strongly suggests that a positive outcome is possible for the majority of patients referred for treatment.

Detoxification

The signs and symptoms of the opiate abstinence or withdrawal syndrome were discussed in detail earlier (see also Chapter 7). When a patient is referred for drug-free treatment, detoxification is the first priority. If withdrawal is evident on examination, detoxification can proceed. If no findings suggestive of withdrawal are present, or if the amount of opiate used may not have been adequate to produce addiction, a naloxone challenge may be carried out in which a small dose of naloxone is given, and objective signs of withdrawal are noted and graded. If no significant withdrawal signs occur, a larger dose is given and observation is continued. If no withdrawal reaction occurs, detoxification is not usually necessary. This test should be carried out with informed consent and by experienced staff, since an immediate, severe, and highly unpleasant withdrawal syndrome may be precipitated and must be treated.

The setting in which detoxification should occur is somewhat controversial because of the absence of good data. Outpatient detoxification may be successful for patients previously stabilized on a methadone program, but is unlikely to be successful for others. Medical detoxification is most likely to be successful if done in a facility with specially trained personnel who are able to offer not only technical expertise but emotional and psychological support. Detoxification on general medical-surgical wards is difficult because of lack of special training, inattention to psychosocial needs, negative staff attitudes concerning drug abusers, and naiveté regarding the manipulative behavior of some addicts. A psychiatric facility may be more appropriate, but treatment personnel with experience in this field must be available. Residential detoxification in non-medical facilities using hospital or in-house medical consultation may offer a viable alternative in some instances.

In patients addicted to most opiates, the conventional method of withdrawal is with decreasing doses of methadone. This drug has the advantages of oral administration, long duration of action (6-12 hours of effective action) and smooth absorption, avoiding peaks and valleys of intoxication and withdrawal. Parenteral drugs should be avoided since they reinforce the "needle habit." A 10 mg dose of methadone is given and the patient is observed for attenuation of the withdrawal symptoms and signs. Additional 5-10 mg doses can be given after 4-6 hours if no relief of *objective* signs occurs. In general, 30-40 mg of methadone per day is adequate for most opiate habits. The dose is stabilized for 48 hours, and then reduced by 5 mg a day until 10-15 mg is reached, and then by 3 mg per day to zero dosage. Alternatively, a fixed daily reduction of 5-10% of total dosage can be carried out. Patient response must be carefully observed, and if intoxication is apparent, doses should be withheld. Conversely, if withdrawal signs reappear, the dosage should be increased to the previous day's dosage and withdrawal carried out more slowly. The appearance of subjective symptoms (e.g., craving, pain, nausea) *without* objective signs (gooseflesh, sweating, lacrimation, dilated pupils) should prompt increased emotional support but not alteration of drug therapy. Some addicts are skilled in producing some objective signs by exposure to heat or cold, rubbing their eyes, and other manipulations, but pupillary dilation cannot be feigned and should be especially noted.

In patients on high doses of methadone (greater than 60 mg) outpatient withdrawal can usually proceed by decreasing the dose by 3% per week over 30 weeks. More rapid inpatient detoxification can be done, but patient discomfort and drug-craving are significant in a 3-week detoxification for patients starting on higher methadone doses than 60 mg. This is most appropriately done only in patients willing to accept long-term drug-free programs. Patients abusing codeine, pentazocine, and propoxyphene are best withdrawn using tapering doses of the original drug over a one-week period, since withdrawal manifestations are rarely severe with these drugs.

Investigational approaches using repeated doses of naloxone to precipitate an intense but short-lived withdrawal have been attempted but have not gained acceptance. Recently, clonidine (an antihypertensive drug) has been found to markedly attenuate withdrawal manifestations, and several protocols using clonidine for both inpatient and outpatient withdrawal have been published (5, 6). Interestingly, clonidine was offered for sale on the streets to addicts before many physicians in this field were aware of its activity for this purpose. Another approach is the use of long-acting oral narcotic antagonist, naltrexone, in detoxified patients to discourage illicit opiate use by eliminating any opiate drug effect. Again, detoxification should be carried out in an appropriate setting by knowledgeable staff, especially if an investigational approach such as clonidine is to be considered.

During the detoxification process, the patient may experience some discomfort, anxiety, and/or depression and insomnia, and should be informed at the outset that these symptoms are likely to occur. When done properly, withdrawal should not be so uncomfortable as to promote lack of compliance with the treatment plan, and strong psychosocial support is essential toward this end. It is clear that while the worst withdrawal manifestations improve within days to weeks, a protracted withdrawal syndrome, lasting weeks to months, may occur. Prolonged anxiety or depressive symptoms, especially sleep disturbance, may occur. The use of sedative-hypnotics and tranquilizers should be strongly discouraged, since they will merely delay the appearance of the sleeplessness-anxiety-depression phase. More importantly, the use of such medications gives the wrong message concerning the desirability of drug-free life. Nonpharmacological methods, such as relaxation techniques, biofeedback, self-hypnosis, and other approaches should be encouraged to deal with these problems. Often, reassurance that such symptoms are usually self-limited will be adequate.

Depression during and following detoxification is very common, and should be treated supportively. Formal psychological assessment in general should be delayed for at least several weeks to avoid misleading results. It is especially important not to label patients with premature and often incorrect psychiatric diagnoses, since this may adversely affect future employment or insurability, as well as producing other adverse effects. The use of antipsychotic and antidepressant medication should be limited to the frankly psychotic or suicidally depressed patient, and then only with appropriate psychiatric consultation. If after detoxification, significant affective or thought disorders are evident, they should however, be aggressively treated.

Specific Treatment Modalities

Multidisciplinary Treatment Centers (MTCs). Most MTCs are primarily designed for alcoholism treatment, but have added special programming and drug counselors to deal with multiple substance abusers and abusers of drugs other than alcohol. These centers provide complex interdisciplinary care, but rely heavily on group therapy, individual drug counseling, and Alcoholics Anonymous or Narcotics Anonymous involvement. These treatment centers may be part of a general hospital or free-standing. Although a limited number of beds may be made available to indigent patients, most patients in MTCs are insured, and this has meant that patients are from at least the middle strata of society. Some MTCs may in fact attract a very affluent clientele by special programming for professional people, athletes, etc. In general, MTCs have not treated large proportions of street addicts, and do not actively seek out this population. Those which target specific programs for special groups (women, minorities, adolescents, professionals) may become more involved with street drug abusers. MTCs may be the most appropriate starting sites for adolescent opiate/polydrug abusers, and may provide comprehensive treatment for some licit drug abusers and most impaired professionals. The staff are frequently recovering people themselves, and most services are provided by certified alcohol and drug counselors, although degreed professionals are an integral part of the therapeutic team.

Drug-Free Programs (DF). Outpatient drug-free programs are often part of the follow-up or aftercare programs of MTCs, but may be independent and provide primary treatment. They vary in treatment philosophy and therapeutic modalities available to clients. Peer group sessions are the major focus, with individual and family counseling provided on a periodic basis. Psychological, psychiatric, and medical interventions may be on-site or provided by consultation. AA/NA groups and philosophy are offered by most. Some DF programs are offered by psychiatric facilities and therapeutic communities (see next paragraph) and these may have different orientations. The staff are usually a mix of degreed professionals (MSWs, PhDs, MDs) and certified counselors.

Therapeutic Communities (TCs). While the therapeutic community has its roots in British psychiatry, the drug-related TC began in the United States with Synanon in 1958. The basic concept was that addicts respond best to other addicts, and that a long-term treatment center would benefit drug addicts by placing them in the company of a highly structured but warm and caring family where there would be incessant demands on the addict to mature and improve. Synanon itself went its own separate way by the mid-1960s, largely because of its insistence that its members could never reenter society and by its rejection of professional or interdisciplinary approaches and of research into treatment modalities and outcomes. There are TCs in most states and some foreign countries, and they also vary widely in techniques and philosophy.

Most TCs have struggled to maintain their core concept of peer-directed treatment, rigorous discipline and structure, while eliminating the excesses (a fraternity hazing or Marine boot camp approach) and developing a professional staff on treatment and administrative levels. TCs have traditionally had charismatic leaders, many of whom are recovering people and TC graduates and this leadership has been both a strength and a weakness. The frequent lack of accountability of such leaders has led, in some TCs, to media revelations of major abuses. On the whole, TCs have upgraded staff and programming and have made use of multi-disciplinary concepts of treatment, including medical, psychiatric, and psychological input. Interestingly, while TCs have borrowed MTC approaches, many MTCs have developed therapeutic communities within their treatment centers, or use TC techniques. TCs have also developed special programming and some are aimed predominately at a target group, such as adolescents or women. Street drug abusers constitute the vast majority of TC clients, although some impaired professionals may require this rigorous treatment.

Methadone Maintenance (MM). This form of treatment began in earnest in 1964, but had antecedants in morphine maintenance programs following World War II and heroin maintenance in Great Britain. While there has been considerable resistance and opposition to MM by some supporters of other programs (chiefly TC and AA/NA oriented programs), methadone maintenance has been an effective mode of treatment when properly carried out in appropriately selected patients. Some MM is offered by private (and profit-oriented) organizations, although most programs are part of public or voluntary institutions. In some centers methadone is dispensed, with essentially token counseling available, and the use of other non-opiate drugs (tranquilizers, sedative-hypnotics) is either not actively discouraged, or such drugs may be prescribed to patients. Other centers offer comprehensive counseling, psychiatric, medical, and psychological services, vocational rehabilitation, and educational counseling. Such centers usually actively discourage other drug use, and make efforts to rehabilitate clients who continue to be involved in antisocial activities.

Methadone maintenance has succeeded in allowing many opiate addicts to successfully reenter society freed from the need to spend most waking hours obtaining drugs and the money to buy them. They have, to a modest degree, reduced some of the societal costs of addiction: criminal behavior, institutionalization, and medical costs of drug complications. Data from MM centers indicate a high relapse rate if detoxification is carried out before two years of stabilization (23). It would appear that the majority of methadone patients do well while on maintenance, but relapse when detoxified. For such patients, lifelong maintenance may be the most practical current solution. It has recently been shown that psychotherapy offered to methadone maintenance patients may significantly improve the outcome in some patients.

Specific Target Groups

Street Drug Abusers. Most patients from this population are treated in outpatient DF programs and MM centers, with a smaller but significant number in TCs. In whichever setting they are treated, the concept of total individual rehabilitation should be respected. Since patients may have needs for all of the services previously discussed, treatment centers should have ready access to all. The success rate (moderately to highly favorable outcomes) is similar in DF, TC, and MM programs, ranging between 51–55%, although the highest percentage of highly favorable outcomes (37%), was in the TC group (17, 23).

Licit Drug Abusers. Patients with chronic pain syndromes are best treated in medically oriented pain programs, although a few may require multidisciplinary treatment centers or even methadone maintenance. A complex array of medical specialists and other health professionals are required to assess the chronic pain patient for remediable problems, and a highly organized team approach is required for successful treatment. Detoxification is usually necessary, and group and individual counseling may be required. Psychological and psychiatric evaluation is desirable in all such patients. Pain-relieving techniques, such as biofeedback, relaxation therapy, self-hypnosis, nerve blocks, and transcutaneous electrical nerve stimulation (TENS), may be helpful in individual cases. Special efforts to educate the patients, their families, and their primary care physicians in the risks of use of mood-altering drugs are often of benefit. Antidepressants and neuroleptic agents, however, may sometimes yield dramatic results in improvement of well-being and relief of pain. No accurate data are available regarding the long-term success of such programs, but short-term results are encouraging. One-half to two-thirds of patients can be detoxified and find pain relief with little or no opiate use required (1).

Impaired Professionals. Doctors, nurses, pharmacists, dentists, and other health professionals constitute a special population of drug abusers who are best treated in MTCs. Several programs aimed at this group have been organized, and some adapt long-term TC techniques to their treatment programs. The involvement of hospitals, professional societies, and state licensing boards in case-finding, intervention, and ongoing monitoring has been important in the success of these programs. While the significant personal resources found in members of this group may allow them to successfully resist entry into treatment for considerable lengths of time, once in treatment their success rate is excellent, with favorable outcomes in the vast majority (7, 8, 9). As with other drug abusers, aftercare is critical, with at least two years of program involvement following treatment. The use of random urine screens on a frequent basis (with the voiding directly monitored to avoid subterfuge) is an important adjunct in these programs and has a significant deterrent effect, as well as allowing early detection of relapse.

Future Directions

Increased efforts to research the relationships among patient characteristics, treatment modalities, and outcome may lead to more cost-effective treatment. There have been increased efforts to "share" effective techniques, such as therapeutic communities for methadone maintenance patients. Some areas in which little is known, such as addiction in women, require increased inquiry. Increased understanding of brain chemistry and the action of neurotransmitters may ultimately lead to breakthroughs in diagnosis, treatment, and prevention. The use of the long-term orally effective narcotic antagonist, naltrexone, may greatly improve treatment outcome in selected cases.

PREVENTION

The addictive potential of opiates became apparent immediately following their introduction, and has led to periodic
attempts to control and prevent the spread of opiate addiction.
Prior to the Harrison Narcotic Act of 1914, opiates were available
in the U.S. without prescription and were widely abused, largely
by white working- and middle-class populations. One percent of
the population (1 million out of 100 million) were believed to be
addicted to opiates in 1910. Current estimates of 750,000 opiate
abusers out of 220 million population (0.34%) would indicate a
reduction in prevalence, with most abusers in lower socioeconomic
strata and/or minority groups (26).

Current preventive efforts involve both governmental and
private sector efforts. On federal, state, and local levels, drug
enforcement officials have mounted massive campaigns to identify
and apprehend high-level dealers and confiscate large quantities
of drugs. Despite spectacular individual successes, the proportion
of drugs confiscated relative to the total amount available is small,
and has succeeded mostly in raising prices, which itself may have
some deterrent effect. International efforts to decrease opium
cultivation, smuggling, and laboratory handling have met with
little success. Local efforts to increase criminal sanctions for possession of large quantities of drugs, or dealing or delivering drugs,
do not appear to have deterred use. More Draconian measures,
such as Singapore's mandatory institutionalization in "political
reeducation" labor camps for those possessing drugs seem
inappropriate in a pluralistic society. Other measures, such as
school and factory locker searches, to both detect current drug
users and deter future drug use, raise serious civil libertarian concerns, and are of unknown efficacy.

In some cases, parental efforts to set appropriate limits and
education of parents about drug abuse antecedents and symptoms
of use, may have preventive effects. Societal efforts to improve
the conditions of those in lower socioeconomic groups may reduce
the poverty and despair associated with drug abuse. However, the
spread of opiate use to higher socioeconomic groups would not
be affected by such measures. Educational efforts directed at these
groups have been increased, but have not been proven efficacious.
Unfortunately, we do not know how to prevent drug abuse, and
research into effective prevention is a national priority. Since

opiate abuse and other forms of drug abuse are multifactorial in etiology and development, prevention, like treatment, will require a multimodal approach.

Drug education programs which both warn of risks and emphasize alternatives to drug use have been the mainstay of private preventive efforts, and involve schools, health professionals, criminal justice authorities, and civic groups, as well as the communications media. There is little evidence that such programs are effective at reducing drug abuse on a national scale, although they may work well in individual situations when properly done. The "scare tactic" techniques (using convicts to talk to students, for example) may be media events, but have not been shown to decrease drug use, and in some cases may have the opposite effect.

SUMMARY

Opiate abuse constitutes a major problem for the individuals and families involved, and for society at large. Personal suffering, loss of productivity, medical costs incurred, enormous crime-related costs and, with impaired health professionals, dangers to their patients, are all components of the high price tag of this abuse. Health professionals, educators, clergy, law enforcement, and other government officials, personnel directors and supervisors, parents, and others may all become involved in case detection, referral, treatment, follow-up care, and prevention.

It is important for those in direct contact with opiate abusers to understand the biological effects of these drugs and other abused substances, and to appreciate the psychosocial aspects of abuse as well. An improved knowledge base and a more positive attitude about rehabilitation of drug abusers go hand-in-hand. With greater knowledge and improved attitudes, it is hoped that there will be increased efforts at early case finding and referral for appropriate treatment.

Treatment facilities should be selected which offer multidisciplinary treatment to meet patient needs, and avoid monolithic or simplistic approaches to this most complex problem. Available facilities include drug-free outpatient programs, therapeutic communities, methadone maintenance, and multidisciplinary treatment centers. Psychiatric hospitals and outpatient programs, pain-control programs, and practitioners of other disciplines (e.g., Transcendental Medication, yoga) may be of benefit in individual cases. The facility chosen should be reputable and employ qualified individuals, provide for needed serivces, and have follow-up programs. In addition, programs should utilize a team or interdisciplinary approach to case management, and be willing to reassess the patient's situation if there is little or no progress.

The overall chances for a favorable outcome are over 50%, although this varies with different subsets, and may be as high as 90% among impaired health professionals. These are encouraging statistics which should prompt us to learn more about addiction and abuse so that we may improve our patients' chances for success. Research in primary prevention remains a priority issue.

Patients who make themselves dysfunctional by their own hands are both frustrating and challenging. As helping professionals, we become impatient with their self-destructive courses, and increasingly unhappy and even resentful over our inability to influence them in a positive manner. However, if we persist in educating, motivating, and persuading drug abusers to enter treatment, a positive outcome can be the gratifying result in many cases. They require the best we have to offer, and we must accept as our responsibility giving them our best.

REFERENCES

1. Brenca, S.F. and Chapman, S.L. (Eds.): *Management of Patients With Chronic Pain.* New York: SP Medical and Scientific Books, 1983.

2. Cox, T.C.; Jacobs, M.R.; LeBlanc, A.E. and Marshman, J.A.: *Drugs and Drug Abuse: A Reference Text.* Toronto: Addiction Research Foundation, 1983.

3. *Diagnostic and Statistical Manual of Mental Disorders,* 3rd Edition. American Psychiatric Association, Washington, DC, 1980.

4. Duberstein, J.L.; Kaufman, D.M.: A clinical study of an epidemic of heroin intoxication and heroin induced pulmonary edema. *American Journal of Medicine, 51:*704, 1971.

5. Gold, M.S.; Pottash, A.C.; Sweeney, D.R. and Kelber, H.D.: Opiate withdrawal using clonidine: A safe, effective and rapid non-opiate treatment. *Journal of the American Medical Association, 243:*343-346, 1980.

6. Gold, M.S.; Pottash, A.C.; Sweeney, D.R. and Kelber, H.D.: Efficacy of clonidine in opiate withdrawal: A study of thirty patients. *Drug and Alcohol Dependence, 6:*201-208, 1980.

7. Green, R.C.; Carroll, G.J. and Buxton, W.D.: Drug addiction among physicians: The Virginia experience. *Journal of the American Medical Association, 236:*1372-1375, 1976.

8. Gualtieri, A.C.; Cosentino, J.P. and Becker, J.S.: The California experience with a diversion program for impaired physicians. *Journal of the American Medical Association, 249:*226-229, 1983.

9. Herrington, R.E.; Benzer, D.G.; Jacobson, G.R. and Hawkins, M.K.: Treatment of substance-use disorders among physicians. *Journal of the American Medical Association, 16:*2253-2257, 1982.

10. Hill, H.E.; Haertzen, C.A. and Davis, H.: An MMPI factor analytic study of alcoholics, narcotic addicts and criminals. *Quarterly Journal of Studies on Alcohol, 23:*411-431, 1962.

11. Hill, H.E.; Haertzen, C.A. and Glaser, R.: Personality characteristics of narcotic addicts as indicated by the MMPI. *Journal of General Psychology, 61:*127-139, 1960.

12. Jaffe, J.H.: Drug addiction and drug abuse. In: *The Pharmacological Basis of Therapeutics,* 6th Edition, Goodman, A.G.; Goodman, L.S. and Gilman, A. (Eds.). New York: MacMillan Publishing Co., 1980, pp. 535-584.

13. Jaffe, J.H. and Martin, W.R.: Opioid analgesics and antagonists. In: *The Pharmacological Basis of Therapeutics,* 6th Edition, Goodman, A.G.; Goodman, L.S. and Gilman, A. (Eds.). New York: MacMillan Publishing Co., 1980, pp. 494-534.

14. Johnson, R.P. and Connelly, J.C.: Addicted physicians: A closer look. *Journal of the American Medical Association, 245:*253-257, 1981.

15. Khantzian, E.J.: Opiate addiction: A critique of theory and some implications for treatment. *American Journal of Psychotherapy, 28:*59-65, 1973.

16. Levine, D.G.; Preston, P.A. and Lipscomb, S.G.: A historical approach to understanding drug abuse among nurses. *American Journal of Psychiatry, 131:*1036-1037, 1974.

17. Lowinson, J.H. and Ruiz, P. (Eds.): *Substance Abuse: Clinical Problems and Perspectives.* Baltimore: Williams and Wilkins, 1981.

18. Martin, W.R.; Hewett, B.B.; Baker, A.J. and Haertzen, C.A.: Aspects of the psychopathology and pathophysiology of addiction. *Drug and Alcohol Dependence, 2:*286-295, 1977.

19. Modlin, H.D. and Montes, A.: Narcotics addiction in physicians. *American Journal of Psychiatry, 121:*358-365, 1964.

20. Monroe, J.J.: Ross, W.R. and Berzins, J.I.: The decline of the addict as "psychopath:" Implications for community care. *International Journal of Addictions, 6:*601-608, 1971.

21. O'Donnell, J.A.; Voss, J.L.; Clayton, R.R.; Slatin, G.T. and Room, R.G.: Young Men and Drugs - A Nationwide Survey. National Institute on Drug Abuse Research Monograph, Series 5, Department of Health, Education, and Welfare Publications, No (ADM) 76-311. Springfield, Virginia: National Technical Information Services, 1976.

22. Roy, R. and Tunks, E.: *Chronic Pain: Psychosocial Factors in Rehabilitation.* Baltimore: Williams and Wilkins, 1982.

23. Sells, S.B.: Treatment effectiveness. In: *Handbook on Drug Abuse*, Goldstein, A. and O'Donnell, J.A. (Eds.). Washington, D.C.: United States Government Pringing Office, 1979.

24. Steinberg, A.D. and Karliner, J.S.: The clinical spectrum of heroin pulmonary edema. *Archives of International Medicine, 122:*122, 1969.

25. Thornton, W.E. and Thornton, B.P.: Narcotic poisoning: A review of the literature. *American Journal of Psychiatry, 131:*867-869, 1974.

26. Wikler, A.: *Opioid Dependence: Mechanisms and Treatment.* New York: Plenum Press, 1980.

Chapter 3

Abuse of Amphetamines, Cocaine, and Other Stimulant Drugs

David Benzer, D.O. and Mary Nold-Klett, PA-C

OVERVIEW

In a sweeping yet detailed and concise manner the authors provide a wealth of information regarding detection, diagnosis, and treatment of disorders associated with use and abuse of amphetamines, cocaine, and other licit and illicit stimulant drugs, including tobacco, caffeine, and pharmaceutical products.

Focusing first on the amphetamines, Ms. Nold-Klett and Dr. Benzer detail the pharmacology and effects of this class of drugs, discuss their now few legitimate medical applications, and describe the physical and psychological effects of their misuse and abuse. The section concludes with a description of the most current approaches to treatment of amphetamine-related disorders.

In much the same manner, and with the same depth and breadth of coverage, the authors address issues related to cocaine. From history (including the interesting role of Sigmund Freud) to pharmacology and actions, to use, abuse, diagnosis, and treatment, the two authors provide AHPs a thorough and complete education regarding cocaine.

In succeeding sections the use and abuse of nicotine and caffeine is fully discussed, including an interesting segment on caffeinism — a legitimate diagnostic category — and a most useful explanation of practical ways to help patients overcome their cigarette abuse and dependence.

A final section on use and abuse of pharmaceuticals — amphetamine-like drugs and antihistamines — is followed by a summary and references, which conclude the chapter.

There is a great fund of interesting and useful information, both theoretic and practical, in this chapter, and AHPs will find this chapter to be essential in learning to recognize and deal with these most-widespread of all disorders of substance use and abuse.

INTRODUCTION

In one form or another, stimulant drugs have been used for centuries. When mentioning stimulant drugs, one most frequently thinks of the pharmaceuticals such as cocaine and the amphetamines; yet the stimulant drugs caffeine and nicotine may be the most popular of all mood-altering drugs, used by a large percentage of our population on a regular basis.

Amphetamines, powerful central nervous system (CNS) stimulants, are popular drugs of abuse among recreational users seeking a euphoric "high." Although they have been employed for a number of medical disorders during the past 100 years, they are currently held in disfavor except for the treatment of narcolepsy and hyperkinesis (minimal brain dysfunction or attention deficit disorder).

Illicit use of amphetamines did not become widespread until the 1960s and 1970s when a number of colonies of amphetamine abusers appeared in isolated areas of the country including New York City, Chicago, and the Haight-Ashbury area of San Francisco. This development occurred during an era of increasing drug experimentation and abuse among a growing youth subculture. Fortunately, such excessive abuse of amphetamines is not as prevalent in this country today as it was in the past. However, AHPs will still encounter patients with problems secondary to amphetamine abuse ranging from the adolescent who becomes ill after abusing "look-alike" stimulants, to the geriatric patient who has been prescribed amphetamines for "weight control" for years and becomes addicted.

Cocaine is a potent stimulant whose popularity as a recreational mood-altering drug has increased dramatically during the past decade. The reasons for this phenomenon are many. Cocaine is erroneously perceived by most users as a status drug having mininal health consequences. It is both a powerful euphoriant and CNS stimulant and has begun to be used by people not previously associated with the drug subculture, especially young professionals. Despite its prohibitive cost of $100-$200 per gram, its use is seen as somewhat of a daring activity by many persons.

The widespread growth of cocaine abuse makes it imperative that AHPs have a working knowledge of this drug and its effects on users. This includes an understanding of the pharmacology of the drug, the recognition and treatment of acute cocaine intoxication, and the availability of treatment for cocaine dependence.

Nicotine is a powerful mood-altering chemical found only in the plant *Nicotiana Tabacum.* Tobacco has been cultivated for centuries and has been either chewed, snuffed, or smoked. Currently, smoking cigarettes is the most popular method of ingesting nicotine in the United States.

Although nicotine is a stimulant drug and as such has effects similar to those of the amphetamines and cocaine, there are major differences between these chemicals. Nicotine has no accepted medical use, is readily available, legal, generally socially acceptable, and relatively inexpensive. Adverse consequences of its use are not immediate; however, they cost the United States billions of dollars per year in health care costs to treat the medical complications of nicotine addiction. These figures ignore the psychological trauma of personal and family illness, permanent disability, and early death. Because of the large number of cigarette smokers in this country, the health consequences of chronic use of tobacco, and increasing interest and concern regarding the use of cigarettes, it is important for AHPs to become familiar with some of the current information concerning nicotine use, and the treatment options available for persons interested in stopping tobacco use.

Caffeine is perhaps the most widely used stimulant drug in the United States. Recently there has been growing interest in the effects of caffeine as a possible drug of abuse. A state of caffeine intoxication, or *caffeinism*, and a caffeine withdrawal syndrome has recently been recognized. It appears as if many heavy coffee drinkers are physiologically dependent on caffeine.

Caffeine, as well as its relatives *theobromine* and *theophylline*, differs from all of the other stimulants discussed in this chapter since its use or abuse is not associated with any known serious health hazard other than that which occurs from an overdose. Its use is even more socially acceptable than that of nicotine, and it is ingested by most people in the form of foodstuffs. It is legal, inexpensive, and readily obtained.

As interest and concern is shifting from the mood-altering chemicals which have been used by comparatively few people, such as heroin and LSD, to the more widespread and frequently used drugs, such as alcohol and nicotine, it seems appropriate to discuss caffeine in the same light as other stimulant drugs. Although caffeine has been used for centuries, it appears as if very little is positively known about the drug as it affects humans, especially on a long-term basis.

While medical problems seen as a result of amphetamine abuse may have declined slightly over the past decade, the evolution of cocaine as a major drug of abuse and the ongoing health problems attributable to nicotine addiction mandate an understanding of stimulant drugs on the part of the AHP. It is hoped that this chapter will provide the information which will aid the AHP in identifying and treating stimulant drug-associated illness in their patients.

AMPHETAMINES

Amphetamine, or *2-phenyl-isopropylamine*, was first manufactured in 1887. Beginning in the 1930s the amphetamines were used to treat obesity, depression, fatigue, hyperactivity, and narcolepsy. During this time they were perceived as relatively safe agents, despite their high abuse potential and reports of the development of dependence and psychosis in some individuals.

Amphetamines have long been used as recreational drugs because of their mood-altering properties. They replaced the stimulant cocaine in popularity with both physicians and the public after the use of that drug was restricted to medical practice in 1914. Illicit use of amphetamines did not become much of a problem in the United States until the 1960s, when experimentation with all mood-altering drugs rose sharply among a youthful subculture. Although experimentation with oral ingestion increased precipitously, in the late 1960s a so-called epidemic of intravenous use occurred in some areas of the country, such as Haight-Ashbury in San Francisco, resulting in the development of a "speed freak" lifestyle known for its associated violence and compulsivity.

In 1970, the Controlled Substances Act relabeled amphetamines as Schedule II drugs (little medical use with high abuse potential). A manufacturing quota was set and limits were imposed, and legitimate laboratories decreased their production of amphetamines. Illicit production of amphetamines did not totally make up for this drop in the pharmaceutical supply.

In addition to the illegal manufacturing of amphetamines in "speed labs" in the late 1960s and early 1970s, a large amount of United States pharmaceutical amphetamine was shipped in bulk to Mexico where it was packaged into capsules and smuggled back into the United States. This supply to the black market was also affected by the rescheduling of amphetamines and the restrictions imposed on legitimate manufacturing, in that these manufacturing restrictions limited the amount of drug available for export. These factors led to an overall decrease in the quality of street amphetamine. "Speed" now sold on the street is often analyzed as containing caffeine, ephredine, or phenylpropanolamine as the stimulant component. These so-called legal stimulants are often misrepresented as amphetamines. They are also openly advertised and sold as "look-alike" speed in some markets. The epidemic pattern of intravenous amphetamine use decreased dramatically during the mid-1970s as the result of both the "burned out" lifestyle of the compulsive "speed freaks" and the poor quality of street drug available.

Some people continue to graduate from oral amphetamine use or abuse to intravenous administration; however, the practice does not appear as widespread as it was a decade or more ago. Unfortunately, abuse of and dependence on amphetamines, whether by the oral or intravenous route, continues to be a significant health problem for a number of individuals and should be recognized as such by the health professional.

Pharmacology

Amphetamines are a class of drugs known for their powerful stimulating effect on the CNS and are pharmacologically related to the naturally occurring catecholamines, epinephrine and norepinephrine. Their method of action is not fully understood, but is thought to be due to cortical stimulation via the reticular activating system. The amphetamines produce a release of the endogenous catecholamines, epinephrine, norepinephrine, and dopamine, and subsequently block their reuptake by the nervous tissue. The euphoria produced by the amphetamines is likely due to an enhanced effect of norepinephrine on the neuron.

The main metabolites of amphetamines are *phenylacetone* and *p-hydroxy amphetamine*, but up to 50% of the drug is excreted unchanged in the urine.

Effects

A low dose of amphetamines results in physical signs and symptoms which include increased respiration, heart rate, peripheral vascular resistance, and diastolic and systolic blood pressure. Other effects include anorexia, diaphoresis, mydriasis and mild relaxation of the smooth muscle of the gastrointestinal tract, the bronchioles, and the urinary bladder. The anorectic or appetite suppressant effect of amphetamines has led to their use as an aid in weight reduction. However, the true appetite depressant effect at therapeutic doses is minimal and will not produce weight reduction unless caloric intake is restricted. Rapid eye movement (REM) sleep is also inhibited. Direct application to the mucosa results in local vasoconstriction, a property which led to the initial use of amphetamine inhalers as a nasal decongestant in the treatment of upper respiratory infections and allergic rhinitis.

Psychological effects include increased wakefulness with a decrease or postponement of fatigue. There is an increase in all types of motor and psychic activity, and an elevation in mood with a feeling of euphoria. Users experience an increase in self-confidence and energy. As the dose is raised there is a concomitant increase in talkativeness, restlessness, anxiety, and irritability, while feelings of powerfulness and superiority surface. Individuals may become suspicious, paranoid, delusional, and experience auditory hallucinations. A state of acute toxic psychosis can also occur.

As emotions are intensified, the development of violent behavior becomes more likely. Violence can often be provoked by a relatively minor incident and at times it may appear as if no provocation existed. This reaction most likely is due to perceptual distortions of reality, feelings of paranoia, and general irritability.

Frequent abusers may experience an increase in repetitive behavior, with an extreme amount of attention being given to relatively minor details. Individuals may become acutely involved in a specific activity which they will perform continually, losing all conception of the passage of time and neglecting to attend to the essential needs of daily living.

A popular belief equates the use of amphetamines and cocaine with heightened sexual sensitivity; however, this most probably is the result of reduced inhibitions.

Tolerance and Withdrawal

Tolerance to any mood-altering chemical develops when increasing doses are required to achieve the same effect, or when the same dose used repeatedly results in a diminished effect. Non-tolerant individuals have been reported to develop severe toxic reactions to 30 mg of amphetamine, while some tolerant persons continue to report euphoric effects with doses up to 2,000 mg. Poisoning can produce convulsions, coma, and death.

The characteristic withdrawal syndrome, which occurs as a result of reduction in or cessation of amphetamine use, includes the symptoms of fatigue, depressed mood, disturbed sleep, and an increase in dream activity or REM sleep. If the withdrawal syndrome is marked, the patient may experience agitation or suicidal ideation as an intensification of the depression. Symptoms occur within one day of reduction in or cessation of amphetamine use and usually peak in 2-4 days; however, depression, irritability, and craving for more stimulant drug may last for months.

Pharmaceuticals

Amphetamine drugs are marketed in a variety of forms. Amphetamine (Benzedrine® - "bennies") is the racemic mixture of the *dextro* and *levo isomers* of amphetamine sulfate, while Dexedrine® exists as dextroamphetamine sulfate. A combination of dextroamphetamine and amphetamine is sold as Biphetamine® ("black Cadillacs"). The dextro isomer has a more pronounced effect on the CNS and less of an effect on the cardiovascular system than the levo isomer. Initially it was thought that since the CNS effect of levo amphetamine was less than that of racemic amphetamine, Benzedrine® was a safer drug than Dexedrine®. However, at doses causing similar CNS stimulation, an individual needs to consume a larger amount of Benzedrine®, which heightens the chances of adverse cardiovascular effects.

Methamphetamine hydrochloride (Desoxyn® - "co-pilots," "speed," "meth," "crystal," "crank," "white cross") is related chemically to both amphetamine and ephedrine and has a profound pressor effect on the cardiovascular system as well as producing nervous system stimulation. It is used in approximately the same dosage as amphetamine and is usually the preferred form of these stimulants for intravenous administration. However, Desoxyn® is now purposely made to be insoluble.

"Look-Alike" Stimulants

The anorectic and stimulant effects of the drugs caffeine and phenylpropanolamine (PPA) have been utilized for years in the over-the-counter appetite suppressants. While the efficacy of these drugs for long-term weight control is doubtful, a combination of caffeine and PPA is available in several preparations (Dexatrim®, Dietac®, Prolamine®). In recent years these two drugs have been packaged so that they resemble the more infamous amphetamines and are sold as "look-alikes." For example, caffeine and/or PPA is put into a black capsule and marketed as "look alike black Cadillacs," which are then sold on the street and even marketed through the mail. These drugs are potentially dangerous. PPA overdose has been associated with seizures, strokes, and psychiatric disturbances (1). The adverse effects of caffeine are discussed later. AHPs should be aware of the potential danger to patients from these drugs whether taken in the form of over-the-counter appetite suppressants or in the form of "look-alike" amphetamines.

Use and Abuse of Amphetamines

Medical Uses. Amphetamines have been employed in the past in inhalers for nasal decongestion; however, abuse of the drugs by this method led to their removal from the market. Other uses for which amphetamines are no longer indicated included epilepsy, central nervous system depression due to sedative-hypnotic drug overdose, fatigue, Parkinsonism, and depression. Currently, the only FDA-recommended uses of amphetamines are in the treatment of narcolepsy, a rare condition characterized by an uncontrollable desire to sleep; minimal brain dysfunction in children (hyperkinesis); and short-term treatment for obesity.

It should be noted that without a decrease in caloric intake, use of amphetamines as a treatment for obesity is ill-founded and generally in disfavor. Also, the potential for developing a drug dependency secondary to the use of amphetamines usually nullifies the benefit of any short-term reduction in weight. Amphetamines can also be used in combination with narcotics for the treatment of severe pain as seen in terminally ill cancer patients. Brompton's Cocktail or Mixture utilizes a combination of amphetamine or cocaine, methadone or morphine, and alcohol. It is felt that the stimulant drugs potentiate the analgesic effect of narcotics.

Due to widespread abuse potential of amphetamines, whether administered by prescription or obtained on the street, any use of amphetamines for legitimate medical purposes should be monitored carefully, both in an attempt to lessen the chances of the diversion of amphetamines for illicit use as well as to prevent the development of abuse or dependence in the patient.

Patterns of Illicit Use/Abuse. Amphetamines can be taken by mouth, inhaled, or injected intravenously. Oral administration results in good absorption by the gastrointestinal tract. Most users of the drug begin with this route. Occasional users of amphetamine have in the past included long distance truck drivers, students (as an aid in studying), athletes (for endurance), and entertainers.

Methamphetamine is usually the preferred form of amphetamine drug for intravenous use. When these stimulants are used intravenously, subjective feelings are intensified in a sudden sensation termed a "rush." Pleasurable feelings are increased and the immediate response to the injection produces a high degree of positive reinforcement for further intravenous use. Although the desired sensations are intensified, they wear off more quickly, often leaving a significant depression, as well as fatigue and irritability. These feelings of dysphoria combined with the desire to again experience the "rush" can lead to a cycle of repeated intravenous use or a "run," lasting from a few hours to a few days. During this time, the abuser usually does not eat or sleep adequately, and may experience a state of sleep deprivation resulting in misperception, irritability, and hallucinations. Repeated use of these stimulants results in a state of exhaustion and depression.

Sedative–hypnotic drugs are often used to offset the undesirable effects of "coming down." Popular use of these two types of drugs produces a cycle of using amphetamines during the day and barbiturates or alcohol at night. At times heroin is used with amphetamines and the combined mixture, a "speedball," is injected. The consequences of repeated use of these drugs in this manner are apparent, as polydrug dependence may occur. When used intravenously, the possibility also exists of developing hepatitis, tetanus, vasculitis, septicemia, subacute bacterial endocarditis, or emboli, especially when the same needles are used repeatedly or shared with other drug users.

Diagnosis

It is important to remember that not all patients who abuse or who are dependent on amphetamines or any other mood–altering chemicals will present to the clinician requesting treatment for their problem. On the contrary, many of these individuals will either deny that a problem exists or will minimize the extent to which they are involved in the use of these chemicals. To allow for proper treatment of the patient who presents with a problem related to amphetamine use, it is imperative than an accurate diagnosis be made. Patients may present with a variety of complaints related to amphetamine abuse. These complaints may vary from an inability to discontinue the use of an amphetamine originally prescribed for weight control to a fulminant acute toxic psychosis secondary to amphetamines. The American Psychiatric Association has devised the following *DSM-III* (2) criteria for amphetamine (or similarly acting sympathomimetic drug) disorders (see Appendix 1). This group includes all of the substances of the substituted *phenylethylamine* structure, such as amphetamine, dextroamphetamine, and methamphetamine, and those with structures differing from the substituted phenylethylamine that have amphetamine–like action, such as methylphenidate (Ritalin®), or other substances used as appetite suppressants.

The DSM-III diagnostic criteria for amphetamine or similarly acting sympathomimetic drugs consist of the organic mental disorders (acute intoxication or delusional disorder), withdrawal syndromes, and substance use disorders. The acute intoxication syndrome is diagnosed by observing at least four of ten symptoms, including psychomotor agitation, elation, grandiosity, loquacity, hypervigilance, tachycardia, pupillary dilation, elevated blood pressure, perspiration or chills, and nausea or vomiting. The diagnosis also requires suspicion of recent amphetamine use as well as behavioral effects such as combativeness, and/or impaired judgment.

Amphetamine Psychosis (Delusional Disorder)

Amphetamine psychosis, or delusional disorder, is actually a toxic reaction which has frequently been misdiagnosed as paranoid schizophrenia, since these two conditions have similiarities. Essentially, the psychosis is an exaggeration of the short–term effects of the drug when taken at high doses and it is more likely to occur when used intravenously. At times, however, the toxic state can evolve after frequent low-dose oral use of the chemical.

Clinical signs and symptoms of amphetamine delusional disorder include feelings of persecution, paranoia, anxiety, compulsive behavior, and at times visual, auditory, and tactile hallucinations. Unlike other drug psychoses, there is no disorientation present. Level of consciousness is also not affected. The syndrome lasts anywhere from a few days to several weeks and symptoms usually subside when intake is ceased and the drug is cleared through the urine. Total excretion occurs after approximately one week of abstinence. Hallucinations appear to subside more quickly than the other symptoms and are thought to be associated with high blood concentration of amphetamine. After the acute psychotic episode has resolved, use of even a small amount of amphetamine can trigger recurrence of the process.

Although amphetamine delusional disorder is rare in occasional users of this class of drug, it is impossible to predict which persons are likely to develop a psychotic reaction. It is also difficult to ascertain what relationship exists between possible pre-existing psychopathology and the effects of the stimulant drug. It appears likely that a psychosis can occur in any individual if he or she ingests high doses of amphetamines for a long enough period of time. However, it is also likely that in a number of individuals, psychiatric conditions may exist that predispose that person to the development of a toxic state as a result of amphetamine use/abuse.

Relatedly, those persons using amphetamines to this degree may be in a deteriorated physical condition, with evidence of REM sleep deprivation and malnourishment. Psychosocial and psychological impairment is also present to some degree, including malfunctioning family and peer relationships, loss of self-esteem, financial difficulties, and possible involvement in the legal system.

The final diagnostic category for amphetamines are the diagnostic criteria for abuse and dependence. These are the standard criteria found in all DSM-III substance use categories, consisting of pathologic pattern of use, impaired social functioning, and/or the presence of tolerance or withdrawal. The criteria are outlined in Appendix 1.

In order for the AHP to accurately make the diagnosis of an amphetamine-related disorder, it is often necessary for family members or friends to be asked to provide necessary information. The patient may be unwilling or unable to provide an accurate history. Only by utilizing all available resources can accurate diagnoses be obtained. Similar to the alcoholic, these patients often exhibit a delusional thought process and may not have the insight needed to relate their deteriorating psychosocial and/or physical being to their drug use. The increasing evidence of multiple drug use and abuse may also lead to an inability to arrive at an accurate diagnosis. It is imperative for health professionals to be aware of these factors when evaluating any patient suspected of using or abusing mood-altering chemicals.

Treatment

Acute Intoxication. Since amphetamines produce a delay in gastric emptying due to relaxation of smooth muscle tissue, lavage can be undertaken with some degree of success. If present, attempts should be made to treat hyperpyrexia. Depending on the degree of agitation and associated symptoms, reassurance or "talking down" may be all that is needed to treat the psychological manifestations of the acutely intoxicated state. If severely agitated, short-term use of a sedative such as diazepam may be necessary.

Delusional Disorder. An acute psychosis due to amphetamine use or abuse with evidence of auditory and/or visual hallucinations, delusionary thought processes, and paranoia should be treated with a major neuroleptic tranquilizer such as chlorpromazine, (Thorazine®), or haloperidol (Haldol®). Chlorpromazine is preferable when agitation is severe. Dosage can be titrated upward until the desired effect is achieved and the patient is stabilized at that dose. The dose is then decreased gradually. The patient's progress is, of course, the primary factor to be considered as the determinant for dosage schedules. Some individuals have been known to have residual effects from drug-induced amphetamine psychosis which may require maintenance on neuroleptics. In these patients it is often difficult to determine if an underlying disorder was present before the use of amphetamines or if these agents were solely responsible for the development of a persistent psychotic state.

Withdrawal. Supportive care is the most appropriate treatment for amphetamine withdrawal. If the psychological depression is severe, hospitalization may be necessary. Physical withdrawal, however, is not a life-threatening syndrome and requires no medication. Death from withdrawal is rare, but can occur as a result of suicide in the severely depressed patient.

Dependence. Most individuals who are either abusers of or dependent on amphetamines or other sympathomimetic drugs do not often present in an acute state. Although a classic picture of physical withdrawal is not seen after cessation of amphetamine drug use as it is seen in individuals dependent on some other mood-altering chemicals, this does not necessarily mean that inpatient treatment for detoxification is not necessary, especially if depression is present. In the addicted patient, hospitalization may be necessary to enable the patient to discontinue amphetamine use, something that may not be possible without the structure and support available in an inpatient setting. Patients addicted to amphetamines experience a profound degree of psychological dependence. Withdrawal symptoms may last for weeks or months and may include feelings of depression, irritability, and craving for more stimulant drug. This is best treated with support and encouragement from the health care team. Specific recommendations for determining an appropriate treatment plan for these chemically dependent individuals are discussed in Chapter 7 and will not be dealt with in depth here. However, it is extremely important to remember that due to the likelihood of long-lasting psychological craving, involvement in some form of long-term treatment, such as group therapy and/or individual counseling, with participation in self-help groups such as Narcotics Anonymous or Alcoholics Anonymous, is imperative in order to help the patient maintain a drug-free lifestyle.

COCAINE

The shrub *Erythroxylon coca* has been cultivated in the Andes Mountain range of Bolivia, Peru, and Colombia for at least 1,200 years. The plant played an important part in the religion of the Incan civilization, and its use and distribution were controlled by the privileged class. Commonly, the coca plant's leaves, which contain approximately 0.6 to 1.8% cocaine, were chewed during religious ceremonies. Leaves were also dispensed to soldiers to facilitate greater endurance and to orators to increase mental capabilities. Around 1860, the alkaloid cocaine was isolated from the coca leaf, and in 1884 Sigmund Freud began to experiment with the use of cocaine in both a personal and medical manner. He became fascinated with the drug, and soon began to hail it as a remedy for a variety of disease states. He advocated its use in the treatment of alcohol and morphine addiction, asthma, digestive disorders, depression, upper respiratory infection, and as an aphrodisiac. He noted its stimulant properties and its ability to increase physical endurance as it alleviated fatigue (3). In a series of articles, the Cocaine Papers, Freud (3) extolled its use, and described his personal experimentation with the drug.

Freud encouraged the use of cocaine among his friends and relatives, and prescribed it for a colleague, Dr. Ernst von Fleisch, as a cure for his morphine addiction. Fleisch progressively increased his use of cocaine which led to mental deterioration and the development of an acute psychotic state. This experience, and the mounting evidence of other toxic effects from the use of cocaine, led Freud to cease his personal experimentation with the drug, as well as his recommendations for its medical uses.

Due to its growing acceptance as a "wonder drug," it began to appear in a number of products during the era of patent medicines. Cocaine was hailed for its restorative powers, and was included in a number of beverages, lozenges, and powders for treatment of a variety of disorders including eczema, asthma, depression, venereal disease, neuralgia, tuberculosis, fatigue, and alcohol and opiate addiction. The most famous of these potions was a syrup called Coca Cola®, which was marketed in 1886 as a tonic for a variety of maladies. Today Coca Cola® contains caffeine as its principle stimulant.

Cocaine began to be viewed with increasing caution by society in general. In addition to its relationship with both physical and mental disability, the drug began to be viewed as a violence-provoking chemical. By the 1920s, recreational use of cocaine had fallen out of popularity by most segments of society.

During the late 1960s experimentation with drugs increased, especially among young people. Cocaine was noted for its stimulating and euphoric properties, and during the last decade its use by individuals not previously recognized as being part of the drug-culture has increased. One of the reasons the use of cocaine has become more commonplace may be due to a tightening of the restrictions and control of another group of stimulants, the amphetamines. Cocaine use has also been perceived as an activity in which members of a higher social class are involved and it is considered by many to be a daring chemical to experiment with.

Recognizing the mounting interest in the illicit use of cocaine, congress in 1970 passed the Comprehensive Drug Abuse Prevention and Control Act which classified cocaine as a Schedule

II drug (high abuse potential with little recognized medical use). Under federal law, illegal possession, manufacture, use, or sale of cocaine is a felony.

Pharmacology and Actions

Cocaine is related to the belladonna alkaloids, and its chemical name is *benzoylmethylecgonine*. Although legally classified as a narcotic it is not an opiate. Cocaine is the most potential naturally occurring CNS stimulant and it is also a powerful local anesthetic. Essentially, the stimulant effects of cocaine are similar to those of the amphetamines. In addition, cocaine is a local vasoconstrictor. Due to its vasoconstrictive properties, it is slowly absorbed if administered either intramuscularly or subcutaneously. It is lipid soluble and passes the blood-brain barrier quickly. As a local anesthetic, cocaine is metabolized by the cholinesterases and pseudocholinesterases in approximately two hours. Pharmacologically, cocaine is both an anesthetic and a stimulant, an apparent paradox. However, one must remember that the local and systemic properties of a drug are not necessarily the same. Cocaine is a *local* anesthetic and has no such property when systemically administered. Systemically, cocaine acts as a stimulant drug.

As a sympathomimetic, cocaine affects the cortical area of the brain. It also increases the heart rate, blood pressure, and respiration rate, and causes anorexia, mydriasis, vasoconstriction, and hyperpyrexia. At higher doses or if used chronically, cocaine can cause insomnia, agitation, weight loss, tremors, and hyperexcitability. Occasionally symptoms also include nausea, emesis, or abdominal pain. Poisoning may result in cardiac arrest, respiratory depression, convulsions, or coma. Although rare, death is possible. Toxicity is dose-related and depends on the individual's tolerance.

As a vasoconstrictor, cocaine increases the likelihood of spontaneous abortion, as well as nasal membrane damage if administered chronically by nasal insufflation. Frequent abusers may experience infections of the nasal mucosa or frequent nosebleeds.

Cocaine is said to have aphrodisiac properties, especially when applied to the vaginal mucosa or male genitalia, allegedly resulting in the ability to prolong intercourse. Some women have resported prolonged levels of sexual excitation without being able to achieve orgasm, while some men have reported transitory impotence after administration of cocaine.

When used as a local anesthetic, cocaine blocks the generation and transmission of nerve impulses for approximately 20-40 minutes. This action ceases once the cocaine is absorbed at the site and distributed throughout the rest of the body. Local anesthesia of the mucous membranes is a medically accepted use of cocaine. When applied to the nose, throat, larynx, or lower respiratory tract in intranasal surgery, bronchoscopy, and emergency nasotracheal intubation, it produces both anesthesia and vasoconstriction. Generally, a 5-10% solution of cocaine is utilized for these procedures. As mentioned previously, cocaine is occasionally used in the Bromptom Cocktail for pain relief in the terminally ill. These are essentially the only medical uses of cocaine.

Although medically employed as a local anesthetic, cocaine holds its primary appeal among illicit users because of its stimulant properties. Employed as a "street drug," users report euphoria with an enhanced sense of well-being, alertness, and friendliness. They become talkative and energized, and experience a decrease in fatigue. Higher doses result in restlessness and anxiety.

Users may experience symptoms of dysphoria after the drug's initial stimulant effects wear off, especially those who use cocaine on a chronic basis. Regular abuse of the drug can produce an acute psychosis which is similar to and can be mistaken for paranoid schizophrenia or amphetamine psychosis. Symptoms include auditory, visual, or tactile hallucinations, paranoia, and delusions.

Tolerance and Withdrawal

Tolerance to the mood-elevating effects of cocaine can develop after repeated use of the drug. Tolerance develops at a different rate for a variety of effects and at times there is a fine line between euphoria and toxicity. Some individuals can learn to titrate their dose of cocaine to that which achieves the most desirous effects; however, this is usually more difficult to do than it is with other mood-altering chemicals, as street cocaine can contain a wide variety of substances that have been mixed in with the original chemical and which also have effects on the CNS.

Although a physical withdrawal syndrome as seen in alcohol, sedative-hypnotic, or opiate drugs is not observed after cessation of chronic cocaine abuse, a psychological abstinence syndrome can occur and may present as depression, insomnia, anorexia, despondency, fatigue, agitation, and/or irritability. The symptoms of cocaine withdrawal are usually transitory in nature.

Adulteration of the Drug

When cocaine is prepared for sale on the street, the powder is mixed with a variety of chemicals that can be added without significantly changing the appearance of the original substance. There are three general categories of chemicals that are usually cut with cocaine. These include local anesthetics such as lidocaine hydrochloride (Xylocaine®) or procain hydrochloride (Novocain®), stimulants such as caffeine or amphetamine, and inactive substances such as mannitol or lactose. In addition, occasionally heroin or phencyclidine (PCP) may be added to cocaine.

Due to the use of adulterants in street cocaine, it is important for the clinician to recognize the possibility of the development of unexpected side effects in individuals who claim that they have used "only" cocaine. Some adulterants can be more toxic than the cocaine, increasing the risk of emboli if injected (benzocaine, cornstarch, Novocain®), or cause an irritation to mucous membranes if administered by nasal insufflation (caffeine, butacaine sulfate). Both stimulants and anesthetics may have an additive or synergistic effect with cocaine, leading to a more noticeable and profound central nervous system stimulation than that experienced with use of cocaine alone.

When street cocaine is purchased, the consumer is usually unable to determine the purity of the substance and the composition of other chemicals which have been added to the sample. Quality control is therefore non-existent and the user persistently runs the risk of not only coming into contact with a variety of unknown and potentially toxic chemicals, but also of ingesting a more pure form of street cocaine than he or she has become accustomed to. This increases the chance of developing a toxic reaction.

Abuse of Cocaine

Despite evidence of significant health hazards (4), cocaine is generally perceived by users as a safe drug that does not produce dependence. It is growing in popularity as both a powerful stimulant and as a euphoric agent, especially among young high-income professionals. Cocaine has a variety of street names including "coke," "snow," or "gold dust." It sells for approximately $100-$200 per gram depending on its purity and the chemicals with which it is mixed, or "cut." A sample of street drug contains anywhere from 10-50% pure cocaine and is usually sold by the gram or half-gram ("spoon").

Chewing or making a tea out of the leaves of the *Erythroxylon coca* shrub has been discussed previously. This method of use has been in practice for at least 1,200 years among the natives of the Andes Mountains. Apparently there is little documentation of adverse effects associated with cocaine use by these methods among the South American natives.

The most common method employed by cocaine users in the United States is by inhaling or "snorting" the crystalized powder through one nasal passage while the other is held closed. The powder is finely chopped with a razor blade and arranged in columns or "lines." One gram yields 35-50 lines and each line of 3-5 centimeters contains approximately 25-30 mg of street cocaine. A "line" of the drug is then inhaled through either a rolled dollar (or $100) bill, a straw, or with the aid of a coke "spoon."

Cocaine taken in this manner is absorbed through the mucous membranes and users experience 15-40 minutes of stimulation and a mild euphoria. Cocaine also produces local anesthesia and vasoconstriction of the mucous membranes with a resultant mild nasal congestion. Frequent repeated use of cocaine by this method has been known to produce chronic rhinitis and in some cases septal perforation due to vasoconstriction. A less commonly used method of administration involves dissolving the cocaine powder and injecting the liquid intravenously. Due to the short-acting nature of the drug, its intensely euphoric effects, and the immediate gratification obtained after intravenous injection, users of this method receive a high degree of positive reinforcement for continued intravenous administration. Cocaine is occasionally combined with heroin for use as the original "speedball." Longer-lasting euphoric effects are achieved when these two drugs are injected simultaneously.

The aftereffects of intravenous cocaine use include irritability and depression; however, the dysphoria produced is both more immediate and more marked than when cocaine is "snorted." These symptoms at times encourage abusers of the drug to employ chemicals of a sedative nature to ease their "coming down." Barbiturates, benzodiazepines, alcohol, or opiates have been used to offset some of the undesirable effects of continued cocaine use.

Intravenous use of cocaine is associated with increased health hazards including the development of hepatitis, bacterial endocarditis, or emboli. Incidence of infectious disease is increased when needles and syringes ("the works") are shared by a number of individuals or used repeatedly. Large doses have been known to cause respiratory depression and cardiac failure due to the local anesthetic effect of cocaine. The development of adverse reactions is further complicated by the adulterants present in the vast majority of samples of street cocaine.

When cocaine is used repeatedly at high doses, a state of chronic intoxication occurs and may produce symptoms of an acute psychosis similar to that seen among some amphetamine abusers. The euphoric effects are replaced by feelings of anxiety, depression, and paranoia. Auditory, visual, and tactile hallucinations can occur and the condition may easily be misdiagnosed as paranoid schizophrenia.

Recently, there has been an increase noted in the smoking of coca paste, or "free-base." This practice is referred to as "free-basing" and imposes some added risk to the cocaine user. The cocaine powder alone cannot be smoked effectively since it is destroyed when burned. A process is required to render the drug useful for smoking purposes.

"Free-base," first introduced on the West Coast of the United States in the mid-1970s, is an extremely volatile substance made from cocaine hydrochloride by the use of a strong alkali such as ammonia or sodium hydrochloride, and ether. As "free-base" is not water soluble, it cannot be injected. The coca paste that is the product of this procedure is either added to a tobacco or marijuana cigarette, melted on a strip of aluminum and smoked through a straw, or smoked in a water pipe, which produces the most intense high.

Use of "free-base" cocaine is associated with a very high degree of positive reinforcement, even moreso than that attributable to intravenous use. The "high" is both very intense and very brief, and is followed by a potentially intense dysphoria which increases the user's desire to repeat the smoking procedure. The "free-basing" process removes all of the sugars that have been cut into the initial product, leaving a much more potent sample. Use of the coca paste can lead to the development of toxicity, psychological dependence, and acute psychosis much more quickly than would be expected if the cocaine was administered by a different route.

Factors to be considered in discussing the practice of smoking coca paste are the consequences that may result from the "free-basing" process itself. Ammonia is used in the procedure and if the user does not rinse off the sample after this step, ammonia poisoning can occur, resulting in kidney disease or kidney failure. There is also a concern that "free-basing" may result in pulmonary complications such as bronchitis or pneumonia. Some users have complained of chest pain, shortness of breath, neck and throat pain, and pharyngitis.

Although the process of "free-basing" is somewhat time-consuming, conversion kits which contain all the necessary materials plus instructions for the procedure have been available at "head shops." However, awareness of the health problems which may occur both due to the use of "free-base" cocaine and as a result of the "free-basing" process itself has led to decreased availability of these kits.

Diagnosis of Cocaine-Related Disorders

Unlike amphetamines, cocaine intoxication is the only diagnosis recognized in *DSM-III* as an organic mental disorder relating to cocaine. The criteria for acute intoxication are identical to those earlier described for amphetamines. The criteria for cocaine abuse are likewise similar to those described for amphetamines.

A separate diagnosis of cocaine delusional disorder, or psychosis, is not described in *DSM-III*, and yet cocaine can cause an acute toxic brain syndrome in some individuals. While cocaine psychosis is usually only seen in chronic abusers of the drug, it is impossible to tell what dose is required for the development of this syndrome as individual variances occur and the quality of street cocaine is not constant.

In the acute psychotic state the patient experiences anxiety, paranoia, compulsive behavior, and feelings of persecution. Auditory, visual, and, at times, tactile hallucinations may occur. Level of consciousness is not affected and there is no disorientation. Differential diagnoses include a manic episode and phencyclidine (PCP) intoxication.

It is difficult to determine in a given individual what relationship exists between pre-existing psychopathology and drug effect. Cocaine psychosis is rare in occasional users of the drug but it is impossible to determine which individuals are at risk for development of a toxic psychosis after use of cocaine. It appears likely that any person has the potential for developing this syndrome if cocaine is used at high enough doses for a long enough period of time.

Since cocaine psychosis is usually observed only in chronic abusers of the drug, other factors often seen in these individuals may play a role in development of the syndrome. A person on a cocaine "run," using the drug continuously for a few days or longer, is usually suffering from insomnia, anorexia, agitation, and depression. He or she may also be experiencing alienation from both society and the drug-using subculture itself due to his or her increasingly bizarre behavior. Since cocaine is expensive and its recreational use is illegal, the user may also be experiencing financial and legal difficulties.

Adulterants used to "cut" the cocaine may also have an effect on the development of a toxic psychosis. This may be especially true if phencyclidine (PCP) is employed as a cutting agent since there have been reports of a psychotic state developing after use or abuse of this drug.

Finally, since the purity of street cocaine can never be guaranteed, a like quantity of different samples of street drug used on successive occasions may produce very different effects.

Treatment

Cocaine Intoxication. Reassurance and "talking down" may be all that is necessary to treat the psychological manifestations of acute cocaine intoxication. If the degree of agitation and associated symptoms are severe, the use of a sedative such as diazepam may be required temporarily.

In the presence of psychotic manifestations of cocaine intoxication, therapy with a major tranquilizer such as chlorpromazine or haloperidol should be instituted, with the dosage titrated upward until the desired effect is achieved. In cases of severe agitation, chlorpromazine is preferred for its sedative properties. The patient should be stabilized for several days and the dosage may be gradually decreased depending on the patient's progress.

It is important for reassurance to continue while the patient is stabilized and maintained on any neuroleptic medication. As stated previously, it is difficult to determine what effect pre-existing psychopathology may have had in the toxic episode.

Cocaine Abuse. Although no true physical withdrawal is present in patients abusing cocaine, the psychological dependence on the drug can be marked. The patient may require inpatient detoxification in order to maintain a drug-free state. The criteria for a decision as to whether to hospitalize a drug-dependent individual are discussed in another area of this book (see Chapter 7) and will not be dealt with in detail here. However, if the patient has expressed an inability to cease use of cocaine on an out-patient basis, or presents in an acutely toxic state, the individual should be hospitalized.

Psychological symptoms of cocaine abuse may last days, weeks, or months and include irritability, depression, and craving for more stimulant drugs. Therefore, treatment needs to be on a long-term basis and should include group and individual therapy. It is essential that the patient remain involved in a self-help group such as Narcotics Anonymous or Alcoholics Anonymous in order to maintain a drug-free lifestyle. Recovery from any drug abuse or dependence is a long and difficult process. It can be achieved if an adequate form of treatment is offered to the patient and if the patient can be motivated to make the necessary commitment to recovery.

NICOTINE

The plant *Nicotiani tabacum* is the only naturally occurring source of nicotine, and has been cultivated for centuries in every area of the world which has an acceptable climate. In the sixteenth century, tobacco was introduced to Europe by the returning Spanish Conquistadors in the form of cigarettes.

The first cigarette-making machine was invented in the 1870s. The population of the United States in 1880 was approximately 50 million and 1.3 billion cigarettes were used in that year. The per capita consumption has increased dramatically since that time.

The potential health consequences of smoking tobacco have been of concern for decades. Congress passed legislation in 1965 requiring cigarette packages to include a warning indicating that smoking may be a health hazard, after the Surgeon General's Committee reported that cigarette smoking was related to lung cancer. The Federal Communication Commission banned radio and television cigarette advertising in 1971.

It is estimated that over 30 million Americans have quit smoking (5). Statistics indicate that per capita consumption of cigarette smoking has decreased in the past twenty years, but from 1963 to 1978 the rate of decrease was less than 0.6% per year (5). There has been an overall decrease in the percentage of people who smoke, yet more women and girls are beginning cigarette use (5).

Pharmacology and Effects of Nicotine

Nicotine is a colorless, volatile, lipid-soluble, bitter liquid having the molecular formula $C_{10}H_{14}N_2$. It exists as an optically active molecule with the levo isomer being much more potent than the dextro. It is a very powerful drug and mucosal absorption of 2-3 drops in an adult would produce death.

Nicotine has never been used as a form of food-stuff, probably because it is quickly metabolized to the pharmacologically inert *cotitine* if passed through the gastrointestinal tract to the hepatic portal system. When absorbed through the lungs or nasal or buccal mucosa, the liver is initially bypassed, allowing for a higher concentration of serum nicotine.

Although most of the nicotine which is absorbed by the lungs or mucosa is excreted by the kidney in its original form, nicotine is also metabolized to nicotine-1-N-oxide. Smokers appear to metabolize nicotine more rapidly than non-smokers, which may be due to enzyme induction. Nicotine is also excreted in sweat, saliva, and human milk.

Nicotine has the ability to simultaneously affect different areas of the brain to produce either stimulation, mild euphoria, depression, or sedation. The effects appear to be dose-related and may also be dependent on the mood and expectations of the user.

The primary effects of nicotine on the cardiovascular system are ones of stimulation, and include an increase in heart rate, blood pressure, cardiac output, stroke volume, and basal metabolic rate. Cutaneous blood flow to the extremities is decreased.

Nicotine stimulates secretion of saliva and decreases contractions of smooth stomach muscle. It also increases colon activity and elimination time. These actions may explain the complaint of constipation given by some ex-smokers during the withdrawal period, which may be due to rebound colonic hypoactivity and resultant increase in elimination time.

The primary effect of nicotine on the central nervous system is one of stimulation. Nicotine use can also cause the development of a tremor.

Larger doses of nicotine may produce a sedative effect. Although viewed primarily as a stimulant drug, many users of nicotine report relaxation with reduction in anxiety after use. The paradox may in part be due to the consumption of larger doses of nicotine to achieve the tranquilizing effect, or may be explained by the alleviation of mild withdrawal symptoms which smokers may experience after short periods without the drug.

Nicotine has also been shown to cause a relaxing effect on skeletal muscle, which is most prominent at peak nicotine blood levels and disappears approximately ten minutes after one cigarette is smoked.

Nicotine increases the excretion of epinephrine from the adrenals and vasopressin from the posterior pituitary. While the former action may allow for the heightened ability of the smoker to cope with stress, the latter action accounts for its antidiuretic affect. The possibility of weight gain is a fear expressed by many smokers who would like to cease their drug use. It appears that smokers generally weigh less than non-smokers despite caloric intake. These apparent metabolic differences are also true of ex-smokers who usually weigh less than non-smokers.

Development of Dependence

Nicotine is only one of over 4,000 chemicals in cigarette smoke. It has been difficult to study nicotine as an entity separate from tobacco-smoking, as the two are so closely related. Nicotine is the chemical considered to be the primary addictive element involved in the development of a tobacco dependence syndrome. However, there may be present in tobacco smoke other reinforcing chemicals which have yet to be identified and which play a part in maintaining smoking behavior.

The only substances that have been smoked on a continual basis by any society are those containing psychoactive chemicals such as cannabis, opium, and tobacco. Apart from the mood-altering effects of nicotine, other variables must be considered when discussing cigarette-smoking as a dependence-producing process.

Unlike other psychoactive drug use, cigarette-smoking has been generally considered a socially acceptable activity. This generalization is true independent of the dose used. Although moderate alcohol use is accepted in most countries, excessive or habitual drinking is generally met with a certain amount of disfavor, unlike excessive use of cigarettes. Recently, it appears as if some of that former social acceptability is waning as non-smokers become more assertive regarding their "right" to a smoke-free environment and laws are passed which restrict the public areas in which tobacco-smoking can occur. Cigarette use is, however, still legal for adults and is likely to continue to be so for some time.

Although often considered excessive, the monetary cost of maintaining a cigarette habit is actually much less than that of other mood-altering chemicals and generally not prohibitive for most of society. Cigarettes are easily obtained and, as long as they are inexpensive, will not likely cause financial difficulties for a large percentage of smokers. However, there are surely large numbers of individuals in lower economic brackets who are making some sacrifice in order to maintain a nicotine habit.

One of the most significant differences between nicotine and most other mood-altering chemicals is the absence of an acute toxic syndrome after ingestion of nicotine. There are no profound physical or behavioral changes that occur after cigarette-smoking like those effects commonly seen after ingestion of alcohol, opiates, amphetamines, hallucinogens, or cocaine. The tobacco smoker does not experience immediate psychosocial dysfunction as the result of behavioral alterations after cigarettes, cigar, or pipe use. Psychosocial dysfunction can occur in the smoker, however, after years of tobacco use as a result of physical disabilities such as lung cancer, emphysema, or heart disease, which may force the patient to limit physical and social activities.

Tolerance, Dependence, and Withdrawal

Nicotine is a mood-altering chemical capable of producing tolerance and psychologic dependence and as such is an addictive drug. Initial tobacco use may result in the adverse physical symptoms of nausea, dizziness, diaphoresis, or palpitation. Tolerance to these adverse effects develops quickly, although the exact mechanism is unknown. A withdrawal, or abstinence syndrome, has been documented in individuals who have ceased use of nicotine after chronic administration of the drug. In some heavy smokers symptoms may occur 20-30 minutes after the last cigarette is smoked. Other smokers may experience few withdrawal symptoms.

Withdrawal symptoms include headaches, irritability, muscular aching, gastrointestinal disturbances such as constipation, anxiety, sore gums and tongue, sleep and visual disturbances, distortion of time perception, and difficulty in concentrating. Associated signs include EEG slowing, a decrease in heart rate and blood pressure, and increased frequency of masseter muscle contractions. Most of the physiological symptoms appear to peak within 3-4 days after cessation of nicotine use, and subside within one week. As with other chemical dependencies, the psychological withdrawal symptoms are usually the most persistent. These are generally viewed as the primary obstacles in preventing the ex-smoker from maintaining a drug-free state.

Since most tobacco users smoke on a regular basis, it is difficult to determine whether they smoke to receive pleasure from the effects of nicotine or other chemicals present, or whether they smoke primarily to avoid the aversive symptoms which occur as a result of a withdrawal syndrome.

Smokers have been shown to titrate their nicotine plasma levels to that which is most desirable by unconsciously adjusting their puff-rate. If heavy, frequent smokers are unknowingly given a cigarette of lower nicotine content than usually smoked, they will often increase the number of puffs taken per minute, or the length of time the smoke is held in their lungs, to obtain an increased plasma nicotine level. Each puff of tobacco smoke contains 50-150 μg of nicotine which is delivered as a bolus to the brain approximately seven seconds after inhalation (6). Switching to a lower-nicotine cigarette may be a positive step in helping the patient eventually stop smoking, but if smokers continue to unconsciously modify their plasma nicotine level to that which they have become accustomed, in effect there has been no benefit gained. In fact, harm may be more likely to occur as the patient is smoking an increased number of cigarettes per day, delivering the same nicotine level but often an increased carbon monoxide level than that previously obtained. Although some newer cigarettes have lower "tar" and nicotine contents than their original counterparts, levels of carbon monoxide and other chemicals are not necessarily also lowered, and at times may be increased. Carbon monoxide impairs the oxygen-carrying ability of the red blood cell and it may also be a factor in the development of vascular disease in smokers.

A bolus model (6) has been offered to account for what appears to be a high degree of nicotine dependence among cigarette smokers. When smoked, nicotine is delivered in puffs, or boli, to the brain a few seconds after inhalation. The effects of nicotine are felt almost immediately after use, causing a high degree of positive reinforcement for continued smoking. In addition, after one cigarette has been smoked, an average of ten puffs, or boli, have reached the brain. Addiction to nicotine can, therefore, occur much more rapidly than with other mood-altering substances, due to its almost immediately perceived effects and the frequency with which the boli are experienced. At a one pack per day habit, a smoker will receive 73,000 boli, or "hits," of nicotine per year.

Coupled with a delay in the development of significant adverse consequences, it becomes easy to understand the potential intensity of the nicotine addiction. The ease with which dependence is produced can be further documented by the small percentage of all smokers who are only occasional or intermittent tobacco users.

It has been postulated that there exists a central nervous system receptor specific for nicotine similar to that discovered recently for opiates (7). The identification of a nicotine receptor would likely be followed by the discovery of endogenous neuropeptides that bind to the same receptor site, producing similar physical and psychological effects as nicotine. These advances may lead to a better understanding of the exact mechanism of the development of central nervous system tolerance to the nicotine molecule.

Medical Complications of Tobacco Smoking

Numerous articles have been written dealing with the health consequences of smoking cigarettes and our purpose here is not to reflect extensively on this aspect of tobacco use. However, in an effort to be complete, the following paragraphs provide significant findings pertaining to cigarette smoking as the practice relates to health.

The short-term effects of nicotine on the cardiovascular/respiratory system have been discussed previously and include increased heart rate, blood pressure, respiration, cardiac output, and stroke volume. Nicotine also causes an increase in circulating free fatty acids and in platelet aggregation, while carbon monoxide leads to a decrease in the amount of oxygen delivered to the heart. These combined effects are considered to result in the higher incidence of heart disease among smokers.

Chronic bronchitis and emphysema are often seen in heavy cigarette smokers. Symptoms include shortness of breath, cough, and increased sputum production. Although medications are available to modify these complaints somewhat, the primary method of treatment is cessation of tobacco use. Pipe and cigar smokers also run an increased risk for the development of these diseases though not to the extent that cigarette smokers do.

Tobacco use has been linked to cancer of the lips, tongue, tonsils, larynx, lungs, stomach, intestines, pancreas, and bladder. Significantly, the form of cancer most correlated with smoking is lung cancer, the incidence of which increases with the number of cigarettes smoked, the amount of inhalation, and the duration of cigarette use. As the number of female smokers has increased in the United States, so has the incidence of lung cancer among women.

Infants born of women who smoke heavily while pregnant are usually of lower birth weight and shorter length than those with non-smoking mothers. The percent of stillbirths and neonatal deaths is also increased.

Fortunately, studies thus far have not shown any significant development differences between children from smoking versus non-smoking women when studied at ages 4 and 7 years.

Diagnosis

The criteria for the diagnosis of tobacco-related disorders has been established by the American Psychiatric Association in its *DSM-III* (see Appendix 1). *DSM-III* describes two tobacco-related disorders. The first diagnosis, tobacco withdrawal, is based on the use of tobacco for at least "several weeks" and a daily consumption of more than ten cigarettes. In addition, following abrupt cessation of cigarette use, withdrawal symptoms including craving tobacco, irritability, anxiety, and headaches appear within 24 hours. The second tobacco-related disability, tobacco dependence, is diagnosed when symptoms of tobacco withdrawal have occurred and when the patient has demonstrated inability to discontinue cigarette use despite specific physical disabilities which are known to be exacerbated by tobacco use.

The American Psychiatric Association (2) notes that in practice, diagnosis of tobacco dependence is to be given only when the individual is seeking professional help to stop smoking, or, in the judgment of the diagnostician, the use of tobacco is seriously affecting the individual's physical health. It should be noted that a heavy smoker who has never tried to stop smoking (and, therefore, who has never developed tobacco withdrawal), and who has no tobacco-related serious physical problem, does not have the disorder of tobacco dependence even though physiologically the individual is almost certainly dependent on tobacco.

Treatment

Tobacco dependence is an addiction and needs to be treated as such. Both psychologic and physical dependence can occur with regular tobacco use, and treatment should address these dependencies if it is to be successful.

Psychologic dependence implies that tobacco has become a significant coping tool for the individual. The tobacco user learns over time to deal with stress, anxiety, and life problems by using tobacco. While this behavior is certainly reinforced by the physiologic action of nicotine, psychologic dependence can occur in patients who are not significantly addicted to the drug nicotine, such as pipe and cigar smokers who do not inhale. In order for tobacco users to successfully refrain from tobacco, they must discover and then utilize substitute coping mechanisms. Often times, these substitutes are themselves harmful. For instance, many smokers have turned to food as a substitute coping agent and as a result gain weight after stopping tobacco use. This negative consequences often discourages smokers in their attempts to abstain and can encourage relapse

Cigarette smoking is unique when compared with other addictions in the sense that so many "doses" of the drug nicotine are received during the course of a day, week, and year. Each cigarette provides at least ten separate doses of nicotine via inhalation of tobacco smoke. Each inhalation provides the drug effect of the nicotine. This results in some powerful behavior modification with important ramifications in smoking cessation efforts. Acquired patterns of behavior become entrenched in the life of the smoker, such as repetitious, subconscious hand movements toward the location of the cigarette, i.e., the shirt pocket or purse. Responding to a ringing phone, answering it and then lighting a cigarette, or having a cigarette with each cup of coffee ingested through the day are other examples. These behavioral patterns need to be addressed in any successful approach to nicotine addiction.

The final component of tobacco dependence is the physiologic addiction to the drug nicotine. Nicotine addiction is best evaluated when the smoker discontinues tobacco use. Because nicotine is a very short–acting drug, the symptoms of withdrawal appear quickly. These include craving for the drug, increased pulse and respiratory rate, and anxiety. These symptoms disappear when the drug is used. Therefore, physical addiction to nicotine, as any other mood–altering drug, presents to the smoker these negative physical consequences as a barrier to recovery from the addiction. Relatedly, in order for the smoker to continue to feel "normal" the addiction must continue. The withdrawal syndrome must be anticipated and appropriately managed in successful smoking cessation programs.

Many smoking cessation techniques have been, and are currently, in use throughout the world, including hypnosis, acupuncture, pharmacotherapy, and aversive therapies. Concise, controlled outcome data have failed to provide the one technique that is clearly superior to the other. Comprehensive reviews are available on the subject of smoking cessation methods (8, 9).

Preparing to Stop. Achieving remission from nicotine addiction is a process which occurs in phases. The first phase consists of planning the strategy in quitting, heightening motivation for achieving the desired goals, and making the decision when to quit. Specific objectives to be achieved during this preparatory phase include: 1) Firmly establishing the benefits of quitting, including health, economic, and social advantages to be obtained by not smoking. These need to be individualized for each patient and specific benefits should be written down. This activity should enhance motivation to quit in the patient. 2) The potential non-smoker should be made aware of what to expect after smoking is stopped. This should include specific details of the symptoms associated with the withdrawal process. This is meant to prepare, not frighten, the patient for the reality of nicotine withdrawal. 3) A specific therapy should be selected to treat the nicotine addiction. This needs to be individualized for the particular patient. Since no single technique has been demonstrated to be significantly superior to the others, the choice of therapy depends on availability of therapeutic modalities and needs of the patient. 4) A target date for quitting should be set. This precludes the "I'll quit tomorrow" rationalization that serves to keep the patient addicted to nicotine indefinitely.

Quitting. The next phase in smoking cessation consists of the actual quitting. The advisability of tapering versus abrupt cessation is still controversial. It would seem that tapering would lessen the intensity of acute nicotine withdrawal. On the other hand, tapering can be drawn out for weeks and months without ever achieving complete abstinence from tobacco. It would seem that a compromise may be possible. The patient may be advised to taper but not over more than 7–10 days, with a firmly established quitting date at the end of that time frame. On the designated quitting day the patient should dispose of all his or her cigarettes and remove all smoking accessories from the living and working areas. Activities designed to keep the hands and mind busy should be substituted. Patients may need to initially alter their social activities by avoiding areas where heavy smoking occurs. Deep muscular and mental relaxation exercises and aerobic exercises should be performed regularly.

A current controversy, centering on the quitting phase, concerns the use of pharmaceutical nicotine to treat the nicotine withdrawal syndrome. In March 1984, the nicotine chewing gum Nicorette® became available via prescription in the U.S. Nicotine chewing gum has been used in Europe for several years to treat tobacco dependency, however, the results and efficacy have been equivocal (10). This is not surprising considering tobacco dependence is an addiction and addictions are not successfully treated by detoxification alone. Detoxification needs to occur first, followed by a therapy which will help maintain remission from the addiction. One would suspect this will prove true with nicotine addiction. Nicotine gum will probably be useful as a detoxification aid (11). If this is then followed by a therapy to help the patient remain off tobacco, the results should be better than when either therapy is used separately. Time and good outcome studies will reveal the veracity of the supposition.

Maintaining Remission. The final phase in treating tobacco dependence consists of maintaining a state of remission from smoking. This is the difficult phase; the majority of the smokers who have made a firm commitment to stop smoking, relapse within the first few weeks of abstinence (8). Relapse prevention strategies for smokers are not well established. Once again, it would seem to make sense to turn to the addiction model of chemical dependence for some guidance on this maintenance phase. The time-tested method for maintaining remission from alcohol and other drug addictions has been through self-help, peer support groups like Alcoholics Anonymous and Narcotics Anonymous. These programs are described in detail elsewhere in this handbook. It seems that maintaining contact with others experiencing the same struggle with the same disease has worked for many patients with these addictions. Why wouldn't peer support groups ("Smokers Anonymous") be helpful for tobacco addicts? Until specific relapse prevention strategies have been proven and established, peer support groups would seem a reasonable approach.

Role of the AHP. The role of the AHP in successfully motivating and maintaining their patients' recovery from tobacco dependence is pivotal. Lichtenstein and Danaher (12) listed five functions of the physician in helping the tobacco dependent patient stop smoking. Most, if not all, are applicable to all AHPs. 1) Act as a model of healthy lifestyle by not smoking. 2) Provide information clarifying the risk associated with smoking and the risk reduction if the patient stops. 3) Encourage abstinence by direct advice and suggestion. 4) Refer the patient to a smoking cessation program. 5) Prescribe and follow up the use of specific cessation and maintenance strategies under his or her own office management.

As in most areas of health care, the team approach is often the best. Each of the allied health professions can function to enhance the chance for successful treatment of tobacco dependence. In doing so, the rewards in terms of decreased morbidity and mortality attributable to tobacco dependence justify any and all efforts expended in fighting this devastating addiction.

CAFFEINE

Pharmacology and Effects

Caffeine (1,3,7-trimethylxanthine) is an alkaloid found in the leaves of tea, some members of the holly family, kola nuts, coffee and cocoa bean leaves, and pods. Caffeine is chemically related to *theophylline* (2-dimethylxanthine) found in tea, and *theobromine* which is found in cocoa. Cafeine has a more pronounced CNS stimulant effect than either theophylline or theobromine. Each of these chemicals belong to the family of methylated xanthines, and are very similar in structure to both the naturally occurring purines, adenine and gaunine, two of the molecules responsible for transmission of the genetic code in DNA synthesis, and to uric acid. Taken orally, caffeine appears in most body tissues within five minutes.

Approximately 1% of caffeine ingested is excreted in the urine. The main metabolites appear to be 1-methylxathine, methyluric acid, and other methyl derivatives of uric acid. It is uncertain whether or not accumulation of caffeine occurs in humans. Plasma half life appears to be 2.5 to 4.5 hours with 12-22% metabolism per hour.

The primary pharmacological actions of caffeine result in stimulation of the CNS and the cardiovascular system. Caffeine stimulates the cerebral cortex and the medullary centers of the brain, causing increased wakefulness, impaired sleep ability, and a delay in the development of fatigue. Mood may be mildly elevated. Caffeine use can generally lead to an increase in the amount of work output except when stress is present or fine motor coordination is required. As with many other mood-altering chemicals, expectation of the drug effect may be a factor in the overall psychological manifestations of drug use.

Caffeine can cause stimulation of the myocardium and results in an increase in heart rate, blood pressure, basal metabolic rate, and cardiac output. Cerebral vessels are constricted, visceral smooth muscle is relaxed, and skeletal muscle is contracted. This last effect can produce a fine tremor. Caffeine stimulates gastric secretion and is a diuretic. Caffeine causes a disturbance in sleep resulting in an overall reduction of REM.

Caffeine and related xanthines are found in a number of foodstuffs, some analgesics and over-the-counter cold preparations, appetite suppressants, and stimulants.

Caffeine is used in some migraine headache medications because of its cranial vasoconstrictor properties. Apparently, analgesia is the only recognized medical use of caffeine at this time; however, caffeine is included in a number of over-the-counter medications ranging from analgesics to "stay-awake" preparations to appetite suppressants. Since caffeine is present in a large num-

TABLE 1

ESTIMATIONS OF CAFFEINE CONTENT
OF VARIOUS SUBSTANCES

Coffee	Instant	61-70 mg/cup
	Percolated	97-125 mg/cup
	Dripolated	137-153 mg/cup
Tea	Domestic or Imported	28-77 mg/cup
	Instant	31 mg/cup
Carbonated Soft Drinks *All cola beverages plus Mountain Dew®*	12 oz. serving	32-65 mg
Cocoa - chocolate products such as candy bars, cake, donuts and brownies	per ounce	3-6 mg caffeine and 30-60 mg theobromine
Over-the-counter pharmaceuticals	Anacin® Excedrin® No-Doz®	32 mg 65 mg 100 mg

ber of foods, individuals are often unaware of their own caffeine ingestion. Others enjoy the stimulation obtained by consuming mild to moderate amounts of the drug, usually in the form of beverages. Patients who take therapeutic doses of theophylline and then ingest caffeine, can experience xanthine toxicity, which is characterized by symptoms seen in caffeine intoxication. AHPs need to warn patients taking theophylline about the potentially hazardous synergism that can occur when caffeine is consumed while theophylline is already in the patient's bloodstream (13).

Although the American Psychiatric Association admits that many heavy caffeine drinkers are psychologically dependent on caffeine, it has not included a diagnosis of caffeine dependence in *DSM-III*. This is not to say that caffeine is not capable of causing life problems in abusers of the drug. An individual consuming large quantities of caffeine may have problems related to the frequent state of caffeine intoxication they experience. These complaints may include palpitations of the heart, anxiety or restlessness, and insomnia (14). When these problems are due to ongoing consumption of the drug caffeine, it would seem reasonable to make the diagnosis of a caffeine abuse or dependency syndrome, despite the lack of formal diagnostic criteria. As in all substance–abuse disorders, the diagnosis is primarily based on ongoing life, health, work, or family problems related to use of a mood–altering chemical.

AHPs should be suspicious of caffeinism in patients presenting with any of the complaints listed under symtpoms of caffeine intoxication.

Diagnosis

The diagnosis of caffeine intoxication is made with a history of recent consumption of at least 250 mg of caffeine with the presence of symptoms such as restlessness, nervousness, insomnia, diuresis, gastrointestinal complaints, rambling flow of speech, cardiac rhythm disturbance, or psychomotor agitation. The diagnosis can be made when known psychiatric conditions that can cause similar symptoms, such as panic attacks or anxiety disorders, have been ruled out.

Treatment of Caffeine–Related Disorders

When a diagnosis of caffeine intoxication has been made, treatment usually requires only reassurance. The patient should be informed about the relationship between the amount of caffeine ingested and the development of symptoms of caffeinism, and be advised to limit caffeine intake in the future. While some of these individuals may present in an acutely intoxicated state, it is more likely that a large number of them are chronically experiencing caffeinism and do not relate their anxiety to caffeine use. These people should be motivated to decrease their caffeine consumption in an attempt to allow the symptoms of what may appear to be a chronic anxiety state to dissipate.

As more articles are appearing in the media which discuss the ill-effects of caffeine, patients may become concerned about their own caffeine intake and request advice from the health professional.

Patients can be reassured that although all of the evidence is not yet available, it appears as if most poeple can tolerate 2-3 cups of coffee, or 300-450 mg of caffeine per day, without ill-effects. However, since some people appear more sensitive to the effects of caffeine, they may not be able to tolerate doses in excess of 150 mg. As with all other drugs, pregnant and lactating women should monitor their caffeine intake carefully since caffeine crosses the placenta and also appears in human milk.

For those people interested in reducing their caffeine intake, advise them to avoid chocolate-containing products and most carbonated soft drinks as well as tea and coffee. Suggest beverages such as milk, water, fruit and vegetable juices, herb teas, hot or cold lemonade, and cider. They may also try drinking a decaffeinated coffee, or a weaker tea or coffee than they have been used to.

It is important when advising patients who appear to have life or health problems related to their consumption of the drug caffeine, to tell them to gradually reduce their daily dose of caffeine. Abrupt cessation can cause symptoms such as headache, lethargy, and some mood disturbances. For example, the patient consuming 15 cups of strong coffee daily and complaining of dyspepsia and insomnia, should be advised to decrease his or her coffee intake by one cup per day, or substitute with a cup of decaffeinated beverage at a rate of one cup per day. In 15 days the patient can successfully and safely be caffeine-free. This also enhances the success rate by avoiding adverse symptoms such as headaches, which when present increase chances of relapse.

OTHER STIMULANT DRUGS

Amphetamine-Like Agents

There are a number of non-amphetamine sympathomimetic amine drugs which are structurally related to amphetamine and exhibit similar pharmacological effects. Each of these has a high abuse potential and the American Psychiatric Association (2) has included these drugs in the diagnosis of disorders relating to amphetamines and similarly acting sympathomimetics.

These chemicals are marketed under a variety of brand names, and are usually indicated for the treatment of minimal brain dysfunction in children (hyperkinesis), narcolepsy, and/or short-term treatment for obesity. Some of the drugs in this class are Ritalin® (methylphenidate hydrochloride), Tenuate® and Tepanil® (diethylpropion hydrochloride), Adipex-P®, Fastin®, Ionamin® (phentermine hydrochloride), Pre-Sage® (chlorphentermine hydrochloride), Pondimin® (fenfluramine hydrochloride), Statobex-G® (phendimetrazine tartrate), Voranil® (chortermine hydrochloride), Didrex® (benzphetamine hydrochloride), Propadrine® (phenylpropanolamine), and Plegine® (phendimetrazine tartrate).

At this time, Ritalin® appears to be the most frequently abused drug in this class. It can be dissolved and injected intravenously, or taken by mouth. Street use of Ritalin® appears to be on the rise, possibly due to the poorer quality of available amphetamine.

The actions of each of these drugs are essentially similar to those of the amphetamines. Although some variations do occur, all appear to be capable of producing either toxicity, depression, or psychosis in some individuals. These areas are dealt with extensively in the section on amphetamine and the reader is referred there for a more detailed explanation of pharmacologic effects, diagnostic criteria, and treatment recommendations.

Antihistamines

Although not commonly considered drugs of abuse, some individuals do abuse these drugs for their mild mood-altering properties. One method of use which has been relatively common among street users is a combination of the opioid Talwin® and pyribenzamine *(Ts and Blues)* for a newer version of the "speed-ball." The drugs are dissolved together and injected as "sets." Abusers can, of course, become dependent on the opiate component, and may seek treatment for this type of drug dependency.

SUMMARY

The use and abuse of stimulant drugs pervades our society. The philosophy that a stimulant drug is always available and should be used whenever a person feels even the least bit fatigued or lethargic is ingrained in our collective psyche and continually reinforced by advertising. The stimulant drug caffeine seems to be ubiquitous and is ingested regularly by almost every age group in the form of chocolates, soda, analgesics, coffee, or tea. Of the many million who use caffeine few will develop problems. However, when one does, the health care professional must meet the diagnostic challenge and think of this drug as a possible etiology for a variety of complaints (15).

The stimulant drug nicotine with its powerful addictive potential, is responsible for many health care problems in patients who use the drug in the form of tobacco. The medical complications of tobacco addiction are myriad and well documented elsewhere. What is equally important for the AHP is not only to know how to treat the medical complications of tobacco addiction, but how to treat the addiction itself, which is the primary illness. Tobacco use cessation techniques should be familiar to all AHPs who should in turn encourage and attempt to motivate their patients to stop using tobacco. This is holistic health care in action, and our patients will be the beneficiaries.

Amphetamine addiction appears to be waning because of tight federal and state control over the manufacture and dispensing of amphetamines. However, the disease of amphetamine addiction still exists and AHPs need to be familiar with its manifestations and appropriate treatment modalities to achieve remission of the addiction. The availability of "look-alike" stimulants makes them a potential problem for the unsuspecting patient who abuses them without knowing the health hazards that may be associated with their use. Caffeine intoxication and phenlypropanolamine toxicity have been discussed and are significant medical complications associated with the abuse of "look-alike," as well as over-the-counter weight reduction preparations.

Finally, the AHP should be adept at diagnosing and treating cocaine addiction. Cocaine, the "drug of the 80s," is appearing as the drug choice for an ever-increasing percentage of patients with unidentified chemical dependency problems presenting for treatment. Patients are appearing in emergency rooms with the acute cocaine intoxication syndrome from inhaling, injecting, or smoking cocaine.

AHPs should take the responsibility to include in their patient evaluation a thorough history of stimulant drug use, both licit and illicit. Health problems related to stimulant drug abuse should be diagnosed and treated; however, that alone is not enough. There must be a treatment plan to deal with the primary problem, the stimulant drug abuse, and not just focus on addressing the complications of the illness. Only by doing this will we have become effective health care providers.

REFERENCES

1. Mueller, S.M.: Phenylpropanolamine, a nonprescription drug with potentially fatal side effects. *New England Journal of Medicine, 308:*653, 1982.

2. American Psychiatric Association. *Diagnostic and Statistical Manual of Mental Disorders*, 3rd Edition, Washington, DC: APA, 1980.

3. Freud, S.: *The Cocaine Papers*, New York: Dunquin, 1963.

4. Gottheil, E. and Weinstein, S.P.: Cocaine risks; a review. *Family Practice Recertification, 5:*78-90, 1983.

5. U.S. Department of Health, Education, and Welfare. Smoking and Health: A Report of the Surgeon General, Washington, DC: US DHEW, 1979.

6. Lichtenstein, E. and Brown, R.A.: Smoking cessation methods: review and recommendations. In: *The Addictive Behaviors*, Miller, W.R. (Ed.). New York: Pergamon Press, 1980.

7. Rosenblatt, M.: Neuropeptides: future implications for medicine, *Medical Times, 11:*31-37, 1983.

8. Hunt, W.A. and Bespalec, D.: An evaluation of current methods of modifying smoking behavior, *Journal of Clinical Psychology, 30:*431-438, 1974.

9. *Proceedings of the Third World Conference on Smoking and Health*, Washington, DC: US Government Printing Office, 1977.

10. Russell, M.A.; Raw, M. and Jarvis, M.J.: Clinical use of nicotine chewing gum. *British Medical Journal, 280:*1599-1602, 1980.

11. Schneider, N.G.; Jaruik, M.E. and Forsythe, A.B.: Nicotine vs. placebo gum in the alleviation of withdrawal during smoking cessation, *Addictive Behaviors, 9:*149-156, 1984.

12. Lichtenstein, E. and Danaher, B.G.: What can the physician do to assist the patient to stop smoking? In: *Chronic Obstructive Lung Disease: Clinical Treatment and Management*, Brashear, R.E. and Rhodes, M.L. (Eds). St. Louis: Mosby, 1978 pp. 227-241.

13. Becker, A.B.; Simons, K.J., *et al.*: The bronchodilator effects and pharmacokinetics of caffeine in asthma, *New England Journal of Medicine*, *310:*743-746, 1984.

14. Greden, J.F.; Fontaine, P., *et al.*: Anxiety and depression associated with caffeinism among psychiatric inpatients, *American Journal of Psychiatry*, *135:*963-966, 1978.

15. Stephenson, P.E.: Physiologic and psychotropic effects of caffeine on man, *Journal of the American Dietetic Association*, *71:*240-247, 1977.

Chapter 4

Abuse of Hallucinogenic Drugs

Jess Johnson, PA–C

OVERVIEW

This chapter opens with a brief history of the religious and cultural uses of natural hallucinogens dating back to pre-Columbian America, and moving forward to the laboratory synthesis of LSD more than forty years ago. The author then goes on to explain in a concise and lucid manner the pharmacology of the major natural and synthetic hallucinogens, indicating their routes of ingestion, usual dosage, and the behavioral, physiological, and psychological effects of their use and abuse. After briefly commenting on past and present epidemiology of hallucinogen abuse, Mr. Johnson then details the signs and symptoms of abuse, and the criteria for making an appropriate diagnosis according to DSM–III criteria. The final section quite fully explicates the accepted methods of treating acute and chronic drug states, which will be of special interest to emergency room personnel and other AHPs.

A summary and references conclude the chapter.

INTRODUCTION

The distinguishing characteristics of the hallucinogens, also known as *psychedelics* or *psychotomimetics*, is their ability to produce distinctive alterations in perception, thought, feeling, and behavior. They are among the oldest known psychoactive drugs, having been used as an adjunct to religious practices in some societies for centuries. One of the earliest uses of hallucinogens is recorded in Central American stone sculptures from 1500 BC. These Mayan sculptures portray hallucinogenic mushrooms from whose stems emerge the heads of gods. Many Indian tribes since the Mayans have a documentable history of hallucinogen use associated with religious rituals. Native American tribes such as the Commanche, Kiowa, and Omaha to this day use the hallucinogen peyote, derived from cactus, in religious ceremonies.

Widespread hallucinogen abuse among American ethnic groups other than Native Americans had its birth with the synthesis of lysergic acid diethylamide (LSD). This compound was indirectly synthesized from a fungus (ergotamine) growing on wet grass and grain, and was first produced by Alfred Hoffmann at Sandoz Laboratories in 1943. However, it was not until the late 1950s and early 1960s that this drug came to prominence as part of a subculture of American youth led by such advocates of hallucinogen use as Timothy Leary. It should also be noted that there was some interest in the use of LSD in the treatment of alcoholism in the late 1950s and early 1960s. Some psychopharmacologists and psychotherapists felt that this mystical and enlightening experience would cause such an aversive experience that people would abstain for life. Obviously we have learned that LSD is not a long-term physiological deterrent to drinking and has, as noted, become a widely abused drug itself (1).

From the initial enthusiasm for LSD, sprang an interest in the traditional hallucinogens used by North Central and South American Indians. "Mushrooms," psilocybae, mescaline, and peyote emerged from the sacrosanct boundaries of religious ceremony to the indiscriminate street usage common today.

PHARMACOLOGY OF HALLUCINOGENS

Lysergic Acid Diethylamide (LSD)

LSD, the prototype hallucinogen, is the most widely abused drug of this class in North America. LSD is an *indole* derivative and the chemical basis of most of the natural *ergot alkaloids*. It is the product of the hydrolysis of the alkaloid *ergonovine (ergometrine)* and its derivatives. Free lysergic acid causes very few psychological effects. Many derivatives have been prepared by substitutions at either or both of the amide and indole nitrogens. Diethyl substitutions at the amide nitrogen of lysergic acid make the most potent hallucinogenic compound, LSD-25.

Physical effect of LSD in humans may include hyperreflexia, restlessness, tremor, ataxia, and spastic paresis (partial or incomplete paralysis). Psychic changes predominate in humans, but are difficult to interpret. Such changes include excitation, mood changes (euphoria, depression), perceptual disturbances, hallucinations and pseudo-hallucinations, depersonalization, and schizoid states. Cognitive functioning may also be affected:

> "Hallucinogenic drug users score more poorly on tests sensitive to cerebral damage than do non-drug users, although presence of gross cerebral pathology has not been established. Testing indicates that hallucinogenic drug use involves some risk to higher cognitive function" (2, p. 281).

LSD produces effects on both sympathetic and parasympathetic activity, which is probably mediated centrally. Sympathetic effects predominate, though parasympathetic effects may be present (e.g., lacrimation, salivation). Pupillary dilation is marked and common. Other effects include hyperthermia, piloerection, hyperglycemia, and tachycardia, all of which are the mesodiencephalic effects of the drug. Hypotension, bradycardia, and respiratory depression may be produced because of the drug's medullary effects. LSD also exerts a weak adrenergic blocking action. For these reasons, effect on blood pressure and pressor response to catecholamines is variable.

Although many investigations have been done to elucidate the mechanism of action of LSD, results are still not conclusive. However, from recent reviews (3) it appears the main action of LSD and other sympathomimetic hallucinogens (psilocybin, mescaline) involves serotonin (increase in the level, decrease in the turnover), although other neurotransmitters may be involved. These hallucinogens interact with serotonin receptors on the postsynaptic membrane, although a presynaptic component of the drug action may exist. The postsynaptic action probably results from competition between serotonin and LSD-25 for common receptors, but it is not yet clear whether these receptors are for serotonin or for tryptamines. In neuropsychological terms this action results in modification of synaptic transmission, possibly facilitation at low doses, and inhibition at high doses. The interference of normal sensory input almost certainly leads to misinterpretation of the sensory information and hence distortion in sensory perception.

The LD-50 (the dose which proves lethal to 50% of the subjects receiving it) of LSD for humans has been assumed to be about 0.2 mg/kg or 14 mg for the average adult male. No death in humans has been known to occur because of the drug's acute toxicity. The usual street dose is 100 μg/kg for an LSD "trip."

Psilocybin and Psilocin

"Sacred mushrooms" have been used for centuries by the Indians of Mexico and Central America during religious ceremonies. Roger Heim, a French mycologist, identified the mushroom as belonging to the genus *psilocybe*. An alkaloid, *psilocybin*, was isolated by Albert Hoffmann, discoverer of LSD, and his colleagues. The major constituent was found to be a potent hallucinogen. Another alkaloid, *psilocin*, which is equally potent, was also found in small amounts. These two alkaloids also occur in several species of mushrooms.

Psilocybin and psilocin are esters of *dimethyl tryptamine*. Psilocybin is relatively unstable, and after its ingestion it is readily hydrolized by alkaline phosphotase. Psilocin appears to be the active metabolite responsible for the effect of psilocybin.

Hallucinogenic effects of the psilocybin are similar to those of LSD in many respects, although they are shorter-lasting (2-6 hours). When equivalent doses of this alkaloid are given to subjects already acquainted with the LSD state, it is impossible for them to tell the difference between the effects of the two drugs. Since a dose of 225 µg/kg produces clinical effects comparable to that caused by 1-1.5 µg/kg of LSD (4), 20 mg of psilocybin is equivalent to the usual 100 µg for an LSD trip. Therefore, LSD appears to be 150-200 times more potent than psilocybin, which in turn is 1.5 times weaker than psilocin.

A clinical syndrome lasting 3 hours can be produced by oral doses of 60-200 µg/kg of psilocybin, while a somewhat longer-lasting syndrome occurs with parenteral doses. Prominent symptoms include dizziness, weakness, nausea, blurred vision, anxiety, dilated pupils, visual effects, dreamy states, impaired coordination, and increased deep tendon reflexes. Visual effects consist of brighter colors, longer-lasting afterimages, sharp definition of objects, and colored patterns and shapes that are reported to be generally pleasing. Induced dilation of the pupils may be a result of central sympathetic stimulation. Performance on psychometric tests decreases for about 1-2 hours after administration of the drug, possibly because of decreased motivation.

Tolerance develops to psilocybin although not as rapidly as to LSD or mescaline. Cross tolerance (as tolerance to one drug in a class develops, tolerance to other substances in that class occur) occurs among all three of them.

The LD-50 in mice was found to be 280 µg/kg for psilocybin. There are no indications of toxic effects in human controlled experiments, nor is any information available as to its cumulative toxicity in the Indians who use the drug in natural form. Cases of poisoning have been attributed to edible psilocybe mushrooms; some have been fatal.

Mescaline

Mescaline is the major active ingredient in the peyote cactus. Peyote is the Aztec term referring to the cacti, *lophophora williamsii* and *anhalonium lewinii*, that grow in northern Mexico. Peyote has been used by Indians from earliest recorded time as an adjunct to religious services to obtain visions for purposes of prophecy and divination, and to induce a trance state in tribal dancing rites. In addition, it has been used to relieve fatigue and hunger, and as a medicine to treat various diseases.

Mescaline, the main alkaloid derived from the cactus, was first isolated by the German chemist, A. Heffterin, in 1869.

Mescaline is one of the eighteen alkaloids derived from the peyote cactus. It is a *phenylethylamine* derivative, and thus differs structurally from LSD, psilocybin, and some other indole–derivative hallucinogens. It is a close chemical relative of the hormone epinephrine and the neurohormone norepinephrine, a fact that led to an interesting hypothesis that aberrant catecholamine metabolism may induce psychosis.

Given in doses of 5 mg/kg, mescaline produces unusual psychic effects and sensory alterations in normal human subjects. In some respects psychic changes are similar to those caused by very small doses of LSD. The equivalent dose of mescaline needed to produce psychotomimetic effects is about 4,000 times higher than LSD. Pseudohallucinations are vivid and consist of brightly colored lights, geometric designs, animals and sometimes people. True hallucinations are not common. Anxiety may develop in normal subjects and may be severe in some schizophrenic patients. Intellectual functioning is transiently impaired and may be a result of the drug effect, or reflect total disinterest on the part of the subject.

Central sympathetic stimulation produced by mescaline is manifested by mydriasis and tachycardia, and a rise in blood pressure very similar to that seen with LSD or psilocybin. In addition, it may produce hyperreflexia of the limbs and tremor. Nausea and vomiting occur frequently.

Alkyltryptamines

Alpha methyltryptamine (AMT) is an analogue of psilocybin and an indole analogue of amphetamine. Compared to psilocybin, AMT has a slower onset of action, but more prolonged effects, sometimes lasting 16–18 hours. Direct stimulation is greater and early symptoms of jitteriness, restlessness, and anxiety are more pronounced. Somatic symptoms are greater in number and intensity. Visual effects and impairment of mental function are much less marked than with psilocybin.

Dimethyltryptamine (DMT)

DMT is the prototype member of the tryptamine subclass of indole derivatives. The drug is the constituent of many of the South American snuffs and drinks that contain other psychedelic indole derivatives. First significant drug effects are noted at doses of approximately 50 mg, whether smoked, or injected. The drug is not active orally unless combined with monoamine oxidase inhibitors. Tolerance develops only after extremely frequent use; there is also cross tolerance between DMT and LSD.

Physiological effects of DMT are similar to those of LSD, but sympathomimetic symptoms such as dilated pupils, heightened blood pressure, and increased pulse rate are more common and more intense. Psychological effects are similar to those caused by LSD but often are more intense since DMT is not taken by mouth:

> "The effects come on suddenly and can be overwhelming. The term 'mind blowing' might have been invented for this drug. The experience was described by Alan Watts as like 'being fired out of the muzzle of an atomic cannon.' Thought and visions crowd in at great speed, a sense of leaving or transcending time occurs, and one experiences a feeling that objects have lost all form and dissolved into a play of vibrations. The effect can be like instant transportation to another universe for a timeless sojourn" (5, p. 19).

Effects of DMT when smoked or injected begin in seconds and reach a peak in 15–20 minutes, a feature that has earned it the name "businessman's trip." The brevity of the experience makes its intensity bearable, and for some, desirable.

Phencyclidine (PCP)

Dissociative anesthetics is the name usually given to a class of synthetic drugs (arylcyclohexylamines) whose most interesting representatives are phencyclidine (PCP) and ketamine. They were

initially used in medicine as analgesics and anesthetics that produce no respiratory or cardiovascular depression. Their effects
have been likened to sensory deprivation, dream-like visions, a
sense of isolation, and often the feeling that the self or soul has
separated from the body. It has been suggested that they stimulate
the central nervous system while disturbing the centers where
sensory impulses are relayed to the cerebral cortex. They are
sometimes said to be intermediate between the anticholinergics
and LSD in their effects.

The drug was patented in 1963 as a surgical analgesic and
anesthetic under the name of Sernyl®, but withdrawn for use with
humans in 1965 because of delirium, agitation, and disorientation
observed among patients on emergence from anesthesia. Since
1967, it has been marketed under the name of Sernylan® as a
tranquilizer and anesthetic for animals. It first appeared on the
street that same year and has since been sold as "crystal," " angel
dust," "super weed," "rocket fuel," and "hog," and also decep-
tively labeled as THC, "synthetic grass," mescaline, psilocybin, or
other drugs. It is easy to synthesize and the precursors are readily
available, so it has become a popular illicit drug. Some persons
are reported to have taken it daily for several years (6).

Phencyclidine can be taken orally, intravenously, or intra-
nasally, but it is most often sprinkled on marijuana or parsley and
smoked. Less than 5 mg is considered a low dose, 5-10 mg moderate, and more than 10 mg a high dose. As used on the street, PCP
should probably be described as a tranquilizer, analgesic, or
euphoriant rather than a psychedelic drug. Vivid visual imagery is
rare; commonly reported effects are relaxation, warmth and
tingling, physical and emotional numbness, floating sensations,
a feeling of emotional or sensory isolation ("sheer nothingness"),
changes in body image, and altered space and time judgment.
Phencyclidine raises heart rate and blood pressure but does not
affect breathing. The effects last 4-6 hours, and a mild, irritable
depression may follow. Residual effects may continue for up to
24 hours. PCP remains in the blood and urine for as long as a
week. Overdose can cause stupor, coma, and even death. There is
also a danger of accidental death, because both judgment and
motor coordination are severely impaired. The most important
adverse effect is a psychotic reaction. Phencyclidine is much more
unpredictable and dangerous in this respect than LSD and other
psychedelic drugs. The symptoms vary but may include depression, manic excitation, sudden mood changes, inappropriate

laughter and crying, catatonic immobility, severe anxiety, blank staring, disordered and confused thought, delusions and paranoid thoughts, fear of dying, and unpredictable violence. Common physical effects are increased nystagmus (vertical and/or horizontal), elevated systolic blood pressure, sweating, vomiting, muscular rigidity of face and neck, opisthotonic posturing, drooling, and repetitive movements. The psychosis may last for as little as a few hours or as long as two weeks, and it is often followed by partial or total amnesia for the period since taking the drug.

Long-term use of PCP is becoming more common, and the effects of it have not been adequately studied. Chronic users are sometimes described as "crystallized," suffering from lethargy, memory and concentration difficulties, and dulled thinking and reflexes. PCP does seem to produce some psychological dependence and some tolerance; withdrawal symptoms have also occasionally been reported. There is no evidence of permanent brain damage.

Ketamine

This drug is chemically related to PCP and was first synthesized in 1962 at Parke-Davis Laboratories in their search for phencyclidine substitutes. The hydrochloride has been available on prescription since 1969 as Ketalar®, and is used as an anesthetic or analgesic with children, to avoid cardiovascular depression.

Although ketamine has excited the interest of adventurers in exotic realms of consciousness, it is not a common street drug and few adverse reactions have been reported. John Lilly's (5) account of his involvement with the drug suggests that prolonged use can cause some of the same problems as PCP, including psychological dependence, psychotic reactions, and a gradual loss of contact with the everyday world.

Anticholinergics

These drugs are not usually regarded as psychedelics, although they have a great deal in common historically, culturally, and pharmacologically with other drugs taken for their mind-altering effect. They are called anticholinergic because they block the action of acetylcholine, a neurotransmitter that controls the contraction of skeletal muscles and also plays a role in brain chemistry. They are also called *deliriants*, because their effects at high doses include incoherent speech, disorientation, delusions, and hallucinations, often followed by depression and amnesia for the period of intoxication. *Belladonna alkaloids* are the principal or classical anticholinergic deliriants.

These *tropane* derivatives, the most powerful of which is *scopolamine*, are found in various plants in the nightshade family or *Solanaceae*, among them deadly nightshade (*atropa-belladonna*), mandrake (*Mandragora Officinarum*), black henbane (*Hyoscyamus Niger*), jimson weed (*Datura Shamonium*), and over 20 other species of henbane and datura. Of all psychoactive drugs, only alcohol has been in used for so long over such a large part of the world. For thousands of years, on all inhabited continents, the belladonna alkaloids have been a tool of shamans and sorcerers, who take advantage of the sensations they evoke to imaginatively leave their bodies, soar through the air, or change into an animal. They also produce toxic organic symptoms such as headache, dry throat, loss of motor control, blurred vision, and greatly increased heart rate and body temperature; death from paralysis and respiratory failure can occur. Belladonna alkaloids are so incapacitating, the physical effects so unpleasant, and loss of contact with ordinary reality so complete,that they are used only with great caution and rarely for pleasure. Ironically, for the same reasons, they are not regarded as a source of drug abuse problem and can be bought in small doses in over-the-counter sedatives and pills for asthma, colds, and motion sickness.

A number of synthetic esters of benzilic and glycolic acid, used in medicine for the treatment of Parkinson's disease and the Parkinsonian effects of antipsychotic drugs, occasionally produce effects like those of the belladonna alkaloids, apparently by the same anticholinergic mechanism. The prototype is Ditran®; others are Artane®, Cogentin®, and Bemactyzine®.

A recent article by Dr. Jonathan S. Rubenstein (4) deals with the abuse of antiparkinsonian drugs. Though abuse of antiparkinsonian drugs has rarely been reported in this country, there is evidence than it is more widespread than generally believed. Dr. Rubenstein (4) reported eight cases of suspected abuse of the drugs. Emphasis here is placed on the need for increased awareness among physicians and Allied Health Professionals regarding the potential abuse of antiparkinsonian agents and greater caution in prescribing them. Case studies (4) clearly indicate abuse of antiparkinsonian drugs: One such study describes a 27-year-old white female schizophrenic who had made numerous trips to the emergency room for refills of her Prolixin® and Artane®. The patient announced she had run out of Artane® ten days after receiving 100 5 mg tablets. A review of her chart revealed she had received large amounts of the drug at frequent intervals, often as much as 600 mg in a two-week period, with no evidence of extrapyramidal symptoms beyond a vague complaint of restlessness.

These findings may indicate that abuse of antiparkinson drugs is more widespread in this country than the paucity of reports would indicate. The fact that all the reported cases in this article were quite easily and quickly collected from the files of a moderately sized mental health facility suggests the problem may be a common one. Such abuse is further suggested by statements of several patients that they have friends who are abusers, and indications are that the antiparkinsonian agents are gaining popularity as street drugs.

EPIDEMIOLOGY

There is a widespread impression that the halcyon days of hallucinogen abuse were in the 1960s and that by the late seventies the use and abuse of hallucinogens had ended. Indeed, *Life* magazine estimated in 1966 that a million people had taken mescaline, LSD, or psilocybin (5). The estimated production capacity of illicit laboratories uncovered by authorities in 1967 was 40,000,000 doses (5), and in 1971 it was estimated that 5,000,000 Americans had used LSD (5). A 1978 report published by the U.S. Department of Health and Human Services (6) shows the number of people who have tried hallucinogens has significantly increased for all ages. Among youth, 7% have tried hallucinogens; 25% of young adults report use, and 5% of those over 25 years report use (6). During the last two decades current use among young adults has more than doubled.

Self-reported use of PCP or angel dust in the 12 to 17-year-old group shows a decrease since 1977 from 6% to 4%. The number of users between ages 15 and 25 has increased significantly; 15% report having tried it (6).

The perception that hallucinogen use is a phenomenon of the past is erroneous. Young people today continue to represent a sizeable segment of hallucinogen abusers within our society.

DIAGNOSIS

Hallucinogen Organic Mental Disorders

The AHPs need to be aware that organic mental disorders are often caused by ingestion of hallucinogenic substances and not necessarily as a result of some metabolic disturbance or dementia. Organic mental disorders are precipitated most often by two types of substances, both of which have hallucinogenic properties: substances that are structurally related to 5-hydroxytryptamine (e.g., lysergic acid diethylamide [LSD] and dimethyltraptamine [DMT]) and substances related to catecholamines (e.g., mescaline). These substances are taken orally.

Hallucinosis. The essential features are characteristic perceptual changes, physical symptoms, and maladaptive behavioral effects due to recent hallucinogen ingestion. The perceptual changes include subjective intensification of perceptions, depersonalization, derealization, illusions, hallucinations, or *synesthesias* (e.g., seeing colors when a loud sound occurs). These effects occur in a state of full wakefulness and alertness. There may be hyperacusis (abnormal sensitivity to sound — sometimes seen in hysteria), and overattention to detail. The illusions may involve distortions of the individual's body image. The hallucinations are usually visual, often of geometric forms and figures, sometimes of persons and objects. More rarely, auditory and tactile hallucinations are experienced.

Physical symptoms include pupillary dilation, tachycardia, sweating, palpitations, blurring of vision, tremors, and incoordination.

Maladaptive cognitive and behavioral effects may take the form of marked anxiety or depression, fear of losing one's mind, ideas of reference, paranoid ideation, impaired judgment, interference with social and occupational functioning, or failure to meet responsibilities.

This category of disorders is called an hallucinosis even though it is recognized that frequently, with low doses, the perceptual changes do not include hallucinations.

Associated features are heavily influenced by the setting in which the syndrome occurs, the dose, and the expectations and personality of the individual. Euphoria is common. Usually the individual realizes that the perceptual changes are due to the effect of the hallucinogen. More rarely, the individual is convinced that he or she has lost his or her sanity and will not regain it.

Imagery and thoughts are often dominated by mystical or religious experiences. For example, the individual may believe that he or she has achieved certain insights not otherwise possible.

The onset of effects is usually within an hour of ingestion. In the case of LSD, the most commonly used hallucinogen, the disorder lasts about 6 hours. For other hallucinogens the duration may range from under an hour to a day or two, or at most, three days.

In rare cases the individual will act irrationally and may harm himself or herself or others. "Flashbacks" (recurrent hallucinations after the hallucinogen is no longer present in the body) can occur. Hallucinogen delusional disorder and hallucinogen affective disorder, both discussed below, are possible complications.

Various substance-induced intoxications, such as that due to cannabis, cause clinical pictures similar to the hallucinogen hallucinosis that results from low doses of hallucinogens. In such cases, if an adequate history is not available, laboratory tests of urine should be used to make the diagnosis (refer to Appendix 1 for DSM-III diagnostic criteria).

Delusional Disorder. The essential feature is an organic delusional syndrome that persists beyond the period of direct effect of the hallucinogen, i.e., 24 hours after cessation of hallucinogen use. The syndrome emerges during or following an hallucinogen hallucinosis and all of the described perceptual changes may occur. In addition, the individual has a delusional conviction that the disturbed perceptions and thoughts correspond to reality.

The course of the disorder is variable, and may range from a brief, transitory experience to a long-lasting, psychotic episode that is difficult to distinguish from a nonorganic psychotic disorder, such as schizophreniform disorder or acute paranoid disorder.

Complications are the same as described for hallucinogen hallucinosis (refer to Appendix 1 for DSM-III diagnostic criteria).

Affective Disorder. The essential feature is an organic affective syndrome that persists beyond the period of direct effect of the hallucinogen, i.e., 24 hours after cessation of hallucinogen use.

Typically, the disturbed mood emerges shortly after hallucinogen use. Most common is the appearance of depression or anxiety; elation is rare. The depressive features often include feelings of self-reproach or excessive or inappropriate guilt, accompanied by fearfulness, tension, and physical restlessness. The individual may be unable to stop talking and may have difficulty sleeping. Such individuals are frequently preoccupied with thoughts that they have destroyed their brains, that they have driven themselves crazy and will be unable to return to their normal state. These thoughts are without delusional conviction. When there is elation, then grandiosity, decreased need for sleep, distractibility, increased activity, and loquacity are also present.

The course is variable, and may range from a brief, transitory experience to a long-lasting episode that is difficult to distinguish from an affective disorder. Complications may include manic and major depressive episodes.

An individual with a preexisting affective disorder may take a hallucinogen to elevate his or her mood and then become more depressed. In such cases it may be difficult or impossible to determine if the increased disturbance in mood is due to hallucinogen affective disorder or is merely an exacerbation of the affective disorder (refer to Appendix 1 for DSM-III diagnostic criteria).

Phencyclidine or Similarly Acting Arylcyclohexylamine Organic Mental Disorders

This group of disorders is induced by substances including phencyclidine and similarly acting compounds such as ketamine (Ketalar®) and the thiophene analogue of phencyclidine (TCP). These substances can be taken orally or parenterally, or can be smoked or inhaled. Within this class of substances, phencyclidine is the most commonly used. It is sold on the street under a variety of names, the most common of which are PCP, "PeaCe Pill," "angel dust," "THC," and "crystal."

Intoxication. The essential features of this disorder are specific physical and psychological symptoms associated with maladaptive behavioral effects due to the recent use of phencyclidine or a similarly acting arylcyclohexylamine. The symptoms begin within one hour of oral ingestion of the substance; if smoked, insufflated, or taken intravenously, onset may be within five minutes. The physical symptoms include increased vertical and horizontal nystagmus, elevated blood pressure, numbness or diminished responsiveness to pain, ataxia, dysarthria, and diaphoresis or increased salivation. Psychological symptoms include euphoria, psychomotor agitation, anxiety, emotional lability, grandiosity, a sensation of slowed time, and synesthesias.

The effects of this class of substance are generally dose-related, although there is great variability among individuals. The effects usually range from a mild, "floaty" euphoria and numbness after ingesting less than 5 mg of phencyclidine; to muscle rigidity, hypertension, and a noncommunicative state following a dose of 5-10 mg; and coma, convulsions, and possible death after a dose of 20 mg or more of phencyclidine. Intoxication may be accompanied by repetitive motor movements, including facial grimacing, muscle rigidity on stimulation, and repeated episodes of vomiting. There may also be hallucinations, paranoid ideation, and bizarre or violent behavior.

In most cases, individuals who are acutely confused following ingestion of phencyclidine or a similarly acting arylcyclohexylamine are alert and oriented within 3-4 hours of admission to an emergency room. Chronic users of phencyclidine report feeling intoxication for 4-6 hours after ingesting the usual "street" dose.

Death from respiratory depression can occur following a high dose. The lethal dose in humans has not yet been established, but in rats it was found to be 179 mg/kg orally, and 16 mg/kg intravenously (3). Suicide is not uncommon during acute intoxication. While an individual is recovering from an intoxicated state, depression, irritability, and nervousness often occur.

Other substance-induced intoxications that cause a similar clinical picture, such as those due to amphetamines and hallucinogens, may be ruled out by the presence of phencyclidine in the urine or plasma (refer to Appendix 1 for DSM-III diagnostic criteria).

Delirium. The essential feature is a delirium due to phencyclidine (PCP) or a similarly acting arylcyclohexylamine. The delirium may occur within 24 hours after use, or may emerge following recovery from an overdose days after the substance has been taken. The disorder may last up to a week, with waxing and waning that is probably a reflection of excretion into and reabsorption from the stomach. Delirium is not as common as intoxication from this class of substances. Associated features and complications are approximately the same as described for PCP intoxication, above. Symptoms such as hallucinations, delusions, and disordered thinking and speech are extremely random and individualistic without evidence of systematization. The course fluctuates, and there is evidence of a clouded state of consciousness with global cognitive impairment. Finally, in delirium there is often a generalized slowing of background activity in the electroencephalogram, and the syndrome's cause is obviously organic (refer to Appendix 1 for DSM–III diagnostic criteria).

Organic Mental Disorder. The essential feature is recent use of phencyclidine or a similarly acting arylcyclohexylamine that has resulted in an illness that involves features of several organic brain syndromes, or a progression from one organic brain syndrome to another. For example, an individual may simultaneously have prominent delusions, hallucinations, and signs of disorientation, or may initially have a delirium, followed by an organic delusional syndrome (refer to Appendix 1 for DSM–III diagnostic criteria).

TREATMENT

LSD, DMT, Mescaline, and Similar Compounds

It is especially important when dealing with abuse of hallucinogens and phencyclidine to provide good supportive medical care, as well as psychiatric care when necessary.

In treating the brain syndromes precipitated by hallucinogens such as LSD, DMT, mescaline, and similar compounds, it is important to rule out other possible causes. Diagnosis depends on history and examination; history should be taken from the user and, whenever possible, any persons accompanying the user. Contacting family and friends is also helpful in history-taking when the patient presents alone. The user is often incorrect about the substance he or she was using. Often the user may be in possession of an unlabeled substance. This observation has been supported by analysis of street drugs, especially with the current look-alike drugs. Up-to-date laboratory analysis of the substances is important so that one can diagnose with higher probability. These analyses are available in some centers but still tend to be slow and difficult to obtain. Thus, AHPs usually find themselves facing a history, mental status, and physical examination which only indicates that the patient has used one or more unknown substances.

With LSD and similar hallucinogens, the usual presenting features include a state of fear and panic due to loss of control of drug effects, sometimes referred to as "freakout." The patient is usually in a state of acute distress marked by fear, paranoid mistrust, suspiciousness, intense anxiety, or depression, with illusions and hallucinations (usually visual) and possible periods of autistic withdrawal. Adverse reactions may include depressed levels of consciousness (as with anticholinergics and some solvents), grand mal seizures (not common but sometimes reported with LSD), or delusional behavior which is a threat to self or others.

Treatment is primarily supportive and requires experience in "talking down" patients. AHPs need to be sympathetic and physically able to provide close observation under controlled circumstances. Relapses may occur as long as several seeks after the original symptoms.

"Talking down" by an experienced staff can help an anxious patient more, help decrease any tendency to depend on drugs, and establish a relationship that may be more useful after the crisis is over. "Talking down" simply involves the process of understanding what the patient is experiencing and helping him or her overcome his or her fears while reestablishing contact with reality by directing his or her attentions to concrete and objective perceptions, and helping control the "trip" through firm, supportive, and reassuring guidance as to where, who, what, how long, etc. It is important to avoid any threatening procedures that are unnecessary, such as gastric lavage, or calling police or parents. The unnecessary use of restraints and sedatives or tranquilizers just emphasizes our own anxieties. It also reinforces the user's need to lean on chemical supports rather than work through the demanding but more rewarding intricacies of interpersonal relationships.

Symptomatic and supportive therapy should be determined by the hallucinogen used. For example, diazepam (Valium®) in appropriate doses, usually 30–50 mg I.M. or P.O. STAT and 10–20 mg every 1–2 hours prn. Use of chlorpramizine is not indicated unless the hallucinogen is known. Once the acute phase of treatment is over, discussion should be centered around referral to an appropriate facility for evaluation and treatment. Also, appropriate psychiatric referral should be facilitated when necessary.

Phencyclidine, or Similarly Acting Arylcyclohexylamines

The majority of individuals acutely intoxicated with phencyclidine are found unresponsive, or present with bizarre or violent behavior. Reassurance or "talking down," a procedure that often works with adverse reactions to marijuana and LSD, is usually ineffective in PCP psychosis. Frequently, young people are brought in by the police when found driving erratically or acting inappropriately after an auto accident. Diagnosis depends primarily on history and examination; history should be taken, when possible, from the user and those with him or her. Important factors are amount taken, route of ingestion, and time of ingestion.

Use of phencyclidine can result in acute psychoses, dyskinesia, seizures, laryngospasm, and respiratory distress. Nystagmus, ataxia, contracted pupils, and hyperreflexia are commonly present. Both opisthotonos and decerebrate rigidity have been observed; myoglobinuria (excretion of muscle hemoglobin in urine, oxygen-transporting protein of muscle) and rhabdomyolysis (acute fulminating disease of the skeletal muslce — potentially fatal — evidenced by myoglobinemia and myoglobinuria) attributed to severe dystonia have been seen. Severe hypertension is occasionally present, and hypertensive crises may ensue. Large doses result in stupor or coma, mimicking head injury.

Chromatographic assay of blood, urine, or gastric contents for phencyclidine may not be available in an emergency, and it is often necessary to proceed with treatment on the basis of a clinical impression. Mild intoxication is ordinarily treated by confining the patient in a non-noxious environment in which visual and aural stimuli are minimized. A calm atmosphere and a reassuring manner on the part of the staff is helpful.

In more severe cases of intoxication, specific therapy has been advocated because phencyclidine is a weak base that is readily ionized in mildly acidic solutions, and is subject to ion trapping in the urine and gastric lumen. The urine concentration of the drug has been reported to be increased 200-fold by lowering the pH below 5. Ammonium chloride, administered in a dose of 2.75 Meq/kg, has been used as an acidifying agent. The ammonium chloride is dissolved in 60 ml of saline and administered via gastric tube, which is then clamped for one hour. The dose is repeated at six-hour intervals until the urine pH is brought to a level below 5. Uusally, two doses of ammonium chloride are required. Urine acidification could be undesirable in patients who have ingested salicylates or phenobarbital. After urine pH is lowered to desired level, furosemide-induced diuresis will greatly enhance the renal excretion of the drug.

In dire emergencies, such as profound coma or intractable seizures, ammonium chloride can be given intravenously in a dose of 2.75 Meq/kg as a 1-2% solution of saline. With ammonium chloride therapy, there should be close monitoring of arterial blood gases, a blood ammonia and electrolyte levels, and renal function.

Both oral (6 gm/day for four days) and intravenous (2 gm/ 20 min.) ascorbic acid have been advocated for acidification. However, these regimens do not appear to lower plasma or urine pH.

Phencyclidine is secreted into the gastric lumen where it can be trapped and removed by gastric lavage and continuous suctioning. A saline laxative should be instilled following the initial aspiration of gastric contents. Continuous gastric suction may be necessary for several days after the patient regains consciousness.

Seizures are usually treated with diazepam, and hypertensive crises with diazoxide.

Chronic brain dysfunction may persist after repetitive use of phencyclidine. Memory gaps, dysphasia, impaired impulse control, and belligerence are among the long-lasting, and perhaps permanent, toxic effects.

Phenothiazines are not recommended while PCP is still in the body because they intensify the anticholinergic effects. There is no indication that phenothiazines shorten the recovery phase, and they may produce severe prolonged hypotension. Diazepam may be used for sedation or if necessary, haloperidol.

As with other drug-abuse patients, after acute phases are over it is important to refer the patient to appropriate treatment centers for evaluation and rehabilitation. Also, referral for psychiatric evaluation is indicated for those who suffer prolonged psychosis.

SUMMARY

Current statistics belie the popular belief that hallucinogenic drug abuse has been on the decline since the 1960s, and Allied Health Professionals need to recognize this when patients present with hallucinations and erratic behavior without other explainable causes.

According to national surveys the use of phencyclidine is on the decline. However, because of the ease of synthesis, this drug has become an attractive adulterant in many street drugs produced through illicit laboratories. Vigilance on the part of the AHP for problems attributable to hallucinogenic drug abuse remains as important today as it was in the 1960s.

REFERENCES

1. Blum, E. and Blum, R.: *Alcoholism: Modern Psychological Approaches to Treatment.* San Francisco: Jossey-Bass, Inc., 1967. pp. 197-200.

2. Acord, L.D. and Barker, D.D.: Hallucinogenic drugs and cerebral deficit. *Journal of Nervous and Mental Disorders, 156:* 281-283, 1973.

3. Pradhan, S.N. and Dutta, S.N.: *Drug Abuse: Clinical and Basic Aspects.* St. Louis: C.V. Mosby Company, 1977, p. 194.

4. Rubenstein, J.: Antiparkinsonian drug abuse: eight case reports, *Journal of Hospital and Community Psychiatry, 30:* 34, 1979.

5. Grinspoon, L. and Bakalar, J.B.: *Psychedelic Drugs Reconsidered.* New York: Basic Books, Inc., 1979, p. 19.

6. Peterson, R. and Stillman, R.: *Phencyclidine Abuse: An Appraisal,* Research Monograph 21. Rockville, Maryland: National Institute on Drug Abuse, 1978.

7. American Psychiatric Association: *Diagnostic and Statistical Manual of Mental Disorders,* 3rd Edition. Washington, DC: APA, 1980, pp. 150-156.

Chapter 5

Sedative–Hypnotic Drug Abuse and Dependency Syndromes

David Benzer, D.O.

OVERVIEW

This chapter opens with a brief historical and epidemiological survey of the use and abuse of sedative-hypnotic drugs from the late 19th century up to the present decade. Following these introductory issues, the author focuses on some of the significant psychopharmacologic properties of these drugs and discusses problems of central nervous system depressant actions, notions of tolerance and dependence, and the paradox of sleep disruption caused by so-called sleeping pills. Dr. Benzer then examines the similarities and differences between the various classes of sedative-hypnotic drugs, such as the barbiturates and the benzodiazepines, pointing out the actions, purposes, and dangers of each group of drugs.

Subsequent sections of the chapter deal with several alternative but complementary approaches to diagnosing abuse and dependency syndromes. The author discusses the American Psychiatric Association's criteria, the appearance of intoxication symptoms, withdrawal syndromes, and laboratory and physical examinations in this context.

The final portions of this chapter deal with matters pertaining to the treatment of intoxication, withdrawal, and the often refractory problems of psychological dependency.

INTRODUCTION

The sedative-hypnotic drugs are among the most widely prescribed drugs in the United States (1). In 1978 alone, there were

112

68 million prescriptions written for just one class of sedatives, the benzodiazepines (2). In light of the fact that millions of Americans are using the sedative-hypnotic drugs, it behooves Allied Health Professionals (AHPs) to become knowledgeable about this class of drugs and to become aware of the possible problems that they may cause in patients using them.

Prior to the 19th century, the only sedative available was ethyl alcohol, a product of the fermentation process. In 1864, barbituric acid was produced from the condensation of urea with malonic acid. Barbituric acid, in itself, is not a sedative drug; however, from it, one of the first synthetic sedative drugs, barbital, was derived. It was first marketed in 1903, under the trade name of Veronal®. Barbiturates remained the most widely prescribed sedative drugs for decades until 1955, when chlordiazepoxide, a chemical of the benzodiazepine class, was synthesized at Roche Laboratories. This drug, better known by its trade name of Librium®, was first marketed in 1960, and by the 1970s, the benzodiazepines had become the most widely prescribed sedative-hypnotic drugs, and millions of people throughout the Western world used them on a regular basis. In the interval between the discovery of barbiturates and benzodiazepines, numberous other sedative drugs were developed and marketed. However, none ever approached the popularity of these two classes of drugs.

It is interesting to note that almost as quickly as a sedative was marketed, a report of abuse or dependence upon that drug appeared in the literature (see Table 1). The consequences of addiction to sedative drugs are dealt with in detail in this chapter, following some preliminary remarks concerning the pharmacology of sedative-hypnotic drugs.

Before an individual can progress to the abuse or dependence stages of sedative use, there must first be an initial exposure to the drugs. Since millions of Americans use sedative drugs every year, exposure to these substances occurs at many levels of society, and no population is spared. Millions of patients receive prescriptions for sedative drugs from their physicians, and few hospitalized patients escape exposure to sedative drugs during their hospital stay. At the other end of the distribution spectrum, many sedative drugs are available on the street as part of the illicit drug trade. Valium® has been one of the most frequently prescribed drugs in the United States for years, and in our experience it is one of the most widely available pharmaceutical sedative

TABLE 1
YEAR OF CLINICAL INTRODUCTION
OF SEDATIVE AND HYPNOTIC DRUGS
AND YEAR OF ABUSE REPORTS

Generic Name	Year of Clinical Introduction	Year of First Abuse Report
Bromide	1838	1877
Chloral Hydrate	1869	1875
Paraldehyde	1882	1887
Barbiturate	1903	1904
Ethinamate	1954	1956
Ethchlorvynol	1955	1959
Glutethimide	1955	1957
Meprobamate	1955	1956
Methaqualone	1955	1967
Methyprylon	1955	1960
Clomethiazole	1959	1961
Chlordiazepoxide	1960	1963
Diazepam	1962	1965
Nitrazepam	1965	1968
Oxazepam	1965	1966
Flurazepam	1970	1973
Lorazepam	1975	1976
Chlorazepate	1972	1977

After Allgulander, C.: Dependence on sedative and hypnotic drugs: A comparative clinical and social study. *Acta Psychiatrica Scandinavica*, Supplementum 270, p. 13, 1978.

drugs in terms of illicit sales as well. As a consequence of the numerous opportunities the average American has to be exposed to the sedative drugs, it can come as no surprise that some of these people develop problems in their lives as the result of their sedative drug use. With the development of life problems because of drug use, these patients are then, by definition, suffering either from an abuse or dependency syndrome secondary to their sedative drug use. No group of patients can be considered not to be at risk of having or developing a sedative drug problem, and several groups are in very high risk categories. Adolescents, with access to sedative drugs on the street and in the schools, and with the constant problem of peer pressure, are certainly at high risk. The woman who sees her physician with complaints stemming from various life problems and is prescribed a sedative drug, is also at risk of developing a dependency on that drug. Similarly, the elderly patient who is prescribed a sedative drug for sleep problems, is a potential candidate for the development of a drug dependency syndrome. Each year, specialists in the treatment of addictions are called upon to treat patients in each of these three groups.

Today's health professional must be cognizant of the widespread use of the sedative drugs, as well as the reality that every year some patients using these drugs develop life problems secondary to them, including problems with family and friends, employment difficulties, or possibly even medical problems such as acute intoxication or withdrawal syndromes (see Chapter 7). Recognition of the sedative drug problem in our patients is impossible without this awareness.

GENERAL PSYCHOPHARMACOLOGIC PROPERTIES

The sedative–hypnotic class of drugs are comprised of two categories, the barbiturate and the non–barbiturate sedatives. Some representative drugs from each category are listed in Table 2. There are several general pharmacologic properties that characterize both the barbiturate and non–barbiturate sedative–hypnotic drugs. Knowledge of some of those characteristics (e.g., tolerance, dependence) is essential to our understanding of the dynamics of chemical abuse and dependency.

Central Nervous System (CNS) Depression

Central nervous system depression is the primary pharmacologic property of the sedative drugs (3). The CNS (i.e., brain and spinal cord) depressant effects are dose–dependent and range from mild sedation at low doses, to symptoms such as ataxia, somnolence, and slurred speech at higher doses. Complete respiratory depression and death occur as a result of overdosing on sedative drugs.

Tolerance

Tolerance is also characteristic of sedative drugs (3), and refers to the fact that with continued use of the drugs, ever-increasing doses are required to maintain the desired effect. The concept of tolerance may be confusing, since there are three distinct types of tolerance.

TABLE 2

COMMONLY USED AND ABUSED
SEDATIVE-HYPNOTIC DRUGS

Barbiturates	Non-Barbiturates
Ultrashort-Acting (half-life, 3-8 hours)	
Thiopental (Pentothal ®)	Alprazolam (Xanax ®)
Methohexital (Brevitol ®)	Triazolam (Halcion ®)
Short- to Intermediate-Acting (half-life 14-42 hours)	
Secobarbital (Seconal ®)	Lorazepam (Ativan ®)
Amobarbital (Amytal ®)	Methaqualone (Quaalude ®)
Butabarbital (Butisol ®)	Glutethimide (Doridan ®)
Pentobarbital (Nembutal ®)	Methyprylon (Noludar ®)
Hexathal (Vital ®)	Meprobamate (Miltown ®)
Allobarbital (Dial ®)	Ethchlorvynol (Placidyl ®)
Butalbital (Sandoptal ®)	Chloral Hydrate
	Paraldehyde
	Oxazepam (Serax ®)
Long-Acting (half-life, 24-96 hours)	
Barbital (Veronal ®)	Chlorazepate (Tranxene ®)
Phenobarbital (Luminal ®)	Diazepam (Valium ®)
	Chlordiazepoxide (Librium ®)

After Goth, A. *Medical Pharmacology*. St. Louis: Mosby Company,
1974, p. 5.

The first, *dispositional tolerance*, refers to the "changes in
the pharmacokinetic properties of the agent in the organism, such
that reduced concentrations are present at the sites of drug
action" (3).

The second, *pharmacodynamic tolerance*, is exemplified in
the phenomenon of enzyme induction by some sedative drugs.
The enzymes, principally hepatic (i.e., of the liver), which are
responsible for the metabolism of the drug, after repeated
exposure to that drug increase their efficiency in eliminating the
chemical from the body. It is now thought, however, that
metabolic tolerance plays a relatively minor role in the overall
development of tolerance to sedative drugs.

The third, *central nervous system or behavioral tolerance*, is
believed to be a major factor in the development of tolerance (3).
The central nervous system rapidly adapts to the repeated
presence of sedative drugs and compensatory modifications

develop in the CNS neurons, allowing tolerance to the effects of the drug to occur. It is the modification in neuronal function that contributes to another uniform property of sedative drugs, namely, the propensity to cause physical dependency.

Dependence

When an individual uses a sedative-hypnotic drug on a daily basis over an extended period of time, and at high dose levels, the CNS adapts to the presence of the drug and the individual is then said to be physically dependent on the drug. That is, the state of CNS depression or sedation becomes the normal condition for that individual. If the drug is then abruptly discontinued, the individual then experiences a "rebound" effect, a period of CNS hyperactivity, which constitutes the withdrawal syndrome. The relationship of the action of the drug to the appearance and duration of the withdrawal syndrome is illustrated in Figure 1. It can be seen that if the drug is abruptly discontinued on day 0, the depressed state of the CNS begins to lift, it approaches the pre-drug state of normalcy, but then, "overshoots" that level and rebounds to the state of hyperactivity before settling back down to the normal level. The onset and duration of the period of hyperactivity is determined by the half-life of the drug. Sedatives or hypnotics with shorter half-lives (e.g., oxazepam, meprobamate, lorazepam), referred to as intermediate-acting sedatives, produce withdrawal symptoms which begin within 24-72 hours after discontinuation of the drug, and may last 5-10 days thereafter. The long-acting sedatives (e.g., chlorazepate, diazepam, chlordiazepoxide) produce a withdrawal syndrome that may not appear until 4-8 days after cessation of the drug, and may last for up to three weeks thereafter. Table 3 provides several examples of dose levels and duration of chronic use needed to produce a state of dependency and a consequent withdrawal syndrome.

Readers are reminded that the type of dependence referred to in this discussion of pharmacologic properties of sedative-hypnotic drugs is purely a physical phenomenon. However, one must keep in mind that these drugs also produce profound psychological dependency, a need in the drug-abusing individual to change the way he feels, or to alter his mood, on an ongoing basis, such that the drug becomes a central focus in the individual's life. (A fuller discussion follows below.)

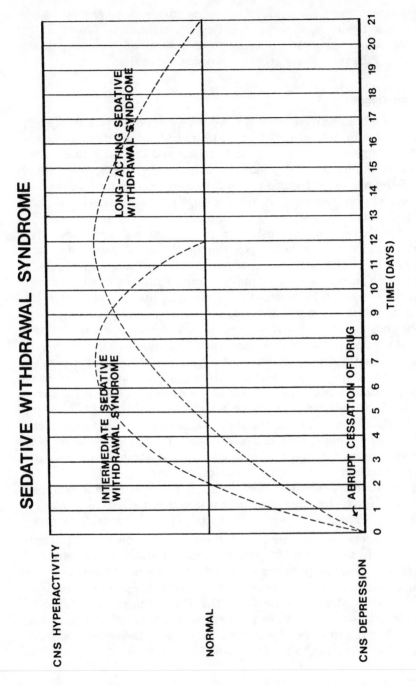

Figure 1. Relationship of drug action to appearance and duration of withdrawal syndrome.

TABLE 3
POTENTIAL FOR PHYSICAL DEPENDENCY
FOR SEVERAL FREQUENTLY PRESCRIBED
SEDATIVE-HYPNOTIC DRUGS

DRUG	Daily dose necessary to produce physical dependency	Minimum time necessary to produce physical dependency	Sedative-hypnotic equivalent doses compared to 30 mg phenobarbital
	Approximate Milligrams	Approximate Days	Equivalent Milligrams
Pentobarbital (Nembutal®)	400 mg	30	100 mg
Meprobamate (Equanil®)	1200 mg	90	400 mg
Methaqualone (Quaalude®)	900 mg	30	300 mg
Diazepam (Valium®)	30 mg	90	10 mg
Chlordiazepoxide (Librium®)	75 mg	90	25 mg

After Fink, R.D.; Knott, D.H. and Beard, J.D.: Sedative-hypnotic dependence. *American Family Physician, 10:*118, 1974.

Cross-Dependence

Cross-dependence is "the ability of one drug to suppress the manifestations of physical dependence produced by another . . ." (3). A situation in which a form of cross-dependence is often seen, occurs when an alcoholic patient undergoes surgery and requires anesthesia. Because anesthesiologists often use the barbiturates to induce anesthesia, an alcohol-dependent patient who already possesses tolerance to the sedative drug alcohol will also display tolerance to the barbiturates and may well require a much larger dose of barbiturate to induce anesthesia because of this tolerance. Cross-dependence or cross-tolerance can be quantified, in that approximate sedative equivalent doses have been assigned to various sedative-hypnotic drugs. This quantification refers to the approximate dose of a sedative drug necessary to produce the same sedation as that dose of another sedative drug used as a standard. The drug often assigned as the standard is phenobarbital.

Disruption of Sleep Patterns

Several sedative drugs that are prescribed for insomnia actually disrupt normal sleep patterns. Sleep is a progressive phenomenon that occurs in repeated cycles of four stages, one of which is known as rapid eye movement (REM) sleep. Most of the dreaming that occurs during sleep occurs during this stage. Some sleep experts feel that the REM periods are the most crucial in achieving complete and meaningful sleep. Some sedative-hypnotic drugs, including alcohol, most of the barbiturates and glutethimide, to name a few, suppress REM sleep (4). This action is a most counterproductive side effect of a drug that is often prescribed and used to promote healthy sleep. The fact remains that most sleep experts feel that no sedative drug should ever be administered as a routine, and that sleeping pills should never be used for a time period of greater than two weeks without a complete assessment of the patient's sleeping difficulties and the alternative therapeutic modalities that might be used to correct these difficulties.

TYPES OF SEDATIVE-HYPNOTIC DRUGS

Barbiturates

The barbiturates, of course, display all of the properties described above. They differ from each other primarily in the length of time they remain pharmacologically active in the body. The duration of action ranges from the ultra short-acting barbiturate such as thiopental (Pentothal®) with a 3–8 hour half-life, to the long-acting compounds such as phenobarbital with a half-life of 36–48 hours (see Table 2) (5). The barbiturates are commonly used as anesthetic agents. Also, since the barbiturates possess significant antiepileptic activity, several of them are used as anticonvulsant agents.

Benzodiazepines

Over the past two decades, the benzodiazepines have surpassed all of the sedative-hypnotic drugs in popularity. Worldwide, they are among the most frequently prescribed drugs. These compounds are somewhat similar to the barbiturates and possess all of the general pharmacologic properties ascribed to sedative drugs, and yet they differ from the barbiturates in several ways.

Unlike the barbiturates, the benzodiazepines are capable of producing relief from anxiety without producing marked CNS depression. This property is the single most significant factor in their tremendous popularity (6). It should be noted, however, that as the dose increases, the signs of CNS depression becomes more apparent. Even so, low-dose antianxiety action is the hallmark of the benzodiazepines. The major difference between the barbiturates and the benzodiazepines is easier to appreciate now that separate and distinct benzodiazepine receptor sites have been demonstrated in human brain tissue (7).

Unlike the barbiturates, the benzodiazepines are known to have skeletal muscle relaxation capability (6), although the exact mechanism of this action is not yet completely understood. The benzodiazepines also display impressive antiepileptic action (6). Because they are most effective in generalized seizure activity, diazepam has become useful in the treatment of status epilepticus.

The ever-increasing number of benzodiazepines available has provided clinicians with a wide spectrum of benzodiazepine drugs with varying half-lives (8). The benzodiazepine with the shortest half-life, 2-3 hours, is triazolam (Halcion®), while oxazepam (Serax®) and lorazepam (Ativan®) with half-lives of approximately 18 hours, are intermediate-acting benzodiazepines. One of the reasons for the shorter half-lives of these compounds is that they have no active metabolites and are excreted unchanged by the kidneys. Conversely, the long-active benzodiazepines such as diazepam (Valium®), chlorazepate (Tranxene®), and chlordiazepoxide (Librium®), have parent compound half-lives of from 20-40 hours. In addition, they have several psychoactive metabolites, each with long half-lives of their own (8). In fact, the half-life of the first metabolite of diazepam, n-desmethyl diazepam, is even longer than that of the parent compound (9).

Other Sedative-Hypnotic Drugs

Methaqualone (Quaalude®), first introduced in 1951, has a short half-life of approximately three hours, and physical dependence can occur in as little as 30 days of continuous use. Methaqualone is known to produce marked respiratory depression. This drug is widely abused, and there are few indications for its use in medical practice.

Meprobamate (Equanil®), is a sedative drug similar to the barbiturates. However, unlike the barbiturates, it has been reported to cause convulsions in epileptic patients.

Glutethimide (Doriden®), Methprylon (Noludar®), and Ethchlorvynol (Placidyl®) can be considered as a group. The first two are structurally similar to the barbiturates, and display sedative action resembling short-acting barbiturates. Ethclorvynol is a tertiary alcohol, also with a brief half-life. All three drugs have the potential for severe and rapid development of physical dependence, and the margin between therapeutic and toxic doses is narrow. All three drugs have been responsible for overdose fatalities. There are few medical indications for their use since the advent of the much safer and equally efficacious sedative drugs such as the benzodiazepines.

DIAGNOSIS OF SEDATIVE-HYPNOTIC DRUG ABUSE AND DEPENDENCY SYNDROMES

Over the years there has been considerable confusion over differentiating use, abuse, and dependency on various classes of drugs. Part of the difficulty arose because of the absence of consensually validated criteria based on consistent clinical-empirical observation. Some of the confusion has been recently alleviated by the publication of the American Psychiatric Association's *Diagnostic and Statistical Manual*, 3rd Edition (*DSM-III*, see Appendix 1) (10), which provides objectively observable behavioral criteria as a basis for diagnosis. In addition, diagnosis is possible on the basis of drug intoxication, the appearance of drug-withdrawal syndrome, and/or the presence of certain physical and laboratory findings. Each of these methods is discussed below.

By DSM-III Criteria

According to the American Psychiatric Association, diagnosis of barbiturate or similarly acting sedative-hypnotic drug abuse can be made if all three of the following criteria are fulfilled.

Pattern of pathological use: inability to cut down or stop use; intoxication throughout the day; frequent use of the equivalent of 600 mg or more of secobarbital or 60 mg or more of diazepam; amnesic periods for events that occurred while intoxicated.

Impairment in social or occupational functioning due to substance use: e.g., fights, loss of friends, absence from work, loss of job or legal difficulties (other than a single arrest due to possession, purchase, or sale of the substance).

Duration of disturbance of at least one month.

To diagnose dependency rather than abuse, the patient must manifest all of the above characteristics, plus either tolerance or withdrawal, defined as follows:

Tolerance: Need to use markedly increased amounts of the substance to achieve the desired effect, or markedly diminished effect with regular use of the same amount.

Withdrawal: Development of barbiturate or similarly-acting sedative or hypnotic withdrawal after cessation of, or reduction in, substance use.

These criteria provide some of the guidelines for the diagnosis of sedative drug problems. In general terms, the diagnosis of abuse depends on demonstrating some life problems that can be attributed to the sedative drug use. These life problems can occur within the family or among friends, with the legal system, with employers, or health problems due to the sedative drug abuse. While the health professional will most frequently recognize the medical complications of sedative drug abuse or dependency, they nonetheless must be aware of the other life circumstances that may lead to the diagnosis. The diagnosis of dependence is made when all of the criteria for abuse are present as well as either the presence of tolerance or withdrawal symptoms.

By Intoxication

The patient who is abusing or dependent upon sedative drugs may appear intoxicated, displaying one or more of the following signs and symptoms.

1. Nystagmus (rhythmic eye movements — barbiturate intoxication)
2. Dysarthria (slurred speech)
3. Ataxia (stumbling gait)
4. Suppressed vital signs
5. Clouding of sensorium and reduced awareness
6. Paranoid ideation
7. Drowsiness
8. Emotional instability
9. Impairment of mental ability

Most of these findings one would see in a patient acutely intoxicated with alcohol. This should be expected in that alcohol is a sedative drug also.

By Withdrawal

At the opposite end of the spectrum from the patient who presents acutely intoxicated, is the patient who presents with physical withdrawal symptoms as a result of abrupt cessation or dose reduction of a particular sedative drug. The clinical presentation of the sedative drug withdrawal may be characterized by some or all of the following signs and symptoms.

Autonomic nervous system hyperactivity, including the signs and symptoms of elevated blood pressure, tachycardia, diaphoresis, tremors of hands and tongue, anorexia, and insomnia (11).

Neuropsychologic symptoms seen in acute sedative drug withdrawal include agitation as well as the possibility of paranoid thinking and hallucinations. Hyperactive deep tendon reflexes are a common finding, and the risk of a grand mal seizure is also present in any sedative withdrawal syndrome. The presentation and timing of the sedative drug withdrawal syndrome seen in any given patient varies somewhat with the following factors.

1. *Dosage.* In general, the higher the dose of sedative drug being consumed by the patient, the more intense will be the withdrawal symptoms (11). The same dose of sedative drug will produce varying degrees of dependency and withdrawal symptoms in patients who vary greatly in body weight.

2. *Duration of use.* The longer the patient has been using a particular drug on a daily basis, the greater the chance of a significant physical withdrawal syndrome being present.

3. *Plasma half-life of the agent.* The timing of the onset of withdrawal is dependent upon this factor. Patients consuming longer-acting drugs have a more delayed and protracted withdrawal syndrome than do patients consuming shorter-acting agents. The example of this is provided in Figure 2, representing patients who were consuming two different classes of sedative drugs (12). Patients in Group II were all consuming alcohol, a short-acting sedative drug described in great detail elsewhere in this book. The patients in Group I were consuming benzodiazepines on a regular basis. One of the patients in this group of 25 was consuming an intermediate-acting benzodiazepine, lorazepam, and experienced a withdrawal syndrome with onset on day 2. All of the rest of the patients were consuming long-acting benzodiazepines, namely, diazepam, chlordiazepoxide, or chlorazepate. Withdrawal syndrome commenced on days

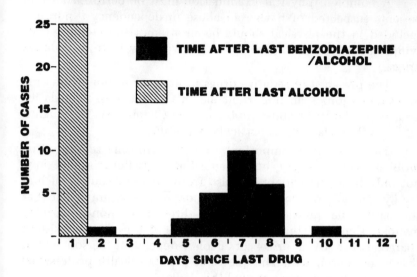

Figure 2.

5-10 with the average day of onset being day 7 following discontinuation of the sedative drugs.

This figure graphically illustrates the variability in the onset of sedative drug withdrawal symptoms as the result of consuming sedative drugs with widely varying half-lives.

4. *Class of sedative drugs.* There is some difference in the nature of the withdrawal syndrome which follows abrupt cessation of the various sedative-hypnotic drugs. Seizures, delirium, and hyperpyrexia are more common in barbiturate withdrawal. Symptoms such as anorexia, insomnia, and agitation predominate in the benzodiazepine withdrawal picture. Even though these are some minor differences between the types of sedative drugs with respect to the withdrawal syndrome produced, the overall picture of sedative-hypnotic withdrawal remains relatively consistent as outlined above.

5. *Individual variability.* Not all patients respond the same to cessation of sedative drugs. One symptom or sign that may be

exaggerated, or even life-threatening in one patient, may be minimal in another.

By Physical and Laboratory Examination

A complete physical examination must be performed on all patients suspected of having an abuse or dependency syndrome. Included in the physical should be an attempt to detect signs or symptoms of either intoxication or withdrawal from sedative drugs.

The presence of sedative drugs in urine or serum at the time of examination is an important aid in the diagnosis of sedative drug dependency or abuse problems (see Chapter 6). The quantitative level, if available, is particularly useful.

The single most important tool in diagnosing sedative drug problems is the history, both medical and pyschosocial, obtained not only from the patient but also from collateral sources such as family, friends, or employer when possible. It is important that the patient be questioned in a non-threatening, non-accusatory manner. Denial of their problems is one of the most consistent characteristics of a drug- or alcohol-dependent person and it should be anticipated. The questions that the health professional asks must attempt to get around this denial.

TREATMENT OF THE PATIENT WITH SEDATIVE DRUG ABUSE OR DEPENDENCY PROBLEMS

Once a diagnosis of a sedative drug abuse or dependency syndrome is suspected, the next step is to attempt to motivate the patient to accept further evaluation and treatment. This step is the most difficult aspect of treating patients with chemical dependency problems. Techniques which can guide health professional in accomplishing this can be found elsewhere in this handbook (see Chapter 11) and are referred to as *confrontation* techniques.

The treatment of the patient with an abuse or dependency syndrome secondary to sedative drugs consists of three possible phases, namely, treatment of the acute intoxication, management of withdrawal, and treatment of the psychologic dependency on the drugs. Each of these will be considered separately.

Treatment of Acute Intoxication

The major threat to the acutely intoxicated patient is respiratory arrest. When caring for a patient acutely intoxicated as a result of sedative drug ingestion, one never knows if the blood level is rising or falling. Also, there is seldom enough time to make adequate determination of which drug was ingested. Therefore, in any acutely intoxicated patient in whom the possibility of overdose exists, several basic steps should be taken, as described by Tanberg (13).

1. Insure and maintain adequate airway and respiration,
2. Maintain cardiovascular performance,
3. Determine level of consciousness,
4. Obtain blood for studies, and
5. Administer 50% glucose solution if patient is comatose, in order to treat possible hypoglycemia that may mimic acute intoxication.

These steps are basic life–support measures that certainly apply to the management of the acutely intoxicated patient. Other measures that may be used in a patient known to have recently ingested large quantities of sedative drugs, or suspected of consuming sedative drugs, are gastric lavage in the unconscious patient, or ipecac (a substance that induces vomiting) administration in the fully conscious patient.

Other than these basic life–support measures, there is no antidote for sedative drug intoxication. Stimulant drugs are of no benefit to the patient suffering from sedative drug intoxication and should never be administered (see Chapter 7 for a fuller discussion).

Treatment of Withdrawal

A sedative abstinence syndrome or sedative withdrawal syndrome may occur anywhere from 12 hours to 14 days after the cessation of drug ingestion, depending upon which sedative drug was used, at what dose, and for how long it had been used on a regular basis. A short-acting sedative drug precipitates a rapid-onset withdrawal syndrome, while the syndrome associated with a long-acting sedative drug might be delayed for as long as 10–14 days after the last dose of the drug.

The treatment goal in sedative withdrawal is to slowly remove the sedative from the system so as not to precipitate an aggressive CNS rebound of hyperactivity (refer to Figure 1). This goal can be accomplished on an outpatient basis in highly motivated individuals, by gradually tapering the dose of the drug. For example, a patient who has been using 40 mg of diazepam daily might have the dose lowered by 5 mg per day each week, such that by the end of eight weeks the drug would be totally discontinued. This procedure affords a safe and gradual tapering of the drug, thereby avoiding the "rebound" withdrawal syndrome that could be precipitated by sudden discontinuation of the drug.

In hospitalized patients, slow tapering may also be utilized. An alternative is to abruptly discontinue the sedative and administer a sedative tolerance test (12). The decision as to when, and if, a sedative tolerance test is to be administered is made on the basis of continual patient-monitoring by experienced nurse observers for sedative withdrawal symptoms. The monitoring begins immediately upon admission to the hospital and is continued until the patient is no longer at risk for experiencing a sedative withdrawal syndrome. A semi-quantitative scale of sedative withdrawal, the Selective Severity Assessment (see Appendix 7) may be utilized in this monitoring process (14). This scale reflects the degree of severity of symptoms and signs that one sees in any sedative withdrawal syndrome. The behaviors and other variables monitored in the Selective Severity Assessment include eating, tremor, sleep, sensorium, hallucination, contact, agitation, sweats, temperature, convulsion, blood pressure, and pulse.

For example, the severity of tremors is rated on a scale of 0-7, in which 0 is the value assigned for the patient with no tremor, and 7 is assigned for severe hand and tongue tremor secondary to sedative drug withdrawal. Our experience indicates that a total score of 20 or more represents the presence of a withdrawal syndrome sufficiently severe to warrant pharmacologic intervention. At that time, the sedative tolerance test is performed. On an empty stomach, after a blood glucose level is determined to rule out a hypoglycemic episode mimicking sedative withdrawal, 200 mg of pentobarbital (Nembutal®) is administered orally. Each hour thereafter, 100 mg of pentobarbital is administered orally until signs of barbiturate intoxication are present, i.e., ataxia, slurred speech, nystagmus, or somnolence. At that point, the total dose of Nembutal® given is the sedative tolerance of the patient. It is important to initiate the sedative tolerance test at the time when significant withdrawal symptoms are present.

If done too early, the results will be falsely low due to the high levels of the original sedative drugs still present in the patient's blood.

Pentobarbital is used because it is a relatively short-acting barbiturate that provides rapid blood levels. Administering a longer-acting drug would result in a delayed sedative effect and would provide confusing results.

The sedative tolerance test is considered positive if the patient is able to take 400 mg or more of pentobarbital without displaying signs of barbiturate intoxication. A positive sedative tolerance test means that the patient is physically addicted to the sedative class of drugs, and he or she then must be slowly withdrawn from these drugs so as not to exacerbate the withdrawal syndrome. To accomplish this, we use phenobarbital, a long-acting barbiturate. Phenobarbital is used in this instance because its long half-life provides stable 24-hour blood levels, and because it is excreted by the kidneys and not as dependent upon hepatic biotransformation. This is important, in that many of the patients to whom a sedative tolerance test might be administered may also have concomitant liver disease. Liver disease may be present because the patient has been abusing not only sedative drugs in the solid form, but also may be abusing the liquid sedative drug alcohol which is severely hepatotoxic. Finally, phenobarbital is an appropriate drug to use in the withdrawal process because patients report that phenobarbital provides them with somewhat of a dysphoric feeling: The patient does not get the feeling of being "high" when using phenobarbital. This makes it much easier when it is time for the medication to be discontinued; the chemically dependent patient seldom complains about stopping the phenobarbital following successful detoxification.

The dose of phenobarbital used is based on the sedative equivalent doses of phenobarbital and pentobarbital. Referring back to Table 3, we note that 30 mg of phenobarbital is equivalent in sedative effect to 100 mg of pentobarbital; therefore, if a patient took 600 mg of pentobarbital in a sedative tolerance test, that would be equivalent to 180 mg of phenobarbital.

$$\frac{30 \text{ mg phenobarbital}}{100 \text{ mg pentobarbital}} = \frac{180 \text{ mg phenobarbital}}{600 \text{ mg pentobarbital}}$$

This equation provides the initial dose of phenobarbital to be used in the withdrawal from sedative drugs. The rapidity with which

one accomplishes the detoxification using phenobarbital is based
upon whether the sedative drug initially used by the patient was a
short- or long-acting sedative drug. If it is a relatively short-
acting drug, such as secobarbital, oxazepam, or methaqualone,
then detoxification can be accomplished more rapidly; for example, in 10 days with a daily dose reduction of 10% of the initial
dose of phenobarbital. For the long-acting sedative drugs such as
diazepam, a 20-day dose reduction period, with a daily reduction
of 5%, is more appropriate.

Continuous monitoring during the course of detoxification
is necessary. If signs of either intoxication or exacerbation of withdrawal symptoms appear, then the dose schedule needs to be
readjusted. A word of warning should be interjected at this point
concerning multiple withdrawal syndromes. Many patients are
consuming more than one drug on a regular basis, and may be consuming drugs in classes other than sedative drugs. In fact, multiple
drug dependency is becoming the rule rather than the exception
among chemically dependent persons. We have observed a number
of cases where patients experienced two or more withdrawal
syndromes, either at the same time or at different times during
the course of their treatment, as a result of physical withdrawal
from more than one drug (15). Health professionals should be
vigilant for this possibility, especially in view of the fact that
patients frequently do not completely reveal the extent of their
multiple drug abuse or dependency when initially questioned
during the taking of a medical history.

Treatment of Psychological Dependency

Management of the intoxication or withdrawal syndromes
represents the more concrete aspects in treating the chemically
dependent patient. Getting the patient to make the changes in
his or her lifestyle and thinking that will be necessary to pursue a
drug-free life, is the more difficult task for anyone treating these
patients. The treatment modality preferred by many professionals
for treating patients with severe psychological dependency on
sedative or other mood-altering drugs is the multidisciplinary
treatment approach (see Chapter 11).

This approach involves a team effort on the part of physician, physician assistants, nurses, counselors, clergy, psychologists,
and other professionals to provide a comprehensive treatment program for the patient, on either an inpatient or outpatient basis. A
description of the multidisciplinary treatment approach, as well as

guidelines for making the decisions as to whether inpatient or outpatient treatment is necessary for a particular patient, can be found in Chapter 11.

Once treatment has been completed, long-term follow-up and involvement in ongoing treatment groups such as Alcoholics Anonymous or Narcotics Anonymous, is crucial to prevent relapse in the patient.

SUMMARY

There are several indications for the use of sedative-hypnotic drugs, including anxiety neuroses and severe stress reactions. A brief course of therapy with small doses of a sedative drug is appropriate use of this medication in these instances. However, the notion that virtually any problem can be made easier to cope with by the use of sedative-hypnotic or anxiety-allaying medication, is one that is quite prevalent today. The fact is that coping with life stresses through the use of these medications is basically nonadaptive. Patients should be encouraged to develop non-pharmacologic coping mechanisms to deal with everyday problems in life. The overuse of sedative drugs to promote sleep is particularly inadvisable, since many of the sedative drugs interfere with rapid eye movement sleep, thereby reducing the quality of the very sleep they were meant to provide. The ritual use of sleeping pills on hospital wards is, for the most part, an attempt to provide the staff, and not the patients, with a peaceful night.

Certainly AHPs must be aware of their potential role in the problem of iatrogenic addiction to sedative-hypnotic drugs. By the same token, the health professions must be the vanguard in re-educating the public as to the dangers of indiscriminate sedative drug use. Life problems cannot be medicated away. An occasional sleepless night present much less danger to the patient than does a potential addiction to a sedative drug.

REFERENCES

1. Hall, R.C. and Kirkpatrick, B.P.: The Benzodiazepines, *American Family Physician, 17:* 131-134, 1978.

2. Greiner, G.E.: Benzodiazepines 1980, *Current Update Psychosomatics (Suppl.), 21:* 3, 1980.

3. Goodman, L.S. and Gilman, A. (Eds.): *The Pharmacological Basis of Therapeutics,* 5th Ed., New York: The Macmillan Company, 1980.

    4. Rodman, M.J.: Protecting your patients from hypnotic drug hazards, *R.N.*, pp. 79-80, July, 1978.

    5. Goth, A.: *Medical Pharmacology*, St. Louis: Mosby Company, 1974.

    6. Greenblatt, D.J. and Shader, R.I.: Benzodiazepines (second of two parts), *New England Journal of Medicine, 291:*1239-1243, 1974.

    7. Braestrup, C. and Squires, R.F.: Brain specific benzodiazepine receptors, *British Journal of Psychiatry, 133:* 249-260, 1978.

    8. Pi, E.G. and Simpson, G.M.: The use and misuse of benzodiazepines: an update, *Continuing Education for the Family Physician, 16:*102-106, January, 1982.

    9. Greenblatt, D.J. and Shader, R.I.: Benzodiazepines (first of two parts), *New England Journal of Medicine, 291:*1011-1015, 1974.

    10. American Psychiatric Association: *Diagnostic and Statistical Manual of Mental Disorders*, 3rd Ed. Washington, DC: APA, 1980.

    11. Fink, R.D.; Knott, D.H. and Beard, J.D.: Sedative-hypnotic dependence, *American Family Physician, 10:*116-122, 1974.

    12. Benzer, D.G. and Cushman, P.C.: Alcohol and benzodiazepines: withdrawal syndromes, *Alcoholism: Clinical and Experimental Research, 4:* 243-247, July, 1980.

    13. Tanberg, D.: Management of acute drug overdose and poison ingestion, *Medical Times, 109:* 1-17, November, 1981.

    14. Gross, M.; Lewis, E. and Nagarajan, M.: An improved system for assessing the acute alcoholic psychosis and related states in alcohol intoxication and withdrawal: experimental studies. In: *Advances in Experimental Medicine and Biology, 35*, Gross, M. (Ed.). New York: Plenum, 1973.

    15. Benzer, D.G. and Cushman, P.C.: Benzodiazepines and drug abuse; clinical observations in chemically dependent persons before and during abstinence, *Drug and Alcohol Dependence, 6:* 365-371, 1980.

PART 2

IDENTIFICATION
AND TREATMENT

Chapter 6

Chemical Screening for the Presence of Substances of Abuse

Robert Lipo, M.D.

OVERVIEW

Following his general introduction, the author discusses important and often overlooked matters pertaining to detection and identification of drugs, including faddish shifts in substances being used, cost–benefit analyses of techniques, the need for communication between clinicians and laboratory personnel, and related issues. Dr. Lipo then explains specific techniques — thin layer chromotography and its several variants, radioimmunoassay, and others — and compares their various advantages and disadvantages, costs, sensitivities, and other variables. In addition, he also provides useful information about techniques for identifying confiscated materials which may be chemicals of abuse, how to monitor patients' compliance with Antabuse regimens, and detection of alcohol in urine, blood, and breath.

Careful reading of this chapter by Allied Health Professionals will provide an ample understanding of some rather technical and highly sophisticated methods in an area of importance often associated with professional detectives and crime labs. Moreover, this chapter penetrates the mystery and misunderstanding surrounding biochemical techniques of drug detection and identification.

A summary and references conclude the chapter.

INTRODUCTION

In the past, alcoholism and other drug addictions were believed to be criminal or sociopathic disorders for which traditional medicine had little to offer except for the treatment of complications when they occurred. Recent expert medical opinion now supports the idea that these are disease states. It has changed our approach to these problems from a punitive to a supportive role. While cure remains improbable, permanent or prolonged remission is possible with the appropriate treatment plan. Implicit in the disease approach is compliance with the prescribed therapeutic regimen. Abstinence from the drugs in question is part of the regimen.

Monitoring patients for compliance with a therapeutic regimen is a part of traditional medical practice. For many years, this was predominantly a historical event — "Are you taking your pills every day?" How often did we get the correct information? How often were we misled? Techniques and methods to prove compliance either did not exist or were too cumbersome to use readily.

Coincident with the change in thinking about alcoholism and drug addiction as diseases was the development of the methods and techniques which permitted easy therapeutic drug monitoring. These same techniques are used to confirm abstinence in the addictive states. These methods are powerful tools for the medical care professional to use in the rehabilitation process if their limitations are understood.

GOALS OF PROGRAM

There are in excess of 60,000 chemicals and several thousand drugs used in industry and medicine. If only a small percentage of these had the potential for abuse, the number of substances for which drug screening might be desirable would number in the thousands. Appropriate methodologies and techniques exist to identify and quantitate many of these substances, but economic realities prohibit such a comprehensive drug-screening endeavor.

A drug-screening program must focus on those drugs and chemicals which experience has shown are likely to be abused within the community being served. Experience has also shown that substance abuse is not a static phenomenon. New substances of abuse are introduced, while others lose popularity. The ability to add to and delete from the screening spectrum, in response to the changing fads of abuse, should be within the capacity of those individuals responsible for monitoring.

Once the decision is made that drug screening will be instituted, the party or parties responsible for designing and implementing the program should seek the advice of their laboratory. When the goals and expectations of health care professionals are explained to the laboratory, an effective program can be designed to meet them. If they are unrealistic or too costly to implement, discussion should lead to a cost–effective compromise.

While sophisticated and sensitive techniques are available to detect small amounts of drug, they are generally expensive, time-consuming procedures which do not lend themselves to automation. These assays are usually specific for a single drug or at most a class of drugs. Since a drug–screening program implies looking for multiple drugs which may be abused, routine analysis utilizing the most sensitive techniques would require multiple and expensive analyses. Cost prohibits this approach, as does the prolonged turnaround time for results of testing. Whatever system is employed, the results of the analysis should be available in a timely fashion to provide the Allied Health Professional with a tool he or she can use if desired. Delays in reporting diminish the usefulness of drug screening.

Cost–benefit analyses force most drug screening programs to use less sensitive, less specific methods which can screen simultaneously for large numbers of drugs economically. The usual basic technique employed is *thin layer chromatography* (TLC) supplemented by *immunoassay*, for example, for screening of drugs deemed important but not detectable on the particular thin layer chromatography system employed.

Thin layer chromatography separation technique allows for testing for the greatest number of drugs for the least amount of money. It is, however, the least sensitive and specific of the techniques available. The most sensitive techniques, *radio immunoassays* (RIA), require the testing for one drug at a time. It is the most expensive of the readily available techniques because of the intensive technical requirements and reagent costs. Intermediate in cost are the *enzyme immunoassays* (EIA). The sensitivity is less than the RIA techniques and better than TLC, but the number of drugs which can be screened is limited by the reagents available.

The lack of specificity of TLC requires that all significant findings be confirmed by a different specific technique, particularly when the presence of a drug triggers a punitive response, e.g., revocation of parole, loss of job, or other such action.

COMMUNICATION REQUIREMENTS

Any system which is instituted must be supported by an open, active line of communication between the persons responsible for the monitoring and the laboratory. The monitoring agent must understand the limitations of the laboratory procedure to properly evaluate the report. Since most Allied Health Professionals are not familiar with laboratories, a dialogue must be opened and sustained to educate both parties to the other's problems, needs, expectations, and limitations.

The laboratorian also needs clinical information. When a patient has a history of drug abuse or the AHP suspects certain substances are currently being abused, informing the laboratory of the specific drugs suspected may allow the laboratories to manipulate the drug-screening system to enhance its sensitivity. Absence of communication between the laboratory and agency ordering the drug screen is probably one of the most serious problems encountered. Without this communication which can educate the parties, clarify the problems, and define the limitations, each party assumes the other is performing at the desired level. The expected level of performance may not be attainable.

A distinction must be made between the concept of *therapeutic drug monitoring* and *drug-screening*. While some of the drugs which are abused may be monitored therapeutically, drug-screening procedures employed may not detect therapeutic drug levels. Therapeutic doses of abused drugs often result in blood and/or urine levels so low that they are beyond the detection sensitivity of common drug-screening methods. If the monitoring agency expects these levels to be detected, it assumes the laboratory is not performing satisfactorily when they do not report them.

In fact, instances have occurred where the monitoring agency wrongly condemned the proficiency of their screening program because of its failure to detect some drugs given in therapeutic doses. Table 1 lists the detection limits for a TLC system, Table 2 lists detection limits for gas or liquid chromatograph systems, and Table 3 lists therapeutic levels of some drugs which may be abused. As indicated, many drugs given at therapeutic levels cannot be detected by these systems.

Communication and an understanding of the limitations of the system employed will minimize the concerns frequently generated by drug-screening programs.

TABLE 1
DETECTION LIMITS OF SELECTED DRUGS

Toxi-Lab System	Detection Limit μgm/ml	Toxi-Lab System	Detection Limit μgm/ml
Acetaminophen	3.0	Methapyrilene	1.0
Amitriptyline	0.5	Methaqualone	1.0
Amobarbital	1.0	Methocarbamol	3.0
Amphetamine	0.5	Methylphenidate	1.0
Atropine	0.5	Methyprylon	0.5
Aprobarbital	0.5	Morphine	1.0
Barbital	5.0	Nicotine	1.0
Benzoylecgonine	1.0	Nordiazepam (serum)	2-3
Benztropine	0.5	Nortriptyline	0.5
Butabarbital	0.5	Orphenadrine	1.0
Butalbital	1.0	Oxazepam (serum)	1.0
Caffeine	0.5	Pentazocine	1.0
Carbamazepine	1.0	Pentobarbital	0.5
Carisoprodol	1.0	Phenacetin	1.0
Chlordiazepoxide (serum)	2-3	Phenazopyridine	1.0
Chlropheniramine	1.0	Phendimetrazine	1.0
Chlorpromazine	1.0	Phenviamine	1.0
Chlorprothixene	1.0	Phenmetrazine	1.0
Chlorazepate	2-3	Phenobarbital	1.0
Cimetidine	3	Phenolphthalein	1.0
Cocaine	1	Phenylpropanolanime	3.0
Codeine	0.5	Phenytoin	1.0
Cyclizine	1.0	Phentermine	0.5
Desipramine	0.5	Prazepam	2-3
Dexchlorpheniramine	1.0	Procainamide	3.0
Dextromethorphan	1.0	Procaine	2.0
Diazepam (serum)	1.0	Propoxyphene	0.5
Diethylpropion	1.0	Propanolol	1.0
Dimenhydrinate	1.0	Protriptyline	1.0
Diphenoxylate	3.0	Pseudoephedrine	3.0
Diphenhydramine	1.0	Pyrilamine	3.0
Disopyramide	1.0	Quinidine	0.1
Doxepin	0.5	Quinine	0.1
Doxylamine	3-4	Salicylamide	3.0
Ephedrine	3.0	Salicylates	100
Ethchlorvynol	3-4	Secobarbital	0.5
Ethinamate	1.0	Spironolactone	1.0
Flurazepam	2-3	Strychnine	0.5
Glutethimide	1.0	Terpin Hydrate	3-4
Hydromorphone	1.0	Thioridazine	1.0
Imipramine	0.5	Thiothixene	1.0
Lidocaine	1.0	Triamterene	0.5
Loxapine	1.0	Trifluoperazine	0.5
Meperidine	1.0	Triflupromazine	0,5
Mephorbarbital (serum)	1.0	Trihexphenidyl	0.5
Meprobamate	3.0	Trimeprazine	0,5
Mescaline	1.0	Trimethobenzamide	3.0
Methadone	0.5	Trimethoprim	3.0
Methamphetamine	0.5	Tripelennamine	1.0

Reproduced by permission of Analytic Systems, Inc., Laguna Hills, California.

TABLE 2
APPROXIMATE DETECTION LIMITS OF SELECTED DRUGS UTILIZING GAS CHROMATOGRAPHY OR HIGH PRESSURE LIQUID CHROMATOGRAPHY

	Detection Limit μgm/ml		Detection Limit μgm/ml
Allobarbital	3	Desipramine	0.05
Amitriptyline	0.03	Diphenhydramine	0.5
Amobarbital	0.05	Flurazepam	0.1
Amphetamine	0.05	Glutethimide	2.5
Butabarbital	3	Nortriptyline	0.05
Butalbital	3	Phenmetrazine	0.05
Chloral hydrate	10	Pentobarbital	3
Codeine	0.05	Secobarbital	3

TABLE 3
BLOOD LEVELS OF THERAPEUTIC DOSES OF SELECTED DRUGS

	Therapeutic Range μgm/ml		Therapeutic Range μgm/ml
Acetaminophen	10–30	Meperdine	0.1–0.8
Amitriptyline	⟩0.12	Mephobarbital (serum)	10–40
Amobarbital	0.3–5.0	Meprobamate	5–15
Amphetamine	0.01–0.10	Methadone	0.05–0.075
Barbital	10–40	Methamphetamine	0.1–0.8
Butabartibal	0.3–5.0	Methapyrilene	2–4
Butalbital	0.3–5.0	Methaqualone	0.4–6.0
Caffeine	10–15	Methylprylon	8–12
Carbamazepine	6–12	Nortriptyline	0.05–0.15
Chlordiazepoxide (serum)	1–3	Oxazepam (serum)	01.–0.4
Chlorpromazine	0.05–0.5	Pentazocine	0.2–0.5
Codeine	0.01–0.10	Pentobarbital	0.1–1.0
Desipramine	0.05–0.15	Phendimetrazine	0.02–0.24
Diazepam (serum)	0.5–3.0	Phenobarbital	10–40
Diphenhydramine	0.025–1.0	Phenytoin	8–20
Disopyramide	2.0–4.0	Prazepam	0.5–3.0
Ethchlorvynol	2.0–6.0	Procainamide	5–30
Flurazepam	0.02–0.10	Propoxyphene	0.05–0.20
Glutethimide	0.2–2.0	Propanolol	0.075–0.1
Imipramine	⟩0.1	Quinidine	2.0–6.0
Lidocaine	1.5–6.0	Salicylates	⟨200
		Thioridazine	1.0–10.0

Disease states, renal and liver function status, state of hydration, route of administration, the type and qualtity of drug ingested, sampling time in relation to drug ingestion, and variations in an individual's metabolism of specific drugs are a few variables which may effect the results of a drug-screen. To minimize problems and maximize the potential information the drug-screen may yield, the laboratory should be given all known information which may effect the procedure. As an absolute minimum, this information should include the drugs suspected of being abused.

The relationship between the monitoring agency and the laboratory must not be allowed to be secretive or adversarial. For example, if a patient is suspected of morphine abuse and the laboratory is informed, it can alter its TLC routine to make the detection of morphine more likely. Approximately 90% of morphine is excreted as the metabolite, morphine glucuronide, and 10% as free morphine. In the usual routine extraction, only the free morphine is obtained. Knowing morphine is suspected, *enzyme hydrolysis* (a technique which converts morphine glucuronide to free morphine) of the specimen could be done prior to extraction. Hence, the communication results in increased sensitivity.

A second example of information given to the laboratory proving useful involves a patient suspected of codeine abuse. The usual source of codeine is a preparation also containing aspirin, phenacetin, and caffeine. While codeine levels, when abused, may stretch the limits of a TLC system, depending upon dosage, sampling time, and other variables, the aspirin, phenacetin, and caffeine are readily detectable long after the codeine has been metabolized. If the laboratory is aware of potential codeine abuse the presence of aspirin, phenacetin, and caffeine assumes more significance.

A fear that the laboratory may be swayed to report what is suspected rather than what is detected may inhibit some AHPs from providing information with the specimen. This position is an adversarial one which can minimize the effectiveness of a drug-screening program. It expresses a lack of confidence in the laboratory, and is a separate problem which should be addressed through a structured program of external quality control. Any reputable laboratory will cooperate in designing a system for the monitoring agency which would test the laboratory's proficiency. The submission of duplicate specimens of known drug content will help evaluate the laboratories' accuracy and reproducibility.

Either blood or urine may be used for drug-screening, but urine is the usual specimen tested because of its relative availability. In addition, most drugs of abuse, with the exception of the barbituates, are more easily extracted and detected in urine than in blood. Specimen requirements will vary from lab to lab, but all will require that some appropriate specimen storage and preservation instructions be followed. The result of testing can be no better than the state of preservation of the specimen. The need for proper specimen identification and handling cannot be emphasized too strongly. Substitution of other liquids for the urine specimen can be prevented by witnessing collection. For valid results, strict control of these variables is mandatory.

A variety of techniques are used to screen and subsequently identify drugs. Chromatography — generally thin layer — is the most widely used screening method. Radioimmunoassay, enzyme immunoassay, gas chromatography, high pressure liquid chromatography and gas chromatography-mass spectometry are usually employed for confirmation and quantitation.

TECHNIQUES UTILIZED

Chromatography

Chromatography is a generic term for techniques which allow separation of a mixture of compounds. The compounds to be separated are added to a mixture of solvents (a carrier or mobile phase) and allowed to interact with and migrate over a stationary phase. As the mobile phase migrates over the stationary phase, the compounds to be separated because of variation of their physico-chemical properties are differentially attracted to the stationary phase.

In solid-liquid chromatography, the stationary phase is a solid, usually alumina, silisic acid or silica gel. These are the usual thin layer systems. In liquid-liquid chromatography, the stationary phase is a liquid which is not soluble in the mobile phase, and is bound to a solid support system. Gas chromatography employs a gaseous mobile phase and either a solid or liquid stationary phase (gas solid or gas liquid chromatography). This differential attraction results in different rates and distances migrated (R_f). Those compounds with the greatest affinity for the stationary phase migrate the least distance at the slowest rate.

Under standardized conditions, utilizing pure known substances as comparative standards, the distance traveled (R_f) or the time taken to migrate to a specified distance (retention time) is used to identify the specific compounts. In TLC, a series of nonspecific chemicals are applied to locate the separated compounds and standards. Comparison of the standard and samples allows presumptive identification.

Gas chromatography, high pressure liquid chromatography, and gas chromatography–mass spectometry often provide positive identification and quantitation because of the specific information given by various detection methods utilized (1).

Extraction of the specimen is the first step in any chromatographic method, and is necessary to isolate the drugs from the complex matrix of biologic specimens. Extraction with organic solvents is commonly used, but ion exchange or resin exchange are alternate methods. Solvent extraction is usually done in an acid and alkaline solution. In the portion of the specimen extracted with solvent adjusted to pH 3.5 (acid), acid drugs and some neutral drugs are recovered. Extraction at pH 9.5, alkaline, recovers organic bases and some neutral drugs.

In TLC, after concentration of the extracted specimen by evaporation, the samples are ready for application as spots to the bottom of the TLC plates. The concentrated samples represent the portion of drug able to be extracted from a specified volume of sample. The sensitivity of the drug–screening procedure is related to this value. Should the extraction solvent system utilized not be optimum for a particular drug, or if the drug is in low concentration, sensitivity may be increased by increasing the volume of sample extracted.

It is impossible to extract all the potential drugs of abuse efficiently with a single solvent system (2, 3). While multiple extraction systems would improve the recovery, it would also increase costs, probably to prohibitive levels. Communication between the laboratory and agency ordering the drug–screen can clarify the limitations of the extraction systems, which may allow adjustment or change in the procedure to improve recovery of a drug deemed particularly important.

After the application of the extracted concentrated samples and appropriate known standards to the TLC plate, it is ready for development or migration of mobile phase solvent over the stationary phase. The choice of a development solvent system recapitulates all of the problems noted above. The development system should:

1. distribute drug chromatographic migrations (R_f) optimally over the plate to separate drugs in the specimen;
2. be sensitive;
3. allow speedy migration or development;
4. be reproducible.

The discrimination of the system, i.e., the probability that the drugs in which we are interested will be separated, is the true test of whatever system is employed. While theoretic R_f values exist for most systems, known standards with R_f values which cover the range of migration patterns must be used if errors are to be minimized. Indeed, standards of all the drugs we wish to identify should be included.

Once the chromatograph is developed, that is, the solvent system is allowed to migrate a specific distance, the plate is removed and allowed to dry.

The process of presumptive identificaton consists of comparing the R_f values and chemical reactions of the drugs and their metabolites, which have been co-extracted from the sample, with known standards. Exposing of the chromatogram to various reagents in sequence results in a known panoply of color changes which allows presumptive identification of the drugs. The confirmatory methods are briefly discussed below. All significant drugs presumptively identified should be confirmed by another method.

Immunoassay

An important advance in immunologic technology was the development of immunochemical assays for the detection and quantitation of physiologic amounts of substances. These substances could only be measured with great difficulty prior to this development. Immunoassays for many of the hormones were quickly introduced (4). Among the first assays were those for thyroid hormones, which found immediate wide acceptance. As a result, almost all laboratories have the capability of immunoassay performance.

Therapeutic drug monitoring, a rapidly growing field which requires sensitive, precise, specific, relatively rapid and readily available measurement of drug levels, is a direct outgrowth of immunoassay technique. The use of immunoassay as a primary method in screening for drugs of abuse is limited; however, it may be employed as an adjunct technique used to screen for a specific drug not easily detected by TLC systems.

The principle involved in radioimmunoassay is based on the consistent observation that I^{125} tagged or labeled antigen (drug) competes for antibody binding sites with unlabeled antigen (drug) in the specimen to be analyzed.

This binding occurs in a predictable, reproducible manner under specified conditions. The competitive binding curve is defined by analyzing the effect of various concentrations of known unlabeled antigen with a constant optimum amount of labeled antigen (drug) and antibody. Increasing amounts of unlabeled antigen result in increased inhibition of binding of labeled antigen to the antibody. Quantitation of the amount of antigen (drug) in an unknown sample is accomplished by comparing the degree of inhibition of binding caused by the unknown, with the degree of inhibition caused by known amounts of antigen (drug), when the analyses are performed simultaneously. Since all the reaction tubes initially contain a constant quantity of labeled antigen, quantitation requires separation of unbound, labeled antigen from labeled antigen bound to antibody.

The variety of methods employed to effect separation of bound from unbound antigen include: gel filtration, dextran-coated charcoal, ammonium sulfate precipitation, and double antibody precipitation. Some of these separations are tedious and require meticulous adherence to technique for consistent results. The appearance of commercially developed kits has simplified separation. In many of these kits, antibody is attached to an insoluble support (the reaction tube). Separation merely consists of a decantation.

Separation in radioimmunoassay is a physicochemical step. In homogeneous enzyme immunoassay, a functional separation occurs. In this technique, the antigen (drug) is conjugated or attached to an enzyme. The enzyme — drug conjugate exhibits enzymatic function in the free state.

When bound to antibody, the enzyme activity is inhibited. Again, the drug in the patient's specimen competes with the enzyme–conjugated drug for antibody sites in a predictable manner. When the specimen containing a drug is mixed with an appropriate quantity of specific antibody, binding of drug to antibody occurs. A known amount of enzyme–conjugated drug is then added to the mixture. It binds with any remaining unfilled antibody binding site. The enzyme activity of the labeled drug is reduced proportionately to the binding, and residual enzyme activity is directly related to the concentration of drug present in the specimen. The mechanism of enzyme inactivation by antibody is not known, but may be the stearic exclusion of the enzyme substrate from the enzymatic active site.

In addition to the lack of a separation step, there are two other advantages to this method. The reaction is measured on a spectrophotometer which is universally available in clinical laboratories. Also, the reagents have a prolonged shelf life. Iodinated isotopic compounds have a shelf life of 5–8 weeks, while enzymatically labeled compounds have a shelf life of 6–12 months. The economic implications are obvious. Finally, since there is no radioactivity, there are no licensing requirements.

While a variety of isotopic labels can be used to tag antigens, tritium or I^{125} is generally used. I^{125} is generally preferred over the tritrated label. Unlike tritrated labels, I^{125} is a gamma emmitter which can be counted in most clinical laboratories. I^{125} labeling offers increased sensitivity to procedure because higher specific activities are had with this label. The enzyme labels in enzyme immunoassay are also varied and include lysozyme, horseradish peroxidase, and glucose-6-phosphate dehydrogenase.

While radioimmunoassay and enzyme immunoassay have gained widest acceptance and use, agglutination inhibition can also be used to detect drugs. Tanned red blood cells or latex particles coated with a specific drug will be agglutinated by drug-specific antibody. If the drug-specific antibody is mixed with free drug contained in serum or plasma, the binding sites on antibody are filled and are not available to react with the drug-coated red blood cells or latex particles. When drug-coated particles are added, agglutination is inhibited if free drug is present in the specimen.

The advantages of immunoassay are its widespread availability, convenience, sensitivity, and small sample requirements, compared to other techniques. The procedure can also be automated. Radioimmunoassay, the most sensitive of the immunoassay techniques, can detect 10 ngm/ml of morphine, for example. The enzyme immunoassays are less sensitive, and cross reactivity occurs. False positives occur and are directly related to the set detection limits. The lower the detection limit, the more false positives occur due to cross reactivity. False positives are difficult to confirm because of the lesser sensitivity of confirmation techniques. Drugs which may cross react at relatively lower levels include phentermine, mephentermine, ephedrin, nylidrin, phenylpropanolamine, and isosupinen, with the amphetamine assay. The morphine assay cross reacts with codeine, malorphine, meperidine, and high levels of dextromethorphan and chlorpromazine. Because of the consequences of a positive result, confirmation by a second technique should be done.

Radio and enzyme immunoassay procedures for many drugs have been reported. However, the number of drugs of abuse assays commercially available is quite limited. The Syva Company's EMIT-dau$_{TM}$ is probably the most widely used enzyme immunoassay system. Table 4 lists the drugs of abuse assays and Syva's published detection limits.

Field Testing of Suspected Drugs

The same chromogenic reagents used to presumptively identify drugs after TLC separation can be used to presumptively identify material suspected of being drugs of abuse. On occasion, an AHP or law enforcement officer may discover substances suspected of being drugs of abuse. While identification of these substances can be very expensive, a reasonable and cost–effective alternative may be to use police field kits (5) as a screening device. Available on the commercial market or through State Crime Laboratories, they are self-contained kits which usually are able to screen for marijuana, opiates, LSD, cocaine, barbiturates, propoxyphene, and amphetamines. Certainly, any positive identifi-

---

TABLE 4
SOME DRUGS OF ABUSE AND THEIR DETECTION LIMITS
BY ENZYME IMMUNOASSAY

	EMIT-dau $_{TM}$ Detection Limits $\mu gm/ml$
Opiate (morphine equivalents)	0.5
Barbiturates	2.0
Amphetamines	2.0
Benzoyl ecgonine	1.6
Methadone	0.5
Oxazepam (benzodiazepam metabolite)	0.7
Propoxylene	2.0

Reproduced by permission of Syva Co., Palo Alto, California.

cations must be confirmed by a specific method. While the number of drugs which can be presumptively identified is small, the availability of these quick, simple screening tests may have immediate confrontational value to the AHP.

Antabuse Compliance

While recent reports indicate that consumption of moderate amounts of alcohol by some persons using Antabuse (disulfiram) does not necessarily result in distress, Antabuse therapy remains an important tool to many alcohol rehabilitation programs. A constant problem for the health care provider is knowing whether or not the Antabuse is being taken. A simple screening test for the detection of Antabuse metabolites in the breath is available (6). It relies on the presence of metabolized sulfhydryl groups in the breath of persons taking Antabuse. Exhaling through a straw into a solution of colorless reagent causes the solution to turn yellow if Antabuse metabolites are present. The reagent is stable, but the color changes, while definitive, are subtle. A similar procedure for urine metabolites is also available through the laboratory.

ALCOHOL DETECTION

Alcohol is still the most widely abused drug in the United States. Should detection of this drug be desired, an enzymatic chemical determination is readily available. If done in volume it can be automated and, therefore, will be cost-effective. The chemical reaction is shown in Figure 1.

The thin layer chromatography systems cannot be used to detect alcohol. Gas and liquid chromatography methods do not lend themselves to a screening program because of the cost of extensive technical time needed.

As noted in Figure 1 the conversion of NAD to NADH as alcohol is oxidized is measured. The alcohol dehydrogenase is not specific, since it catalyzes the oxidation of primary straight chain alcohols other than ethanol, i.e., some secondary alcohols, hydroxyacids, polyalcohols, and amino alcohols. However, the levels of these substances required to produce changes in the analytical system would clinically be extremely toxic. A second source of false-positive identification may be storage of specimen in plastic tubes, since substances may leach from the plastic and

Ethyl alcohol + NAD _____ ADH ____→ NADH + acetalydehyde

NAD = nicotinamide − adenine dinucleotide

ADH = alcohol dehydrogenase

NADH = nicotinamide adenine dinucleotide reduced

Figure 1. Chemical reaction in testing for the presence of alcohol.

react with the reagents. The commonest source of false positives is cleansing the skin with an alcohol wipe prior to venipunctures. It is important to cleanse skin with aqueous based cleansers, never alcohol or other volatile solvents.

False negatives may also occur if specimens are stored improperly, since bacteria in urine and red blood cells in blood are capable of metabolizing alcohol. Specimens must be refrigerated if testing is delayed. Separation of red blood cells from plasma, and refrigeration of plasma, should be done if storage of the blood specimen is necessary. As alcohol is volatile, storage containers must be air-tight and as full as possible to minimize dead air space.

The ratio of concentration of alcohol in blood to that in urine is from 1.2 to 1.5. When measured alcohol concentration in urine is multiplied by 0.7, the resulting value approximates the blood concentration at the midpoint of time during which urine was formed. Comparing simultaneous blood and urine concentration allows determination of absorption and elimination stages.

SUMMARY

The goals of a drug screening program are:
1. testing for a wide spectrum of abused substances;
2. the ability to rapidly change screening to include current faddish drugs;
3. to utilize the most sensitive and specific methods cost constraints will allow.

These goals can be met by a program utilizing thin layer chromatography supplemented by immunoassay. This system, for the most part, will allow good sensitivity, but lacks specificity. Therefore, all *positives must be confirmed* by another equally sensitive, but more specific method. The confirmatory methods will usually be radioimmunoassay, gas or liquid chromatographic methods.

The value of all screening programs can be enhanced by an open line of communication between the AHP who orders the procedure and the laboratory. By working together, the system can be manipulated to provide the maximum amount of information at the least cost. The limitations of the system must be emphasized to those involved to avoid inappropriate expectation levels.

REFERENCES

1. Wheals, B.B., and Jane, I.: Analysis of drugs and their metabolites by high performance liquid chromatography. *Analyst, 102:*626, 1977.

2. Owen, P., Pendelbury, A., and Moffat, A.: Choice of thin layer chromatography systems for the routine screening of neutral drugs during toxicological analysis. *Journal of Chromatography, 161:*197, 1978.

3. *Ibid., 161:*195.

4. Butler, V.P., Jr.: Immunologic assay of drugs. *Journal of Pharmacology and Experimental Therapeutics, 2:*103, 1977.

5. *Field Testing Kit.* Wisconsin Department of Justice, Division of Law Enforcement Services, Crime Laboraotry Bureau, 4706 University Avenue, Madison, Wisconsin 53702.

6. Paulson, J., Kraus, K., and Ibert, F.: Development and evaluation of a compliance test for patients taking disulfiram. *Johns Hopkins Medical Journal, 141:*119, 1977.

Chapter 7

Identification and Treatment of Acute Drug Abuse Problems

Paul Cushman, Jr., M.D.

OVERVIEW

The goal of this chapter is to acquaint AHPs with the variety of acute effects they are likely to observe in the course of working with patients who have been using or abusing drugs. This information will be particularly relevant for hospital and clinic emergency room personnel, since many acute drug-effects represent medical emergencies. Psychological or behavioral emergencies, such as acute fear or panic reactions, disorientation, and other mental effects, however, are equally frequent and require immediate attention.

This chapter begins, then, with a definition of terms, the classification of four types of acute effects, and some general considerations relevant to all acute drug-effects. It proceeds to a specific and detailed discussion of the acute effects of particular categories of drugs and other substances, including opioids, inhalants, sedative-hypnotics, alcohol, cannabis, stimulants, and hallucinogens. A brief summary concludes the chapter.

Although the emphasis of this chapter is on the hospital and clinic setting, the information provided can be equally useful to AHPs working in or with schools, the courts, police stations, walk-in counseling centers, telephone hotlines, suicide and other crisis-intervention facilities, or on the streets. The ability to rapidly identify and appropriately deal with acute effects of drug use and abuse is an increasingly important skill in the clinical armamentarium of AHPs.

INTRODUCTION

Because many acute problems resulting from drug use and abuse are often unrecognized as such, and hence may be untreated or improperly treated, well-educated AHPs can provide a valuable service by learning to recognize and manage acute drug-induced states. Some such states may be produced when excessive amounts of a drug are used or the user is idiosyncratically sensitive to a drug (a *toxic* effect). Other such states may be produced only when the user abruptly discontinues ingestion of the drug (a *withdrawal* effect). Some drugs only rarely, while others quite frequently and regularly, produce effects requiring professional intervention. Hence AHPs are well-advised to recognize and manage those drug-related problems whose treatment may range from quiet verbal reassurance to cardiopoulmonary resuscitation and other emergency life-saving efforts.

Acute drug-effects may be classified and defined according to the following schema. An *overdose* refers usually to the effects caused by a dose large enough to impair normal functioning, and the effects are moderate to extreme exaggerations of the normal and expected actions of a standard (therapeutic) dose. Overdose may be accidental or intentional. While the effects of overdose are usually physical, one may also observe an *acute organic mental syndrome* (see Chapter 16), which may include a state of confusion, impairment of orientation (to time, place, and person), disturbances of memory, impaired intellectual functioning, disturbed perception and cognition, and a variety of hallucinations, and delusions. *Acute withdrawal effects* are observable only when the drug-dependent individual abruptly discontinues use of his or her drug, or when an antagonistic drug is administered. (Such withdrawal effects are also referred to as *abstinence syndromes.*) Finally, if acute drug-effects spontaneously reoccur some time after an earlier use of that drug, such phenomena are called *flashbacks.*

Several general considerations are in order regarding the detection and management of acute drug-effects. For example, suspicion of drug-caused problems should be aroused when individuals appear sedated, stimulated, uncoordinated, angry or paranoid without provocation, have bizarre ideation, or display otherwise inappropriate behavior. Observe the patient carefully for helpful diagnostic and management clues. If the overdose patient is agitated, then amphetamines, LSD, or PCP may be suspected.

If he or she shows slurred speech, or is apathetic, sluggish, stuporous, somnolent, or comatose, the sedative drugs are more likely. A panicky patient may be reacting to the acute sensory distortions of marijuana. Pulse irregularities and tachycardia suggest amphetamines, cocaine, or tricyclic antidepressants. Hypertension also suggests abuse of stimulants or PCP. Pupils are dilated with amphetamines, LSD, and occasionally with marijuana. If pupils do not react, then an anticholinergic drug such as atropine may be suspected. Heroin and other opioid use results in pinpoint pupils. Nasal perforation implies past cocaine use. Nystagmus suggests thiamine deficiency in alcoholics or PCP intoxication.

For the diagnosis of withdrawal, one expects signs opposite to those of the acute effects of the drug. For example, dilated pupils suggest narcotic withdrawal. Agitation, restlessness, insomnia, and tremor suggest sedative withdrawal; while drowsiness and lethargy suggest cessation of stimulants.

The most serious problem is the unconscious patient. Here immediate life support is essential. If cardiac function is inadequate, as reflected by weak or no palpable pulses, then immediate cardiac resuscitation is warranted by external cardiac massage, simultaneously summoning physician assistance. If respiratory efforts are ineffective or absent, then establish an airway (remove obstruction such as dentures or position of the head) and start artificial respiration, usually by mouth-to-mouth breathing. Prior awareness of cardiopulmonary resuscitation is highly desirable.

With this background information in mind, we can proceed now to individual and specific discussions of those classes of drugs whose use and abuse often lead to acute effects requiring professional intervention and management.

OPIOID REACTIONS

The acute intoxication with narcotics ranges from "nodding" — a semisomnolent state in which the subject sits quietly, as if immersed in dreams, yet can be aroused — to stupor, all the way to deep coma. Generally, the larger the dose, the greater the sedation, but individual tolerances may vary importantly. Usually hypotension, bradycardia, and hypoventilation are present in the severe cases. These are urgent, often fatal, problems if not properly and swiftly treated. Pupillary constriction is marked, no matter how long narcotics were used.

Immediate treatment of opioid overdose includes life support, as indicated, and prompt administration of naloxone, a pure opioid antagonist. Optimally, given 0.4 mg as an IV push, naloxone generally will completely reverse the symptoms of narcotic overdoses; occasionally a second or third dose a few minutes apart is needed for full effect. Intramuscular doses also work, but more slowly. Because the longer-acting opioids, such as methadone, remain active in the body for longer than naloxone, relapse may occur after the naloxone wears off. Hence all methadone overdose patients should be observed in a hospital for at least one day for repeat doses of naloxone as indicated. Because naloxone is not known to be harmful in itself, it is now routinely administered in all cases of non-traumatic stupor or coma in the emergency rooms of major city hospitals. If the patient fails to respond to three successive naloxone doses. It is discontinued and the clinical diagnostic presumption is made that no narcotic component was present if the patient's stupor is established.

Opioid withdrawal syndromes are typically composed of tearing, anxiety, disturbed sleep, nausea, vomiting, diarrhea, pain, restlessness, rhinorrhea, and related symptoms. While distressing, these symptoms are not life-threatening in themselves. Objective findings, helpful in establishing this diagnosis, include goose flesh and dilated pupils. Many patients will require tapering doses of opioids, usually methadone, to alleviate these symptoms, enroute to detoxification. Major opioid withdrawal reactions are uncommon with the exception of the methadone-maintained patients.

INHALANT REACTIONS

Occasionally, inhalant users will show acute toxic reactions, with sedation, slurred speech, unsteady gait, and difficulty speaking. Cues may include local drug effects, such as irritation of the nasal and ocular tissues, or as a foul odor to the breath. Paint on the body or clothing are helpful indicators. The psychological symptoms resemble those of alcohol use, with excitation, depression, impulsiveness, and exhiliration present in some degree. Only rarely has a serious depression with confusion or delirium been observed. Treatment is supportive, and occasionally life supports or drugs to combat undesired cardiac rhythms may be needed. No withdrawal syndromes occur.

SEDATIVE-HYPNOTIC REACTIONS

As with alcohol, barbiturates, methyprylon, chloralhydrate, meprobamate, and others produce sedation, somnolence, disinhibition, staggering gait, slurred speech, and related symptoms. Serious overdoses present with exaggerated somnolence, even coma. Generally, respiration, pulse rates, and reflexes are also depressed. Alcohol odor, while helpful, cannot be considered diagnostic since it merely denotes recent contact with alcohol.

Some overdoses represent overt suicide attempts. Some result from inadvertent ingestion of larger than intended amounts of drugs; the drug-sedated patient may be confused, not recall the immediate past drug use, and take more.

The most important sedative drugs, the barbiturates, vary in their speed of action, distribution throughout the body, and mechanisms by which they are excreted. A deeply depressed barbiturate-overdose patient should have life support. When the airway is secure and no chance remains of inhalation of stomach contents into the lungs, then an attempt should be made to remove from the GI track all as-yet unabsorbed portions of the drug by gastric lavage through the tube. Instillation of activated charcoal may help sequester the drug from being further absorbed. Fluids and diuretics may be helpful.

For methaqualone, meprobamate (Miltown®), and chloralhydrate, the overdose features are very similar to those of the barbiturates. Chloralhydrate has gastric irritating properties which induce vomiting. Ethchlorvynol (Placidyl®) may produce an especially protracted coma, when ingested with alcohol in the setting of liver disease. Glutethemide (Doriden®) may have fluctuating signs of overdose. Because of its long duration of action and very slow excretion rates, its detection in an overdosed patient may require prolonged support, and a special variety of hemodialysis to accelerate the drug's disposal rates.

Although the benzodiazepines have a high margin of safety, they may sometimes cause an overdose reaction. They represent the most frequently identified drug group in biological fluids in toxicological laboratories. By themselves they usually present few problems, but when used in combination with other drugs, they add an important component of sedation. Many persons are unaware of the possible importance of the prolonged activity of the more commonly used benzodiazepines: Valium®, Librium®, and Dalmane®. Accordingly, unexpectedly greater sedation may arise with alcohol, sedating antihistamines, or antidepressants, when combined with recent, or not so recent, benzodiazepine use, compared to the effects of the same drugs taken alone.

Sedative withdrawal can be suspected when a patient presents with sympathetic nervous system hyperactivity. Some symptoms may be classified as minor, such as insomnia, restlessness, tremor, anxiety, poor sleep, loss of appetite, and limb twitching. The major withdrawal signs are severe agitation, seizures, fever, and even a delirium tremens type of reaction identical to that of alcohol withdrawal. Because of the possible life-threatening nature of severe sedative withdrawal, such patients should be hospitalized. An oral pentobarbital (Nembutol®) challenge is usually done to determine the level of sedation to tolerance and to gauge the initial sedation requirements for the gradual detoxification.

Most sedative withdrawal reactions will occur within a few hours after the last drug use, but others may arise only after several days in the case of the long-acting benzodiazepines (see Chapter 5).

ALCOHOL REACTIONS

Alcohol overdose ranges from the mild inebriation — the well-known humorous, pathetic, or belligerent drunk — to the arousable but sleepy person, all the way to a deeply comatose and life-threatening state.

Recognition of immediate-past alcohol use is easy; however, the establishment of the degree of seriousness of alcohol-induced impairment requires some sophistication and attention to detail. Not all alcohol-related emergencies are directly attributable to its intoxicating effects. For instance, the alcohol user may have consumed other drugs in addition to alcohol, a very common practice in this decade, especially among the younger alcohol users. This mixed or polydrug use may require urgent attention to the other drug component or to the combined effects of all drugs together. Also, the alcohol user may have had recent head trauma, which can be sometimes obscured in the initial appraisal. Thus, a confusional state may relate more to a concussion than to the pharmacologic effects of alcohol. Past head trauma, rather common in many indigent alcoholics, may also result in the late appearance of subdural hematomas. This neurosurgical emergency often presents with a cloudy mental state, unequal pupillary size, seizures, and focal neurological signs and symptoms. The alcohol user may also have occult bleeding. If the blood loss is of significant magnitude, the alcohol user may be pale and have evidence of inadequate blood flow to the brain or coronary arteries, manifested by dizziness or chest pain.

Furthermore, the alcohol user may have hypoglycemia, a major medical emergency which, if inadequately treated, may have damaging sequelae. The symptoms are those of excessive catecholamines, i.e., tachycardia, sweating, anxiety, dizziness, headache, dilated pupils, hunger, and cloudy mental state. These symptoms are abrupt in onset and are most often seen in the heavy drinker who has not had recent food. Especially vulnerable is the stuporous person with little history, brought to the hospital by ambulance.

Therefore, the initial appraisal of the alcohol user should include a blood or breath alcohol determination. The latter is non-invasive and very easy to accomplish; it is as valuable as the blood level provided that 20 minutes or more have elapsed since the last drink, in order for the mouth to clear the local effects of the beverage so that the breath now measures alcohol excreted by the lungs. A measurement of the alcohol levels helps document alcohol use and quantify the alcohol load. The chronic alcoholic may have considerable tolerance to many of the effects of alcohol, therefore, the blood level may be surprisingly high in relation to the degree of drunkeness clinically displayed. If higher than expected levels of alcohol are found, this patient should be viewed as likely to have an important withdrawal syndrome.

The mildly intoxicated alcohol abuser usually needs only general assistance. For example, arrange for a place to sleep it off, plan his or her return home to avoid driving, and for some supervision. It may be useful to initiate treatment for alcoholism, although most inebriates are unable or unwilling to consider this step effectively at the time.

The more severely intoxicated patient should be thoroughly appraised for other complicating factors. If cleared, then he or she usually can be managed in the same way as the mild inebriate.

The deeply stuporous or comatose patient needs immediate hospitalization for life support as warranted, and detoxification, if their alcoholism has progressed to the stage of physical dependency. Management of whatever medical problems may emerge in association with alcohol abuse, and encouragement to enter treatment for alcohol abuse when sober, are also important components of proper case-management.

Several recent studies purport to show a reduction in alcohol-induced sedation and an improvement in mental status of deeply somnolent alcoholics with IV administration of naloxone. The proposed mechanism of action of naloxone involves some as-yet undefined interaction of alcohol and the opiate system in the body, as the endorphins. Although controversy has risen about the effectiveness of naloxone for this purpose, it is without toxicity. Thus, its use is safe, and possibly beneficial in the routine management of alcohol overdose.

CANNABIS (MARIJUANA OR HASHISH) REACTIONS

It is uncommon for a cannabis user to have a serious reaction. Occasionally a beginning cannabis user, experiencing the usual cannabis distortions of time, space, sound, color, and other stimuli, may panic. They are anxious about whether they might have "blown their minds," might not return to normal, or may experience loss of control of themselves. They need mainly reassurance until the cannabis effects wear off. Rarely, an acute organic mental syndrome, with disorientation, paranoia, and confusion may ensue after cannabis use. There is no clinical withdrawal syndrome after cessation of cannabis.

STIMULANT (COCAINE OR AMPHETAMINE) REACTIONS

In general, acute stimulant reactions produce signs and symptoms of overactivity of the sympathetic nervous system.

Since the duration of action of cocaine is very short, cocaine users rarely present for emergency care. When they do, they usually have consumed extraordinarily large amounts of cocaine. The acute toxic effects are confusion, paranoia, restlessness, irritability, tremor, anxiety, tachycardia, and hypertension. In extreme cases there may be high fever, convulsion, or coma, which constitute a need for intensive hospital inpatient care.

Much more common are amphetamine abusers. Amphetamines produce effects similar to those of cocaine. An amphet-

amine psychosis typically consists of a gradual onset of suspiciousness and paranoia, but without confusion or change in orientation.
There may also be delusions or hallucinations, including an
imagined invasion of the body by small creatures which they may
constantly try to pick off. The stimulant-induced psychosis may
closely mimic schizophrenia.

Treatment is generally supportive. For most cases, a calm and
non-threatening environment, and possible use of appropriate
doses of antipsychotic drugs, as haloperidol, chlorpromazine, etc.
Most stimulant-induced psychoses clear in 2-7 days.

The withdrawal stage after a run on stimulants may include
somnolence, depressive mood, fatigue, and often a strong desire to
obtain more stimulants. While the post-cocaine state quickly
passes, the amphetamine user may have these symptoms for some
hours. Reassurance and encouragement to enter treatment for
drug abuse are recommended.

HALLUCINOGEN REACTIONS

Although less common today than a decade or two ago, LSD
overdoses still occur. They usually present with a panic reaction,
together with active hallucinations, loss of contact with reality,
and profoundly disturbed behavior. The onset of the reaction may
occur minutes or several hours after the drug was purportedly
taken. While the psychological findings predominate, there are
also increased pulse, blood pressure, and perspiration, and blurry
vision.

After the diagnosis, the first step is to reach the patient with
calm, supporting, and reassuring words. Then with continuous
reassurance, he or she can be gradually helped to reorient himself
or herself and "talked down" to his or her usual mental baseline.
Flashbacks, some time after the drug was last used, are a benign, if
exaggerated and frightening, self-limiting episode, managed rather
similarly to the acute toxic episode.

PCP, an hallucinogenic substance with anesthetic and opioid
properties, has decreased in importance recently. Abundant and
widespread disclosures of its toxic potential seems to have tempered its use. Phencyclidine has numerous aliases: Angel Dust,
Peale, Pill, PCP, THC, Horse Tank, and others, and may or may
not be recognized by its consumer. Accordingly, the history of
drug ingestion may be of little clinical value.

The acute reactions vary with dose. Low doses (1-5 mg) produce, 1-8 hours later, distortions of body perceptions of diverse sorts. Staggering gait, nystagmus, drooling, and nausea, are combined with symptoms of anesthesia or numbness. Some users display irritability or aggressiveness and may become assaultive. Sometimes completing this clinical picture are hallucinations and paranoia. Blood pressure and pulse rate rises. With larger doses (5-20 mg) more bizarre features appear. A blank catatonic state, tremors, agitation, stupor, and seizure can be added to the previous symptoms. Very heavy intoxications have fever, seizures, and deep coma. PCP intoxication is much more accurately recognized, although the initial appraisal of such patients is frequently quite erroneous. Precise diagnosis of PCP intoxication requires suspicion and its measurement in biological fluids (blood quantitatively and urine qualitatively).

Initial management includes life support if needed; supportive care with continuous reassurance; avoidance of provocation; removal of PCP by gastric lavage and instillation of activated charcoal; and enhancement of PCP excretion by ascorbic acid (cranberry juice). Most patients need hospital care.

SUMMARY

The preceding material gives the AHP an indication of the extent to which he or she can provide necessary services in working with the patient who is experiencing an acute drug problem, regardless of the nature or cause of such problems. From toxic reactions to overdoses to impending withdrawal, there are many ways, and many settings, in which AHPs are active in direct patient care. Whether providing emergency or life-sustaining procedures, or "talking down" an anxious, frightened, or agitated patient, or explaining the circumstances to a concerned family member, a good working knowledge of the causes and symptoms of acute drug problems is mandatory for AHPs. Since many persons who are experiencing acute drug problems may be unable to communicate the nature and cause of their current state, either because of mental confusion, unconsciousness, or for other reasons, it is essential for AHPs to understand what physical and behavioral signs to look for in determining the appropriate course of action. Once that appropriate course of action has been determined, the principles and procedures described in this chapter can be appropriately followed and applied, leading to a favorable outcome and the reduction or elimination of more serious physical and behavioral sequelae. Frequently, in many cases, it will be important for the participating AHP to follow up acute care with the necessary recommendations and encouragement toward getting the patient into an appropriate long-term or rehabilitative treatment program. Hence, dealing with the acute stages of drug-induced or drug-related problems is seen as only an initial step in the continuum of care in which the AHP will be involved.

Chapter 8

The Role
of Allied Health Professionals
in the Recovery Process

George Jacobson, Ph.D.
and Roland Herrington, M.D.

OVERVIEW

The purpose of this chapter is to provide the widest possible range of allied health professionals (AHPs) with an improved understanding of the changes which frequently occur among persons experiencing recovery from alcohol abuse and alcohol dependence. Just as there are symptoms of illness there are also signs of recovery, and such signs must be adequately understood by patients, their families and friends, and the health professionals who care for them. Thus, the information in this chapter will promote improvement of services provided by AHPs, and will assist you in educating your patients and their "significant others" regarding the changes they might expect in the course of the recovery process.

Three major points are emphasized in this chapter. First, because only approximately 25–30% of treated alcoholics do *not* experience at least a brief return to alcohol use during the first year or two of the recovery process, the occurrence of a relapse (resumption of drinking) can be legitimately considered as a phenomenon of the recovery process. In fact, alcoholism has been defined as a "remitting, relapsing disease," and treatment personnel ought to know how to deal with such an eventuality. Second, recovery is a long process and it is not unusual to observe the signs of beneficial changes taking place over a period of two and three years of continuing abstinence. It is important to realize, therefore, that recovery is a *process*, not a *product*. Third, just as the development of illnesses may be idiosyncratic and widely variable, so may there be great individual variability for the signs of recovery, in terms of sequence, duration, intensity, and frequency. There are, of course, some reasonable and worthwhile generalizations that can be made, but readers should keep in mind the idea that recovery phenomena can be varied and unpredictable.

Since prolonged alcohol abuse and alcohol dependence involves virtually all systems of the body, as well as behavior, attitudes, thoughts and ideas, feelings, and all other aspects of human physical and psychological functioning, so all aspects of soma and psyche may be involved in recovery. Similarly, social, occupational, financial, spiritual, environmental, and other changes in the course of recovery must be considered in the overall ecology of the changing person.

A practical and theoretic framework for understanding and dealing with the recovery process is presented. Based on the observation that most of the major effects of alcohol are exerted by suppression and/or distortion of central nervous system functioning, signs of recovery are generally interpreted in terms of psyche and soma attempting to regain a measure of their relatively normal pre-disease state of homeostasis. Usually some degree of compromise is effected, and it is those compromises which are the subject of this chapter.

INTRODUCTION

The alcohol dependency syndrome has been thoroughly discussed elsewhere (see Chapter 9), and need not be explained in detail here. The role of a multidisciplinary approach to comprehensive treatment of the alcoholic person and his or her family has also been amply explained in this handbook and no further explication is needed. But a brief review of some general information regarding the development of the syndrome and its treatment may be useful for understanding, explaining, recognizing, and, when necessary, treating the phenomena associated with the recovery process.

First, it is necessary to keep in mind that although this chapter is written in terms of generalizations, there will always be exceptions and a wide range of individual differences. Just as the development of the alcohol dependency syndrome varies in appearance, sequence, frequency, intensity, and duration of constituent symptoms, so will the signs of recovery. For example, the presence of alcoholic "blackouts" is a defining characteristic of alcohol dependency, but recent research reveals that approximately one-third of treated alcoholic patients have never experienced one. The point is, then, that as thorough or comprehensive as we attempt to be in discussing the recovery process, some patients may manifest only a few or very mild signs of recovery, some will show many or very marked signs of recovery, and others may show unique signs that are not even considered here. So the rule is to be prepared for surprises. Your ability to assist the patient through the recovery process can be limited only by your own flexibility and adaptiveness.

The second necessary reminder is about the very pervasive and encompassing nature of alcohol abuse and alcohol dependence, and the extent to which virtually all aspects of a human's life and functioning are affected. Unlike most other diseases, illnesses, or health problems, most of whose effects tend to be relatively localized, what is commonly called "alcoholism" more closely represents an altered state of being, a different style of existence, which can impinge on all facets of physical, psychological, and social functioning. Virtually all aspects of the nervous system are affected by prolonged and/or repeated abuse of alcohol, as is the gastrointestinal system, cardiovascular/circulatory system, reproductive/urogenital system, endocrine system, muscles, skin, bones, and so on, necessitating the participation of a wide range of medical specialists, physicians' assistants, nurses, and other personnel in the prolonged recovery process. Relatedly, nutritionists and dietary consultants must perform educational and restorative functions. Clergy must participate in the spiritual recovery. Physical therapists can further enhance the return to optimal functioning. Occupational, recreational, and activity therapists add other dimensions to recovery of functioning. Certainly mental health professionals — psychiatrists, psychologists, social workers, rehabilitation counselors, alcoholism counselors, and others — must play a central role throughout all phases of treatment and recovery. Other allied health professions and ancillary personnel must provide significant supportive functions: counseling the spouse for marriage or divorce; returning the patient to his or her family, friends, and community; preparing the patient to cope with recovery at work or in school; resolving any sequalae of earlier involvement with legal authorities, and so on.

Perhaps the most important part of the role of all Allied Health Professionals is providing the patient the ongoing understanding, support, and encouragement needed to help him or her throughout all phases of the often protracted process of recovery.

For all these reasons, then, the body of this chapter is written in such a way as to provide AHPs an easily used guide to common or frequent signs of recovery, for their own use and for providing patients and their "significant others" with useful and supportive information. This information is accompanied by brief statements regarding implications of the recovery phenomena for relevant health personnel.

One final introductory comment will enable readers to have a better grasp of how and why many of the recovery phenomena occur. By way of analogy, consider what happens when you press down on a resistant spring and then suddenly release the pressure. The spring does not simply return to its original size and shape, but instead it may fly up and bounce off the floor and roll around before it returns to its normal resting state. That same sort of "rebound" phenomenon may occur in the nervous system, although more slowly and gradually. Thus, when the "pressure" of alcohol, a central nervous system depressant, is suddenly removed, all sorts of rebound effects may continue to occur until the nervous system eventually returns to its normal state. (Of course, if one presses too hard or too long on the spring, it may lose its flexibility or elasticity and be unable to return to its previous state; the same reduction or permanent loss of function is also possible in human physiological and psychological processes.) Relatedly, various parts of the nervous system, and other organ systems, may become overactive. You can demonstrate this sort of phenomenon yourself: After standing in a darkened room for five or ten minutes, suddenly shine a bright flashlight into your wide-open eyes, and you'll experience a sensation of shock and pain as a result of your body's attempt to protect itself against, and adjust to, the sudden overstimulation. In a similar manner the recovering alcoholic may experience related phenomena in all spheres of psychologic, somatic, and social functioning, necessitating a prolonged period of gradual readjustment. (In fact, one interesting theory of the etiology of alcoholism suggests that some individuals may come to abuse alcohol as a result of their initial use of that drug for coping with a chronic state of "sensory overload.")

With these ideas in mind, then, we can look more closely at some of the signs and problems of the normal recovery process.

THE PROBLEMS OF RELAPSE

The construct of an extended recovery process in the rehabilitation of alcoholics and other chemically dependent persons is a generally accepted one among treatment personnel, who tend to conceptualize that recovery period in terms of two to three years of gradual resumption of functioning. When the active drinking and drug-taking behavior is interrupted, there is a gradual improvement in many areas of the individual's life. However, it would be a serious error to assume that all of the disabilities that had been associated with the chemical abuse or dependency will quickly and automatically clear. During the period of active substance abuse or dependency, most persons experience a retardation or regression in nearly all aspects of personal and psychological functioning, most particularly in the sphere of interpersonal relationships. Hence the chemically dependent person becomes, or remains, immature, impatient, impulsive, selfish, self-centered, and narcissistic. If employers, spouses and other family members, friends, relatives, treatment personnel, and perhaps the patient himself/herself, have the unrealistic expectation of a quick return to full and normal functioning, a heavy and unmanageable burden may be placed on the patient. Very frequently, the resultant sense of frustration, disappointment, and impending failure may precipitate a resumption of drinking or drug use — a relapse.

It is useful to identify and define two levels of relapse: *brief* (minor) and *significant* (major). The former is a return to alcohol or other drug use for a period of less than one month, without the reappearance of any important problems or disabilities. By contrast, a significant relapse refers to the resumption of substance use for a month or more, with consequent life problems appearing. Health care professionals would be well-advised to consider *any* relapse as cause for concern, and as a symptom that must be detected and treated at the earliest possible moment.

The greatest problem during the first year of recovery is the struggle to remain free of alcohol and other mood-altering drugs. The majority of relapses occur within ninety days after discharge from an active period of treatment, and only about one-third of all treated persons can report total and continuous abstinence for one year after discharge. The longer the relapse is allowed to continue, the more life-problems that accumulate, the more likely the patient is to regress physically, psychologically, and socially, and the more difficult it becomes to motivate the individual to return to abstinence and sobriety. An individual who experiences any degree of relapse should have his or her long-term treatment plan reviewed by the appropriate treatment personnel, to assess the following relevant factors.

1.   It is important to identify the individual, interpersonal, and/or environmental event(s) that may have triggered the relapse, since some modifications of the precipitating events are usually possible, such that future relapses may be avoided. A variety of potential sources of precipitating events are systematically identified in subsequent sections of this chapter.

2.   The extent of the patient's compliance with all aspects of his/her treatment program must be determined, and the importance of full compliance and cooperation should be re-emphasized. For example, to what extent was the patient participating in AA/NA activities, and would one or more additional weekly meetings be useful? If the patient was fully engaged in the program at the time of relapse, then the program should be re-evaluated and modified as needed.

3.   The status and role of the patient's spouse or "significant other" should be examined to determine if that other person should be more fully involved in the patient's treatment, or perhaps in a treatment program of his or her own.

4.   Because substitute addictions are frequent causes of relapse, one ought not to assume that the original substance of abuse is the agent of relapse, and specific inquiries (or biochemical assessments; see Chapter 6) are necessary. Rehospitalization for detoxification may be needed.

5.   Give careful consideration to the possibility that the relapse may be attributable to an underlying psychiatric disorder which may have been undetected during the initial period of treatment. Quite often — in perhaps as many as 25% of cases — substance abuse patients have been found to have significant problems of anxiety or depression for which they were using alcohol or some other drug to medicate themselves or ameliorate their symptoms. Unless the psychiatric problem is appropriately treated, future relapses may be inevitable.

Patients who experience a significant relapse may require rehospitalization for detoxification, for increased environmental controls to disrupt the substance abuse behavior, and for greater intensity of treatment programming. Brief relapses, on the other hand, are more frequently manageable on an outpatient basis. Once the first post-discharge year has been completed, the probability of relapse is reduced. However, treatment personnel should remain vigilant, since the second year of recovery poses its own problems. As chemically dependent persons become increasingly healthy they may overestimate their capacity for work, activity, and productivity, and the resultant over-ambitious expectations may lead to disappointment, frustration, and a loss of precious and hard-earned self-esteem, possibly setting the stage for relaspe. By the end of the third year in the recovery process the probability of relapse is even further reduced. If sobriety has been uninterrupted, or if relapse has been only brief, the individual will have developed significant inner and outer resources to allow him or her to become fully invested in a lifestyle characterized by feelings of happiness, contentment, satisfaction, and the ability to enjoy interpersonal relationships that are deep and meaningful. While relapse may remain a potential problem throughout the recovery process, the incidence is relatively low once this level of development has been attained.

Although relapse is the single greatest problem in the recovery process, recovering individuals do experience a host of other difficulties. These may range from being merely transient, annoying, or puzzling, to those which are frightening, long-lived, and a threat to sobriety. It is to these other problems in recovery that we now turn our attention.

THE SPECIAL SENSES

Because sustained use of alcohol at relatively high dosage levels has some direct and/or indirect disruptive effects on all of the special senses (as well as the possibility that some persons who become alcoholic may have pre-existing problems of sensation and perception involving the special senses), it is not surprising to note that the recovery process may affect that full array of one's sensory systems.

Regarding vision, for example, research has suggested that approximately 3-4% of the normal adult male population may have significant color-vision defects. Among hospitalized alcoholics, however, the rate may be as high as 38% for men and women, with special problems in blue-yellow and red-greed perception (1). Studies have shown, however, that one of the side-effects of chronic alcoholism is a loss of color vision acuity, and for those persons who were not truly color blind prior to their abusive drinking, one can expect a gradual return of that function (2). A sign of recovery, then, is a renewed interest in, and attention to colors. Restoration of normal function can be accelerated by alert nutritionists who are aware of the need for vitamin therapy in this aspect of recovery. Relatedly, a heightened sensitivity to bright lights may be another sign of recovery, so that special problems such as driving at night may be anticipated.

Hearing is another of the special senses whose return to normal functioning may be manifested in signs of recovery. For example, prolonged abusive drinking can result in impairment of the ability to discriminate differences among sounds, and in one group of hospitalized alcoholics 39% of the patients reported experiencing a nearly constant sensation of ringing or buzzing (called *tinnitus*) in their ears. Not surprisingly, then, as recovery continues and hearing returns to normal, alcoholic persons may experience a sense of pleasure over being able to enjoy a wider and deeper appreciation of sounds. On the other hand, this return to normal auditory acuity may result in heightened irritability in response to loud, intrusive sounds and noise. Audiological examinations can be useful in monitoring the return of normal hearing, and patients and their families who are informed of these changes can perhaps cooperate in limiting or avoiding a potential source of annoyance and discomfort.

Since even low doses of alcohol impair sensitivity to tastes and smells, these special senses also can return to normal functioning during the recovery process. As with hearing, the recovering alcoholic may react with a great deal of pleassure and displeasure to the returning gustatory and olfactory sensitivity. It has been suggested that sudden and unusual food binges which some recovering alcoholics experience may be related to restoration of normal olfaction and gustation, although empirical evidence is inconclusive on this point. It is likely, however, that the recovering person may develop sudden and strong aversions to particular smells and tastes, such that family members — particularly those with responsibility for preparing meals — may have to make some special efforts at accommodating to these changes.

The special senses related to perception of pain and temperature also undergo marked functional alterations, some of which can bring pleasurable changes in sensation, and others of which may require special attention of AHPs. Since alcohol has anesthetic and analgesic properties, discontinuation of the drug often leads to the re-experiencing of a wide variety of old aches and pains. More importantly, however, many persons while intoxicated sustain all sorts of minor injuries, the effects of which may not be realized and experienced until one is well along in the recovery process. Untreated strains, sprains, fractures, and other physical trauma which occurred during periods of intoxication can become quite painful during abstinence and sobriety, and physical therapists and other AHPs may be called upon to provide treatment. Of course, special care must be exercised to avoid the use of any analgesic medications which may be addicting.

Whereas temperature perception and regulation may not be properly considered one the the "special senses" because of its mediation by vascular, muscular, and hypothalamic processes, it is nonetheless reasonable to briefly discuss the sensory/perceptual apsects of it in the context of this chapter. Many alcoholics while drinking may disrupt the natural mechanisms which govern thermoregulation, resulting in sensations of feeling too hot or too cold inappropriately, and chronically cold hands and feet are experienced by many persons. The return of normal thermoregulatory processes is generally perceived as one of the pleasurable aspects of recovery.

Other changes in skin sensitivity may also occur. One clinician (3) has reported that among his recovering patients there are frequent reports of severe itching, particularly of the lower leg, and frequently, the disappearance of some contact allergies which had developed during chronic abuse of alcohol. He suggests that such signs of recovery may occur between three and six months after withdrawal of alcohol.

Other interpretations of these recovery phenomena are available, of course. Since alcohol does serve to blockade many aspects of consciousness, it is possible that these phenomena are representative of a return to, or exaggeration of, normal processes of attention and perception. Of course, they may also be due to real changes in peripheral and central nervous system physiology, or some combination of both. Regardless of the underlying causes, however, these are some of the signs of recovery which you and your patients may anticipate.

SLEEP AND DREAMS

While there is some experimental evidence which suggests that some individuals develop alcohol dependence as a result of

their use of that drug as a remedy for insomnia or other sleep disorders, it has been very consistently observed that one of the
effects of alcohol is an alteration of the structure and physiology
of sleep. One of the more significant effects, for example, is a
suppression of that state of sleep during which rapid eye movements (REMs) and dreaming usually occurs. It is not surprising,
therefore, that significant changes in sleep and dreaming patterns,
with consequent alterations of related behaviors, occur during the
recovery process.

One such change may involve a difficulty in falling asleep at
night (sleep-onset or initial insomnia, which may have contributed
to the abuse of alcohol in the first place), with frequent disruptions of sleep throughout parts or all of the night (intermittent
insomnia). Some research has shown that, during early stages of
recovery, alcoholics may experience two to three times as many
spontaneous awakenings during the night as do most non-alco-
holics. The usual outcome of these sleep problems is a feeling of
fatigue, tiredness, and perhaps some irritability during the day. If
such sleep problems occur during recovery and excessive daytime
sleepiness (EDS) results, perhaps one or two brief naps during the
day — particularly during the afternoon or early evening — may be
necessary until the regular sleep cycle readjusts itself. Making the
bedroom as conducive to sleep as possible, or the development of
some pre-sleep ritual, may also be useful. The important point to
emphasize again, however, is that such problems ought to be
viewed and understood within the context of the recovery process,
rather than being causes of alarm and over-concern. Nothing
causes insomnia more often than worrying about insomnia, and it
is doubtful that anyone will die from missing a bit of sleep.

Somewhat more dramatic, but no more likely to be fatal, are
the aftereffects of prolonged REM-sleep suppression or deprivation which occurs with alcohol abuse. No one knows the purpose
of REM sleep and dreaming, but it does appear to be necessary to
good physical and mental health. As a result, recovering patients
may experience a rebound-type of phenomenon in which they
dream more, or more often, or more vividly. For some persons this
may be frightening — especially if such dreams are threatening or
have a mightmare-like quality — and for most it may be disturbing. Also, transient and brief episodes of dream-like visual experiences are possible during "microsleep" episodes which may occur
during the day when one appears to be fully awake. Again, these
are generally temporary aspects of recovery which, if logically

explained by AHPs and recognized as such by properly informed patients and their families, can be tolerated and dealt with appropriately.

SEXUAL FUNCTIONING
AND REPRODUCTIVE CAPACITY

Although it is commonly believed that alcohol has aphrodisiac qualities, its long-term effects work quite to the contrary. Whereas small doses of alcohol may serve to reduce some sexual inhibitions, perhaps by blocking some cortical brain activities, and thereby give an appearance of heightened sexuality, in fact larger doses of alcohol or chronic abuse of the drug actually reduces sexual functioning. Moreover, continued heavy abuse of alcohol can lead to reduced production of necessary sex hormones, and morphological changes in reproductive organs, with consequent impairment of reproductive functioning. Then too, it has been frequently noted that many men and women have disturbed, inadequate, or ineffectual sexual relations and performance prior to the onset of alcohol dependence, and perhaps those pre-existing characteristics contribute to the development of the alcohol problem.

These data and observations must be kept in mind throughout the recovery process, may require professional treatment by sex therapists or specially trained counselors, and must be dealt with in a sensitive but direct manner. Although some of these problems are self-limiting and may show spontaneous remission during recovery, others are more persistent and serious and demand attention if one is to avoid further deterioration and/or resumption of destructive drinking. For example, the impaired potency of some men may be spontaneously restored simply through sufficiently prolonged abstinence. Similarly, male infertility attributable to the sperm-damaging qualities of alcohol, may also show some spontaneous reversal, and patients and their families should be appropriately advised if they are to avoid unexpected pregnancies. Relatedly, women whose menstrual cycles had been disrupted or irregular during heavy drinking may find spontaneous recovery of functioning during continuing abstinence.

On the other hand, other sexual and reproductive problems may be more enduring and resistant to improvement. A pre-existing problem of uncertain or inappropriate gender identity, sexual taboos, feelings of sexual inadequacy or incompetence, and related issues are unlikely to go away simply because one remains abstinent. For example, recent research has revealed a surprisingly high rate of sexual abuse or incest among women who are, or will later become, alcoholic. Therefore, the point must be emphasized that early recognition and treatment of such problems must be attended to during recovery, and that patients and families must be appropriately informed to anticipate such difficulties lest they become unnecessarily alarmed, pessimistic, or despondent. The need for patience, understanding, cooperation, and support of the spouse or other sexual partner is absolutely essential.

MEMORY, INTELLECTUAL, AND COGNITIVE FUNCTIONING

Significant disruptions and impairments of memory, particularly short-term retention and recall, frequently occur as a result of prolonged alcohol abuse, and these problems can be expected to continue during the recovery process. If drinking has been extremely heavy and prolonged, there is some doubt as to whether this function can ever be fully restored, particularly among older persons, so that recovering alcoholics and their families may have to adapt to the associated difficulties. It seems now that the capacity for new learning is affected, such that the alcoholic's ability to encode material into memory, and/or to retrieve new material from memory storage, is no longer fully functional (4). Some memory problems can be compensated for, and researchers have recently been developing new rehabilitative techniques for retraining impaired persons (5), so the prognosis for recovery may be better. Again, patience and understanding will be useful and necessary throughout the recovery process. Of course, if the patient's state of deterioration approaches that seen in cases of Korsakoff's syndrome, then the prognosis for recovery is far less optimistic, since adaptive capacities and strategies are far more limited (6).

In this regard, AHPs involved in treatment and recovery programs would be well-advised to keep in mind several notions. First, memory, intellectual, and cognitive impairments, even among social drinkers, seem to be more closely related to quantity of alcohol ingested per drinking episode, rather than to actual duration of drinking history (7). Therefore, it is most important that you obtain from the patient, and his or her family and other sources, as complete and accurate a record of past drinking behavior as possible, since this information can be used as a rough guide to prognosis and plans for recovery. Second, it is now believed that alcohol may act to accelerate the aging process, and therefore, the patient's actual chronological age will also play a role in the restoration of memory, intellectual, and cognitive functions during recovery (8). Third, you must have a clear picture of the patient's premorbid level of development in order to assess the extent to which adaptive capacities existed initially. It is becoming increasingly more evident, for example, that many persons who become alcoholic in adulthood may have had a diagnosable learning disability in childhood, and this knowledge can be used to realistically plan for recovery. It may be to your, and to the patient's advantage, then, to consult school records, interview parents and older relatives, and in other ways obtain the fullest information possible. Fourth, and this is especially critical in the early weeks and months of recovery, you must keep in mind the newer research evidence which suggests that for at least two to five weeks or longer after the detoxification period, the patient's impairment is such that he or she is unlikely to benefit much from treatment involving a need for cognitive skills or intellectual participation. Hence, it may be best to postpone until later, or to repeat, the cognitive/intellectual components of treatment. Fifth, and finally, many persons who become alcoholic may do so because they lack, or have not developed, cognitive skills and capacities necessary for coping with and adapting to life-problems, and may have come to abuse alcohol because of low-level problem-solving abilities. So, be realistic in your expectations throughout the recovery period.

Returning to some of the specific issues which, in addition to the memory problems discussed above, will play a significant role in recovery, other cognitive and intellectual functions may be slow to return, if they were present initially. Language ability in general seems to be little affected by long-term alcohol abuse, as though it were so fundamental a human characteristic that nature has provided it some special protection. The appearance of relatively intact verbal skills may be misleading, however, as some associated processes remain impaired. For example, abstract reasoning and concept formation, if well-developed before the addictive process began, may return very slowly during recovery, and in some patients full restoration will not occur. Consequently it may be necessary for you, as a member of a treatment team or as an independent practitioner, to be quite concrete and specific in your approach to rehabilitation, to be able to explain, clarify, demonstrate, and repeat if necessary, those aspects of treatment for which you are responsible. This by no means implies that alcohol impairs general intelligence, because that appears not to be the case; rather, it implies only an understanding that certain memory, intellectual, and cognitive skills may not return to normal as quickly and as fully as others during the early weeks and months of recovery.

In recognition of these observations, and out of respect for the wide range of individual human differences, necessary modifications of your management of rehabilitation practices, and a full and candid explanation to patients and their families, can certainly facilitate the recovery process. Keeping in mind any inherent pre-existing limitations among patients will also enable you and them to more realistically plan appropriate recovery strategies.

EMOTIONAL, BEHAVIORAL, AND PSYCHOLOGICAL FUNCTIONING

In these spheres of human functioning it is best to keep in mind two basic *caveats:* There will be a bewildering array of individual differences in behavior during recovery, and the problems which predisposed and precipitated the development of alcoholism will continue beyond the alcoholism–treatment period *per se.* One of the major effects of alcohol abuse is to retard the development of emotional, behavioral, and psychological growth, to inhibit problem–solving ability, to limit the range of one's adaptive choices and alternatives. The recovery period offers an opportunity for renewed growth and development, and at the same time elicits many of the old and troubling feelings, thoughts, ideas, behavior patterns, and other problems. Without an understanding of this, and a readiness to apply the greatest range of flexibility and creativity to resolving these issues, you and your patients are apt to be disappointed and confused, and a return to drinking may be virtually inevitable. That is to say that one of the most consistent and destructive failings of many rehabilitative efforts is the mistaken belief that if drinking can be interrupted and the patient can remain abstinent, then somehow, magically, all of the other problems will be solved. Quite the contrary, if one is to believe the statistics on relapse rates: Life without alcohol may be unendurable, and few of the old problems simply go away, other than those most directly attributable to drinking *per se.*

Thus, signs of recovery are both encouraging and troubling, and must be dealt with appropriately if a return to drinking is to be avoided. It is at this time that referral to mental-health specialists may be most appropriate and beneficial. Recall, for example, that self-enhancement is a frequent motive for, and reinforcer of, alcohol use, in terms of social facilitation, perceived mental and personal benefits, and related reasons. People drink because it allows them to feel smarter, more handsome, sexier, more assertive, less shy or awkward or timid or inhibited, more comfortable or relaxed, and so on. The underlying problems of low self-esteem, poor self-concept, inadequate or inappropriate social skills, anxiety and tension, must be addressed once the earliest stages of treatment have been passed, and a variety of therapeutic interventions may be valuable. Alcoholics Anonymous, individual and group psychotherapy, occupational and recreational counseling, socialization training, biofeedback, and other rehabilitative modalities may be appropriate in assisting the patient to overcome these obstacles to full recovery.

Wide fluctuations in energy and behaviors may be seen during the extended recovery period. Freed of the enervating and depressing effects of alcohol, patients may demonstrate enormous energy, enthusiasm, and euphoria for work and play, followed by periods of lethargy, sadness, or loss of interest. Projects may be impulsively started and then spontaneously aborted, emotions may be extreme, and in other ways the human pendulum may vacillate wildly before settling down to a moderate level of homeostatic balance. Grandiose plans, unlimited ambition, unrealistic ideas and expectations, impulsive buying and spending, compulsive eating or other oral activities, may be rapidly and unpredictably followed by withdrawal, anger, frustration, confusion, and inattentiveness, as the organism seeks its own steady state in replacement of that which alcohol had supplied. Patients and families, friends, and employers who are aware of these possibilities will be better able to cope with these behaviors if they occur.

Periods of depression, grief, remorse, guilt and loss appear to be frequently reported phenomena during recovery. Some persons who may have been using alcohol as a self-selected drug for treatment of pre-existing depression may require special care, but many alcoholics may experience these feelings to some degree. Whatever the underlying problems, continued counseling may be needed during a two- to three-year recovery period.

FAMILY PROBLEMS IN RECOVERY

As discussed in Chapter 13, family counseling during recovery may be particularly valuable since families, like individuals, tend toward a homeostatic balance. It is unfortunate but true that some families, and particularly spouses of alcoholics, may need to maintain the dependency and irresponsibility of the drinker and may, therefore, subtly sabotage the patient's progress. The patient's increase in independence, autonomy, self-esteem, and self-reliance may become a threat to the spouse, and couples and/or family therapy can assist in uncovering such problems and helping the family to achieve new and more healthy means of dealing with problems, needs, and conflicts. For some couples, however, separation or divorce may be the only reasonable solution for irreconcilable conflicts, and counseling for that possibility may be necessary.

RECREATIONAL AND SOCIAL ASPECTS OF RECOVERY

Time can be both an ally and enemy of recovery. Over time, much of human behavior can be changed, but for the non-drinking alcoholic empty hours can be devastating. For many people the time spent in drinking and related activities and functions, the time spent in being intoxicated, may stand open and threateningly unfilled when drinking stops. Avocational counselors, recreational and activities counselors, and other AHPs can serve a vital function in training people to use leisure time, interests, and skills to advantage. Relatedly, research has demonstrated that physical fitness and mental health are positively related. Recovering alcoholics who maintain active programs of physical fitness (e.g., jogging, running, bicycling, swimming) have lower resting pulse rates and blood pressure, greater self-esteem and more favorable self-concept, experience less tension, anxiety, and depression, have improved sleep and eating patterns, greater stamina and endurance, less fatigue, and other health benefits.

A note of caution must be introduced to balance the tone of general optimism regarding the possibilities of long-term recovery. Although the plasticity of the human psyche and individual behavior is great, there are certainly limits to adaptability which must be recognized and respected. Age, temperament, personality, intelligence, education, health, and other variables must be considered in determining the realities of recovery. To be unrealistically optimistic and falsely encouraging, is as great an error and as counter-productive as an attitude of despair and hopelessness, and a rational balance must be maintained by AHPs if patients are to achieve that same objective.

SPIRITUAL ASPECTS OF RECOVERY

Finding a purpose in life, some special meaning, and developing a sense of engagement and commitment can be a powerful force for continuing successful recovery. Research has consistently indicated that purpose in life, spirituality, and commitment is associated with improved prognosis. Whether one finds that through the rituals of organized traditional religions, the "higher power" of AA doctrine, commitment to family or community, or some private experience of deep feeling and lasting meaning, such phenomena are all of significant consequences. Hence, members of the clergy and other spiritual and community leaders can play an important role in the continuing process of recovery.

SUMMARY

Of the many common problems in recovery, relapse is one of the most frequent, and certainly a difficult one to deal with, and prevention of its occurrence is preferable. A heightened awareness of the probability of relapse, and a familiarity with the conditions that may precipitate it, can be most useful in our prevention efforts. If relapse does occur, then it is important to return the patient to abstinence as soon as possible, and without undue or unnecessary recriminations — you can be sure that the patient will generally experience sufficient guilt, remorse, and self-punishment without our adding to it.

In addition to the significant problem of relapse, a host of other difficulties can be reasonably anticipated, and often overcome, in the course of the 2-3 year recovery process. Effects of prolonged alcohol abuse on the nervous system, and problems associated with abstinence from alcohol, may be represented in both pleasant and unpleasant changes in the patient's senses of sight, hearing, taste, and smell, pain, temperature, and other sensory processes. Again, anticipating these problems and explaining them to patients, while perhaps not eliminating the problems will at least reduce the confusion, fear, and discomfort associated with such phenomena. Similarly, the frequently observed changes in sleep and dreaming can be made less bewildering and frightening.

A more sensitive issue, that of sexual functioning and reproductive capacity, may require referral to appropriate specialists (e.g., sex therapists, endocrinologists, etc.) and the AHP who is aware of such problems can provide some support and reassurance while directing the patient to the relevant facilities. Also, a familiarity with the memory, cognitive, and intellectual changes that occur in recovery — and an awareness of those that may not occur — enables AHPs to smooth out the sometimes rocky road of the recovering patient.

Perhaps most troubling, for patients and AHPs, is the enormous range and depth of emotional, behavioral, and psychological changes which can occur during recovery. Anger, depression, euphoria, self-esteem, activity level, and a great array of other processes may change, perhaps rapidly and unpredictably. Knowledge and forewarning of these potential problems, and knowing how to deal with them, may reduce the probability of relapse and keep the recovery process moving forward.

Although discussed only briefly in this chapter (but at length in Chapters 11, 13, and 14), the role of the family, the importance of recreational and social functioning, and the significance of the spiritual aspects of being human, must be recognized by AHPs as playing integral parts in the overall recovery process.

Throughout this chapter there have been frequent references to the need to maintain a balance of reasonable optimism and a realistic and rational appraisal of the patient's potential for full recovery and rehabilitation. To this end, AHPs and the patients they serve must have an adequate understanding of the problems in recovery, while at the same time not stimulating any undue alarm or concern in the patient. It is not sufficient to simply interrupt the drinking behavior and thereafter assume that all related problems will be solved. An active and continuing role is demanded of the full array of AHPs participating in the ongoing process of recovery.

REFERENCES

1. Varela, A.; Rivera, L.; Mardones, J. and Cruz-Coke, R.: Color vision defects in nonalcoholic relatives of alcoholic patients. *British Journal of Addiction, 64:*67-73, 1969.

2. Mardones, J.: Evidence of genetic factors in the appetite for alcohol and alcoholism. *Annals of the New York Academy of Sciences, 197:*138-142, 1972.

3. Massman, J.E.: Normal recovery symptoms frequently experienced by the recovering alcoholic. In: *Currents in Alcoholism, Vol. VI: Treatment, Rehabilitation, and Epidemiology,* Galanter, M. (Ed.). New York: Grune & Stratton, 1979, pp. 51-58.

4. Guthrie, A. and Elliott, W.A.: The nature and reversibility of cerebral impairment in alcoholism: treatment implications. *Journal of Studies on Alcohol, 41:*147-155, 1980.

5. Hansen, L.: Treatment of reduced intellectual functioning in alcoholics. *Journal of Studies on Alcohol, 41:*156-158, 1980.

6. Cermak, L.S.: Improving retention in alcoholic Korsakoff patients. *Journal of Studies on Alcohol, 14:*159-169, 1980.

7. Parker, E.S. and Noble, E.T.: Alcohol consumption and cognitive functioning in social drinkers. *Journal of Studies on Alcohol. 38:*1224-1232, 1977.

8. Parker, E.S. and Noble, E.T.: Alcohol and the aging process in social drinkers. *Journal of Studies on Alcohol, 41:*170-178, 1980.

Chapter 9

Alcohol Abuse
and Alcohol Dependence:
Treatment and Rehabilitation

Roland Herrington, M.D.

OVERVIEW

In this chapter on the alcohol abuse and alcohol dependence syndromes, which are collectively referred to as alcoholism, the author first provides information about the epidemiology of the disease, followed by an attempt to derive a rational and consensually valid working definition that encompasses most of the frequently observed phenomena associated with the disorder. He then proceeds to a discussion of some of the issues relating to detection and diagnosis of alcohol abuse and alcohol dependence, including explication of three specific approaches or techniques to deal with this matter. He includes also a discussion of pertinent issues pertaining to appropriate and early interventions. There is even a guide with suggested questions that can be used to elicit diagnostic information from the patient.

The bulk of the chapter focuses on the identification, clarification, and elaboration of those five symptom groups which most often characterize the alcoholism syndromes: psychological dependence, physical tolerance, impaired control over the use of alcohol, physical dependence on the drug, and pathologic organ changes. In related sections the author provides useful information on the diagnosis and treatment of the several stages of the alcohol withdrawal syndrome and other matters pertaining to the treatment and clinical management of the patient.

The chapter concludes with a summary and references.

INTRODUCTION

Whether one is working in a clinical laboratory, taking x-rays, nursing, or otherwise involved with patients, alcoholism should be of major concern to all Allied Health Professionals (AHPs). It is essential to bear this disease in mind, since alcoholism is a great mimicker, often confused with some of its complications. For instance, unhappiness or depression is often diagnosed when in fact the heavy ingestion of ethyl alcohol, a depressant drug, is the basic problem. Toxic psychosis may be a consultant's opinion of an alcoholic in severe withdrawal. Medical conditions such as pancreatitis, anemia, or malnutrition, are all examples of illnesses which are commonly diagnosed in alcoholics without mention of the underlying alcoholism.

Other psychiatric problems such as conduct disorders or personality disorders may be diagnosed instead of, rather than in addition to, the concomitant alcoholism. Hence, regardless of one's specialty or area of functioning, one's suspicions ought to be raised when encountering one or more of these conditions which are often caused by, and/or associated with, the abuse of alcohol.

The magnitude of the problem is suggested by the fact that, in the United States, alcoholism is estimated to affect as many as ten million adults and three million children and adolescents (1). Males seem to be involved more often than females by a ratio of approximately three to one (2). So widespread is the disorder that individuals from the very young to the very old have been affected. The majority of our patients have either attended or graduated from college, while nationally a very high percentage have completed at least a high school education. Although our patients tend to be professional or managerial types, alcoholism is common among manual laborers, white collar workers, students, homemakers, retirees, doctors, and most other groups. Occupational and economic achievement in no way immunizes one from this disease; alcoholism is no respecter of sex, age group, or socioeconomic status. There are significant national, cultural, and religious differences, however. For instance, because some Moslem countries prohibit the use of alcohol and the punishment for violating this law may be extremely severe, such countries tend to have low rates of alcoholism. The same religious proscriptions, and consequent low rates of alcoholism, are found among Mormons. Italians tend to consume alcohol, particularly in the form of wine, on a daily basis, but have low rates of alcoholism and alcoholic liver disease. The Jewish religion and culture has always included regular use of alcohol, often as part of religious symbolism, and yet low rates of alcoholism have persisted over the years for the Jewish culture. However, in recent years, with increasing tendency for intermarriage and cultural assimilation, one is seeing a rising incidence of alcoholism and indeed, numerous Jewish alcoholism awareness groups have come into being to help combat this growing problem.

It is generally agreed, however, that alcoholism is a world-wide problem, and while some groups may generally appear to be less vulnerable to the disorder, others appear to be more at risk, and it has consequently been suggested that there may be some racial or genetic factors involved. For example, among some Oriental groups even a small dose of alcohol leads to flushing of the skin, changes in blood pressure and respiration, and a subjective report of uncomfortable feelings of dizziness and nausea (3). Interestingly, the flushing of the skin (actually a change in the body's blood distribution) and other signs of discomfort are also present in the infants of such Oriental groups, when tested within hours after birth (4). For that reason — although many other factors are likely to be involved as well — many Oriental peoples have a low incidence of alcoholism.

On the other hand, it has long been known that alcoholism seems to be familial — it "runs in the family" — and we have consistently observed that approximately 45% of our patients have one or both parents who are alcoholic. Of course, our present state of knowledge does not allow us to conclude whether nature (heredity) or nurture (environment) is solely responsible, but recent research suggests that heredity may play a more important role than initially believed. For example, Schuckit (5) suggests that some familial alcoholics may lack a particular enzyme needed for normal metabolism of alcohol. Relatedly, Goodwin and his colleagues (6) have reported that the children of alcoholic parents, even when raised by nonalcoholic foster parents, still have an unusually high rate of alcoholism; that rate is even higher for twins, also raised apart by nonalcoholic foster parents, than it is for non-twin siblings born of alcoholic parents.

These are all examples of the fact that while some individuals and groups appear to be differentially vulnerable to the development of alcoholism, there are no absolute immunities. We are dealing with a health problem that is virtually global in its distribution. These are also examples of how religious, socioeconomic, cultural, racial, and genetic factors may all be involved in the epidemiology of alcoholism. The overall points to be kept in mind, however, are these: With 9-10 million adult alcoholics and perhaps another 3 million juvenile alcoholics in this country; no signs of a downtrend in the incidence of new cases; and a virtually world-wide use (and proportionate rates of abuse) of beverage alcohol; it is highly unlikely that any AHP will not encounter alcoholics among their respective populations of patients, irrespective of patients' age, sex, race, ethnic background, socioeconomic status, country of origin, religion, or other factors. Although the etiology of alcoholism remains unknown, there is considerable evidence that it is multifactorial in nature. More specifically, alcoholism, like other diseases, is an interaction between an agent, a host, and the environment. The agent in the case of alcoholism is ethyl alcohol, or beverage alcohol; factors that influence this agent in the development of the disease include its availability, its toxicity, as well as biogenetic factors related to its metabolism. Host factors include constitutional factors, probable genetic predisposition in some cases, and individual personality structure and character. Other factors which interact in the production of the syndrome of alcoholism are environmental variables which include such things as the external environment, presence or absence of family, stress, etc. These factors interact with each other in a unique way for each individual. In any given case, one or more of these factors may dominate as opposed to the others, with great variability being present.

DEFINITIONS AND FUNDAMENTAL CONSIDERATIONS

It can be seen, then, that while alcoholism may be present in virtually every part of our world, there remain many unanswered questions about its possible causes, and probably owing to the complexity of the illness we have not even achieved consensus on a definition of it. For example, The American Medical Association defined alcoholism as "an illness characterized by preoccupation with alcohol and loss of control over its consumption which usually leads to intoxication if drinking is begun; by chronicity; by progression; and by the tendency toward relapse. Typically associated with physical disability and impaired emotional, occupational, and/or social adjustments as a direct consequence" (7, p. 6).

The National Council on Alcoholism (8) defined alcoholism as "a chronic, progressive, and potentially fatal disease. It is characterized by tolerance, physical dependency, pathologic organ changes, or both, all of which are the direct or indirect consequences of the alcohol ingested" (p. 249). One of our leading authorities, Dr. Stanely Gitlow (9), defined alcoholism as "a disease characterized by the repetitive and compulsive consumption of any sedative drug, ethanol representing but one of this group, in such a way as to result in interference with some aspect of the patient's life, be it health and marital status, career, interpersonal relationships, or other required societal adaptations."

Although other examples could be cited, there are certain commonalities among them. Most definitions emphasize dependence on the drug (ethanol), tolerance, and at times, impaired control over the use of ethanol, either in the form of drinking more than planned, or an inability to refrain from drinking. For our purposes we shall consider alcoholism to be a *chronic, recurring, usually progressive disease, characterized by strong psychological dependence on the drug (ethanol), resulting in compulsive drinking, tolerance to ethanol, and impaired control over the use of alcohol.* In addition, we know that *most alcoholics will at some time in the course of their illness show evidence of pathologic organ changes and physical dependence on alcohol.* While some definitions of alcoholism are overly simplistic, at the other end of the spectrum there are overly complicated definitions which try to refine the definition of alcoholism far beyond the available knowledge. We see our definitions as a reasonable compromise, a tentative working statement, which incorporates most of the frequently observed and clinically relevant phenomena, without being too broad or general (inclusive) nor too narrow or specific (exclusive).

Sound clinical judgment and responsible practice of our health care professions dictates that we must be cautious and avoid diagnosing alcoholism where it does not exist. Equally if not more important, however, is our responsibility to be vigilant for the presence of alcoholism if there is *any* reason to suspect it. False-negative identification, or failure to diagnose alcoholism where it is present, often has far more serious implications for the patient's health status than does a false–positive identification. Unfortunately it is generally more common to fail to diagnose alcoholism, to focus instead on symptomatic treatment (see Chapters 10 and 16), while overlooking the causal addictive process, which then tends to continue unabated, creating further physical, mental, social, and spiritual problems.

For these reasons it is our bias to recommend that AHPs view as *possible*, *potential*, or *suspected* alcoholic any patient who has consistent, ongoing, or deteriorating problems in any area of his or her life which appear to be caused by, exacerbated by, or associated with, the use of alcohol. To confirm or disconfirm such suspicions, and to make a positive diagnosis, we are convinced that a thorough and comprehensive history and physical, a competent clinical interview, and appropriate laboratory work is essential. Additionally, as discussed below, there are known signs and symptoms, attitudes and behaviors, which should serve to increase your index of suspicion. There are also some structured and formalized or standardized interviews, pencil-and-paper tests, questionnaires, and diagnostic schema that can be applied, with varying degrees of certainty, and these are also discussed below.

First, however, it is helpful to understand the distinctions of drinking, drunkenness, and alcoholism. Clearly, no one consciously or intentionally starts out to be an alcoholic, and each alcoholic person began his or her drinking career as some kind of social drinker; i.e., the drinking was not initially associated with any kind of problem, including significant periods of intoxication. Normal drinkers, true social drinkers, have no consistent or compelling *need* to drink, and are free to choose when, where, and how much alcohol they will consume. While most individuals remain in the normal drinking category, there are significant numbers, estimated to be as large as 20% of all drinkers, who fall into the heavy-drinking category. A significant number of these individuals may consume an average of five to ten alcoholic drinks on each drinking occasion and suffer little or no disability in their lives as a result. But there are a number of drinkers in the heavy-drinking category who appear to be in the early stages of alcoholism, and it is the timely differentiation of these individuals from the heavy-social-drinker with no problem that is difficult yet so important in achieving the earliest possible intervention. Health care professionals need to be aware of the first signs and symptoms of this disease, in order to identify these individuals in time to prevent many of the physical, social, and other tragedies which are later concomitants of alcoholism. Indeed, if one waits to make the diagnosis of alcoholism until cirrhosis is present, or the individual has lost his or her job or family, then indeed we are diagnosing alcoholism on the basis of its complications, rather than on the signs and symptoms of the underlying basic addictive process.

The presentation of alcoholism, however, shows wide variations in both the time of onset and in the signs and symptoms which are manifest. The variations are sufficiently numerous to encourage those who wish to divide the subject into its many parts, an opportunity to thoroughly confuse the clinical picture. The professional literature reveals numerous models of alcoholism in an attempt to explain the variations which are commonly seen in the presentation of this disease. The tendency to divide the subject into its many parts and variations has led to a common saying in the field: "I don't know how to define alcoholism, but I know an alcoholic when I see one." Be that as it may, it is probably useful and clinically advantageous to view alcoholism as a *syndrome*, a group of signs and symptoms which collectively represent a disease. The signs and symptoms may vary greatly in the presentation of the disease; e.g., *blackouts* are said to be an early or late sign of alcoholism, depending on which authority one chooses to believe. However, not all alcoholics have blackouts, and therefore, a blackout *per se* is not synonomous with alcoholism. Having a blackout in the course of heavy drinking is not necessarily a symptom of anything other than a bout of heavy drinking, whereas repeated blackouts are a significant sign pointing to the probable presence of underlying alcoholism.

In spite of the great variability in the expressions of this disorder, it is nonetheless possible to concentrate on those signs and symptoms which are most frequent and which tend to appear with the greatest regularity. In our description of alcoholism, we acknowledge that many variations occur and these are important in diagnosing atypical cases, but to understand and conceptualize the disease in a more general sense, we must focus our attention on those signs and symptoms which present with the greatest frequency. At the same time we reserve the right to talk about atypical cases, unusual symptoms, and unusual presentations of almost any disease; alcoholism is no exception.

PRINCIPLES OF DETECTION
AND EARLY INTERVENTION

There are at least 15 recognized methods, techniques, and approaches to the detection, assessment, and diagnosis of alcohol abuse and alcohol dependence; all of these are described, evaluated, and critiqued extensively in the professional literature (10, 11, 12) and are available to qualified health care professionals. It is unnecessary to discuss all such approaches here; instead, we will focus on those three which seem to have the greatest applicability in the widest range of clinical settings. Readers should keep in mind, however, that this does not constitute an endorsement of any particular method, since all of them have their shortcomings and disadvantages.

The first of these, perhaps the most widely used and highly publicized, is the Michigan Alcoholism Screening Test (MAST) (13). The MAST is reproduced here in Appendix 2. As can be seen, the MAST is a 25-item questionnaire to which respondents answer yes or no. The questionnaire can be administered in the form of a structured interview on an individual basis, requires little more than 15 minutes for completion, and has been successfully used by medical students, social workers, research assistants, nurses, doctors' receptionists, and others, after only brief and minimal training. Alternatively, the MAST can be self administered by virtually any English-speaking patient with an eighth grade education. Recent research has indicated, however, that the interpersonal interview method of administration generally yields more valid and reliable results (12). Questions are quite direct: "Have you ever been in a hospital because of drinking?" "Has drinking ever created problems for you and your spouse?" Item weights range from 0-5, with three of the questions having direct diagnostic significance. That is, a yes response to either question 9, 20 or 21 has a scoring weight of 5, which is generally used as a cut-off point for identifying the presence of alcoholism. Total scores can range from 0-53, with scores of 3 or less indicating the absence of alcoholism, a score of 4 presenting the suspicion or suggestion of possible alcoholism, and scores of 5 or higher being presumptive evidence of alcoholism. Several recent revisions and modified versions are available including a 10-item brief MAST, a 13-item brief MAST, and a 24-item self-administering version (see [12] for a review of all revisions and modifications).

Despite the widespread use and general acceptance of the MAST, several problems exist which detract from the value of this identification technique. For one thing, it has very high face validity; that is, there is no attempt to disguise the nature and purpose of the MAST, and consequently many patients can and do, either intentionally or unintentionally, misrepresent themselves in responding to the interview or questionnaire, particularly if they have reason to deny the presence or severity of their symptoms. For another, recent research (see [11, 12]) has indicated that the MAST does not so much detect the process of alcoholism as it does identify people who are willing to admit their alcoholism. Additionally, the MAST has a built-in bias, such that people of lower socioeconomic status are more likely to be identified as alcoholic, because they do not have the resources needed to avoid many of the consequences of their own drinking. Finally, it has been demonstrated that a cut-off score of 5 is probably too low, too sensitive, and therefore will produce an unacceptably high rate of false-positive identifications (12). Consequently, we are firmly recommending a cut-off score of 12 as a more valid detection indicator.

The next of the three major approaches is that which was developed by the Criteria Committee of the National Council on Alcoholism (8). Because of the involvement of a large number of nationally and internationally recognized authorities, recruited from a variety of professional disciplines, the NCA Criteria (CRIT) has the weight and imprimatur of organizations behind it, including the prestigious American Medical Association, World Health Organization, and others. Again, however, this should not be viewed as an endorsement, nor as a statement about the validity and reliability of the approach; instead, that serves as an indication of the time and effort that went into the development, application, and testing of the CRIT. The complete CRIT is reproduced in Appendix 3. As can be seen, this is a complex, multilevel, highly detailed, and well-delineated series of charts listing major and minor signs and symptoms of alcoholism and their respective diagnostic significance, categorized as either physiological and clinical, or behavioral, psychological, and attitudinal, and labeled as being early, middle, or late manifestations of alcoholism. Further complicating the picture, diagnostic levels are designated according to the assumed significance of the symptoms in the diagnostic picture. Thus, diagnostic level 1 includes those criteria which are closely associated with alcoholism and which therefore make the diagnosis classical, definite, or obligatory; diagnostic level 2 includes those criteria which should arouse suspicion of alcoholism, but for which other corroborative evidence should be sought, and which make the diagnosis probable, frequent, or indicative; diagnostic level 3 includes those signs and symptoms which are only potential, possible, or incidental, and although common among alcoholics and certainly suspicious, are not sufficient for diagnosis. The early, middle, and late manifestations are said to follow the so-called progression of the disease, but apply only to the minor criteria. Another complexity is added by the fact that only the minor criteria are designated as being either direct or indirect effects. Thus, there is a sometimes bewildering array of 84 or more signs and symptoms of alcoholism, and the use of all of them would require the personnel and facilities of a hospital and clinical laboratory, a barrage of tests, extended periods of observation, many hours of the time of a multitude of health care professionals, and would probably cost several hundreds of dollars. Readers will note, incidentally, that some of the symptoms are identifiable only on autopsy, and by then, diagnosis serves little clinical value.

Of perhaps more immediate and direct value is a modified version of the NCA Criteria (MODCRIT), which was developed by Jacobson and his colleagues (14, 15, 16, 17). The MODCRIT has been tested with a variety of patients and other populations, in a number of different clinical and non-clinical settings, and has been shown to be acceptably valid and reliable when used by Allied Health Professionals who received appropriate brief training in its use.

The MODCRIT, shown in Appendix 4, retains many of the features which were part of the initial CRIT; however, it has been vastly simplified for use, and retains only those 35 signs and symptoms which are readily recognizable through interviews and observation. A brief training manual is available, with suggestions for establishing rapport or eliciting information, conducting the interview, and scoring the outcome. Jacobson's research (12) has determined that a score of 5 points on the MODCRIT represents a definite or obligatory diagnosis of alcoholism, when each of the diagnostic level 1 symptoms is accorded a weight of 5, and each of the diagnostic level 2 symptoms is accorded a weight of 1. Thus, any patient with one or more diagnostic level 1 symptoms, or five or more diagnostic level 2 symptoms, or any combination of both, would necessitate a positive identification. Those few diagnostic level 3 symptoms which have been retained in the MODCRIT have no point value; affirmation or endorsement of those symptoms do, however, serve to alert the health care practitioner to those signs and symptoms which may require further investigation.

The third systematic approach to the detection and diagnosis of alcoholism is that which was introduced by the American Psychiatric Association in their *Diagnostic and Statistical Manual of Mental Disorders (Third Edition) (DSM-III)* (18). In that book, they introduce the notion of a general class of so-called mental disorders which they refer to as *substance use disorders*. This diagnostic category remains questionable and controversial, since there is some doubt as to whether or not heavy cigarette smoking and heavy coffee drinking represent mental illness. Nevertheless, the diagnostic schema is useful, primarily because of its specificity. That is, the distinctions between alcohol abuse and alcohol dependence are valuable ones, and the appropriate and widespread use of that diagnostic nomenclature should eliminate much of the confusion brought about through the inappropriate use of the more generic term, alcoholism. Instead, we now have two readily identifiable alcoholism *syndromes*, one of which appears to be more severe than the other, and which provide implications for differential treatments and thereby may bring about improvements in existing treatment systems. Additionally, the new diagnostic system allows greater specificity in describing the causes of the syndromes.

As can be seen in the descriptions of the signs and symptoms (see Appendix 1), all of the information required for appropriate diagnosis should be available to Allied Health Professionals through appropriate interview, history and physical, and observation.

Clearly, major advantages of this last diagnostic approach reside in the consistency and uniformity of meaning now made explicit in the terms alcohol abuse and alcohol dependence. Relatedly, insurance companies and other third party payers have consistently recognized the validity of the diagnoses rendered through or yielded by consistent application of this schema. It is hoped that such a system, and the more precise terminology therein, will replace the more colloquial, less meaningful, and confused and confusing term, alcoholism.

Irrespective of which of these three detection approaches may be preferred by health care practitioners, it should be noted that there exists among them a fairly consistent core of symptomatic behaviors which may represent what is generally considered to be, according to *DSM-III* terminology, the alcohol abuse syndrome. We have identified and described below those eight symptoms which most frequently and consistently appear to be relevant to a diagnosis of alcohol abuse. It is interesting to note that even though alcohol abuse is considered to be a disease, a mental illness, the symptoms are all behavioral, rather than physical, with the possible exception of blackouts.

Preoccupation with alcohol or the next opportunity to drink.

Increased Tolerance for alcohol. Can usually drink much more than others and still function relatively well.

Gulping Drinks. Usually drinks a "double" or consumes the first 1-2 drinks fairly fast.

Drinks Alone, which may include drinking in public in bars, but by oneself.

Use as a Medication for relief of tension or anxiety or as an aid to sleep.

Blackouts. Drinking quantities sufficient to cause "amnesia" for some of the events of the drinking episode.

Secluded Bottle. Having a bottle secreted in the home or elsewhere in case a drink is "needed."

Non-Premeditated Drinking. Drinking much more than anticipated, or drinking differently than one had previously planned.

Most alcoholics do not initially recognize themselves as such, nor are they always so identified by others. They may refuse to acknowledge that their drinking pattern is different, and subconsciously defend themselves from this knowledge. Therefore, considerable skill is needed to choose the right questions to ask the alcoholic in order to secure an accurate history. To facilitate this process, the following questions are suggested for eliciting information about the above. If four or more of the eight criteria are fulfilled with a "yes" or "sometimes" answer, this constitutes a non-social drinking pattern and provides positive evidence of alcoholism (19).

Preoccupation. Do you find yourself looking forward to the end of a day's work so you can have a couple drinks and relax? Do you look forward to the end of the week so you can have some fun drinking? Does the thought of drinking sometimes enter your mind when you should be thinking of something else? Do you sometimes feel the need to have a drink at a particular time of the day?

Increased Tolerance. Do you find that you can sometimes drink more than others and not show it too much? Have friends ever commented on your ability to "hold your liquor"? Have you ever wondered about your increased capacity to drink and been somewhat proud of this ability? Do you usually have an extra drink for yourself when mixing drinks for others?

Gulping Drinks. Do you usually order a double or like to drink your first two or three drinks fairly fast? Do you usually have a couple of drinks before going to a party or out to dinner?

Drinking Alone. Do you sometimes stop in a bar and have a couple of drinks by yourself? Do you sometimes drink at home alone or when no one else is drinking?

Use as a Medicine. Do you usually drink to calm your nerves or reduce tension? Do you find it difficult to enjoy a party or dance if there is nothing to drink? Do you commonly use alcohol to help you get to sleep at night? Do you commonly use alcohol to relieve physical discomfort?

Blackout. Following a drinking episode, have you ever had the experience of not being able to remember everything that happened while you were drinking? Have you ever had difficulty recalling how you got home after a drinking episode?

Secluded Bottle. Do you sometimes store a bottle away around the house in the event you may "need" a drink? Do you ever keep a bottle in the trunk of your car or office desk "just in case" you might need a drink?

Non-Premeditated Drinking. Do you sometimes stop in to have a drink or two and have several more than you had anticipated? Do you sometimes find yourself stopping in for a drink when you had planned to go straight home or someplace else? Do you sometimes drink more than you think you should? Is your drinking sometimes different from what you would like it to be?

Denial is a cardinal symptom of alcoholism, making the diagnosis difficult for those who are unfamiliar with the intricacies of the disease. As one of the dozen or so basic human defense mechanisms thought to protect us from unpleasant reality, denial is extreme in the alcoholic person, although its intensity may fluctuate at varying stages of the disease. It has been said that the alcoholic uses denial not only to avoid facing the unpleasant prospect that his or her own alcoholism exists, but more perversely that denial exists to permit the continued drinking of alcohol, in spite of a whole variety of contraindications to this. The basic psychopathology of alcoholism, from a phenomonologic approach, includes denial and other defense mechanisms, together with the observations that alcoholics under the influence of alcohol tend to fantasize in such a way as to distort the reality of their lives. In so doing, significant insight is lost and the patient comes to believe that he or she does not have a drinking problem; that if they do have a problem, it is being caused by some external factor; and if any intervention is required, it should be directed toward the thing or person responsible for the patient's drinking. Because the disease progresses slowly, in most instances, two to five years will have transpired since the onset of heavy drinking and before the disease is well established. Hence, the person does not understand the reality of his or her situation, and in fact, is unable to reach out for help. A basic understanding of this circumstance is essential to any type of intervention proceeding. Since the patient often lives in a world of non-reality or fantasy, he or she comes to believe that the fantasies, aided and abetted by defense mechanisms, represent the true situation. It is difficult for those not experienced in the treatment of alcoholics to understand the intensity of this process and to realize that only through patient and carefully planned confrontations, often on a slow and graduated basis, can the denial and other defenses be overcome. Unless this is accomplished, all of our present treatment methods, which are basically non-specific, are without avail. Therefore, a basic issue in all treatment, both initial and ongoing, is a thorough destruction of a patient's basic denial pattern.

PHENOMENOLOGY OF ALCOHOLISM

Because of the absence of any consistent, firm or convincing evidence for the superiority of any one particular theory over any other which purports to explain the etiology of alcohol abuse and alcohol dependence, it is perhaps more productive to focus instead on the phenomenology of alcoholism. We can thereby narrow our attention to an empirical, clinical description of those behaviors which appear to define the disorders, and which are relevant to treatment.

Psychological Dependence

The foundation upon which alcoholism rests, as well as all other forms of drug abuse and addiction, is psychological dependence on the drug. It should be remembered that psychological dependence is not an all-or-nothing phenomenon; it can be mild, moderate, or severe. When considering the diagnosis of the disease of alcoholism, however, we are not talking about mild or moderate dependence; indeed, we are talking about very strong dependence, so strong that the need to drink represents a compulsion, an irresistible impulse to perform some act contrary to one's better judgment or will. Therefore, continuing to drink, despite contra-indications known to the patient, represents the critical difference between the alcoholic person and the person who is a heavy social drinker. Examples of compulsive drinking include continuing to drink in spite of warnings to the effect that one will lose a desired job, a family member, and, of course, classically, the person who is told that he or she has liver disease and continues drinking will result ultimately in advancement of the liver disease and probable death. Non-compulsive drinkers are able to respond to these warn-ings if they so wish. The alcoholic person, while perhaps desiring not to suffer these consequences, will continue the drinking because the urge to do so is compulsive. In each example, we are talking about an insatiable, strong, and uncontrollable desire or craving for alcoholic drink.

Tolerance

Tolerance is a pharmacological phenomenon in which more and more alcohol (or other drug) is required to achieve the desired effect, or when drinking the same amount, the desired effect is not achieved to the same degree. Tolerance is of different types, including brain tolerance, metabolic tolerance, and distributional tolerance. However, when this term is used without qualification, we are referring to brain tolerance; i.e., an adaptation occurs in which, in spite of increasing amounts of alcohol, the basic signs of alcohol toxicity — namely intoxication — are significantly sup-pressed. In fact, individuals with significant alcohol tolerance may sustain very high blood alcohol concentrations (BACs) without showing the staggering gait, slurred speech, or nystagmus com-monly seen in naive or non-tolerant drinkers. Law enforcement personnel commonly ask an individual they suspect of driving under the influence of alcohol to walk a straight line and do the finger-to-nose test in an attempt to detect impairment of coordi-nation. These tests, together with knowledge of the BAC, may give the experienced observer considerable insight into the nature of the drinking problem. For instance, a recent case in point involved a young adult who two years previously had been arrested while driving under the influence of alcohol. At that time, the individual had a BAC of 0.15% and could not pass the straight line test or the finger-to-nose test. Two years later, when the same individual was again arrested for driving under the influence of alcohol, the BAC was again 0.15%. However, the patient was able to pass the straight line and the finger-to-nose test. This case suggests the possibility that the person had developed increasing tolerance since his arrest two years previously, assuming a reasonably similar interpretation of these two tests. The blood alcohol determination is extremely useful in evaluating people who have drinking problems. The interpretation of the BAC, however, has to be within the confines of the patient's tolerance as well as such factors as whether the BAC is in the process of increasing or decreasing. Generally speaking, in an adult the BAC should decline at a rate of approximately 0.15 gm% per hour. The health care professional will do well to understand the signs and symptoms to be expected from any given blood alcohol concentration in both the naive drinker and in the drinker with significant tolerance (see Table 1).

Tolerance is the phenomenon which precludes alcohol from being a truly workable and satisfactory drug to alter one's mood. Tolerance develops quite rapidly in a matter of hours and days. The individual, therefore, is required to drink more and more

TABLE 1
CLINICAL EFFECT OF A GIVEN BLOOD ALCOHOL LEVEL* IN A NON-TOLERANT INDIVIDUAL

Blood Alcohol Concentration	Clinical Effect
20 mg% to 99 mg%	Muscular incoordination. Impaired sensory function and changes in mood, personality, and behavior.
100 mg% to 199 mg%	Marked mental impairment, incoordination, a prolonged reaction time and ataxia.
200 mg% to 299 mg%	Superimposes nausea, vomiting, diplopia, and marked ataxia on the clinical condition.
300 mg% to 399 mg%	Hypothermia, severe dysarthria, amnesia and Stage I anesthesia develop.
400 mg% to 799 mg%	Coma, respiratory failure and death** occur.

*Blood alcohol level can be estimated by assuming that 1 oz. of 100 proof whiskey (50% ethyl alcohol by volume) raised the blood level of a 70 kg adult by about 25 mg%.

**The lethal dose of alcohol is variable. In adults the lethal dose is about 5 to 8 gm/kg of body weight, while in small children it is approximately 3 gm/kg. If alcohol is ingested rapidly in the absence of food, which slows absorption, death may occur before a full dose of 5 gm/kg can be absorbed.

alcohol to get the same effect. The new result of this is that the individual ends up drinking alcohol in amounts which have the potential to cause pathologic organ changes or which have the potential to produce dependence on alcohol.

Alcoholics will, at some time or other, exceed their tolerance and show signs of intoxication. The extent to which alcoholics exceed their tolerance, however, varies considerably, so much so in fact, that some alcoholics, as part of their denial, claim to have never been drunk. Tolerance tends to decrease in the late stages of alcoholism, attributable to an apparent decrease in the adaptation of the brain which resulted in the initial tolerance. A decrease in tolerance is also commonly seen with advancing alcoholic liver disease.

Impaired Control of Alcohol Use

Impaired control over the use of alcohol, often referred to as *loss* of control, is perhaps one of the most important signs of this disease. The emphasis given to this sign by experts in the field is varied, from absolutely diagnostic to those who question its very existence. However, clinically speaking, one can distinguish those patients who have impaired control over the use of alcohol from the uncomplicated heavy social drinker. Impaired control over drinking is of two types. The most common type seen in the United States is the loss of control associated with the inability of the individual to consistently limit his or her drinking once having started, most often seen in early-middle-stage alcoholism. This contrasts with the second type, in which the person cannot consistently abstain. Such inability to refrain is seen in individuals who are drinking in response to the alcohol withdrawal syndrome, or in certain types of individuals with extremely poor impulse control. The precise mechanisms involved in impaired control over drinking are not known, although many theories have been offered in an attempt to explain this phenomenon.

It is important to understand that in the development of alcoholism, *loss* of control is neither a sudden nor total phenomenon, hence *impaired* control over the use of alcohol is the preferred term. Individuals who are developing alcoholism will control their drinking at times, and at other times show impaired control. Generally speaking, as the disease progresses, one sees more and more impairment of the control mechanisms, whatever they may be. Impaired control over drinking can be detected by questioning the patient. A typical response is that at the time an individual begins drinking, intending to have a set number of drinks and then to go on to some other activity, the limit is exceeded and the individual will continue to drink, not infrequently until he or she runs out of money or until the drinking establishment closes (in spite of many social contraindications to such behavior). Impaired control over drinking is a phenomenon which alcoholics seem to understand better than the experts.

Physical Dependence

Physical dependence, like psychological dependence, is not an all-or-nothing phenomenon and it may be mild, moderate, or severe. The presence of physical dependence for many years has been deemed necessary to make a diagnosis of alcoholism. That clearly is not the case, since the development of physical dependence relates primarily to the drinking pattern that each individual has developed. Since ethyl alcohol has a short half-life, it is necessary to consume a significant quantity of it on a daily basis for a number of weeks or months to develop physical dependence. Thus, individuals who have a weekend drinking pattern would not necessarily develop physical dependence. They would, however, have tolerance and have progression indicating the disease of alcoholism. Furthermore, alcoholics may have physical dependence for a period of time only to alter their drinking pattern, slip into a period when they are not physically dependent, and develop physical dependence again at some later date. Far too much emphasis has been placed on physical dependence as a criterion for the diagnosis of alcoholism. It is true, however, that if the patient has physical dependence, then the diagnosis of alcoholism is certain.

Pathologic Organ Changes

Alcoholics show wide variation in the presence or absence of significant pathologic organ changes (see Chapter 10).

Once the health professional has evaluated the presence or absence of these five factors in any given patient, he or she should be able to conceptualize the presence or absence of the addictive process in a given patient. The presence of this process can then be confirmed by its complications. The complications of the addictive process can be found in the physical, mental, and social areas of the individual's life. This is part of the history which uncovers family problems, job problems, health problems, and those emotional problems which one often sees as the result of the basic process. It is also useful to combine this information with an alcoholism screening test or one of the other instruments described above. The health care professional is then in a position to examine the *DMS-III* diagnostic criteria and to select appropriate nomenclature to be applied in any given case. The criteria of the National Council on Alcoholism should also be consulted, particularly as it relates to some of the minor criteria and groupings of criteria derived from laboratory data and other non-specific signs which, when grouped in combination, strongly support the diagnosis of alcoholism.

In many instances, early in the disease, it is not possible to differentiate heavy social drinking from early-stage alcoholism, other than by observing the patient over time, sometimes for as long as several months to several years. Alcoholism is not unlike many other diseases, such as multiple sclerosis, in which the early signs are not clearly diagnostic and require a period of observation to detect progression. The important element is the *suspicion* that alcoholism may indeed be present in its early stages, and the health care professional should see that adequate follow-up is pursued in order to determine the correct diagnosis at a relatively early stage.

During such a period of observation, the health care professional has the golden opportunity of discussing with the patient how much alcohol is too much in terms of the production of physical illness. This counseling, together with the patient's ability to respond positively to the advice, is a further indicator of the true nature of the underlying disorder. Guidelines for the health care professional in counseling individuals whose drinking still resides in the heavy social area, or in the grey area between heavy social drinking and alcoholism, are available. For instance, in the middle 1800s, an English pathologist by the name of Anstie (20) studied the question of how much alcohol is too much from the standpoint of maintaining physical health. He concluded that 1½ ounces of pure ethanol, the equivalent of around three ordinary drinks a day, was the upper limit which an adult in otherwise good health could ingest on a regular daily basis without running the risk of developing pathologic organ changes. A recent international symposium on alcohol and nutrition concluded that Anstie may indeed have been close to his mark. The National Institute of Alcohol Abuse and Alcoholism (1) identified anyone consuming two or more drinks a day on a regular basis as "a heavier drinker." It is well known that certain susceptible individuals who are heavier social drinkers may develop liver disease and be totally unaware of its presence until a very late stage. These individuals are totally capable of moderating their drinking or discontinuing their drinking as they do not have the disease of alcoholism as manifested by compulsive drinking with impairment of control. This grey area of how much is too much is extremely significant, both in terms of proper counseling of patients, and in terms of understanding the progression of those who pass through the grey area into clear-cut alcoholic disease.

IDENTIFICATION AND TREATMENT
OF THE ALCOHOL WITHDRAWAL SYNDROME

The alcohol withdrawal or abstinence syndrome is an expression of physical dependence on the drug ethanol. It is the signs and symptoms of the withdrawal syndrome that tells us the organism's physical adaptation to ethanol, called physical dependence, has occurred. Physical dependence may be defined by a *latent hyperactivity of the central nervous system (CNS)*. In other words, when an individual has a sufficiently high concentration of ethanol in his or her system, that person feels well, and has no manifestation of the abstinence syndrome. However, when the BAC falls below a certain critical level for that person, then the CNS hyperactivity becomes overt. Many of the signs and symptoms of the abstinence syndrome clearly are related to increased psychomotor and autonomic activity.

The cerebral effects, which are the ultimate expression of this syndrome, include hallucinatory experience, disorientation, and acute reversible organic psychosis.

Physical dependence is not an all-or-nothing phenomenon. It may be mild, moderate, or severe, and the severity of the process appears to depend on a variety of factors, including the quantity of alcohol consumed and the period of time over which such consumption occurred. The expression of this complication of alcoholism varies all the way from slight agitation and tremor to full blown delirium tremens. The sedative properties of ethanol, at sufficient concentrations of this drug, will control or suppress this syndrome. However, as the alcohol concentration falls, the individual may begin to experience CNS hyperexcitability. Generally speaking, these signs and symptoms of withdrawal do not occur until the BAC drops to .15 gm% or less, and indeed sometimes not until the concentration has reached zero. When the process is severe, however, the signs of the abstinence syndrome may appear at very significant BACs. We have not infrequently seen the onset of tremor and diaphoresis at blood alcohol levels of .25 gm%. When this occurs, it signifies that the physical dependence in that individual is extremely severe and that the withdrawal syndrome, as manifested by CNS hyperactivity, is so intense that it is breaking through the sedative-depressant effect of the drug ethanol.

There have been numerous attempts, since Victor (21) defined the withdrawal syndrome in terms of a *minor* syndrome and a *major* syndrome, to develop a classification of withdrawal which would be more clinically useful in terms of monitoring the patient, and allowing for more accurate assessment of the need for sedative drugs when such exists. For the purposes of this chapter, we are dividing the alcohol withdrawal syndrome into alcoholic epilepsy and three stages.

Alcoholic Epilepsy

Alcohol withdrawal seizures occur in individuals who are physically dependent on ethanol. Convulsions are separated from the three main stages of withdrawal only because occasionally a seizure may be the sole manifestation of the withdrawal syndrome. These seizures tend to have their peak incidence about 22 hours after the last drink. They are *grand mal* in type, and are said to be differentiated from the grand mal seizures of idiopathic epilepsy by the fact that there is no aura. After 24 hours, the incidence of seizures drops off rather rapidly, and it is unusual to see withdrawal seizures beyond the third or fourth day after the last drink. The seizures are most often single, but not infrequently are multiple, and only rarely is *status epilepticus* seen in the individual who has no underlying seizure disorder. The incidence of seizures in hospitalized alcoholics is approximately 5%.

Alcohol withdrawal seizures, in an individual with no previous history of such seizures, do not lend themselves to pharmacological preventive measures.

The basic treatment of all alcohol withdrawal seizures is continued abstinence from alcohol. There have been attempts to prevent these seizures by giving Dilantin® to all individuals. However, unless one uses significant loading doses, effective anti-convulsant levels are not obtained until after the danger of seizures has passed. In addition, using larger doses of Dilantin® in order to obtain adequate anti-convulsant levels is frequently associated with untoward effects. Most notable of these are cardiac arrhythmias. Therefore, one should not give large loading doses of Dilantin® without having at one's disposal the medications and monitoring equipment needed to detect and adequately treat whatever arrhythmias may result. For a single seizure, no medication would be given. If the seizure is repeated, one would consider intravenous diazepam, 5 to 10 mg, injected over two or three minutes. Diazepam is perhaps the only drug capable of stopping the seizure that is in progress. Generally speaking, sufficient diazepam may be given to control multiple seizures when this is the case. Patients should be observed carefully, vital signs should be monitored every fifteen minutes for the first two hours, and every four hours for the next 24 hours. The patient should be carefully examined to determine if there was an internal or external injury as a result of falling. It is important to note on the patient's record that such an examination was done following the seizure, and to specify either the absence of physical findings, or to enumerate the objective findings on the chart.

Patients who give a history of having previous withdrawal seizures, but no history of idiopathic epilepsy or other type of seizure disorder, may be given Phenobarbital®, 2 to 5 mg per Kg of body weight, in either a single or divided dose for approximately four days, following which the Phenobarbital® should be tapered off for another four days. Finally, patients with a history of idiopathic epilepsy, who have been taking anti-convulsant drugs, should be maintained on these drugs from the time of admission. Many of these patients have stopped taking their drugs because of the mental state induced by a recent drinking bout, and therefore are very vulnerable to seizures. In fact, a leading cause of grand mal seizures in the United States is probably the abrupt discontinuation of Dilantin® by the patient, the physician, or by other health care professionals.

The differential diagnosis, in addition to the various forms of epilepsy, should always include hypoglycemia. Alcoholics are vulnerable to hypoglycemia, the signs and symptoms of which closely mimic those of early-stage alcohol withdrawal, occasionally with seizures. It is an error to treat such a patient with chlordiazepoxide or some other sedative drug. It is a simple matter to obtain a stat blood sugar in these cases, or to use a Dextro-stick® to make sure that one is not dealing with the ubiquitous hypoglycemia.

Stage I Withdrawal

Stage I alcohol withdrawal represents nearly 90% of all of the cases of the alcohol withdrawal syndrome that the health care professional will encounter in clinical practice. This syndrome begins approximately 6-12 hours after the last drink, and is manifested first by tremor of the hands, then increasing agitation of the patient. The alcohol withdrawal tremor is coarse, and it may, if the process is severe enough, extend to involve all of the upper extremities, and even the trunk. The health care professional should check for this tremor by having the patient extend both upper extremities and spread the fingers, as the tremor is an intention tremor in the early stages. At the same time one is checking for hand tremor, it is helpful to ask the patient to stick out his or her tongue and to note the presence or absence of tongue tremor. Tongue tremor indicates a very severe process. In addition to agitation and tremor, one sees increased autonomic activity as the process becomes more severe. The autonomic response is characterized by tachycardia, systolic hypertension, increasing rate and depth of respiration, and intermittent diaphoresis. At this point, one should always test for the deep tendon reflexes, which will uniformly be hyperactive. Insomnia and anorexia are also part of Stage I alcohol withdrawal. The mental state is one of alertness and extreme anxiety. The patient is oriented to time, place, and person. The quality of contact with the patient is within normal limits and there is no evidence of hallucinatory activity.

It should be emphasized again that the alcohol withdrawal syndrome is not an all-or-nothing phenomenon, so that we see all manifestations from very mild to very severe, with *all stages of alcohol withdrawal.* Most patients with Stage I alcohol withdrawal will not manifest all of the signs and symptoms, but if the process is severe, then all of these signs and symptoms will appear, sometimes in exaggerated form. This fact permits quantification of the severity of the syndrome by using the Selective Severity Assessment described by Gross (22) or its modification as indicated in Appendix 7. It is important to attempt quantification of the severity of the syndrome so that the appropriate treatment may be administered at the correct point in time. We have found that approximately 80% of the patients we have encountered with Stage I withdrawal can be talked down and kept quite comfortable, by having the staff use various methods of reassurance. More specifically, if we encounter such a patient and expend a reasonable amount of time reassuring this patient, one can expect to see a marked improvement in the Stage I symptomatology. This would indicate to the health care professional that reassurance is the appropriate treatment of the patient at that particular point in time. It is necessary, however, to keep monitoring the patients using the Selective Severity Assessment as previously mentioned. In our experience, the presence of a tongue tremor is an indication for beginning pharmacological intervention because there is a continuum in the most severe cases from Stage I to Stage III or delirium tremens. If Stage I and Stage II are appropriately treated, one may consistently prevent the onset of delirium tremens. This is a most important point because Stage I and Stage II are not usually associated with mortality, whereas the mortality rate from Stage III, or delirium tremens, across the United States is still approximately 10–15%. In addition, one spares the patient and his or her family the rigorous experience of the acute reversible organic psychosis that we refer to as delirium tremens.

The cornerstone of pharmacological intervention in the alcohol withdrawal syndrome is sedation. This syndrome responds well to any of the sedative drugs which are cross-tolerant with ethyl alcohol. Currently, the drugs providing the best control and the widest margin of safety are of the benzodiazepine class. In the United States, chlordiazepoxide is the most widely used member of this drug group. There are many physicians who recommend other members of the group, such as diazepam or Tranxene®. Experience is accumulating with numerous other members of this drug group. It is clear that no one drug is the drug of choice, but rather the health care professional should become familiar with the properties of one or more of these agents in the management of patients with the alcohol withdrawal syndrome. It is more a matter of skill in the utilization of the drug rather than the characteristics of a specific member of this group. We shall describe our method of using chlordiazepoxide (Librium®) simply as an example of one correct way of handling Stage I alcohol withdrawal. Before we do this, however, it is important to understand certain basic principles which guide the health care professional in the utilization of these drugs.

Principle 1. It should be understood that the health care professional is, in fact, titrating the patient's central nervous system hyperactivity against the sedative properties of the drug he or she is using, against the liver function of the patient, and against the patient's age. In general, a patient's tolerance for the sedative drug decreases as liver function decreases. Significant liver impairment increases the half-life of the drug, and therefore calls for a reduced dosage of such drug. In addition, a patient's tolerance for sedative drugs decreases with age, particularly after the age of 65.

Principle 2. Reasonable control of alcohol withdrawal without producing oversedation or coma is the desired endpoint. It is indeed a mistake to oversedate these patients as many of them have associated pulmonary disease. A decrease in the cough reflex due to central nervous system depression may result in bronchopulmonary accumulation and the onset of pneumonia.

Principle 3. The sedative drug employed should be given orally whenever possible. Some drugs of the benzodiazepine group are not readily absorbed from intramuscular depots, and therefore if oral treatment is not possible because of vomiting, it may occasionally be necessary to give the drug intravenously. Where this is the case, precautions should be taken to administer the drug very slowly according to the stated recommendation for the drug in question. In the case of chlordiazepoxide (Librium®) it is recommended that the drug not be given faster than 12 mg per minute. Injecting the drugs intravenously, rapidly as a bolus, frequently results in apnea and the need to intubate the patient and place the patient on a respirator. This problem can be avoided in most instances by judicious slow injection of the medication.

Principle 4. There should be one hour between doses.

Principle 5. The systolic blood pressure should be 100 or above prior to the administration of the next scheduled dose.

Our chlordiazepoxide regimen calls for a three-hour schedule. The initial dose is 100 mg, followed in three hours by 50 mg, and the third dose three hours after the second is 25 mg. Thereafter, 25 mg every three hours until the signs and symptoms of Stage I alcohol withdrawal are reasonably controlled for a period of approximately 12 hours. Following this, the chlordiazepoxide is reduced to 25 mg qid for one day, and then further reduced to 10 mg qid on the following day. The drug is then discontinued. This regimen, if administered in accordance with the principles enumerated above, will control approximately 90% of the cases of Stage I alcohol withdrawal. There are, however, very severe cases of Stage I which require additional administration of chlordiazepoxide. These supplemental doses need to be given appropriately. For example, a patient who is given 100 mg of chloradiazepoxide as the initial dose should be checked by the health care professional in one hour. At this time, if the patient is not slightly improved, or if the intensity of the withdrawal is increasing, one would immediately supplement with an additional 100 mg. One would then follow the regimen, and three hours from the first dose, administer 50 mg. As many supplemental doses as needed to control the situation may be administered, provided there is one hour between doses and the systolic blood pressure is 100 or above. The scientific literature indicates that in an adult, the 24-hour dose of chlordiazepoxide should not exceed approximately 1500 to 2000 mg. The uncomplicated Stage I case will require approximately 300 to 500 mg of chlordiazepoxide in the first 24 hours and less in the subsequent 24 hours. Larger doses are given in Stage I, but these very rarely exceed 700 mg in 24 hours. Cases requiring more than this are almost invariably cases of delirium tremens, which are treated with a different regimen.

Problems associated with the use of such a regimen relate to the following issues:

1. Failure to supplement when the patient is not moving in the right direction, or failure to supplement adequately so that the patient is moving in the direction of control of Stage I withdrawal symptoms.

2. Failure to distinguish correctly between severe Stage I and Stage III (delirium tremens). Delirium tremens need to be treated more aggressively on the basis of the schedule which follows. Attempting to treat delirium tremens with the Stage I regimen is often complicated by temporary control of the withdrawal symptoms, only to have the process reappear when the supplementations decrease. Reinstitution of the Stage I regimen at a later stage for delirium tremens is commonly associated with oversedation, and certainly one runs the risk of serious respiratory depression.

3. Oversedation may occur if the signs and symptoms which are being monitored are the result of agitation produced by acute anxiety reaction or an acute psychotic process. It should be remembered that for any method to be effective, the signs and symptoms must be due to alcohol withdrawal and not some other process.

4. Focal seizures should always be considered due to something other than alcohol withdrawal until proven otherwise. It is particularly important in these instances to rule out intracranial lesions.

Stage II Withdrawal

Stage II represents a continuum from Severe Stage I. This stage includes everything in Stage I, plus auditory hallucinations for which the patient has insight. Typically, the patient who has evidence of tremor, sweats, and agitation indicates that he or she hears voices coming out of the light plug, or out of the television set which is turned off. Such a patient will acknowledge that this is impossible and wishes to know from the health care professional what is happening. The auditory hallucinations are not infrequently threatening, in that what is being heard is of an uncomplimentary nature. In Stage II, the hallucinations less commonly may be visual, but are generally associated with insight into the fact that the hallucinatory material is not reality. The differential diagnosis should separate delirium tremens, in which all of the hallucinations are primarily visual but may also be auditory. However, in delirium tremens there is clouding of the consciousness which is not present in Stage II. It is important to differentiate Stage II from the organic hallucinosis produced by alcohol. The time of onset of alcoholic hallucinosis is in the first few days of abstinence from alcohol. This syndrome generally appears without the severe signs of psychomotor and autonomic activity described under Stage I alcohol withdrawal. However, any organic hallucinosis may have superimposed on it an acute alcohol or drug withdrawal syndrome. Therefore, no hard and fast rule can be stated. The differential diagnosis rests on observation of the patient, and proper treatment of any alcohol withdrawal syndrome which may exist. Alcoholic hallucinosis may typically last for a few hours to a few days, but there are a minority of instances which may go on for several weeks, or even several years.

A further differential feature is the fact that patients with alcoholic hallucinosis respond to the hallucinations as if they were real. Patients have been known to harm themselves trying to avoid the consequences of threatening auditory hallucinations for which they have no insight. The Treatment of Stage II alcohol withdrawal is precisely as for Stage I.

Stage III Withdrawal (Delirium Tremens)

Patients with delirium, or Stage III alcohol withdrawal, are suffering from an acute reversible organic psychosis which used to be called acute brain syndrome. The onset of this syndrome is typically 72 hours after the last drink, although occasionally it may present sooner. It is always preceded by signs and symptoms of Stage I alcohol withdrawal. Stage III is differentiated from Stage I and Stage II by the fact that the patient manifests clouding of the sensorium, i.e., a reduction in clarity of awareness of the environment. The patient experiences difficulty in sustaining attention to both external and internal stimuli. The patient experiences sensory misperception and an extremenly disordered stream of thought. In approximately 30% of instances, the patient will experience a grand mal seizure prior to the onset of delirium. It has been reported in the scientific literature (23) that once the patient has developed delirium, further seizures related to alcohol withdrawal do not occur. The significance of this report is that seizures occurring in a patient with alcohol withdrawal delirium are not due to the withdrawal process. The health care professional should seek the cause in hypoglycemia, intracranial pathology, or elsewhere. Disorientation, at least to time, is present. Not infrequently, disorientation is also present for place, and occasionally one sees a patient with alcohol withdrawal delirium who is experiencing global disorientation. The common hallucinations in alcohol withdrawal are visual. These hallucinations are characterized by the following features:

1. The patient has no insight into the hallucinations, and reacts to the hallucinatory material as if it were reality.

2. The hallucinations are vivid and colorful.

3. The hallucinations are characterized by macropsia and micropsia, i.e., hallucinatory material appears smaller or larger than in real life.

4. The hallucinations, more often than not, represent some type of threat to the patient. This feature may lead the patient to some type of panic reaction to avoid the consequences of the threatening hallucination.

Patients experience extreme anxiety and fear, as a result of their hallucinatory experience, may fall out of bed, jump out of bed, and sometimes have been known to jump out of the window. This behavior apparently represents a panic reaction to the perceived threat involved in the hallucinations, Many patients who jump out of general hospital windows are, in fact, suffering from alcohol withdrawal delirium. It follows, therefore, that appropriate measures, including restraints when necessary to protect the patient from themselves, should be used.

Hallucinations may also be auditory, fused audiovisual, tactile, and rarely, olfactory. Fused audiovisual hallucinations are said to have prognostic significance, indicating a severe process.

A further diagnostic feature in alcohol withdrawal delirium is misidentification. In these instances, the patient misidentifies an individual as someone out of his or her past or present. This, occasionally, is seen in the early stage of delirium tremens when the diagnosis may be difficult. Patients who misidentify, and who have the autonomic and psychomotor hyperactivity described for Stage I should clearly be diagnosed as having delirium tremens.

The patient's emotional state is most often variable and subject to rapid change. The patient at various times may experience great anxiety, fear, depression, anger, euphoria, apathy, and irritability. A classical feature of delirium tremens is the tendency for the emotional state to become more agitated and hyperactive after sunset. Darkness, whether produced by sunset, or artificially by drawing drapes and turning out lights, appears to increase the hyperactivity. Therefore, the patient's room should remain brightly lighted at all times. Engaging the patient in conversation, even though the patient is not capable of sustained thought patterns, will keep the patient from closing his or her eyes and experiencing further hallucinations. This points out the extreme importance of helping the patient build a bridge to reality, an extremely significant aspect of the supportive treatment required to attain reasonable results with these patients.

The patient with Stage III alcohol withdrawal is differentiated from severe Stage I and Stage II withdrawal by the clouded sensorium, disorientation, at least to time, and not infrequently, to place and person, visual hallucinations for which the patient has no insight, often associated with auditory and other types of hallucinations, misidentification, and a marked increase in the psychomotor and autonomic hyperactivity described for Stage I and Stage II. It should be particularly noted that the heart rate generally exceeds 120 bpm, and both systolic and diastolic hypertension are often present. The diaphoresis one sees is more marked and more generalized, being characterized by drenching sweats. A febrile response is common. The literature reports (23) that the body temperature may be elevated to 102° Fahrenheit solely as a result of the withdrawal process. This author's experience indicates, however, that one should have a high index of suspicion that the fever may represent some underlying medical complications when it exceeds 101° Fahrenehit.

Stage III is a process very much like Stage I alcohol withdrawal in that once established, the process will continue until it clears as a result of its own limitations. It is for this reason that the purely symptomatic management of the withdrawal process is fraught with great dangers. The health care professional should understand that he or she is treating a process which has a natural history. In the case of Stage II alcohol withdrawal, this process will usually run its course in three to five days.

The variations in the length of the process seem to be dependent on a number of variables, including the intensity of the physical dependence and the presence or absence of underlying medical complications. The presence of a significant underlying medical complication is thought to predispose a patient in alcohol withdrawal to develop delirium and to result in a more protracted course. It is important to recognize that this syndrome carries a mortality rate in the range of 10-15% across the United States today. This figure is down considerably from ten years ago, partly because of the recognition that delirium tremens may be prevented if Stage I and Stage II alcohol withdrawal are adequately treated. There has also been a vast improvement in the understanding of the underlying metabolic problems, particularly as they relate to the patient's fluid and electrolyte balance (see Chapter 10).

Clinical Management

It should be emphasized once more that, unless the patient *presents* with Stage III withdrawal, it can be prevented by recognizing Stage I and Stage II, and providing adequate treatment as previously outlined. However, when the syndrome exists, the management is on a multiple front. It is critical to diagnose and adequately treat any underlying medical complication. It is estimated that approximately 5% of hospitalized alcoholics develop delirium tremens. A characteristic of this group is the observation that they have been drinking in the neighborhood of one quart of distilled spirits a day, or its equivalent in beer or wine, for five to ten years. It, therefore, follows that manifestations of alcohol toxicity in the form of pathologic organ changes would be more marked in this group. This appears to be the case, with almost half of these patients exhibiting significant alcoholic liver disease. The whole gamut of medical complications, however, may be represented.

Recognition and treatment of the associated fluid and electrolyte disturbances is another critical area. Here, it is recommended that the patient have an indwelling Foley catheter. These patients with delirium, as a rule, are not capable of asking for the urinal and therefore tend to develop bladder distention and overflow incontinence. This problem results in an increase in the patient's agitation and precludes an adequate urinary output record. Careful estimates of the sensible/insensible losses are also important because significant amounts of hypotonic fluid may be lost in this way. Daily measurements of the principal ions and of the blood gasses is recommended.

The question of restraining these patients because of their hyperactivity is an important one. It is well-documented that restraints increase the patient's agitation and are, therefore, undesirable. However, unless a responsible person is with the patient at all times, restraints are usually necessary. When used, they should be of the full leather type, and should be applied for the shortest period of time necessary to obtain appropriate control of the patient's agitation.

Sedation of the patient is more intense than in Stage I or II alcohol withdrawal. The same basic principle in the utilization of sedation outlined for Stage I alcohol withdrawal should be followed in Stage III. A large number of sedative drugs, which are cross-tolerant with ethyl alcohol, have been used in the treatment of delirium tremens, as well as some anti-psychotic medications. While there is not total agreement on this subject, a benzodiazepine derivative is most often viewed as the drug of choice. We shall continue to use as an example chlordiazepoxide (Librium®). This drug is used in a more intense way in Stage III than in Stage I. Specifically, chlordiazepoxide may be given orally in doses of 100 mg each hour, providing there is one hour between doses and the systolic blood pressure remains at 100 or above. This process may be continued until the patient goes to sleep. Sleep is regarded as the endpoint, and the hourly dosage should be discontinued. Chlordiazepoxide has a long half-life, and there is generally sufficient drug in the patient's body to carry the patient through the rest of the Stage III process without additional supplementation. Occasionally, it may be necessary to give small doses following discontinuation of the hourly schedule on an as-needed basis. It should be recalled that the amount of sedation that a human being can tolerate is largely dependent on the amount of psychomotor activity exhibited by the patient. As the withdrawal process peaks and begins to decline in intensity, the patient's psychomotor activity decreases. It is at this time that the patient is vulnerable to oversedation.

How does the health care professional know that his or her treatment of a given case of Stage III alcohol withdrawal is proceeding according to schedule? It should be recognized that Stage III may be mild, moderate, or severe, so that the following examples may be used only as rough guidelines. Assuming that all medical complications, including fluid electrolyte imbalance, are appropriately managed, the following may indicate an appropriate course. The best one can hope to achieve is to have the patient rational most of the time, and taking oral fluids within 24 hours. If this condition is obtained in 48 hours, the result may be viewed as good, and if this result requires 72 hours, the result may be viewed as satisfactory. Failure to obtain the above state within 72 hours suggests that an unrecognized medical complication may be present. One rather uncommon cause of a prolonged course is the evolution of the amnestic syndrome (Korsakoff's Syndrome). The treatment of this syndrome is different from the treatment of delirium tremens. Usually one sees a marked decrease in the patient's hyperactivity, but a continuation of mental confusion. Confabulation, which is often a part of the amnestic syndrome, is said not to occur in the first week after its onset, and should not be considered essential to the diagnosis of this syndrome.

Patients recovering from Stage III alcohol withdrawal or alcohol withdrawal delirium are often weak. They frequently have slow thought processes and tend to be somewhat depressed and apathetic. This state improves gradually with proper nutrition and elimination of the sedative drug required to treat the syndrome. The presence or absence of other underlying medical complications will also influence the patient's course. Rehabilitation programs for these patients should take into consideration the profound metabolic and neurological consequences of this syndrome. The mortality rate in well-conducted cases would probably be no more than 1%, although this may vary with the population being served by any given facility. The morbidity, however, may be quite severe. Generally speaking, longer-term, structured-type rehabilitation programs play an important role in the recovery of many of these patients. In the case of severe underlying medical complications, a medically oriented extended-care facility would seem to be appropriate.

FURTHER TREATMENT CONSIDERATIONS

While alcoholism treatment historically began with care of its medical complications, the social complications were referred for attention to the criminal justice system and a variety of social agencies. This approach often prolonged life and assisted families, but it did little to interrupt the basic underlying addictive process discussed earlier. When Alcoholics Anonymous (AA) was founded in 1935, the Twelve Step Program of AA soon demonstrated that many alcoholics could recover (see Chapter 14), thereby providing the impetus for the modern system of multidisciplinary AA-oriented treatment programs in the United States. While there are other emerging treatment systems, including, for example, primary psychiatric care, social-model programs, religious (conversion) approaches, and others, most of the attention in the last decade has been paid to the multidisciplinary AA-model programs.

Since the causes of alcoholism remain unknown, most treatment tends to be non-specific. Indeed, we know that *alcoholism* is a general term, like *cancer*, and alcoholics do not represent a homogeneous group. There may be several alcoho*lisms* as suggested by Jacobson (11), or we may be talking about variations in the presentation of the disease as it relates to age, sex, culture, occupation, environmental stress, and other variables.

Because long-term longitudinal observation reveals that a given patient's drinking status can be highly variable, and the collective experience of clinicians who have worked with alcoholics for many years shows the need to adopt long-range flexible treatment strategies over a period of years, we should be talking about a *continuum* of care which will meet a given patient's needs at a particular point in time. What is needed, then, is the ability to accurately assess a patient's needs and be able to refer to a variety of treatment modalities on a more individualized basis. Much has been made of the fact that treatment outcome in unselected patients tends to be similar for inpatient and outpatient treatment. It is likely that patients properly screened for given modalities, and continued in long-range individualized treatment programs, will show improved outcomes. The State Medical Society of Wisconsin, through its Committee on Alcoholism and Other Drug Abuse, has made a beginning in establishing criteria for different treatment phases (see Appendix 5).

Another treatment issue relates to abstinence as a primary goal. It is generally understood that alcoholism is usually a chronic and relapsing disorder. The studies (24) available to support controlled drinking in bona fide alcoholics are seriously marred, and many patients who return to drinking tend to show serious life problems as a consequence, if followed for a sufficiently long period of time. At this point in time, it is safest to propose abstinence for all alcoholics. Abstinence is strongly related to work adjustments, health status, interpersonal relationships, and social stability. Treatment must also address the patient's major psychological and social problems as well as the drinking behavior. Involvement of appropriate family members in the recovery process is now considered essential by most treatment providers. Early and continued Alanon and Alateen participation by appropriate members of the family is often helpful (see Chapter 14).

As one aspect of the continuum of care, inpatient treatment may occur in a general or psychiatric hospital, or free-standing alcoholism treatment center. During this phase of treatment the patient, medically pre-screened, undergoes a careful history and physical examination, laboratory and x-ray studies are performed, and a provisional differential diagnosis is established. Detoxification from alcohol and other drugs is accomplished along with whatever other medical complications require immediate attention. While these physical problems are being assessed and treated, the basic underlying alcoholism is also targeted for active treatment. Any symptomatic denial, which may be total or partial, is initially confronted compassionately and objectively. Early involvement of a family member, employer, or friend, may be important in motivating the patient to remain for the subsequent medically directed psychosocial rehabilitation program.

Transfer of the patient from the medical ward to a peer-group rehabilitation unit as soon as safety permits, is often an important variable in the patient's making a commitment to recovery. The patient is then ready to begin peer-group and individual counseling. In addition, the patient participates in a variety of educational activities aimed at increased awareness of the problem. A thorough introduction to the Twelve Step program of Alcoholics Anonymous occurs in most facilities, and the patient is often asked to progress through the first five steps while in an inpatient program. This requirement is facilitated by actual attendance at AA meetings in the facility and in the community. Progress through this process is monitored closely by the multidisciplinary team, under the direction of a physician knowledgeable in addictive diseases. The patient is staffed by this team on a weekly basis, and it is therapeutic for the patient to be present at these staffings to obtain additional feedback and to express his or her concerns.

Progress is judged by a reduction in the degree of denial and dependence, improved attitude, and willingness to be involved in an ongoing treatment program upon discharge from the inpatient phase. The ultimate purpose of inpatient treatment is this motivation for ongoing treatment.

Outpatient treatment of alcoholism may encompass the same basic principles as the inpatient phase. The program should be designed for those in the earlier stages of alcoholism with fewer physical and psychosocial problems, as well as those improving patients who have successfully completed an inpatient-treatment program. Implicit in this mode of treatment is the patient's possession of a better support system, less need for environmental controls, and no untreated major physical or psychiatric complications. Ability to refrain from drinking is another essential requirement (see Appendix 5), and Antabuse may or may not be suggested for this group. Retention in outpatient treatment is often more difficult and high dropout rates are not uncommon. This treatment should be open-ended, but usually follows a prescribed four- to six-month course. Ongoing additional outpatient treatment may include support groups, individual counseling, and family and couples treatment. There may be specialty programs for adolescents, professionals, minorities, elderly, and other groups either as primary treatment or as a secondary continuum following specialized inpatient treatment.

Recovery homes provide extended residential treatment for those individuals whose level of acceptance of treatment, sense of personal responsibility, and motivational strengths need additional attention. Lack of an adequate support system is also an indicator for this extended residential treatment. These programs tend to last three to six months, but may be open-ended.

Specialists' care, provided by psychiatrists knowledgeable in addictive diseases, is a significant component for those patients with major psychiatric disorders. We have found that expressive/supportive psychotherapy enhances the recovery process in terms of "quality sobriety" for many patients (25).

Sheltered workshops may provide more-disabled patients with opportunities to re-establish discipline and self-respect in their lives. These vocational programs often lead to reintegration in the nation's work force.

The continuum of care should also include specialized nursing homes for extended treatment of those patients with late-stage physical and psychiatric complications. Treatment in such facilities must be low-keyed and within the capabilities of each patient. With appropriate extended care, many patients will be able to resume independent living.

Early diagnosis and treatment of relapse is an essential part of this continuum of care for an estimated minimum of 50% of patients, regardless of whether treatment is inpatient, outpatient, or residential. The early identification of relapse, with appropriate adjustments to the treatment plan, will salvage many of these patients. Relapse is most common in the first year following formal treatment, and a monitoring program which keeps in touch with the patient's progress is essential to good clinical practice.

Treatment outcome is judged by maintenance of abstinence, decreasing symptomatic denial, acceptable occupational functioning, improving family relationships, and ultimately, the patient's ability to relate normally and comfortably with other human beings.

The number of treated people who ultimately recover varies with the population treated and the continuum of care provided, but the range is from 30% to 80%. These numbers are likely to improve when we match the patient, the patient's disease stage, and their therapy in an ongoing continuum. We prefer to follow our patients over a period of at least two years for those without significant complications, and open-ended for those with significant relapses and behavioral difficulties (25). Although spontaneous improvement has been observed to occur in 2-15% of cases, it is more likely to occur in older persons with good social adjustment and less general psychopathology. Thus, access to a complete and ongoing continuum of care is likely to be needed by most patients.

SUMMARY

Alcoholism is a chronic, recurring, usually progressive disease. The disease process, from a phenomenologic point of view, includes strong psychological dependence, tolerance, and impaired control over the use of alcohol. This process, as it develops, causes complications both physical and social in nature.

How much alcohol is too much? This question is answered by citing Dr. Francis Anstie's observation that 1.5 ounces of pure ethyl alcohol on a daily basis is sufficient to place most human beings at risk of developing pathological organ changes. Such drinking on a daily basis also places the individual at risk of developing addiction in view of the propensity with which tolerance develops with escalation of the intake of ethyl alcohol.

The many complications of alcoholism include physical dependence and the alcohol withdrawal syndrome. Appropriate diagnosis and treatment of this entity is an essential first step in the management of alcoholism when physical dependence is present. Concomitantly, the other physical complications of alcoholism should be carefully assessed and treated early in the process.

The treatment of alcoholism includes the continuum of care from very early intervention and counseling, to very complicated hospital inpatient programs, to residential treatment, and in the more advanced cases, to extended-care nursing home facilities. It is extremely important to match the patient's particular problems in any stage of their disease, and then find the suitable facility and personnel to deal with these problems on an individualized basis. A significant number of patients have, in addition to their alcoholism, some underlying significant psychiatric illness. Here again, the importance of differential treatment is emphasized. The objectives of inpatient treatment are to manage the alcohol withdrawal syndrome when present, and concomitantly treat any other medical complication which may exist. Motivation of the patient for ongoing treatment is the objective of the psychosocial rehabilitation program, which includes confrontation of denial and the other defense mechanisms as well as a very careful appraisal of the individual's problem areas. Once the patient becomes motivated for ongoing treatment, a wide variety of outpatient and inpatient residential programs are available.

Treatment needs to be continued at some level for at least one to two years to assure reasonable outcome. Abstinence from alcohol and other mood-altering chemicals is a major goal in the treatment of alcoholism. It is not, however, the only objective. Improvement in the patient's interpersonal relationships ultimately attest to significant progress. Numerous psychological issues which affect the patient's self-esteem and the discipline of everyday living are involved in the long-term treatment process. Family relationships invariably need some attention. Vocational maladjustments need to be addressed when these exist. Alcoholism is a disease with a high recurrence rate, and consequently, it is essential to detect relapse at the earliest possible moment, and to provide additional support and treatment at this point.

REFERENCES

1. Alcohol and Health: Fourth Special Report to the Congress. National Institute on Alcohol Abuse and Alcoholism. Washington, DC: US Government Printing Office, 1981.

2. Schuckit, M.A.; Morrisey, E.R.: Alcoholism in women: some clinical and social perspectives with an emphasis on possible subtypes. In *Alcoholism Problems in Women and Children*, Greenblatt, M., and Schuckit, M.A. (Eds.). New York: Grune & Stratton, 1976.

3. Stamatoyannopoulos, G.; Chem, S.H.; Fukui, M.: Liver alcohol dehydrogenase in Japanese: high population frequency of atypical form and its possible role in alcohol sensitivity. *American Journal of Human Genetics*, 27:789-796, 1975.

4. Wolff, P.H.: Ethnic differences in alcohol sensitivity. *Science, 175:* 449-450, 1972.

5. Schuckit, M.A.; Rayses, V.: Ethanol ingestion: Differences in blood acetaldehyde concentrations in relatives of alcoholics and controls. *Science, 203:*54-55, 1979.

6. Goodwin, D.W.; Schulsinger, F.; Hermansen, L.; Guze, S.B.; Winokur, G.: Alcohol problems in adoptees raised apart from alcoholic biological parents. *Archives of General Psychiatry, 28:*238-243, 1973.

7. American Medical Association: *Manual on Alcoholism.* Chicago, Illinois: AMA, 1968.

8. Criteria Committee, National Council on Alcoholism. Criteria for the diagnosis of alcoholism. *Annals of Internal Medicine, 77:*249-258, 1972.

9. Gitlow, S.E. and Peyers, H.S. (Eds): *Alcoholism: A Practical Treatment Guide.* New York: Grune & Stratton, 1980, p. 3.

10. Jacobson, G.R.: *Diagnosis and Assessment of Alcohol Abuse and Alcoholism.* Washington, DC: Alcohol, Drug Abuse, and Mental Health Administration, 1975 (US DHEW Publ. No. [ADM] 80-228).

11. Jacobson, G.R.: *The Alcoholisms: Detection, Assessment, and Diagnosis.* New York: Human Sciences Press, 1976.

12. Jacobson, G.R.: Detection, assessment, and diagnosis of alcoholism: current techniques. In *Recent Developments in Alcoholism, Vol. 1,* Galanter, M. (Ed.). New York: Plenum Press, 1983. pp. 377-413.

13. Selzer, M.L.: The Michigan Alcoholism Screening Test: the quest for a new diagnostic instrument. *American Journal of Psychiatry, 127:*89-94, 1971.

14. Jacobson, G.R.; Niles, D.H.; Moberg, D.P.; Mandehr, E.; Dusso, L.: Identifying alcohol and problem-drinking drivers: Wisconsin's field test of a

modified NCA Criteria for the diagnosis of alcoholism. In *Currents in Alcoholism, Vol. VI: Treatment, Rehabilitation, and Epidemiology*, Galanter, M. (Ed.). New York: Grune & Stratton, pp. 273-293, 1979.

15. Jacobson. G.R.: Identification and assessment of problem drinkers. In *Proceedings of the 2nd National DWI Conference*. Falls Church, Virginia: AAA Foundation for Traffic Safety, pp. 35-43, 1980.

16. Jacobson, G.R.; Lindsay, D.: Screening for alcohol problems among the unemployed. In *Currents in Alcoholism, Vol. VII: Recent Advances in Research and Treatment*, Galanter, M. (Ed.). New York: Grune & Stratton, pp. 357-371, 1980.

17. Jacobson, G.R.; Moberg, D.P.; Lindsay, D.: Screening for alcohol problems among the unemployed: II. Further development of rapid identification procedures, referral for treatment, and outcome of treatment. Final Report to the Governor's Employment and Training Office, 1980 (unpublished).

18. American Psychiatric Association: *Diagnostic and Statistical Manual of Mental Disorders, 3rd Ed.* Washington, DC: APA, 1980.

19. Heilman, R.C.: Symposium on the problems of the chronic alcoholic. *Mayo Clinic Proceedings, 42:*705-723, 1967.

20. Anstie, F.E.: On the dietetic and medicinal uses of wine. *Practitioner, 4:*219, 1970.

21. Victor, M.: Treatment of alcoholic intoxication and the withdrawal syndrome. *Psychosomatic Medicine, 25:*636-650, 1966.

22. Gross, M.M.; Lewis, E.; Hastey, J.: Acute alcohol withdrawal syndrome. In *The Biology of Alcoholism, Vol. 3*, Kissin, B. and Begleiter, H. (Eds.). New York: Plenum Press, 1974, p. 214.

23. Wolf, S.M.; Victor, M.: The physiological basis of the alcohol withdrawal syndrome. In *Recent Advances in Studies of Alcoholism*, Mello, N.K. and Mendelson, J.H. (Eds.). Washington, DC: US Government Printing Office, 1971, pp. 188-199.

24. Pendery, M.C.; Maltzman, I.M.; West, L.J.: Controlled drinking by alcoholics? New findings and a reevaluation of a major affirmative study. *Science, 217:*169-175, 1982.

25. Herrington, R.E.; Benzer, D.G.; Jacobson, G.R.; Hawkins, M.K.: Treating substance-use disorders among physicians. *Journal of the American Medical Association, 247:*2253-2257, 1982.

Chapter 10

Medical Complications of Alcoholism

David Benzer, D.O.

OVERVIEW

In this chapter on the medical complications of alcohol abuse and dependency the author very systematically reviews the myriad of dysfunctions — some of them potentially fatal — which AHPs can expect to see among alcoholics. In his opening section on gastrointestinal complications, Dr. Benzer details the diseases of the oropharynx, esophagus, stomach, small intestine, pancreas, and liver which are directly and/or indirectly attributable to excessive alcohol ingestion. He focuses next on the circulatory system, citing the prevalence of cardiomyopathy, hypertension, and coronary artery disease. Special attention is paid to the potentially life-threatening effects of cardiac abnormalities during acute withdrawal from alcohol.

Lung abscesses, pneumonia, and tuberculosis — particularly among skid row residents — are among the pulmonary diseases experienced by alcoholics, which are explicated in the third major segment of this chapter.

In a section on neurologic complications the author delineates several major problems likely to be encountered among alcoholic patients. Because alcoholism is appropriately conceptualized, diagnosed, and treated as a biobehavioral health problem, this section illustrates particularly well the interaction between alcohol's insult to the cortex and the behavioral changes which signify alcohol abuse and dependency.

Several types of anemias, immunologic problems, and blood-coagulation defects are discussed in the section on hematologic and immunologic complications. Next addressed are metabolic complications, including glucose metabolism, and fluid and electrolyte imbalances. Special attention should be directed to this section, because of the many apparent similarities between symptoms of hypoglycemia and those of the alcohol withdrawal syndrome.

In the closing segments of this chapter, the author focuses on some miscellaneous medical complications of alcoholism, including accidental trauma, and skin and muscle disorders. He then discusses some of the effects of alcohol on the endocrine and reproductive system, with special emphasis on what we now recognize as the Fetal Alcohol Syndrome, the most preventable form of birth defects. Ways in which alcohol affects human sexual behavior are also clarified for readers. This section is followed by a summary of the new clinical information regarding possible associations between alcohol and cancer.

Overall, this chapter provides an excellent review of the causes and treatments of a wide array of medical and psychiatric complications of alcohol abuse and dependency.

INTRODUCTION

Alcoholism is a disease that is responsible for extensive morbidity and mortality on a worldwide basis (1). No human organ system is spared from the deleterious effects of this drug when it is consumed in abusive quantities. Research has consistently demonstrated that alcohol is directly or indirectly responsible for the hospitalization of as many as 25–30% of the patients on general medical wards (2), and yet the diagnosis of alcoholism is disproportionately under-represented on these medical records. Instead, the complications of alcoholism are recorded assiduously with only infrequent reference to the primary cause of the disability, the alcoholism itself. For example, the patient whose chart documents the presence of a skull fracture often neglects the fact that acute alcohol intoxication may have been the underlying cause of the trauma that created the fracture. In such cases, and many other similar ones, physicians are reluctant to record a diagnosis of alcohol abuse or alcohol dependence, even when there is little doubt about the patient's alcoholism. It would appear, then, that there is an attitudinal problem among physicians and other allied health professionals (AHPs), possibly attributable to the real or imagined social stigma associated with outmoded, incorrect, but still prevalent, notions about alcoholism.

The math is all bad.

A related issue is the matter of determining at what point alcohol use — social drinking — becomes alcohol abuse. The question is how much alcohol is too much? Relatedly, what are the limits of alcohol consumption which are not associated with an increased risk of medical complications? The range provided by a review of the literature on this subject is from 30-120 grams of ethanol consumed daily (1). There are roughly 30 grams of ethanol in one ounce of pure alcohol. Therefore, there are 15 grams of ethanol in one ounce of a 50 percent ethanol solution such as 100 proof distilled spirits, the same as in 12 ounces of beer and in 4 ounces of wine. It is crucial to be aware of this fact: It makes no difference which alcoholic beverage is consumed with regard to the development of medical complications of alcoholism. It is the absolute quantity of alcohol consumed, and not the beverage in which it is found, that is the determining factor.

More recent data indicate that consumption of as little as 40-60 grams of ethanol daily (2-5 drinks) can induce hepatic disease and increase the risk of developing certain cancers (1). This quantity is the approximate maximum level of consumption that was delineated by Dr. F.E. Anstie more than 100 years ago (3). Dr. Anstie noted that a daily consumption of 1.5 ounces of absolute alcohol (approximately 45 grams), was "about the limit of what can be habitually taken . . . without provoking symptoms of chronic malaise indicative of actual alcohol poisoning" (3). This estimate, known as *Anstie's limit*, has withstood the test of time and is probably as accurate as any we have today, although by no means an absolute guide to "safe drinking."

Another issue that has recently been given a great deal of attention both in the medical and non-medical literature is the subject of moderate drinking versus abstention. A recent study demonstrated a slightly higher mortality rate from cardiovascular disease among abstainers when compared to moderate drinkers (4). However, recent revisions of these studies reveal that the initial conclusions may be misleading. It has been found in two recent studies that the risk of mortality from cancer and stroke is higher in the social drinkers than in the abstainers (5, 6). Furthermore, the studies show that the *overall mortality* in social drinkers is higher than that of abstainers when all causes of death are investigated.

Alcohol used in quantities greater than 30-40 grams daily clearly is associated with increased morbidity and higher mortality rates. The influence of alcohol on morbidity rates is reflected in

50% by wt. → 100 proof
too rough
No
30 cc vol = 24 g wt.
density of alc.
.79 × H₂O at 60°
12 oz beer = 16.2 cc or ≈ 13 g
4 oz 12% wine = 14.4 cc ≈ 11.5 g

12 oz beer / 13 g   4 oz wine / 11.5
1 oz 100 proof = whiskey ~12 g

Anstie's limit 45 g 45 cc = 36 g → a short 3 beers (39)
→ a long 3 wines (34.5)
→ exactly 3 oz   ale at 100 proof
(36)

the increased frequency of hospital admissions among alcoholics, who are admitted to hospitals 2-3 times more freqeuntly than nonalcoholic patients (2). Overall mortality rates in alcoholics are consistently found to be at least twice that seen in nonalcoholic patients (1).

The use of alcohol in doses greater than Anstie's limit is clearly a risk factor in patients seen and treated by AHPs, and a thorough familiarity with the possible consequences of this action is essential. A description of the medical consequences of alcoholism in each organ system is provided in the following pages. Hopefully this knowledge will help reverse the trend that has made the disease of alcoholism one of the most underdiagnosed illnesses in the health care field.

GASTROINTESTINAL COMPLICATIONS OF ALCOHOLISM

Alcohol is truly a multi-system toxin, but no organ system is more drastically affected by alcohol than the gastrointestinal (GI) system. The oropharynx, esophagus, stomach, small intestine, liver, and pancreas are all prone to the deleterious consequences of alcohol abuse. Alcohol's action on each of these areas will be examined separately.

Oropharynx

The oropharynx is the first part of the body to come in contact with the ethanol. There seems to be an increased risk of developing oropharyngeal carcinomas in an alcoholic population (7). The relationship between alcohol and cancer is reviewed in a separate section of this chapter.

Additional oropharyngeal problems that may be seen in alcoholics include poor oral hygiene with resultant increase in dental caries, and in Vitamin B deficient alcoholic patients, an atrophic, smooth, beefy red tongue. Finally, easily bleeding gums may signal end-stage alcoholic liver disease with concomitant coagulation defects in the alcoholic patient.

Esophagus

Alcoholics have an increased susceptibility to esophageal carcinoma (8). More commonly seen is the problem of *reflux esophagitis.* Alcohol is responsible for relaxing the lower esophageal sphincter (a tight ring of tissue at the lower end of the esophagus that prevents the highly acidic stomach contents from flowing back up into the sensitive esophagus), such that the back-flow of gastric contents occurs more readily. Also contributing to this problem is the tendency for alcoholics to assume the supine position after drinking, which facilitates the back-flow of gastric contents into the esophagus. All of these factors increase the frequency with which gastric contents come in contact with the esophageal mucosa, resulting in an irritation of the mucosa of the esophagus and the consequent reflux esophagitis (heartburn). The patient with reflux esophagitis may complain of burning in the mid-epigastric or lower sternal areas of the chest. The pain is usually relieved by antacids, which neutralize the acid that is causing the irritation. Another consequence of reflux esophagitis may be bleeding of the inflamed esophageal tissues. It is always necessary to rule out reflux esophagitis as a possible etiology of upper GI bleeding.

Another untoward effect of alcohol on the esophagus is related to the fact that alcoholics are frequently plagued by excessive nausea and vomiting. This may be due to either direct irritation of the gastric tissue by alcohol, or as a result of the effects of alcohol on the central nervous system (CNS). The pressure exerted on the walls of the esophagus may be too severe during a bout of protracted vomiting, and the wall may then tear longitudinally. This clinical occurrence is known as the *Mallory Weiss Syndrome* and the majority of the patients with the syndrome are alcoholic (9). The Mallory Weiss Syndrome must be considered in the differential diagnosis of any alcoholic patient experiencing GI bleeding.

The alcoholic patient may also develop *esophageal varices,* enlargement of veins that result from an impedance of blood flow through the venous system. In the case of esophageal varices, the problem results from obstruction of venous flow secondary to a cirrhotic liver. This obstruction results in an increase in pressure in the veins leading to the liver and is known as *portal hypertension.* The increased pressure is then transmitted to the esophageal veins and can cause them to distend. Esophageal varices are quite susceptible to being broken or punctured, which in turn leads to massive bleeding into the GI tract. This complication of alcoholism carries with it a very high mortality rate. Treatment of esophageal varices is usually surgical (10).

Stomach

Alcohol is a toxin which disrupts the integrity of the stomach's mucosal barrier, a clinical finding first noted by Beaumont (11) in 1833. The precise pathogenesis of this insult to the stomach's protective lining has not been eludicated; however, the consequences of the phenomenon are quite clear. Inflammation of the gastric tissue progressing to tissue breakdown and bleeding are frequent sequelae of excessive alcohol use. This is clinically known as *gastritis*, and when alcohol is the cause, *alcoholic gastritis* is the appropriate diagnosis. Patients suffering from alcoholic gastritis often complain of early morning mid-epigastric pain and burning that is relieved by antacids or milk.

The compromised integrity of the gastric mucosa would not unexpectedly then predispose to the development of peptic ulcer disease, and indeed, there seems to be an increased incidence of peptic ulcer disease in an alcoholic population when compared to a nonalcoholic group.

Small Intestine

It has long been recognized that alcoholics are prone to malnourishment and vitamin deficiency states (12). The etiology of these disorders is two-fold. First, in the heavily drinking individual, there is frequently a poor dietary intake. Alcohol provides large numbers of so-called *empty calories*, calories unaccompanied by other nutritional components. There are, for example 9 calories per gram of pure ethanol. In 1 ounce of 100 proof distilled spirits, there are 125 calories with virtually no other nutrients. The second factor which predisposes to nurtitional deficiencies is intestinal malabsorption. Malabsorption of the carbohydrate D-Xylose, Vitamin B_1 (thiamine), folic acid, Vitamin B_{12}, and fat, is known to occur in alcoholic patients (12). There can be some devastating consequences of this malabsorption, especially involving the vitamins. Thiamin deficiency is the cause of the *Wernicke-Korsakoff Syndrome*, a particularly debilitating neurologic disorder seen in alcoholics. Folic acid deficiency can lead to anemia.

Another intestinal complication attributed to alcohol was recently explained when it was found that alcohol inhibits Type I mixing waves in the jejunum while stimulating Type III propulsion waves. The net effect of these influences is to create a rapid transit of intestinal contents and the result of this is diarrhea, often termed *alcoholic diarrhea*. This alcoholic diarrhea generally resolves within one week of cessation of drinking.

Pancreas

Acute *pancreatitis* is a disease entity whose clinical spectrum ranges from a mild process lasting only a few days with minimal morbidity, to a disease with a fulminate and fatal course. There are multiple etiologies of pancreatitis in alcoholism (13). From 30-60% of all the cases of pancreatitis can be attributed to alcoholism. The second most common cause of pancreatitis is biliary disease.

The most plausible pathogenesis to date concerning the etiology of alcohol-induced acute pancreatitis involves alcohol's tendency to precipitate protein from pancreatic fluid followed by inspissation, or condensation, of protein plugs in the pancreatic ducts. This process results in a backup of pancreatic enzymes and subsequent autodigestion of the pancreas.

Alcoholic pancreatitis may be classified into three types: acute pancreatitis, acute relapsing pancreatitis, and chronic pancreatitis (13). Acute and acute relapsing pancreatitis are characterized by complete restoration of the pancreatic histology and functioning following resolution of the attack of pancreatitis. In contrast, chronic pancreatitis is often associated with late sequelae of the disease, including calcification of the pancreas, diabetes mellitus, and digestive disorders secondary to exocrine-function defects in the pancreas.

The clinical signs and symptoms of acute pancreatitis are often non-specific. Subsequently acute pancreatitis must be considered in the differential diagnosis when searching for a cause of a wide variety of back, abdominal, and thoracic complaints. The primary clinical symptom of acute pancreatitis is pain. The most common presentation is pain localized in the upper abdomen with radiation to the back. Other clinical signs and symptoms include vomiting, abdominal muscle spasm, guarding, and pleural effusion. The laboratory findings in pancreatitis include elevations in serum amylase, lipase, blood sugar, and the amylase/creatinine ratio.

The treatment of acute pancreatitis includes nasogastric suction, intravenous fluid replacement, and analgesics. Every attack of acute pancreatitis must be treated as the potentially life-threatening condition that it is. The mortality rate from acute pancreatitis is 8-10%; however, with the very severe form of acute pancreatitis known as *acute necrotizing pancreatitis*, the mortality rate soars to anywhere between 40 and 85%.

The single most important point to remember concerning acute pancreatitis is that unless treatment is received for the underlying etiology of the acute pancreatitis, namely alcoholism in at least 30% of the cases, one is merely treating a recurring symptom of the primary disease. The prognosis is indeed poor for the patient who has had acute pancreatitis but continues to drink.

Liver

Alcoholism is responsible for the majority of the cases of chronic liver disease seen in this country (14). Cirrhosis of the liver is one of the major causes of death in males between the ages of 25 and 60 (14). Although a great deal of research has been done and many questions regarding the nature of alcoholic liver disease have been answered, there remains many more that continue to elude the clinical investigators. We will begin our discussion of alcoholic liver disease with a discussion of the pathogenesis of this condition.

There are three stages in the progression of alcoholic liver disease, which often overlap in any given patient and are probably an oversimplification of the disease process. Also, it must be kept in mind that the definitive diagnosis concerning which stage or stages are present in any given patient can only be made by liver biopsy.

The first stage of alcoholic liver disease is known as *alcoholic fatty liver*. In this stage, there exists an intracellular accumulation of fats (principally triglycerides) within the liver cells, attributable both to alcohol having replaced the lipids as an energy source for the liver, and to a defect in the transport of lipids out of the liver cells (15). However, accumulation of lipids is not the sole reason for the liver enlargement seen in alcoholic fatty liver. There is also an accumulation of intracellular protein within the liver cells which acts osmotically to retain water within the cells (15). Therefore, the *hepatomegaly* seen in alcoholic fatty liver is a result of both the accumulation of fat, protein, and water within the liver cells.

The clinical picture of fatty liver disease is, on physical examination, one of liver enlargement with possible tenderness and pain. Laboratory findings may include an elevation in the blood level of liver enzymes and an increase in mean corpuscular volume of red blood cells.

Alcoholic fatty liver may then progress to the next stage of alcoholic liver disease which is *alcoholic hepatitis*, an inflammation of the liver secondary to several possible causes. Among these possible etiologies are a disruption of the normal hepatic cellular architecture by the fat and water accumulation, an increase in autoimmunologic activity induced by the alcohol, or possibly an alteration in the blood flow in the liver tissue as the result of alcohol being present. The precise mechanism by which alcoholic hepatitis develops has not been elucidated; however, suffice it to say that alcohol is most definitely the etiology (15). The clinical presentation of alcoholic hepatitis varies from the patient being virtually asymptomatic, to a patient presenting with severe right upper quadrant pain, fever, jaundice, leukocytosis, and abnormal liver function studies.

The final stage in the progression of alcoholic liver disease is *alcoholic cirrhosis*. This process involves the deposition of fibrous tissue amidst the liver parenchyma in response to tissue damage that occurred during the fatty liver and hepatitis stages. The process is similar to scar formation anywhere in the body. The severe medical sequelae often associated with alcoholic liver disease occur in the cirrhotic patient. Complications such as jaundice, testicular atrophy in males, bleeding esophageal varices, and the accumulation of fluid within the abdominal cavity (known as *ascites*) are all possible consequences of this severe alcoholic liver disease. Even more serious conditions such as blood coagulation defects or *hepatic encephalopathy*, (a form of toxic brain syndrome leading to a comatose state, brought about by the accumulation of poisonous waste products that the diseased liver is not able to detoxify) are also potential complications of cirrhosis. All of the consequences of cirrhosis are the result of either widespread destruction of hepatic tissue and resultant failure on the part of the liver to perform its metabolic function, or as the result of a resistance to the flow of venous blood through the diseased liver, known as *portal hypertension*.

The cornerstone of treatment for any stage of alcoholic liver disease is abstinence from alcohol. Studies have shown that the mortality rates of patients with alcoholic liver disease at any stage who continue to consume alcohol is markedly higher than for the patient who abstains from alcohol (14). Other than abstinence, the therapy for the liver disease process itself is mainly nutritional and vitamin therapy. Treatment of complications such as hepatic encephalopathy, ascites, coagulation defects, and varices is much more extensive.

Surprisingly, not all alcoholics develop alcohol liver disease, thus raising some interesting questions regarding susceptibility of the individual to the development of liver disease. Why is it that given the same history of consumption, some alcoholics develop little or no sign of liver disease, while others can experience a fulminant and rapidly fatal course with their liver disease?

While it has not been possible to precisely correlate completely the amount, duration, or type of alcoholic beverage ingested with the development of alcoholic liver disease, there are several factors that are known to greatly enhance the risk of developing alcoholic liver disease. Certainly, consuming greater than 80 grams of ethanol a day markedly increases the risk of developing alcoholic liver disease. Also, a daily drinker, as opposed to an episodic drinker, has an increased risk of developing alcoholic liver disease. Even these risk factors are not absolute, in that there are daily drinkers consuming more than 80 grams of ethanol a day who do not develop any significant alcoholic liver disease.

For many years it was believed that nutritional factors were involved in the evolution of alcoholic liver disease. The hypothesis was that the alcoholic who did not maintain a proper nutritional state was more susceptible to the appearance of alcoholic liver disease than were those alcoholics who continued to eat properly. This belief was disproved by Lieber and his colleagues (15), and it is now recognized that good nutrition does not prevent the untoward effects of the toxin ethanol on liver tissue.

All that is then left to explain the variance in individual susceptibility to alcoholic liver disease are constitutional and genetic factors that vary from patient to patient. It is almost certain that the status of the immune system plays a vital role in the susceptibility of a particular alcoholic patient to the development of alcoholic liver disease, much as it does in patients with viral liver infections. Some patients with viral liver infections have no problem after the acute infection has passed while others who apparently have some form of immunologic susceptibility go on to have a stormy and chronic course as the result of that initial infection. The final answers to the perplexing question of susceptibility to alcoholic liver disease lie in future research.

CARDIOVASCULAR COMPLICATIONS

The fact that alcohol influences the cardiovascular system has been recognized for nearly a century (16). Small doses of alcohol produce an increase in heart rate, a concomitant increase in cardiac output, and some rise in blood pressure. Another cardiovascular consequence of alcohol ingestion is a decrease in cutaneous vascular resistance producing flushing of the skin and a compensatory visceral vasoconstriction.

Over the last few years, several new issues concerning alcohol and cardiovascular function have been raised and some old issues rekindled. Five of these topics will be addressed here, namely cardiomyopathy, alcohol–induced arrhythmias, hypertension, coronary artery disease, and cardiovascular abnormalities found in the acute alcohol withdrawal syndrome.

Cardiomyopathy

In 1785, William Withering (17) reported that 16 of his 163 patients treated with foxglove for cardiac abnormalities were alcoholic, probably the first suggestion of *alcoholic cardiomyopathy*. The syndrome was further elucidated by Bollinger (18) in Munich at the end of the 19th century, who noted the appearance of signs of what is now recognized as *congestive heart failure* in chronic beer drinkers. This syndrome became known as the *Munich Beer Heart*. In the ensuing 80 years, alcoholic cardiomyopathy has become an accepted and recognized cardiovascular complication of alcoholism and part of the differential diagnosis in any patient presenting with congestive heart failure.

The precise pathogenesis of alcoholic cardiomyopathy is not yet known, however the concensus now is that this disorder is indeed due to the direct toxic effect of either alcohol, or its first metabolite acetaldehyde, or both, upon cardiac tissue (19). The notion that nutritional factors have a role is no longer popular. Electron microscopy has revealed characteristic intracellular changes in cardiac muscle damaged by alcohol, including a depletion in contractile proteins and an increase in the number of swollen, disrupted mitochondria.

The diagnosis of alcoholic cardiomyopathy is a difficult one to make early in the course of the disease, but it must be considered in the differential diagnosis of any alcoholic patient who presents with any cardiac abnormality. Early symptoms include tachycardia and a narrow pulse pressure. As the course of the disease progresses, the classic signs and symptoms suggestive of congestive heart failure, including rales, edema, third and fourth heart sounds, and venous congestion, begin to appear. The electrocardiographic and roentgenographic findings are somewhat nonspecific in alcoholic cardiomyopathy. EKG may reveal T–wave abnormalities, but there are no distinctive electrocardiographic changes in alcoholic cardiomyopathy. A chest x-ray might reveal the typical picture of congestive heart failure.

It becomes apparent that the diagnosis of alcoholic cardiomyopathy is one of exclusion. If the other known causes of congestive heart failure have been eliminated, and there is a history of alcoholism, the diagnosis of alcoholic cardiomyopathy can be made. The treatment once again involves abstinence from alcohol. The remainder of the therapeutics are the same as would be used in any case of congestive heart failure, including modification of diet in order to decrease sodium chloride consumption, and the judicious use of diuretics and digitalis.

Alcoholic cardiomyopathy is a serious consequence of alcoholism and almost half of the patients with this diagnosis progress rapidly to death. Clearly the most desirable treatment for the condition is one of prevention, which means early recognition of alcoholism in patients before the onset of alcoholic cardiomyopathy.

Cardiac Rhythm Disturbances

Cardiac arrhythmias without coexistent cardiomyopathy can be induced by alcohol ingestion. One such arrhythmia is called the "Holiday Heart Syndrome." Patients with this syndrome complain of cardiac palpitations after a drinking episode often following a holiday celebration (20). Recently, cardiac rhythm disturbances were documented after the ingestion of only about three ounces of 80 proof whiskey in 14 patients with a history of regular alcohol consumption and complaints of palpitations and/or syncope after drinking. The documented rhythm disturbance included more frequent premature ventricular beats and tachyarrhythymias (21). Clearly, then, alcohol can produce and/or exacerbate cardiac rhythm disturbances.

Hypertension

The relationship between alcohol consumption and hypertension has for years been confusing at best. Some light was shed on the subject when, in 1977, the Kaiser-Permanente Multiphasic Health Data on alcohol consumption and blood pressure in 84,000 people, revealed that men and women who consumed two or fewer drinks per day had blood pressure similar to those of nondrinkers (22). Men and women who had three or more drinks daily (remember Anstie's limit) had blood pressure higher than the nondrinkers. This study demonstrated that the prevalence of clinical hypertension (blood pressure greater than 160/95) was twice as common in men and women who consumed six or more drinks daily when compared to persons who abstained or had two or less drinks daily. This relationship between alcohol and hypertension was independent of regular salt use, coffee use, cigarette smoking, race, sex, or age. The implications of these findings are important, and the data correlate with the clinical experience of many experts in the field of alcoholism who report a high incidence of hypertension in alcoholic patients. Also, we have found in our experience with hypertensive alcoholic patients, that many previously diagnosed *essential hypertensives* become normotensive upon cessation of alcohol ingestion. This change does not occur with all hypertensives who are alcoholic because some of these patients indeed have true essential hypertension, but it is contrary to the notion that once a patient has developed hypertension they will have that disease throughout their life. It is apparent that some patients who have hypertension as a result of alcoholism can become normotensive after their drinking has been eliminated.

Coronary Artery Disease

Toward the end of the 1970s, several reports were published relating "moderate" alcohol consumption to a lessened risk of developing coronary artery disease. One such report was the Honolulu Heart Study, which examined alcohol intake and incidence of coronary artery disease in Japanese men in Hawaii (4). They found that an inverse relationship existed between the habitual moderate drinking of alcohol and the development of coronary artery disease. Results such as these were widely publicized by the press and were music to the ears of drinkers everywhere. However, as is so often the case, the early results did not fully examine all of the implications of the data. Three years after the initial report was released, a follow-up study was reported using the same group of patients (5). This time, when the patients were scrutinized for total mortality, the investigators found the death rate from cancer and stroke increased progressively with rising alcohol consumption. When the overall mortality rate was compared for drinkers and abstainers, the drinkers now had a higher mortality rate. It seems that alcohol is anything but "medicinal" and that teetotallers do fare better than drinkers in the long run.

Cardiac Abnormalities in the Withdrawal Syndrome

In the midst of the explosion of autonomic hyperactivity present during the alcohol withdrawal syndrome, it should not be surprising that the cardiovascular system, so richly supplied with autonomic nerve fibers, is often influenced by this autonomic hyperactivity. The cardiovascular manifestations of withdrawal include sinus tachycardia, elevated systolic and diastolic blood pressures, sinus arrhythmias including atrial fibrillation, and premature beats of both atrial and ventricular origin (23). Since 24-hour cardiac monitoring is seldom performed on patients experiencing an alcoholic withdrawal syndrome, many of these abnormalities are not recognized. Also, most of these arrhythmias and premature beats disappear with the resolution of the withdrawal.

Several important points should be kept in mind regarding all cardiac abnormalities seen in the acute alcohol withdrawal syndrome. First, many fluid and electrolyte problems are seen in a patient experiencing alcohol withdrawal, which are a consequence of heavy, prolonged drinking and include hypokalemia, hypomagnesemia, hypophosphatemia, hypocalcemia, and overhydration. All may exacerbate cardiac abnormalities or actually be responsible for them. The importance of careful fluid and electrolyte monitoring of any patient in alcohol withdrawal cannot be overemphasized. The second point that needs emphasis is that unless the cardiovascular manifestations seen as a consequence of withdrawal are associated with particular symptoms or are life-threatening, they need not be treated. With proper management of the alcohol withdrawal syndrome using appropriate sedation as well as maintaining fluid and electrolyte balance, most of the abnormalities will resolve and will not adversely affect the patient. Even the hypertension associated with the alcohol withdrawal syndrome will respond to proper management of the alcohol withdrawal, and antihypertensive agents are rarely needed.

PULMONARY COMPLICATIONS

In 1943, Benjamin Rush noted that "The following diseases are the usual consequence of the habitual use of ardent spirits: hoarseness and a husky cough, which often terminates in consumption, and sometimes in an acute and fatal disease of the lungs" (24).

Alcohol's direct effect on the lungs is not entirely clear. There have been suggestions that ethanol may be directly toxic to the lung parenchyma, that it may inhibit mucociliary action, or that it might produce dehydration or the mucous layer of the tracheobronchial tree (25). Any of the conjectured direct effects of alcohol on the lung would undoubtedly predispose the alcoholic patient to a variety of pulmonary diseases. Despite not knowing the precise pathology of alcohol's action on the lung tissue, we do know of several pulmonary problems seen more frequently in the alcoholic patient. Among these conditions are *pneumonia*, including *aspiration pneumonia*, *lung abscesses*, and *tuberculosis.*

Before discussing these disease processes, it must be made clear that alcohol, in many patients, is but one factor that may be contributing to pulmonary pathology. Over 90% of all alcoholics also smoke cigarettes, and tobacco use may also play a role in the predisposition to any lung disorders seen in these patients. It is also often difficult to single out the influence of other pulmonary toxins, such as industrial pollutants, as contributing to the development of various pulmonary diseases. It is with these qualifying statements in mind that we embark upon a discussion of the pulmonary complications of alcoholism.

Pneumonia

Gastric contents may be introduced into the tracheobronchial tree as a result of the inspiration of vomitus in an acutely intoxicated patient. This is a very serious pulmonary complication of alcoholism called *aspiration pneumonia.* Once the bacteria and/or gastric contents enter the pulmonary system, the second deficit induced by alcohol comes into play. An immunologic impairment, manifested by decreased leukocyte mobilization, interferes with the patient's ability to destroy pathogens that invade the lung tissue (26). In the midst of these deficiencies, several organisms opportunistically invade the pulmonary system and initiate a pneumatic process (27).

There are five groups of bacteria that are most often implicated in pneumonias in alcoholic patients. The anaerobic bacteriodes (primarily from the mouth), strep pneumoniae, klebsiella pneumonia, E.coli, and hemophilus influenza, are the principal bacterial organisms that are the etiologic agents of pneumonias in alcoholics (27).

Prompt recognition and treatment of pneumonia in alcoholics is essential. The mortality rate from pneumonia in an alcoholic population has been found to be three times higher than in a nonalcoholic group. The treatment of alcoholic pneumonia is, of course, based on antibiotic therapy as in any other pneumonic process. Until sputum culture results are available to confirm the type of bacteria causing the pneumonia, antibiotic choice is usually made on an empirical basis. When aspiration pneumonia is present, oftentimes a combination of antibiotics is used to combat this life-threatening process.

Lung Abscess

A lung abscess is an air- and fluid-filled cavitation within the lung tissue, seen on x-ray as a cavity with an air-fluid level. Several studies have demonstrated that alcoholics comprised from 24 to 74% of all patients with lung abscesses (28). Abscess formation is a pulmonary complication frequently seen after an episode of aspiration pneumonia. While the incidence of lung abscess seems to be diminishing in our hospitals, when present it is one complication of alcoholism that must be vigorously treated. The patient with the lung abscess presents most often as an alcoholic with poor oral hygiene who has a history of persistent low grade fever, weight loss, and occasionally a cough productive of foul-smelling sputum.

The diagnosis of lung abscess can be made after other diseases that may present as a cavitary lung lesion have been ruled out, such as carcinoma, fungal infections, etc. A chest x-ray, sputum cultures, and transthoracic aspiration of the lesion can aid in making the proper diagnosis. The treatment of lung abscess consists of long-term antibiotic therapy and postural drainage. If these measures fail, surgery may be necessary.

Tuberculosis

The incidence of tuberculosis in this country has been steadily declining over the past several decades since the advent of effective pharmacologic treatment for this disease (29). Among alcoholics, the overall incidence is similar to that seen in the general population, with the exception of the skid row alcoholics, among whom there remains a large pool of inadequately treated cases of tuberculosis. When patients within this special group are seen by health professionals, routine sputum cultures for acid-fast bacilli and chest x-rays should be obtained. Successful outcome depends on adherence to the treatment protocols, which in turn is greatly affected by the presence or absence of continued drinking in these patients.

NEUROLOGIC COMPLICATIONS

The neurologic complications of alcoholicsm are myriad. Alcohol-induced pathology within the nervous system extends from the highest cortical centers to the most distant peripheral nerves. There are two mechanisms by which alcohol damages the nervous system, the first of which is alcohol-induced nutritional deprivation. Alcohol is responsible for the intestinal malabsorption of thiamine, leading to a thiamine-deficiency state that predisposes the alcoholic patient to several central nervous system (CNS) diseases, including the *Wernicke-Korsakoff Syndrome*. The second mechanism by which alcohol effects the nervous system is via direct neurotoxicity, in which alcohol itself is a toxin to the cells of the nervous system.

Thiamine Deficiency Syndromes

Alcoholics absorb thiamine very poorly from the gastrointestinal tract, with some absorbing as little as·5% of the thiamine hydrochloride they ingest. This malabsorption, frequently combined with poor dietary intake, results in a propensity for thiamine deficiency in the alcoholic patient. There are three specific clinical syndromes which may occur as a consequence of this deficiency.

Alcoholic polyneuropathy, the first of these syndromes, is a metabolic peripheral neuropathy quite similar to other metabolic peripheral neuropathies, including that associated with diabetes mellitus (30). Alcoholic polyneuropathy is a sensorimotor deficiency that is usually symmetric, in that both sides of the body are affected equally. The etiology is thiamine deficiency, and the most common presentation is a *sensory parasthesia*, often in the form of a burning type of pain, usually in the lower extremities. In addition, one might see some muscle weakness and wasting, diminution of deep tendon reflexes, and generalized distal sensory impairment. The condition may be alleviated with nutritional and vitamin therapy along with the discontinuance of alcohol use, although occasionally the deficits persist despite treatment.

The second syndrome is *alcoholic cerebellar degeneration,* also associated with thiamine deficiency secondary to alcoholism (30). The patient with this syndrome usually presents with *ataxia,* which is a lack of coordination of the lower limbs and trunk. The arms are relatively spared. This disorder may respond to thiamine administration and abstention from alcohol.

Of the three thiamine-deficiency syndromes associated with alcoholism, the *Wernicke-Korsakoff Syndrome* is responsible for the majority of the morbidity and mortality within the group (31). This syndrome, actually two separate clinical presentations of the same disease process, is a CNS complication of thiamine deficiency. The two syndromes are *Wernicke's encephalopathy* and *Korsakoff's psychosis.* Symptoms of the former include confusion, ataxia, and oculomotor disorders (nystagmus and bilateral sixth nerve palsy). The symptoms may appear suddenly over a period of a day or two, or may evolve more slowly over a period of weeks.

Sometimes the patient then develops Korsakoff's psychosis, a syndrome characterized by severe memory deficits. Frequently, this amnesia is associated with an unconscious attempt to cover up the fact that the patient cannot retain or remember events of the recent past. *Confabulation,* one means by which patients accomplish this, is the process of making up a story to provide answers to questions that are unanswerable because of the Korsakoffian amnesia. It is quite characteristically, but not exclusively, found in Korsakoff's psychosis, and is a diagnostic hallmark. Korsakoff's syndrome is often called the *amnestic-confabulatory syndrome.*

Polyneuropathy and ataxia secondary to cerebellar degeneration often occur with the Wernicke-Korsakoff Syndrome. This is not surprising since all have an identical etiology, namely thiamine deficiency. Treatment of the Wernicke-Korsakoff Syndrome is once again thiamine administration. In a patient suspected of having a Wernicke-Korsakoff Syndrome, a dose of 500-1000 mg of thiamine should be administered intramuscularly immediately. Thereafter, a daily dose of 100 mg of thiamine orally three times a day is recommended. It is a common practice in alcoholic treatment centers, and in emergency rooms when patients are suspected of being alcoholic, to give them 100 mg of thiamine intramuscularly upon admission. Such a dose of thiamine is harmless and may prevent cases of impending Wernicke-Korsakoff Syndrome from becoming full blown.

Recovery from the Wernicke-Korsakoff Syndrome is variable. The oculomotor deficits usually respond relatively rapidly with thiamine administration. In contrast, the memory deficits may, in some cases, be permanent. Roughly one quarter of the cases demonstrate significant improvement in time, one half show some improvement with time, and one quarter experience permanent disability.

Alcohol Induced Seizures

Seizures of the grand mal type are frequently seen among alcoholic patients (30). They occur most often after the cessation of drinking, although they may occur any time the blood alcohol level (BAL) is declining. The majority of seizures occur within the first two to three days after the last alcohol consumed, and therefore, are termed *alcohol withdrawal seizures.* After seven days of abstinence from alcohol, withdrawal seizures *generally* do not occur. Occasionally, a grand mal seizure may herald the onset of the most severe stage of alcohol withdrawal syndrome, *delirium tremens.* Some neurologists recommend that alcoholic patients who are entering a treatment or health care facility receive a seven to ten day course of anticonvulsant therapy if there is a history of alcohol withdrawal seizures. Phenytoin (Dilantin®) is the drug most often used for this purpose. Phenobarbital may also be used in these patients at the discretion of the individual physician. Other physicians contend that it is difficult to attain a therapeutic blood level fast enough to abate alcohol withdrawal seizures and, therefore, do not recommend prophylactic treatment with anticonvulsants. The decision to treat or not is left to the discretion of the individual physician at this time. Hopefully, future studies will help settle this controversy.

Sequelae of Trauma

Alcoholics are quite susceptible to trauma as a result of accidents and falls (32). These incidents often lead to serious neurologic problems. Complicating this situation is the fact that alcoholic patients often appear in the emergency rooms in a state of altered consciousness, namely intoxicated, and this can make the diagnosis of other neurologic problems difficult. To further complicate the diagnosis, the patient is often unable to remember the events that led to the injury. As a result, major neurologic conditions such as subdural hematoma may go unrecognized.

Any alcoholic patient appearing for emergency care must be considered at risk for having major neurologic problems, including subdural hematomas, skull fractures, cerebral contusions, and peripheral nerve trauma and palsies. A careful physical examination must be performed on all of these patients in order to diminish the chances of missing one of these conditions.

Three Rare Syndromes of Uncertain Etiologies

Tobacco-Alcohol Amblyopia, an ophthalmologic syndrome, is most often seen in nutritionally deficient, tobacco-using alcoholics. It first presents as decreased visual acuity in the patient, and may go on to include difficulty in distinguishing colors, scotomata (defects in the visual field), or optic atrophy. Usually the ocular abnormalities respond to nutrition and vitamin therapy.

The second, *Central Pontine Myelinolysis*, is a rare disease seen in nutritionally debilitated alcoholics. A variety of neurologic signs and symptoms may be present, reflecting widespread destruction of pontine and brainstem neurotissue. Quadraplegia, dysphagia, ophthalmoplegia, and coma may occur. Hyponatremia has been noted in a number of cases, raising the question as to its possible role in the etiology of this disease. Abstinence, correction of fluid and electrolyte imbalance, and nutritional therapy are the mainstays of treatment for this disorder.

In *Marchiafava-Bignami Disease*, demyelination of the corpus callosum results in a wide array of possible neuropsychiatric symptoms, including impairment of language, gait, and motor skills, and seizures and hallucinations. Once again, malnutrition is thought to have a role in the disease progression. Although the syndrome is quite rare, it is seen most often in the alcoholic patient, and can be confirmed only by autopsy.

Brain Atrophy and Organic Brain Syndrome

With the advent of modern noninvasive neuroanatomical diagnostic instruments such as computerized axial tomography (CAT) scanning, the relationship between brain atrophy and alcoholism has proven to be far more prevalent than previously suspected (33). Recent studies, in which groups of alcoholic patients selected at random from alcoholic treatment center populations underwent routine CAT scanning, have demonstrated an incidence of brain atrophy in as high as 50% of all alcoholic patients scanned

[handwritten annotations: "DEMONSTRABLE!!", "can you get functional without atrophy?", "organic brain syndrome"]

(33). If neuropsychological testing is performed on patients with demonstrable cortical atrophy, functional deficits that accompany the structural abnormality can sometimes be observed. The range of neuropsychologic deficits runs from minimal cognitive deficits to a profound organic brain syndrome secondary to the alcoholism.

The practical implications of these data are important. First, in any alcoholic patient with a history of drinking ten years or more, the possibility of brain damage on either a structural or functional basis, or both, must be suspected. In a large percentage of patients some deficits will be uncovered. Abstinence from alcohol for these patients is, of course, mandatory. Following cessation of drinking, the rapidity and degree of recovery from the central nervous system deficits will vary with the severity of the impairment. Mild cases of brain atrophy and dysfunction can usually regain complete function within six months after arresting the alcoholism. This resolution can be demonstrated by repeating neuropsychologic testing at this interval. The more severe cases may require years to resolve. Milder cases can often maintain sobriety following conventional treatment for alcoholism. Patients with severe organic brain syndromes often require long-term residential treatment in extended-care facilities. Even then, some will never recover completely from their alcohol-induced organic brain syndrome.

HEMATOLOGIC/IMMUNOLOGIC COMPLICATIONS

Anemia is the most common hematologic complication of alcoholism (34). There are a number of possible etiologies for the anemia seen in an alcoholic patient but the most common cause is *folic acid deficiency.* As many as 80-90% of all alcoholics will demonstrate *macrocytosis,* or enlargement of red blood cells, on their complete blood count (CBC). This abnormality is quantified by using the measure of mean corpuscular volume (MCV). The macrocytosis is due to a decreased supply of the vitamin folic acid available to the developing red blood cells. In alcoholism folic acid deficiency is from two causes. First, there may be a lack of folic acid in the diet of the alcoholic. Secondly, and more important, is that alcohol inhibits proper absorption of folic acid in the small intestine. The net result is an insufficient quantity of folic acid available to the developing blood cells, causing the creation of larger, more immature red blood cells. Later on, with the progression of the deficiency, there will be an actual decrease in the production of red blood cells and a resultant anemia. The macrocytosis and/or anemia in the alcoholic patient due to folate deficiency, can be easily corrected by abstaining from alcohol and administering supplemental folic acid for several days.

A second type of anemia that may be found in alcoholics is *iron deficiency anemia* (34). As described above, alcoholic patients are particularly prone to GI bleeding in the form of gastritis, esophageal varices, or peptic ulcers, and the chronic blood loss results in a reduction of total body iron stores and subsequent ineffective erythropoesis. Health care providers must be vigilant for possible sources of blood loss in alcoholics. Appropriate treatment for the bleeding may be followed by the administration of supplemental iron to correct the iron deficiency anemia.

Finally, the alcoholic may present with a *multifactorial anemia*, that is, one with more than a single cause. It is possible to observe both iron and folate deficiencies in the same patient. Also, the alcoholic patient with severe liver disease may have red blood cell defects as a result of this liver disease.

Anemias in the alcoholic can be complicated, but with early recognition, they are quite correctable. Also, it is important to keep in mind that any time a patient appears with an anemia from one of the aforementioned etiologies, the possibility of alcoholism must be considered, and a thorough history and physical may provide additional clues to the diagnosis of alcoholism.

Immunologic Impairments

Alcohol is known to inhibit the production and functioning of white blood cells which are responsible for the body's immunologic, or defense system. Not only may there be a reduction in the absolute numbers of white cells available to combat infections (leukopenia), but also there are defects in the functioning of these white cells (26). These defects include inhibition of white cell migration to the site of an infection, and a decrease in production of the white cell's antibodies necessary to help destroy invading pathogens. The net result of all of these factors is that the alcoholic has an increased susceptibility to infection, and once infectin is present, has more difficulty combating that infection with his/her immune system. Consequently, the alcoholic patient must be carefully monitored for infection. Once infection is diagnosed, prompt and vigorous treatment should be instituted.

Alcohol-Induced Coagulation Defects

Proper hemostasis or coagulation of the blood after an injury occurs requires a combined effort of the platelets and a group of proteins within the blood known as the coagulation factors. Alcohol abuse can result in malfunctioning of both of these components (34).

Platelets are small cellular blood components which upon injury to a blood vessel, will come together to help form a plug to stop bleeding from the broken vessel. Alcoholism results in a decreased number of platelets available for this function and also results in decreased functioning of the platelets that are available. A decrease in the absolute number of platelets in the blood stream is known as *thrombocytopenia*. The phenomenon of decreased functioning of the platelets themselves as the result of the toxin alcohol has recently come to be known as *storage pool disease of platelets* (35).

Alcohol also results in a deficiency in the coagulation factors of blood proteins available for hemostasis. There are coagulation factors that bind together to form the protein *fibrin*, a substance that helps bind the platelet plug into a tight mass that effectively prevents further blood loss. Alcoholism and subsequent alcoholic liver disease prevent proper production of the coagulation proteins via two mechanisms. First, there is a malabsorption of Vitamin K in the small intestine. Vitamin K is crucial in that four of the coagulation proteins need Vitamin K in order for them to be synthesized. Secondly, because all of the coagulation proteins are manufactured in the liver, severe liver disease results in a decrease in the amount of healthy hepatic tissue available for the synthesis of these proteins. The net result of these two deficiencies is a decrease in the available coagulation proteins and subsequent impairment of hemostasis.

The treatment for these coagulation deficiencies obviously requires discontinuing the use of alcohol. Upon cessation of drinking, the platelet count usually rises. Also, as the liver begins to heal and proper Vitamin K absorption commences, the coagulation factors begin to be replenished.

The efficiency of the coagulation system can be monitored by utilizing the laboratory test known as *prothrombin time*. This test measures the clotting time of blood in a test tube. Severe cases of alcoholic liver disease with markedly prolonged prothrombin time, may require, concomitant with the cessation of alcohol use,

Vitamin K administered intramuscularly for several days, for a rapid correction of coagulation defects. In very severe cases, even Vitamin K injections may not be enough to help, and some patients with end-stage alcoholic liver disease will die from uncontrollable bleeding as a consequence of coagulation defects.

METABOLIC COMPLICATIONS

Glucose Metabolism

Glucose, a simple sugar molecule crucial to life, is the only energy-producing nutrient that human CNS cells can utilize. Without glucose available as an energy source, coma and brain death will occur.

Alcohol has several significant effects on the body's metabolism of glucose. After ethanol has been ingested, the rate of anaerobic breakdown of glucose, known as *glycolysis*, is increased. *Gluconeogenesis*, the production of glucose from noncarbohydrate sources, is inhibited. Finally, the synthesis of the glucose storage molecule, *glycogen*, is diminished. How these changes effect the blood glucose level depends upon whether or not an adequate supply of glucose has been ingested prior to the alcoholic being seen by the AHP.

If inadequate amounts of carbohydrate have been consumed, the alcoholic patient may present with severe hypoglycemia even to the point of hypoglycemic coma. In the alcoholic, three factors combine to cause hypoglycemia. First, the alcoholic whose diet is poor may not be consuming enough carbohydrates to begin with. This eventually results in diminished glycogen stores, which act as a reservoir for glucose molecules. In addition, alcohol-induced suppression of gluconeogenesis contributes to the paucity of glucose available to the alcoholic. Subsequently, blood glucose levels fall and hypoglycemia develops. This is clinically very significant. An alcoholic patient may present as being tremulous, diaphoretic, and agitated, and AHPs might assume an alcohol withdrawal syndrome is present. However, because these are also the clinical manifestations of hypoglycemia, every patient who is considered a candidate for alcohol detoxification should have an assessment of blood sugar done first, to rule out the possibility of a hypoglycemic episode mimicking the alcohol withdrawal syndrome. By the same token, any unconscious alcoholic should have an immediate blood glucose determination and then have intravenous glucose administered routinely in the event that severe hypoglycemic coma is present.

The alcoholic patient may also present in a *hyperglycemic* state. In this case the alcoholic has been eating properly and ingested an adequate quantity of carbohydrates in addition to the alcohol. When this state occurs it is possible that the alcohol-induced block of glycogen production may prevent an adequate *fall* in blood sugar levels. Glucose molecules are the building blocks for glycogen molecules. When alcohol prevents glycogen formation, the blood levels of glucose begin to rise, hence a temporary hyperglycemia may be present. With several days of abstinence, this hyperglycemia usually abates and immediate treatment for what is essentially a false diabetic condition is unnecessary. If the hyperglycemia persists, then diabetes mellitus must be considered and appropriate diagnostic and therapeutic procedures should be employed.

Water Balance

A great deal of myth and confusion has traditionally attended this subject. Our knowledge today allows us to replace this myth with some facts. Anyone who has consumed an alcoholic beverage can testify to the fact that alcohol promotes an increased production of urine. Indeed, in the presence of a rising blood alcohol concentration (BAC), antidiuretic hormone (ADH) production is inhibited, resulting in an increased renal clearance of solute–free water. However, this only pertains to the acute drinking episode in the presence of a rising BAC. In chronic alcohol ingestion, there is an alcohol-induced retention of water and an actual increase in the total body water. Hence, the chronic alcoholic often presents not as being dehydrated, but with an increase in total body water, often with edema being present. Patients presenting like this have been described as "pseudo-Cushings," and are discussed later in this chapter.

Alcohol-Induced Electrolyte Imbalance

Failure to recognize electrolyte imbalance early in the treatment of the alcoholic can have catastrophic consequences. Most health facilities are fastidious in monitoring the electrolytes surveyed on routine laboratory electrolyte panels, namely sodium, potassium, chloride, and bicarbonate. However, in the disease of alcoholism there are two other electrolytes that must be carefully followed, namely the phosphorus anion and the magnesium cation.

Hypophosphatemia. Diabetic ketoacidosis and alcoholism are the two most common causes of hypophosphatemia (36). Any alcoholic patients admitted to health care facilities should be monitored in the first week of treatment for hypophosphatemia. Often patients are admitted with a normal serum phosphorus level, only to experience hypophosphatemia on the third or fourth day (36). The consequences of hypophosphatemia vary from the patient being totally asymptomatic with minimal depression of phosphorus levels, to disastrous clinical complications of profound hypophosphatemia including breakdown of muscle tissue (*rhabdomyolysis*), CNS deficiencies, red blood cell dysfunction, and heart failure. Prompt administration of supplemental phosphorus is mandatory, either intravenously in severe cases, or orally in less critical patients.

Hypomagnesemia. Severe hypomagnesemia in the alcoholic patient may result in a number of problems such as muscle cramp- and delirium (37). Replacement therapy with magnesium, orally or parenterally, is the treatment of choice in patients with hypomagnesemia.

The precise mechanism by which phosphorus and magnesium deficiencies are created as a result of alcoholism is not yet clear. Suffice it to say that the clinical consequences of ignoring these electrolyte imbalances may be disastrous, and the prompt recognition of them is of the utmost importance when treating the alcoholic patient.

OTHER MEDICAL COMPLICATIONS

Trauma

In any emergency room in the United States, a significant number of the patients seen in a year are there as a result of trauma sustained while under the influence of alcohol. The types of trauma that occur are widely disparate (32).

Head trauma is common in an alcoholic population. In any patient with head trauma, and especially the alcoholic patient, subdural hematoma must be ruled out. The behavior or level of consciousness that results from a subdural hematoma might mistakenly be assumed to be the result of acute intoxication. The AHP must be wary of falling into this trap.

Motor vehicle accidents are recognized worldwide as one of the most serious consequences of alcoholic behavior. The intoxicated driver has markedly impaired cognitive and motor skills and as a result, 50% of all of the motor vehicle fatalities in this country are alcohol related.

Other forms of trauma such as burns, injuries, drowning, farm accidents, and home and industrial accidents are often associated with intercurrent alcoholism. It behooves AHPs to suspect alcoholism in any of the aforementioned traumas.

Dermatologic

Conclusive evidence that there is a causal relation between the development of specific dermatologic diseases and alcoholism is lacking. One dermatologic condition that has historically been linked with alcoholism is *rosacea*, a facial eruption characterized by erythema and acne-like lesions (38). A form of rosacea, known as *rhinophyma*, is recognized as the stereotypic red, bulbous nose of alcoholics. However, while rhinophyma, like rosacea, may be exacerbated by alcoholism, it is not directly caused by alcoholism and it may occur in nonalcoholic individuals.

Other cutaneous changes which *may* point to alcoholic liver disease include *palmar erythema, vascular spiders, Dupuytren's contracture,* and *white nails.* However, it should be remembered that these are cutaneous signs of not only alcoholic liver disease, but *any* significant hepatocellular dysfunction regardless of etiology.

Alcohol-Induced Muscle Disease

Alcoholics are susceptible to a particular form of muscle disease known as *alcoholic myopathy,* which may present acutely or in a more insidious, chronic manner (39). The acute form of alcoholic myopathy is characterized by muscle weakness, tenderness, edema, and even *myoglobinuria,* (the appearance of the oxygen-carrying protein of muscle, myoglobin, in the urine). Chronic alcoholic myopathy presents as a more insidious process with few symptoms appearing until actual muscle wasting and weakness has occurred. Up until this point the only abnormality that one might find would be unexpected serum elevations of muscle enzymes especially creatine phosphokinase (CPK), and aldolase.

As in alcoholic cardiomyopathy, the etiology of alcohol-induced skeletal muscle myopathy is unclear. Possible causes are a direct toxic effect of ethanol on muscle tissues or alcohol-induced hypophosphatemia.

The only effective treatment of alcoholic myopathy is abstinence from alcohol. With cessation of alcohol consumption and improved nutritional states, most patients with alcoholic myopathy will experience a remission of the pathologic process and a resolution of symptomatology.

REPRODUCTIVE AND ENDOCRINE COMPLICATIONS

Fetal Alcohol Syndrome

It has been suspected for centuries that alcohol use during pregnancy is ill-advised. Abstinence from alcohol was recommended for women as early as 2500 years ago; "Behold, thou shalt conceive, and bear a son; and now drink no wine or strong drink . . ." (Judges 13:7). But it was not until 1968 that Lemoine (40) described a pattern of growth and developmental retardation, facial, limb, and cardiac anomalies in the progeny of alcoholic women who drank during their pregnancy. A very similar syndrome was independently described by Jones and Smith in 1973 (41). Since then, a great deal of research has been directed to what is now called the fetal alcohol syndrome (FAS).

The precise pathogenesis of FAS is not understood. The most plausible current hypothesis is that ethanol disrupts protein synthesis *in utero*, thereby predisposing to the anomalies seen in the syndrome. What is clear is that FAS is not an exotic syndrome rarely seen. Current estimates are that its frequency of occurrence is between 1-2 births per 1,000 (42), and it is speculated that partial occurrence of the syndrome is even more frequent.

There are three elements of the FAS. The first is *growth deficiency*, which may occur either prenatally, and manifest as a small for gestational age newborn, or postnatally as a delay in reaching growth milestones. Most FAS children remain more than two standard deviations below the mean height and weight for children of their age group. The second abnormality found in FAS children is *central nervous system dysfunction*, the most common manifestation of which is mental retardation. The majority of FAS children have intelligence levels below average. Additional CNS dysfunction may include microcephaly, irritability or hyperactive children, and poor coordination. The final characteristic of these children is *facial dysmorphia*. A short palpebral fissure, a hypoplastic upper lip with thinner upper vermillion border, and a diminished to absent philtrum (the median groove on the external surface of the upper lip) are common facial characteristics in fetal alcohol syndrome children. The facial anomalies make FAS children a visually identifiable group.

There are other congenital anomalies occasionally seen in FAS children, particularly cardiac and ocular malformations; however, the triad of growth deficiency, CNS impairment, and facial anomalies are the mandatory features needed to make the diagnosis of FAS. Patients in whom one of these features is missing, can be termed a suspected case.

There is not doubt that the fetal alcohol syndrome is real, but the question remains, who is at risk? Certainly, zero risk is afforded only to those mothers who abstain from alcohol throughout their pregnancy. For women who do drink during their pregnancy, there is a spectrum of severity of the effects of alcohol on their children, shown in Figure 1. Clearly, both the risk and severity of the syndrome rise precipitously when daily consumption of alcohol exceeds six drinks. Equally clear is the fact that the "social drinker," consuming 2–3 drinks per day, is not free from the risk of having a child affected by the teratogen alcohol.

There are many questions still unanswered concerning the FAS. What is the specific mechanism that results in alcohol-induced changes *in utero*? Do other drugs commonly used by pregnant women, such as caffeine and nicotine, play a role in the development of fetal anomalies? Precisely how much alcohol during pregnancy is too much? The answers to these questions are not yet available, but AHPs will be called upon by patients to give an opinion on some of them. One in particular will be as to whether or not it is safe to drink at all during pregnancy. It would, at this time, seem prudent to recommend that all women planning on conceiving, or all women who are already pregnant, abstain from as many drugs as possible. These include alcohol, caffeine, nicotine, as well as all other pharmacologic agents with the exception of those prescribed and monitored by their attending physician. Until all the data are available concerning the effect of alcohol and drug use on pregnancy, it would be best to follow this approach. The 1981 Advisory from the Surgeon General echoes this opinion (43). Furthermore, any pregnant woman who is unable to stop drinking upon receiving this advice, should immediately be referred to comprehensive treatment for alcoholism, in order to avoid any further exposure of the fetus to alcohol.

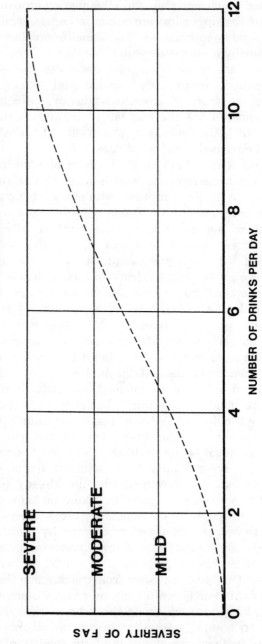

Figure 1.

One final word on alcohol and pregnancy. While it is now quite clear that consuming alcohol during pregnancy can induce fetal damage, it is becoming apparent that alcohol can also enhance the chances of spontaneous abortion, particularly in the second trimester (44). A recent study (44) cited the risk of spontaneous second-trimester abortion to be normal for women drinking less than one drink daily, doubled for those drinking from 1-2, and more than tripled in those women consuming 3 or more drinks daily. In light of the degree of fetal damage and wasting apparently induced by alcohol, there would seem to be no justification at this time for its use during pregnancy.

Alcohol and the Human Sexual Response

William Shakespeare's observation that alcohol "provokes the desire, but it takes away the performance" has been substantiated in recent scientific research indicating that alcohol heightens sexual interest but impairs actual responsiveness and activity. In males, penile tumescence (firmness of erection) decreases as blood alcohol level increases (45). Among women, impaired sexual arousal was demonstrated in subjects receiving alcohol, versus those receiving none (46). It is apparent, then, that Shakespeare's dictum represents sage advice.

Hypothalamic-Pituitary-Gonadal Function

When the disease of alcoholism is present, sexual dysfunction may progress well beyond the point of diminished responsiveness, to actual hormonal and organic damage and disease. In male alcoholics, serum testosterone levels can be depressed by a combination of ethanol's toxic effects on the hypothalamic-pituitary hormonal control center and directly upon testicular testosterone production (47). In addition, endogenous estrogen levels in alcoholic males may rise because of the ethanol-induced impairment in metabolizing those endogenous estrogens secreted by the adrenal cortex (48). The clinical correlates of this endocrine dysfunction in alcoholic males are testicular atrophy, impotence, and loss of libido (sexual interest and energy). Sexual dysfunction among alcoholic males is probably more common than has been suspected: Masters and Johnson (49) reported that alcoholism was the second leading cause of impotence in male patients.

In women, the toxic effects of ethanol on ovarian function are not as clearly documented. While incomplete ovarian failure and premenopausal amenorrhea have been associated with alcoholism, the precise route by which alcohol produces those toxic effects is unclear (47). Alcoholic women do not seem to have diminished serum estrogen levels which would be analagous to the depressed testosterone levels found in alcoholic males (47). The most compelling evidence of ethanol-induced impairment in female reproductive functioning is the FAS, discussed above.

Adrenal Dysfunction

In 1960 Kissin and his colleagues (50) reported elevated plasma cortisol levels associated with alcohol ingestion. Later, Smals and his colleagues (51) reported increased cortisol levels in three alcoholic patients, associated with a "pseudo-Cushings syndrome." The clinical findings in these patients included facial edema, elevated blood pressure, central obesity, and muscle wasting. The same symptoms could be found in a patient with Cushings Disease, caused by an overproduction of corticosteroids by the adrenal glands. What differentiated the pseudo-Cushings patients from the Cushings patients was that, in the former, their symptoms disappeared when drinking stopped. These observations help explain the paradox alluded to earlier in this chapter (see Alcohol and Water Balance) regarding alcohol's ability to promote diuresis in social drinkers while producing fluid retention and edema in chronic alcohol abusers.

ALCOHOL AND CANCER

In the past four decades there has been increasing concern over the effects of external environmental factors on the development of cancer. Many epidemiological studies have been undertaken to sort out the impact of these various factors. Cigarette smoke and lung cancer was one of the first associations to be made. Soon after, investigators began looking at the incidence of cancer in a population of heavy alcohol users. They discovered a statistically significant relationship in several areas.

Upper alimentary tract cancers are the neoplasms most clearly associated with excess alcohol use (7). There is an increase in the risk of developing cancer of the oral cavity, larynx, and esophagus with increased alcohol consumption. There is an even more dramatic risk in developing these neoplasms in patients using both alcohol and tobacco. For instance, one study (52) indicated that the risk of developing esophageal carcinoma is 45 times greater in an individual consuming greater than 20 grams of tobacco and 80 grams of alcohol daily, than in an individual consuming little or none of these substances.

Alcoholism has been implicated with increased risk of developing several other cancers. Primary hepatic carcinoma is seen more often in an alcoholic population with cirrhosis of the liver (8). Similarly, there have been reports of a disproportionate number of alcoholics among patients with rectal and pancreatic cancer (53). The relationship between these neoplasms and alcoholism is not yet as clearly defined as it is for upper alimentary tract tumors.

The mechanism by which alcohol, with or without tobacco, predisposes to cancer is uncertain. Several mechanisms have been proposed (7, 8, 52). First, the direct contact by alcohol and/or tobacco with cells in the upper alimentary tract may play some part in carcinogenesis in these areas. Secondly, it has been postulated that low levels of carcinogens are present in alcoholic beverages and that these are responsible for the development of neoplasms. Thirdly, it has been theorized that alcohol acts as a solvent to facilitate the transport of other carcinogens, such as those found in tobacco, into cells where the carcinogens stimulate neoplastic cell growth. These are only several of the postulated mechanisms by which ethanol may induce cancer. While the mechanisms are speculative, the fact that alcoholics do have an increased risk of developing cancer is a certainty. Therefore, it behooves AHPs to be vigilant for the detection of neoplasms in any alcoholic patient. In any form of cancer, the earlier the neoplasia is detected, the better the chance for cure.

SUMMARY

Alcoholism is a disease that accounts for the expenditure of billions of health care dollars each year, as well as thousands of hours of time on the part of the health care providers. Unfortunately, the majority of these dollars and hours are spent treating the complications of the disease, while alcoholism itself remains one of the most underdiagnosed health problems in America. The alcoholic patient is often labeled with the appropriate secondary diagnosis such as gastritis, depression, or skull fracture. while the primary diagnosis which was responsible for the development of the secondary condition is missed. This oversight results in alco-holic patients having to suffer further sequelae of their disease without the benefit of receiving appropriate treatment and, hope-fully, putting an end to the succession of complications of the alcoholism. All too often the diagnosis of alcoholism is not made by the health care provider until end-stage sequelae are present, such as the Wernicke-Korsakoff Syndrome or cirrhosis of the liver. By that time, the patient may well have suffered irreparable dam-age as a consequence of alcoholism, long ago unrecognized by the health care system.

REFERENCES

1. Schmidt, W. and Popham, R.E.: Heavy alcohol consumption on physical health problems: a review of the epidemiological evidence. *Drug and Alcohol Dependence, 1:*27-50, 1976.

2. Barchha, R.; Stewart, M.A. and Guze, S.B.: The prevalence of alco-holism among general hospital ward patients. *American Journal of Psychiatry, 125:*681-684, 1968.

3. Anstie, R.E.: On the dietetic and medicinal uses of wine. *Practi-tioner, 4:*219, 1870.

4. Yano, K.; Rhoads, G.C. and Kagan, A.: Coffee, alcohol and risk of coronary heart disease among Japanese men living in Hawaii. *New England Journal of Medicine, 297:*405, 1977.

5. Blackwelder, W.C.; Yano, K.; Rhoads, G.C., *et al.*: Alcohol and mor-tality: the Honolulu heart study. *American Journal of Medicine, 68:*164-170, 1980.

6. Kozararevic, D.J.; McGee, D.; Vojvodic, N., *et al.*: Frequency of alcohol consumption and morbidity and mortality: the Yugoslavia cardio-vascular disease study. *Lancet, 1:*613-616, 1980.

7. Mashberg, A.; Garfinkel, L., and Harris, S.: Alcohol as a primary risk factor in oral squamous carcinoma. *A Cancer Journal for Clinicians, 3:*146-155, 1981.

8. Lieber, C.S.; Seitz, H.K.; Gario, A.J., *et al.*: Alcohol related diseases and carcinogenesis. *Cancer Research 39:*2863-2886, 1979.

9. St. John, D.J.; Masterton, J.P.; Yeomans, N.D., *et al.*: The Mallory Weiss Syndrome. *British Medical Journal, 1:*140-143, 1974.

10. Orloff, M.J.; Charters, A.E.; Chanoler, J.G., *et al.*: Portocaval shunt as emerging procedure in unselected patients with alcoholic varices. *Surgical Gynecological Obstetrics, 141:*59-68, 1975.

11. Beaumont, W.: *Experiments and Observations on the Gastric Juice and the Physiology of Digestion.* New York: Dover Publications, Inc., 1959.

12. Roe, D.A.: Nutritional concerns in the alcoholic. *Journal of the American Dietary Association, 78:*17-21, 1981.

13. Sheehy, T.W.: Acute alcoholic pancreatitis. *Continuing Education for the Family Physician, 3:*87-109, 1980.

14. Mendenhall, C.L.: What to do for alcoholic liver disease. *Consultant, 12:*23-77, 1978.

15. Lieber, C.S.: Pathogenesis of alcoholic liver injury. In: Geokas, M.C., Moderator. Ethanol, the liver and the GI tract. *Annals of Internal Medicine, 95:*198-211, 1981.

16. McGuire, R.: Acute dilation of the heart produced by alcoholism. *British Medical Journal, 1:*1215, 1887.

17. Rahimtoola, S.H.: Digitalis and Wm. Withering, the clinical investigator. *Circulation, 52:*969-971, 1975.

18. Meister, R.P.: The "Munich beer heart" — revisited. *Beitraegezur Pathologie, 157:*1-13, 1976.

19. Ganz, V.: The acute effect of ethanol on the circulation and on the oxygen mebatolism of the heart. *American Heart Journal, 66:*494-497, 1963.

20. Ettinger, P.O.; Wu, C.F.; De LaCruz, Jr., C.; Weisse, A.B.; Ahmed, S.S.: Regan, T.J.: Arrhythmias and the "Holiday Heart": alcohol-associated cardiac rhythm disorders. *American Heart Journal, 95:*555-562, 1978.

21. Greenspoon, A.J. and Schaal, S.F.: The "Holiday Heart": Electrophysiologic studies of alcohol effects in alcoholics. *Annals of Internal Medicine, 98:*135-139, 1983.

22. Klatsky, A.L.; Friedman, G.D.; Sieglaub, A.B., *et al.*: Alcohol consumption and blood pressure — Kaiser Permanente Multiphasic Health Examination Data. *New England Journal of Medicine, 296:*1194-1200, 1977.

23. Regan, T.J.: Ethyl alcohol and the heart, *Circulation 44:*957, 1971.

24. Rush, B.: An inquiry into the effects of ardent spirits upon the human body and mind. *Quarterly Journal of Studies on Alcohol, 4:*321-341, 1943.

25. Lyons, H.A. and Saltzman, A.: Diseases of the respiratory tract in alcoholics. In: *The Biology of Alcoholism*, Vol. 3, Kissin, B., Begleiter, H. (Eds.). New York: Plenum Press, 1974, pp. 403-431.

26. Brayton, R.G.; Stokes, P.E.; Schwatz, N.Y., *et al.*: The effect of alcohol and various disease states on leukocyte mobility phagocytolysis, and intracellular killing. *New England Journal of Medicine, 282:*123, 1970.

27. Sen, P. and Lauria, D.B.: When a drinker is too good a "host." *Journal of Respiratory Diseases, 6:*44-48, 1980.

28. Schweppe, H.I.; Knowles, J.H., and Kane, L.: Lung abscess: an analysis of the Mass. Gen. cases 1943-1956. *New England Journal of Medicine, 265:*1039-1043, 1961.

29. Glassroth, J.; Robins, A.G., and Snider, D.E.: Tuberculosis in the 1980s. *New England Journal of Medicine, 302:*1441-1450, 1980.

30. Jaklecki, C.: Neurologic complications of alcoholism. *Continuing Education for the Family Physician, 1:*23-25, 1982.

31. Centerwall, B.S. and Criquim H.: Prevention of the Wernicke-Korsakoff Syndrome. *New England Journal of Medicine, 299:*285-289, 1978.

32. Moessner, H.: Accidents as a symptom of alcohol abuse. *Journal of Family Practice, 8:*1143-1146, 1979.

33. Lee, K.; Hardt, F.; Moller, L., *et al.:* Alcohol-induced brain damage and liver damage in young males. *Lancet II:*759-761, 1979.

34. Steinberg, S.E. and Hillman, R.S.: Adverse hematologic effects of alcohol. *Postgraduate Medicine 5:*139-147, 1980.

35. Khurana, M.S., *et al.:* Storage pool disease of platelets. *Journal of the American Medical Association, 244:*169, 1980.

36. Knochel, J.P.: The pathophysiology and clinical characteristics of severe hypophosphatemia. *Archives of Internal Medicine, 137:*203-220, 1977.

37. Frankushen, D.; Raskin, D.; Dimich, A., *et al.:* The significance of hypomagnesemia in alcoholic patients. *American Journal of Medicine, 37:* 802-812, 1964.

38. Rosset, M. and Oki, G.: Skin diseases in alcoholics. *Quarterly Journal of Studies on Alcohol, 32:*1017-1024, 1971.

39. Oh, S.J.: Alcoholic myopathy: a critical review. *Alabama Journal of Medical Sciences, 9:*79-95, 1972.

40. Lemoine, P.; Harousseau, H.; Borteyru, J.P., *et al.:* Les enfants des parents alcoolques: anomalies observees. *Question: Semeio-Logie Medicale, 25:*476-482, 1968.

41. Jones, K.L.; Smith, D.W.; Ulleland, C.N., *et al.:* Pattern of malformation in offspring of chronic alcoholic mothers. *Lancet, 1:*1267-1271, 1973.

42. Clarren, S.K. and Smith, D.W.: The fetal alcohol syndrome. *New England Journal of Medicine, 298:*1063-1067, 1978.

43. Infant botulism. *FDA Drug Bulletin, 11:*11-12, 1981.

44. Harlap, S.; Shiono, P.H.: Alcohol, smoking and the incidence of spontaneous abortions in the first and second trimester. *Lancet, II:*173, 1980.

45. Wilson, G.T. and Lawson, D.M.: Expectancies, alcohol, and sexual arousal in male social drinkers. *Journal of Abnormal Psychology, 85:*587-590, 1976.

46. *Ibid., 87:*358-367, 1978.

47. Van Thiel, D.H. and Gavalor, J.S.: The adverse effects of ethanol upon hypothalamic-pituitary-gonadal function in males and females compared and contrasted. *Alcoholism: Clinical and Experimental Research, 6:* 179-185, 1982.

48. Gordon, G.G. and Southren, A.L.: Metabolic effects of alcohol on the endocrine system. In: *Metabolic Aspects of Alcoholism,* Lieber C.S. (Ed.). Baltimore: University Park Press, pp. 249-302, 1977.

49. Masters, W.H. and Johnson, V.E.: *Human Sexual Inadequacy.* Boston: Little, Brown and Co., 1970.

50. Kissin, B.; Schenker, V., and Schenker, A.L.: The acute effect of ethanol ingestion on plasma and urinary 17 hydroxycorticoids in alcoholic subjects. *American Journal of Medical Science, 239:*690-704, 1960.

51. Smals, A.G.; Kloppenborg, P.W.; Njo, K.T., *et al.:* Alcohol-induced Cushingoid Syndrome. *British Medical Journal, 2:*1298, 1976.

52. Tuyns, A.J.; Pequignot, G., and Jensen, O.M.: le cancer de l'oesophage en ille et Vilaine en fonction dex niveaux de consommation d'alcool et de tabac. Des risques qui se multiplient. *Bulletin du Cancer, 64:*45-60, 1977.

53. Tuyns, A.J.: Alcohol and cancer. *Alcohol Health and Research World, 2:*20-32, 1978.

Chapter 11

Recognizing, Confronting, and Treating the Alcohol- and Drug-Abusing Patient: the Multidisciplinary Approach

David Benzer, D.O.

OVERVIEW

In this chapter the author provides detailed information on several absolutely critical areas of knowledge and practice in dealing with substance-abuse and substance-dependent patients. In the first portion of the chapter he has carefully documented the procedures of identification and diagnosis of a wide variety of substance-use disorders, noting the similarities and differences in physical findings, laboratory tests, and psychosocial variables among patients.

Following this information, AHPs are provided a virtual step-by-step guide in the "how to" of successful and productive confrontation or intervention. Significant issues are addressed and problems are identified, enabling the AHP to anticipate difficulties and deal with them appropriately.

Varieties and modalities of treatment are next discussed, with emphasis on the preferred model of the multidisciplinary-team approach. The roles of the physician's assistant, nurse, psychologist, addictions counselor, and other AHPs are addressed.

In the closing sections of the chapter, advice and information is provided regarding matters of prognosis and recovery, a summary is offered, and references are listed for further reading.

INTRODUCTION

Not unlike the process used in the treatment of any other chronic disease, the recognition and treatment of the patient with an alcohol or other drug-abuse problem should proceed in an orderly fashion. In fact, a parallel can be drawn between the recognition and the treatment of a patient with diabetes mellitus and one who has a chronic disease such as a drug- or alcohol-abuse problem. The first step in both cases involves recognition of the disease process, and maintenance of a high index of suspicion for such diseases characterizes all good health professionals. A patient's complaints of polyuria, polydipsia, urinary frequency, and/or a propensity to frequent infection, should heighten the index of suspicion of the allied health professional (AHP) toward the possible diagnosis of diabetes mellitus. Similarly, the presence of unanticipated liver dysfunction, a recent arrest for operating a motor vehicle while intoxicated (OWI), and/or conflict among family members of a patient, should make the AHP suspicious of the possible diagnosis of a substance abuse or chemical dependency problem.

Once a diagnosis is suspected, one must proceed to support the diagnosis. In the case of diabetes, the diagnosis is made on the basis of one or more elevated blood glucose readings. In chemical dependency, the diagnosis is arrived at through the use of somewhat more complicated diagnostic criteria, such as the *Diagnostic and Statistical Manual of Mental Disorders, Third Edition (DSM-III)*, of the American Psychiatric Association (1), or the Diagnostic Criteria of the National Council on Alcoholism (2) shown in Appendices 1 and 3 respectively. When properly used, either of these sets of criteria enable the AHP to make prompt and accurate diagnoses of alcohol- and other drug-dependency syndromes.

The next step in the continuum of chronic disease management consists of informing the patient of the existence of the disease. In the case of diabetes, this generally is not difficult and patients, more often than not, accept the diagnosis without difficulty. In the case of substance abuse, however, the task of informing the patient of the diagnosis is a bit more complicated. In fact, the process has a special name that reflects this greater difficulty: *intervention* or *confrontation*. In an intervention session, the patient is presented with the evidence that leads to the diagnosis of an alcohol- or other drug-dependency syndrome. One can expect *resistance* on the part of the patient when it comes to accepting this diagnosis, but if the resistance is anticipated and planned for, it need not be a barrier to getting the patient to accept treatment for his or her disease. Once the patient has been made aware of the presence of a chronic disease, the AHP's next task is to help to decide on appropriate therapy. In the case of diabetes, dietary modification or weight reduction may be the initial therapies. Following that, a physician may prescribe oral hypoglycemic agents, or insulin therapy. The patient may initially be treated on an inpatient or outpatient basis.

For the alcohol- and drug-abusing patient, the same decision must be made. Should the initial therapy be on an inpatient or outpatient basis? What therapeutic modalities are available for use in this patient population?

This chapter provides the AHP with some information on recognition and intervention techniques that may be useful in dealing with substance-abusing patients. Alternative treatment approaches, both outpatient and inpatient, are discussed and a multidisciplinary treatment approach — which is a team effort on the part of the multiple health care professionals — is highlighted. We continue our model comparing the treatment of diabetes to that of substance abuse for a look at the recovery process, and some of the factors enhancing a favorable prognosis are examined.

RECOGNITION OF ALCOHOL- AND OTHER DRUG-DEPENDENCY SYNDROMES

Unfortunately, there is no single symptom that will lead to the diagnosis of substance abuse of dependency, nor is there any one laboratory test that will confirm such a suspicion. This lack makes diagnosing alcohol- and other drug-dependency syndromes more challenging than identifying some other chronic diseases. An unfortunate corollary of this state of affairs, is that substance-abuse problems are often underdiagnosed among patients, even those on general hospital wards (3). The AHP must be sensitive for diagnostic clues from multiple life areas of the patient, including employment problems, legal difficulties, and family crises. We will examine all of these areas, but first we will concentrate on physical and laboratory findings that may suggest a substance abuse diagnosis.

Physical and Laboratory Findings

A comprehensive listing of physical and laboratory findings in patients with alcoholism can be found in the NCA Criteria (2) in Appendix 3. While NCA Criteria provide numerous signs and symptoms of alcoholism, it is to the patient's advantage that we strive for the earliest diagnosis possible. Diagnosing alcoholism when end-stage cirrhosis of the liver is present is not particularly difficult, but it would have been much better for the patient to have had the diagnosis made ten to twenty years earlier. At that time, more subtle findings may have been present, such as a slight elevation of the liver enzyme gamma glutamyl transpeptidase (GGTP), or an elevated mean corpuscular volume (MCV). These signs are often much earlier laboratory clues to the diagnosis of alcoholism (4).

Patients abusing drugs other than alcohol experience social, behavioral, and psychological problems similar to those outlined for alcoholics in the NCA Criteria. The physical and laboratory findings in these patients are outlined in the chapters on sedative/hypnotics, opioid, stimulant, and hallucinogenic drugs elsewhere in this volume. They tend to be distinct from those seen in an alcoholic population.

Social Circumstances

Life problems associated with drug and alcohol abuse are crucial in making the diagnosis. Social complications of chemical use are an integral component of the NCA and *DSM-III* diagnostic criteria, some of which are described below.

Marital conflict. Marriage problems, including separation and divorce, are common in the family with one chemically-dependent spouse.

Parent-child conflict. Strained relationships between children and parents occur in families when one or more family member, parent or child, are chemically dependent.

Spouse battering and child abuse. These forms of family violence tend to be more frequent in families with a chemically dependent member (5).

Employment problems. Frequent absenteeism, unreliability, loss of job, and frequent job changes, may mark the employment record of the chemically dependent individual.

Legal complications. Arrests for possession of controlled substances, drunk and disorderly conduct, burglary, truancy, and OWI, are some of the legal problems which may suggest a chemical dependency problem.

Evidence of diagnostic clues, from any *single* area presented here, either medical or social, is not sufficient to make the diagnosis of substance use disorder. This diagnosis requires that criteria from several categories be met. However, the AHP will find that with some study and practice, making the diagnosis of an alcohol- or other drug-dependency syndrome can become as routine as diagnosing diabetes or hypertension.

A RATIONAL APPROACH TO CONFRONTING THE DRUG- AND ALCOHOL-ABUSING PATIENT

As noted in the Introduction to this chapter, confronting the chemically dependent patient with evidence for your diagnosis can be difficult if one does not prepare properly for an anticipated response. One must always remember that denial is often an integral problem in chemical dependency disorders. Drug- or alcohol-dependent patients spend a great deal of effort attempting to convince others, and ultimately themselves, that they are merely social users of alcohol or other drugs. Any negative consequences that have accrued due to alcohol or drug use are often seen by the patient as simply the result of bad luck or unfortunate circumstances. Another common twist of this denial is to attempt to rationalize their chemical use with comments such as, "If you had my job, you would drink too," or, "If you were married to my spouse, you would use drugs too."

The chemically dependent patient may use these techniques or other defenses when confronted with evidence for a drug or alcohol problem, and *this must be anticipated by the AHP.* The denial of chemical dependency is often so strong in the afflicted patient, that it frequently prevents them from seeking help voluntarily. Most often, patients are referred to treatment as a result of being confronted by family, employer, or health-care provider. Therefore, it is important that the AHP be aware of proper confrontation techniques. Families and employers will often seek out the AHP for help in arranging and carrying out confrontation sessions. Some suggestions that may be helpful to remember when planning a confrontation follow.

Strategies

Multiple participants. It is important to involve as many significant people in the patient's life as possible, including spouse, children, other family members, employer if possible, clergyman, and others. It is not particularly productive to confront an addicted patient alone. It is too easy to dismiss the evidence from a single person with phrases such as, "What do you know about it?" or "Don't you ever drink a little yourself?" It is much more effective to confront with a group; there is, indeed, strength in numbers.

Present specific evidence related to chemical abuse. Each confronter should present their own evidence for a chemical dependency problem. Children, for example, can cite instances of broken promises resulting from chemical abuse. An employer can present work records, and the health-care provider can present medical/laboratory data substantiating the chemical dependency diagnosis. Each confronter should assiduously relate each example to drug or alcohol abuse.

Timing of the confrontation. Deciding upon an appropriate time to conduct an intervention session is crucial to the success of the venture. It is important that some of the evidence presented is current. Therefore, a good time to confront the chemically dependent person is soon after a crisis precipitated by chemical use. At such times the identified patient is more willing to listen to the evidence presented, and treatment may be accepted more readily. A second factor to remember is that a confrontation should *never* be attempted when a patient is intoxicated or in a significant withdrawal. At these times, cognitive functioning is markedly impaired and the decision-making processes are distorted. The intervention session should be planned at a time when cognitive functioning is closer to normal.

Location of the intervention. An intervention should occur in a quiet, non-threatening, private location. Many locales will meet these criteria. Some that do not include hallways, busy public places, or hospital corridors.

Anticipate defenses. As noted above, denial can be expected. Confronters must be prepared for counter-accusation, rationalization, minimization, and all other defense mechanisms that may be employed by the chemically dependent individual. One must also be prepared for the possibility of anger and criticism from the patient being confronted.

Demonstrate genuine concern. Each confronter should make it clear to the chemically dependent person that their motivation for participation in the confrontation is concern for the well-being of the addicted individual. This attitude has been appropriately referred to as "tough love." This attitude can also be implicitly communicated to the addicted individual by demonstrating respect and consideration for them through the session.

Understand chemical dependency. It is critical that each member of the confrontation team have some understanding of alcohol- and other drug-dependency syndromes. The more knowledgeable the confronters are, the more determined and effective they will be in the session.

Present treatment alternatives. This ability is another special area for the AHP's expertise. The chemically dependent person needs to be presented with realistic treatment alternatives that meet their current needs. This is discussed later in this chapter in the section on treatment alternatives.

Prepare responses to outcome. If the confrontation session results in the patient accepting treatment alternatives offered, the only necessary response on the part of the confronters would be to warmly congratulate the chemically dependent person on making such a good decision.

If the chemically dependent patient does not accept treatment recommendations, the confrontation team, and each member individually, must be prepared with a response. The team must decide if they will accept a compromise. Most chemically dependend patients feel they can cure themselves, hence, a frequent compromise offered by the patient is, "If I have one more drink, then I'll get some help." The team must decide in advance if such compromise will be acceptable. Because the patient may also try to delay the onset of treatment, the team must decide in advance how much, if any, procrastination they will accept. These are just two examples of possible compromises. In general, compromising is a dangerous action during confrontation, since it may result in a loss of gains made during the session.

Finally, each individual member of the team must voice a commitment not to "enable" the chemically dependent patient from that point forward. This commitment signals an end to covering up for the actions of the person who is dependent on alcohol or another drug. The addicted person must, from that point forward, be made to feel completely responsible for the consequences of his or her dependency.

TREATING THE ALCOHOL- AND OTHER DRUG-ABUSING PATIENT

Decision on Where to Treat: Inpatient or Outpatient

Recently, the Medical Society of Wisconsin's Committee on Alcohol and Other Drug Abuse published criteria for the treatment of the chemically dependent patient (6). The criteria (Appendix 5) suggests appropriate treatment modalities for patients with varying conditions and circumstances. Basically, any patient experiencing withdrawal symptoms, medical complications, or lacking adequate environmental or social support systems is a candidate for inpatient treatment. The patient without withdrawal signs and/or symptoms of medical complications, and who is able to stay drug-free long enough to become involved in the treatment process, may be appropriate for outpatient treatment. It should be remembered that these are basic guidelines, and the decision as to where to treat a patient must be carefully determined on an individual basis.

Choosing a Treatment

Inpatient treatment. If a person is admitted as an inpatient to a general hospital, the first course of action would be to treat any withdrawal problems and all physical complications resulting from the addiction. Then, one must determine whether a patient requires continued inpatient treatment in a drug and alcohol treatment unit, or whether outpatient treatment would be adequate.

The treatment of the withdrawal and physical complications, and the treatment of the addiction, can be accomplished at the same location if a patient is treated in a specialty hospital, such as a multidisciplinary substance-abuse treatment facility.

Outpatient treatment. An individual might be referred to an outpatient services facility following inpatient treatment in a hospital, or may be referred directly to an outpatient facility for primary treatment. As an outpatient, one may receive individual or group counseling, Antabuse therapy, marriage counseling, or family therapy. The treatment modalities utilized can be tailored to the patient's needs.

THE MULTIDISCIPLINARY TREATMENT APPROACH

There are several treatment models available in this country for the treatment of chemical dependency. These include the psychiatric model, the social model, and the multidisciplinary model. The model favored by the editors of this handbook is the multidisciplinary model, which employs a wide array of health-care professionals working in concert and functioning as a team to treat the patient with an alcohol- and other drug-dependency syndrome, on both an inpatient and outpatient basis. The roles of the team members are described below.

Physicians, Physican Assistants, and Nurses

These health-care providers are essential in the triage or screening process alluded to above. They help decide which patients require more extensive monitoring of physical and psychiatric status: Some patients may need to begin their treatment with a hospital stay, while others may be directly referred to an outpatient facility. These health professionals also provide detoxification services and treat co-existing medical complications of addiction. In addition, they should be instrumental in helping to formulate a treatment plan to meet the specific needs of the patient.

Psychologists

Psychologists should be able to provide several services within the multidisciplinary treatment system. Initially they may provide psychological evaluation and testing services to help uncover the presence of co-existing psychopathology, or neuropsychological damage that are sequellae of substance abuse. Following assessment, the psychologist's skills are invaluable in providing ongoing therapy for the addicted individual and his/her family.

Alcohol and Other Drug Counselors

These health care professionals, who often are themselves successfully recovering from chemical dependency, are essential members of the multidisciplinary team. They can be relied on to spend hours with the patient in both group and individual therapy, helping the patient to understand their defenses and ultimately helping them gain insight into, and acceptance of, their chemical dependency.

Dieticians

These AHPs help the chemically dependent patient begin to achieve well-being through nutrition. The substance-abusing patient often presents with evidence of inadequate nutrition. They need not only replenishment, but also re-education, so that they can continue to use good nutrition as part of their overall recovery program.

Clergy

An awakening spirituality is part of the AA/NA tradition (see Chapter 14). Among the leaders in the reawakening are the clergy, whose role, among other things, is to hear the important "Fifth Step" of the AA Twelve Step program. The clergy can be an important source of support for addicted individuals and their families, especially early on in recovery (see Chapters 13 and 14).

Occupational and Activity Therapist

The alcohol- or other drug-dependent patient often lacks interests and hobbies, usually because the time involved in procuring and ingesting mood-altering chemicals becomes central to his or her life, to the exclusion of other activities. The ability to use leisure time, so necessary for the recovering individual, is poorly developed or has been lost. The occupational and activity therapist can help the patient rediscover the value of meaningful use of leisure time. Interest in lost hobbies can be rekindled. Through exercise and sports, physical health can complement improving mental health.

All of these health care providers bring their particular expertise to the treatment effort. The result is a comprehensive treatment approach which maximizes the chances for recovery of the patient with chemical dependency.

Self-Help Groups

In this discussion of treatment for the substance-abusing patients, we have addressed elements of inpatient and outpatient treatment, as well as a preferred model for facilitating treatment — the multidisciplinary model — in either locale. However, one final statement needs to be made concerning treatment: most individuals in whom the diagnosis of alcohol- or other drug-abuse has been made, are appropriate for referral to either Alcoholics Anonymous or Narcotics Anonymous. No treatment modality has been found to be more effective in maintaining long-term recovery for the substance abuser than these self-help groups. The

AHP should make it a point to become familiar with these groups, and learn how to make referrals to them (see Chapter 14).

PROGNOSIS AND RECOVERY

Prognosis

One of the first things one learns in treating chemically dependent patients is that it is very hazardous to assign prognosis. Any professional in this field can remember "hopeless" cases who turned their life completely around to become pillars of the recovering community. By the same token, we recall patients who performed well in treatment, only to see them rapidly progress to a fatal outcome. One lesson is that prognosticating is quite dangerous in patients with alcohol- and other drug-dependency syndromes. An even more important lesson is that there truly is no such thing as a "hopeless" case. The AHP must exert 100% effort with each case; the patient deserves no less.

Recovery

Going back to our original comparison between the chronic diseases of diabetes mellitus and chemical dependency, we once again find a parallel, this time with respect to the recovery process.

The diabetic has a recovery program that includes diet and medication. Deviation from this program may well result in relapse to uncontrolled hyperglycemia with its attendant complications. The alcohol- or drug-dependent patient also has a recovery protocol. Here too, deviation from the program can result in a relapse to drug or alcohol use with its attendant complications in varied life areas.

The AHP's response to a relapse by a patient with either of the diseases should not be to blame or condemn; instead, the AHP should help the patient correct errors in the way in which the recovery program was worked, and, in a nonjudgmental fashion, set about reestablishing a workable, successful recovery program.

If these principles are followed, the AHP will achieve success in treating patients with virtually any chronic, relapsing disease.

SUMMARY

As with any human disease or health problem, appropriate treatment can not be initiated without accurate diagnosis. In properly identifying the varieties of substance-use disorders, AHPs must have a working knowledge of physical and laboratory findings, as well as the diagnostic significance of marital problems, disturbed parent-child relations, job-related difficulties, legal problems, and other social and behavioral consequences.

Once the substance-use disorder has been correctly identified and the diagnosis confirmed, very often the abuser refuses to accept the diagnosis or acknowledge his or her chemical dependency. In such cases, a direct confrontation may be required, in which the AHP, the patient's family, employer, and other significant persons in the patient's life must join forces to persuade the patient of the need for treatment. If the confrontation is not successful, all concerned parties must allow the patient to assume full responsibility for his or her own decision.

If the confrontation is successful, then appropriate treatment should be initiated at once. Regardless of whether inpatient or outpatient treatment is selected, most experts generally agree that an integrated multidisciplinary treatment approach has the greatest probability of successful outcome. Physicians and physician's assistants, psychologists, alcohol and drug counselors, dieticians, occupational and activity therapists, members of the clergy, and other AHPs all work together to bring their particular skills, training, and experience to bear on the illness which affects the patient and his or her family.

Because prognosis and recovery are so often highly individualistic matters, no general rules have been formulated, but one: There are no hopeless cases.

REFERENCES

1. American Psychiatric Association: *Diagnostic and Statistical Manual of Mental Disorders, Third Edition.* Washington, DC: APA, 1980.

2. NCA Criteria Committee: Criteria for the diagnosis of alcoholism. *American Journal of Psychiatry, 129:*127-135, 1972.

3. Barchla, R.; Stewart, M.D., and Guze, S.B.: The prevalence of alcoholism among general hospital ward patients. *American Journal of Psychiatry, 125:*133-136, 1968.

4. Bates, H.M.: GGTP and alcoholism: a sober look. *Laboratory Management, 3:*17-19, 1981.

5. Goodstein, R.K.; Page, M.D.: Battered wife syndrome: overview of dynamics and treatment. *American Journal of Psychiatry, 138:*1036-1044, 1981.

6. Wisconsin State Medical Society Committee on Alcohol and Other Drug Abuse: Guideline admission criteria for chemical dependency treatment services. *Wisconsin Medical Journal, 80:*5, 1981.

Chapter 12

The Role of Nursing
in the Treatment
of Substance Use Disorders

Mark Daley, R.N., M.S.N.

OVERVIEW

Because the role of nurses in prevention, identification, intervention, and treatment of substance-use disorders is a major and ubiquitous one, this chapter examines their functions in both medical and nonmedical settings. In the former, emphasis is placed on the activities of nurses in acute-care facilities. Hence, the author focuses first on dealing with acutely intoxicated patients, including the identification, assessment, and treatment of alcohol- and other drug-induced states. The subsequent focus is on the identification, assessment, and treatment of withdrawal states, with emphasis on the application of the recently developed, objective, Selective Severity Assessment instrument.

In quasi- and nonmedical settings nurses play a continuing and significant role in the continuum of rehabilitative care, and the author consequently focuses on their participation with the individual patient and his or her family. Recognizing the need for an analytic, non-judgmental, supportive attitude on the part of the nurse, the author provides relevant and pertinent suggestions regarding the confrontive yet therapeutic stance needed for maximum effectiveness. As recovery proceeds, and both expected and unexpected problems arise, the nurse continues his or her facilitative and supportive functions within the family/environmental systems.

Invoking also a community health-systems model, there is next an examination of the nurse's role in determining the epidemiologic patterns of substance-use disorders, and his or her function as a social-change agent. This focus greatly expands the more traditional view of nursing, and significantly broadens the reader's understanding of how AHPs may beneficially affect not only individuals and their families, but wider segments of society as well.

A summary and references conclude the chapter.

INTRODUCTION

Nurses encounter the chemically dependent individual in their personal and professional lives in varied settings and situations. For example, the nurse in the emergency room may see the hostile, belligerent inebriate who disrupts the emergency room, or the overdose victim who arrives in a comatose state. The community health nurse may come across liquor bottles scattered throughout a home and witness the disintegration of family roles and relationships. Others may have worked a shift to cover for a peer who reported to work intoxicated or imbibed while working.

To many nurses, chemical abuse, misuse, and dependency may mean nothing but frustration. The nurse may often feel inadequate in dealing with this patient population and may shift responsibility to others, including the affected individual. In many communities there is a paucity of resources for the chemically dependent individual and his or her family, or if they are available, the nurse may be unaware of their existence or lack necessary skills needed to develop linkages between the patient and the community resources.

The purpose of this chapter is to delineate the role of the nurse and to examine the processes and methods that are most frequently utilized by nurses to identify and deliver care to individuals, families, and communities that are affected by chemical dependency problems. The models most frequently used by nurses to evaluate the chemically dependent population are the individualized and community health approaches. The individualized approach relies heavily on the nursing process and concentrates on the individual and his or her family. The community health approach evaluates the health status of a community, specifies the vulnerability for developing chemical dependency problems, and mobilizes or develops linkages to respond to the identified needs of this population.

As a member of the health care team, nursing makes a unique contribution to the total continuum of care for the chemically dependent population. The recent Social Policy Statement adopted by the American Nurses Association (1) delineates the nature and scope of nursing practice. The policy statement assigns nursing the responsibility for the diagnosis and treatment of human responses to actual or potential health problems. Often it is the nurse who is called upon to deal with the multifaceted and complex responses associated with chemical dependency. Some of the responses may be direct consequences of chemical dependency while others may have contributed to its development. The progression and severity of a chemical dependency problem will display wide variation. The nurse is in a position to deal with the feelings, concerns and needs of the chemically dependent individuals and their families. The social, psychological, spiritual, and physiological problems associated with chemical dependency may have progressed insidiously and escaped detection by the affected individual and his or her family. It is the nurse who has frequent close contact with these parties during critical periods of time, and is in the most opportune position to make recommendations effecting responses that can precipitate, delay, or prevent recovery. Therefore, it is important that the nurse acquire as much expertise as possible in the area of chemical dependence.

EVALUATION AND TREATMENT OF THE PATIENT

The following sections look closely at the processes and methods employed by nurses to identify the needs of the chemically dependent patient in the acute care settings, as well as the chemically abusing and dependent population within the community.

Acute Intoxicated States

In the acute care setting the nursing processes which focus on the individual patient are utilized regularly. A general assessment of the chemically dependent patient, as with all patients, begins with the collection of data and should proceed in an orderly manner. The nursing history (Appendix 6) utilizes information obtained from the patient, family, significant others, the nurse's observations, and those of other health care providers. Based on the history, a nursing diagnosis is made and a plan of care is formulated and evaluated on an ongoing basis to determine the effectiveness of the nursing care. When necessary and appropriate, modifications in the plan are made. The nurse must be aware of his or her own limitations and strengths and should not hesitate to seek assistance from other members of the health care team.

In assessing the chemically dependent patient the nurse must be aware of his or her attitude toward the chemically dependent population. If working with the chemically dependent population is a negative experience and the nurse is nontherapeutic, it would be more beneficial for both the nurse and the individual if the nurse referred that individual or family to someone else or requested a change of assignment. The nurse, to be effective, must convey acceptance and support to the individual and family. The ability of the chemically dependent individual to make decisions and engage in affiliative relationships is impaired; self-image, feelings of personal worth, and perceptions of health are distorted. As a result of limited insight, the individual is unable to identify the relationship between his or her chemical use and current difficulties. Conflicting information may be obtained from patient, family, and significant others. Histories of other subjective data must be reviewed with skepticism. Since denial may be a symptom of chemical dependency, strong objective evidence that there is a problem must be compiled. Input from family, significant others, and physicians may be used for this purpose. It is also important to remember that one should never assume that chemical dependency is always the major or only problem. Constantly ask yourself the question, "Is what I'm seeing due to alcohol or other drug abuse, or is something else causing these problems?" The nurse must be cognizant of common pathophysiology as well as dysfunctions that are prevalent in the chemically dependent population. Such anomalies may be directly or indirectly related to the uncontrolled use of mood–altering chemicals. The medical complications of alcoholism and other drug abuse are summarized in Table 1. For more detailed analysis of these entities, the reader is referred to Chapter 10.

Sedative Drugs: Alcohol, barbiturates, benzodiazepines. Intoxication, an acute toxic brain syndrome, is clinically identified by observing staggering gait, slurred speech, nystagmus and/or drowsiness (see Chapter 7). One or all of these signs may be present and must be correlated with a recent history of chemical use. If the patient's clinical condition allows it, the nurse

TABLE 1	
MEDICAL COMPLICATIONS OF ALCOHOL AND OTHER DRUG ABUSE	
Alcohol-Related Medical Complications	*Medical Complications of Drug Abuse*
Trauma due to accidents, fights, fires, murder, suicide attempts	Serum Hepatitis
Esophagitis, esophageal varices, esophageal carcinoma	Bacterial Endocarditis
Gastritis, gastric ulcers	Overdose
Malabsorption	Pulmonary emboli from infected debris or dilutents
Hepatic disease (fatty liver-hepatitis-cirrhosis)	Arrhythmias
Pancreatitis	Trauma
Cardiomyopathy	Psychosis
Skin and skeletal muscle disease	
Hypoglycemia	
Peripheral neuropathy, neuritis, cerebellar degeneration	
Convulsions	
Birth defects	

should obtain a drug history and ascertain the duration of the most recent drug consumption episode, type(s) of drug used, previous patterns of use, previous treatment for chemical dependency, and date and time of last usage.

It is important that the level of sedation be quantified. For the individual that is being seen in the emergency room, or on a chemical dependency unit, or other acute care setting, the level of alcohol intoxication may be determined objectively by obtaining an immediate blood alcohol level or completing a breath analysis test. Simultaneously, a urine specimen or serum sample should be collected for a drug screen (see Chapter 6). Results of these tests may provide objective measures of the degree of intoxication or some clue as to drug usage. Due to the subjective nature of self-reported drug histories, it is important that this adjunctive test (drug screen) be performed in order to identify drugs that have been inadvertently forgotten or intentionally unmentioned during the initial interview. The breath or blood alcohol level is used clinically to assess the degree of intoxication and prevent the unnecessary use of medication while the patient remains inebriated. The possibility of oversedation and its concomitant array of complications such as respiratory or cardiac arrest must always be a consideration. It is known that alcohol is metabolized at a constant rate which cannot be modified or improved. Therefore, if a breath or blood alcohol level is 0.15 mg percent (150 mg/100 ml), the patient usually will not require any sedation unless, due to extraordinary metabolic and CNS tolerance, the individual experiences withdrawal symptoms at elevated blood alcohol levels. Similarly, the individual who has ingested other sedative drugs (barbiturates and non-barbiturate sedative-hypnotics) and has elevated serum levels is not a candidate for additional sedation.

If the use of breath or blood alcohol testing is restricted or unavailable, another technique that can be utilized by the nurse is evaluation of the level of consciousness. The state of awareness of one's self and one's environment is the most reliable indicator of neurological status. The nurse assesses the individual's capacity to react to verbal stimuli by evaluating the accuracy and speed of answers to questions about person, place, and time. For example, does the individual correctly respond to simple questions such as: "What is today's date? Where are you? Who is the President of the United States?" Responsiveness to verbal stimuli should then be noted. Reaction to painful stimuli would then be assessed. This may be accomplished by exerting pressure on the individual's fingertips between the examiner's thumb and index finger, or pressing the Achilles tendon for a bedridden patient. Minimal pressure that evokes a response should be employed. Appropriate responses may be a grimace, withdrawal, or noises and should be noted. Based on the nurse's findings, a determination would be made whether to contact the physician immediately for further medical evaluation.

Narcotics. Intoxication and toxicity from narcotics represents an additional area of concern for the nurse. As with other depressant drugs, the initial assessment focuses on determining a level of intoxication and a level of consciousness. Toxicity from narcotic ingestion is a life-threatening situation which requires supportive care and maintenance, including assuring a patent airway and adequate ventilation (see Chapters 2 and 7).

One of the most effective antidotes for narcotic overdose is Narcan®. This drug acts by competing for cellular receptors in the drug-depressed neurons and it restores normal respiration and rouses the victim from stupor or coma.

Stimulants: Amphetamines, cocaine. Intoxicated individuals may display hyperactivity, talkativeness, loss of appetite, and bruxism (teeth grinding) (see Chapter 7). Although the individual who has ingested large doses over prolonged periods of time is not at risk for developing signs and symptoms of physical withdrawal, the abrupt cessation of these drugs may lead to serious psychological problems, and in some cases, include a psychosis accompanied by hallucinations and delusions. The individual may also state that he or she feels the sensation of bugs crawling under the skin (formication). The nurse must assess the psychological status of the patient and be cognizant of the psychological highs and lows (euphoria/dysphoria) demonstrated by the patient (bipolar affect). The patient may also experience fatigue and must be protected from physical injury. The physician should be kept apprised of the patient's psychological status so that medication and/or therapy may be ordered when indicated.

Hallucinogens: LSD, PCP. The nurse may encounter the toxic effects in individuals who have ingested hallucinogens. However, the nurse must be aware that signs and symptoms of physical withdrawal do not occur. The aporoach with these patients should be a calm, firm, supportive demeanor. There must be sensitivity to the psychological status of the patient when the patient is belligerent or acting out. Patients must be protected from harming themselves or, in some instances, others. The patient may exhibit disorientation, paranoia, hallucinations and/or delusions (see Chapter 7). Physical restraints may be necessary in some cases. The nurse must refrain from exhibiting fear and must reassure the patient and reinforce an orientation to reality. Talking the patient down is the most effective mode of treatment. For those patients who experience residual effects from the chemicals (hallucination, delusions), pharmacological intervention such as a major tranquilizer and ongoing psychotherapy under the direction of a physician may be indicated.

The nursing care of the patient who has ingested phencyclidine (PCP) (an animal tranquilizer that is a derivative of ketamine) is somewhat different due to the potential for violent behavior during the toxic phase. The acutely confused patient is best managed by sensory isolation with observation at a distance. Minimizing verbal and tactile stimulation does not preclude the monitoring of vital signs. Important functions to monitor are respiration, blood pressure, muscle tone and activity, renal function, and temperature. Ideally, the patient would be placed on a cushioned floor in an isolation room with a monitor present. In some instances, protection of the patient and staff necessitates the use of restraints. Urine samples are obtained at the time of admission and screened for phencyclidine as well as other drugs.

Marijuana, hashish (cannabinoids). Therapy for the psychological dependence associated with cannabinoid abuse is undertaken in an environment that provides supportive psychological treatment. Treatment for cannabinoid abuse is supplemented by early involvement in the rehabilitation phase of treatment. For those patients who have ingested cannabinoids concurrently with other sedative drugs, there is a synergistic effect which increases the level of sedation. When taken by themselves, physical withdrawal from cannabinoids does not occur.

Withdrawal States

In working with chemically dependent patients, the most frequent concern expressed by nurses is: "What am I going to do if a patient goes into withdrawal?" To respond to such a question, the following matters must first be explained: What is withdrawal? How is it identified clinically? How is it evaluated? The mysteriousness surrounding withdrawal states must be dispelled and nurses must become comfortable with their assessment skills.

The withdrawal or abstinence syndrome occurs in those individuals who have developed tolerance to and physical dependence on mood-altering chemicals. For sedative and narcotic drugs, the central nervous system hyperexcitability associated with abrupt cessation of these drugs manifests itself clinically with a specific set of signs and symptoms (see Chapters 2 and 5). With stimulants and hallucinogenic drugs an abstinence–related psychosis may appear. In any event, the discontinuation of any mood–altering drug where there is physical and/or psychological dependence will precipitate craving and anxiety, and the nurse must be capable of identifying and responding to this problem.

Withdrawal problems occur as the level of the mood–altering chemical decreases. The simplest form of withdrawal can be demonstrated by examining what occurs following an evening of drinking to excess. The following morning the hangover or withdrawal effect is exemplified by headache, fatigue, gastrointestinal disturbance, and sweating.

For the chemically dependent individual who has developed tolerance to, and physical dependence on, sedative drugs (including narcotics), the discontinuation of the chemicals result in signs and symptoms that are greater in intensity. With the awareness that withdrawal problems begin to occur as the level of the drug declines, the progression of withdrawal problems becomes predictable. If identification and intervention occur in early stages, more severe problems may be avoided or moderated.

Sedative-Hypnotic Withdrawal Syndromes

In order to effectively assess withdrawal problems, the nurse has available at his or her discretion assessment tools that assist in quantitatively evaluating withdrawal. Signs and symptoms of sedative-hypnotic withdrawal are described in Table 2 (also see Chapter 5).

The pathophysiology for this syndrome is presented in Chapter 5. One tool used to measure sedative withdrawal is the Selective Severity Assessment (SSA) (see Appendix 7). This tool quantifies the severity of sedative withdrawal and is used to evaluate withdrawal from ethanol, barbiturates, benzodiazepines, and non-barbiturate sedative-hypnotics such as glutethimide, methaqualone, and ethchlorvynol. Based on objective and subjective data, it reduces the need to medicate patients. The SSA examines twelve different symptom groups including eating, tremor, sleep patterns, hallucinations, quality of contact, clouding

---

TABLE 2
SIGNS AND SYMPTOMS
OF SEDATIVE-HYPNOTIC WITHDRAWAL

Stage I   Hypertension, tachycardia, hyperthermia, diaphoresis (paroxysmal), tremor, nausea, vomiting, anorexia, insomnia, agitation.

Stage II   All of Stage I plus hallucinations (auditory or visual). Patient has insight into the benign nature of these hallucinations.

Stage III   All of Stage I and II plus disorientation, misidentification, hallucinations, and profuse diaphoresis.

Seizures may occur during any Stage

of the sensorium, agitation, sweating, temperature, pulse, blood pressure, and convulsions. Each area is evaluated and assigned a numerical value based on objective data using the nurse's sense of touch, sight, smell, and hearing. The sections which follow below examine the signs and provide the rationale for doing the evaluation. The reader is encouraged to have the SSA available for reference (see Appendix 7).

Eating. The nurse must be aware that eating disturbances occur frequently in the chemically dependent population and dysfunctions related to nutritional problems are possible, e.g., hypoglycemia, B-vitamin deficiencies. Drug-induced gastritis and malnutrition represent additional problems that are encountered in the chemically dependent population. The nurse must, therefore, assess whether the individual has been eating or is able to eat based on the individual's recall of the meal(s) prior to the exam. Nausea, anorexia, and vomiting are additional problems that can occur following the abrupt cessation of consumption of mood-altering chemicals. It is also advisable to obtain a longitudinal picture of how the individual has eaten in the last 24 hours as well as in the past week. Any special dietary needs should also be evaluated at this time. The state of hydration including skin turgor, as well as the ability to masticate food, must also be evaluated. It is not uncommon to find patients who are edentulous and unable to chew their food.

Tremor. This sign is evaluated by having the patient sit up in a chair or on the side of a bed and extend the arms and hands and spread the fingers. If the patient remains lying in bed in a fetal or tense position it is possible to mask the severity of the withdrawal and ultimately lead to more serious withdrawal problems. The nurse's sense of touch is important in feeling the tremor prior to seeing it. The nurse should also ask the individual to open his or her mouth and stick out his or her tongue. For those individuals who exhibit a tongue tremor, a value of 7 should be recorded. The prognosis for such patients is poor and the likelihood of these patients developing more severe withdrawal problems is high. In the majority of these cases, the patient is immediately started on medication. Another type of tremor that patients exhibit is a flapping tremor (asterixes). To evaluate, the nurse may ask the individual to extend his or her arms to the side and touch his or her nose with his or her fingertip. The nurse should observe for flapping of the hands as the individual completes the exam. The nurse may also use the palm of his or her hand to press against the individuals fingertips; after release, the individual's hand will flap. This type of tremor occurs most frequently in individuals who are cirrhotic and are unable to remove nitrogenous wastes — the by-products of protein metabolism — from their system. They may develop hepatic encephalopathy which can progress to hepato-renal failure and death. Vital signs in this individual are depressed and there is no hallucinosis. The most significant factor in the care of these patients is that they *must not be sedated* or respiratory depression and/or cardiac arrest may occur, resulting in death.

Sleep, psychomotor activity. When evaluating the nature of the individual's sleep pattern and disturbances, as well as other CNS agitation and increased psychomotor activity, the nurse relies heavily on observation, and information provided by the individual and family or significant others. When the sedative action of ingested drugs wears off, the individual demonstrates an increase in psychomotor activity. Such action may seem paradoxical but due to the limited sedative action of these drugs the individual may become restless, belligerent, agitated, and insomnolent. If the nurse is able to observe the sleep pattern and psychomotor activity over a twenty-four hour period, an objective perception of these areas may be formulated. It must be recalled that sleep patterns are very individualized and the nurse must appreciate and be sensi-tive to differences that may be present in individuals who work nights or split shifts. In such an instance, the individual's sleep pattern may be erroneously labelled abnormal. Such individual differences are important in planning nursing care. The nurse must ascertain if the individual wakes frequently, is easily aroused from sleep, or sleeps soundly. Subjectively, this information can be provided by the patient and when feasible it should be substan-tiated by obtaining information from family or others.

Quality of contact-agitation. The Selective Severity Assess-ment includes a thorough evaluation of the quality of contact. Is the individual aware of the examiner and other people around him or her? Individuals who are experiencing the most severe stage of withdrawal (III) are unaware of the presence of the examiner or others. Knowing that individuals who experience early-stage with-drawal will become progressively detached, the nurse will need to plan more intensive nursing intervention. This can be accom-plished by contacting the physician if the patient is hospitalized or arranging for transportation to a medical facility from the person's home. Simultaneously, while evaluating the quality of contact, the nurse is able to evaluate the degree of agitation that the individual is experiencing. Does the individual pace during the interview? Is he or she unable to sit and answer questions? The amount of movement must be evaluated and is related to the CNS hyperexcitability. Before quantifying the degree of agitation it is advisable to allay any anxiety by sitting down with the patient and reassuring him or her that he or she will be evaluated frequently, that signs and symptoms of withdrawal will be monitored closely, and that if necessary, medication may be ordered by the physician.

Sweating. The sense of touch becomes important for the nurse. The nurse may feel the forehead and arms of the patient to determine if he or she is sweating. While completing this procedure, the nurse may once again reassure the patient. The clothing and/or the bed must also be checked. Soaked linen would indicate drenching sweats. In many cases, the sweating is paroxysmal and the need for frequent evaluation must not be underestimated.

Clouding of the sensorium. In evaluating the sensorium, the nurse must differentiate between confusion and disorientation. The latter is exemplified by loss of appreciation of person, place, and time, whereas confusion is a mental state characterized by unstable attention, poor perception of present reality, inability to act coherently, plus disorientation. Therefore, confusion is a much more comprehensive problem that encompasses the quality of contact, clouding of the sensoirum, and hallucinations.

Hallucinations. To evaluate hallucinations, the individual should be asked if he or she has ever seen or heard things that were not really there. Is the individual aware of your presence or is he or she hearing voices or seeing people or things? If auditory hallucinations are occurring, what is the content? How often does the individual hear them and what is their intensity? For visual hallucinations, the same questions may be raised including whether they are colorful, macroscopic, or microscopic. The individual may be picking at his or her clothing or linen because he or she sees bugs or rats. Hallucinations are often depicted as frightening but this is not always the case. The individual may see "little Mexican dancing girls," or "little construction people with air hammers," or see himself "out on a lake fishing." For those individuals experiencing hallucinations, it is important that the nurse refocuses the individual on reality and reassures the individual that he or she will be safe. Some sources in the literature (2) also report olfactory hallucinations but they are very difficult to evaluate.

Seizures. Seizures may be precipitated by multiple etiologies, including cessation of sedative drug consumption. The nurse must, therefore, be cognizant that seizures can occur as the blood and tissue level of a chemical decreases in the individual who is physically dependent on a drug. The incidence of such seizures is most common in patients who are addicted to alcohol, barbiturates, benzodiazepines, and nonbarbiturate sedative-hypnotics. Withdrawal seizures only occur as the name implies; during the withdrawal phase. Generally, no aura precedes this event. It is also possible that a seizure can be the precursor for delirium tremens. If this were the case and another seizure occurred following the onset of delirium tremens, contact the physician immediately. The probability of severe neurological damage is imminent and a neurology workup is necessary. Because seizures may also occur as the result of hypoglycemia, which is prevalent in alcoholics, hypoglycemia should be ruled out before starting any withdrawal medication regimes. Symptomatically, it mimics Stage I alcohol withdrawal (emotional lability, tachycardia, and sweating). Use of a Dextrostix® (blood glucose testing strip) or blood sugar level done by the laboratory would be conclusive in determining a blood sugar value. In some cases, the patient will experience both hypoglycemia and alcohol withdrawal simultaneously. The treatment ordered for each problem differs. For hypoglycemia, the drug of choice is 50% dextrose 50 cc which may be administered intravenously. For alcohol or other sedative withdrawal, sedation may be ordered.

Blood pressure, pulse, and temperature. Hypertension (blood pressure in excess of 140/90) is common in the alcoholic population and may decline when the consumption of ethanol stops. The nurse must monitor blood pressure and be concerned about one that either remains high or continues to increase following the cessation of sedative medication. If left untreated, hypertensive crisis could ensue. Therefore, the blood pressure must be monitored but must be evaluated within the context of the entire SSA. The pulse and temperature must also be monitored. CNS hyperexcitability is often demonstrated by tachycardia and an increase in temperature, although it must be remembered that within the chemically dependent population there is a higher incidence of infection. Anxiety may also contribute to these elevations. It must be reiterated how important it is that fear and anxiety be minimized when evaluating an individual.

The SSA is used by the nurse and a numerical value is assigned for each specific clinical category. The numbers are then added and the total is used as an indicator to quantify the severity of the withdrawal state. If the total is calculated and is less than 20, the patient is said to be experiencing mild withdrawal. In such a situation, the nurse should be able to talk the patient down. The nurse would provide a concrete statement to the patient about his or her clinical condition and reassure the patient that he or she will be evaluated frequently and if necessary, medication will be requested from the physician. The nurse must also attempt to focus on the long-term recovery process and assure the patient that during the acute phase he or she will be monitored closely for medical problems. Utilization of such an approach can decrease the need for medication and underscores the importance of frequent contact and adequate nursing care. However, the nurse must not rely solely on the number tabulated but must also use sound clinical judgment. For instance, someone with an SSA total of 14 may be shaking uncontrollably and require pharmacologic intervention. Remember, the intent of the tool is not to subject the patient to unnecessary discomfort by withholding medication. If, on the other hand, the nurse can be reassuring and indicate that the patient will be continually monitored on a regular basis, the patient's status may improve. The efficacious utilization of the SSA assists the nurse in the assessment. When notifying the physician regarding a patient's status, it is imperative that data be objective and subjective. In totalling the SSA, do not deviate from numerical weights assigned each item. The rule of thumb is 0-19: mild withdrawal; 20-24: moderate withdrawal; 25 or greater: severe withdrawal. The evaluator is encouraged to compare each reading with the previous reading to determine if clinical status has improved or deteriorated. Once a patient has been placed on a withdrawal medication regime, the nurse must not be lulled into a sense of false security. Continuous monitoring is necessary to ensure that withdrawal symptoms are controlled. For those patients whose withdrawal problems are not adequately controlled, the physician will need to be contacted. If necessary, supplemental doses of medication may be ordered. These may be administered every hour if necessary, but it must be remembered that there must be at least one hour between each dose of sedation. If the systolic blood pressure drops below 100, the physician should be notified. Due to the similarity among the drugs in the sedative-hypnotic class, the SSA may be used effectively for the evaluation of other sedative-hypnotic drugs besides alcohol. However, some minor differences between alcohol, barbiturate, and benzodiazepine withdrawal should be noted. With barbiturate withdrawal, there may be postural hypotension, cardiovascular collapse, and in some cases death within 24 hours of the last dose if withdrawal is undetected or left untreated. Benzodiazepine withdrawal is more subtle and clinically mimics a psychiatric syndrome and often occurs anywhere from two to ten days after the last dose. Elevation in blood pressure is slight and the tremor associated with the withdrawal is fine rather than gross. Often there is a state of paranoia with preoccupation for a particular event or person. Cognizant of the progression of withdrawal and its time sequence, the nurse is able to quantify its severity. The SSA, which has been adopted from the original work of Gross and his associates (3) enables the nurse to objectively evaluate the severity of sedative-hypnotic withdrawal. This tool, along with the clinical skills of nursing staff, has proven effective in reducing and minimizing the need for pharmacological intervention in the treatment of the withdrawal syndrome.

Narcotic Withdrawal Syndrome

Patients addicted to narcotics are another problem encountered by nurses. The first step necessary to evaluate these patients is to obtain an accurate drug history. If the history depicts heavy use, the attending physician may decide to administer Narcan®. With the purity of street drugs highly suspect, medical staff may choose to administer Narcan® to this population in order to differentiate between the individual who is physically addicted to narcotics and the "pseudo" addict who gives a history of heavy narcotic use but is not physically dependent. Following the intravenous push infusion of Narcan® by the physician, the physically addicted patient would exhibit signs and symptoms of narcotic withdrawal (Table 3) within 90 seconds.

However, if medical staff choose not to utilize such a process, the narcotic withdrawal worksheet (see Appendix 8) can be used to ascertain if withdrawal is occurring, and to assess its severity. The abstinence signs appear sequentially and are predictable. If objective signs and symptoms of withdrawal are present, the physician should be notified and medication may be ordered to control the symptoms. For individuals experiencing the abstinence signs of narcotic withdrawal, the physician may choose to detoxify the individual with the patient's drug of choice or may select Methadone. Either technique is pharmaceutically sound but Methadone offers the advantage of a 24 hour half-life, which allows the withdrawal process to proceed more smoothly. The time frame for starting and completing this regimen, irrespective of the with-

TABLE 3
SIGNS AND SYMPTOMS OF NARCOTIC WITHDRAWAL

Grade 0	Craving, anxiety
Grade 1	Yawning, perspiration, lacrimation, rhinorrhea
Grade 2	Increase in above signs plus mydriasis, piloerection, tremors, muscle twitches, hot and cold flashes, aching bones and muscles, anorexia
Grade 3	Increased intensity of Grade 2 plus insomnia, hypertension, tachypnea, tachycardia, restlessness, nausea
Grade 4	Increased intensity of Grade 2 and 3 plus febrile facies, position curled up on hard surface, vomiting, diarrhea, weight loss (5 lbs. daily), spontaneous ejaculation or orgasm, hemo-concentration

drawal medication employed, should not exceed seven days (see Chapter 2 for complete information).

PSYCHOSOCIAL ASPECTS OF CHEMICAL DEPENDENCY: THE NURSING PERSPECTIVE

The nurse must be capable of dealing with the acute medical problems experienced by the chemically dependent patient. Detoxification and physiological stabilization during the acute phase represent the initial focus of treatment. The psychosocial dysfunctions associated with chemical dependency must also be assessed and cannot be perceived as isolated from the patient's physical condition. A holistic approach must be employed. The nurse must be sensitive to physical problems, but after stabilization must refocus on the primary problem, chemical dependency. In the following sections, special attention is given to examining the effects of chemical dependency on psychosocial functioning and well-being.

Evaluation and Treatment of the Family

Chemical dependency has far-reaching effects on family members and, therefore, it is critical that members of the family be involved in the recovery process (see Chapter 13).

Nurses in general and specialty hospitals, as well as nurses in the community, can observe many of the major ramifications of chemical dependency encountered by the individual and family members. These may include depression, anger, pain, feelings of helplessness, divorce, domestic violence, and suicide, as well as psychological impairment that can result in runaways, drop-outs, and chemical use and abuse problems that occur later in life. If the nurse is aware of the Protean manifestations of alcoholism in the family, recommendations can be made that will assist the family in their recovery, i.e., Alanon, Families Anonymous, family therapy (see Chapters 13 and 14).

When interviewing family members, the nurse must be non-judgmental and elicit information from each family member while promoting interaction among family members around the presenting problem. As a facilitator the nurse must be cognizant of communication pathways and alliances. Redirecting the family away from usual pathways enables the nurse to test hypotheses regarding these pathways and determine the flexibility or rigidity of a family. Rules that are either formal or informal may also be identified. The interview should be concluded by stating the presenting problem and any other associated problems. For example, "James beats you up when he is drunk and spends half of his check before coming home, and you are seeking ways to help him improve lines of communication." The nurse, unless trained as a family therapist (Chapter 13), must rely extensively on intervention and referral. A referral to Alanon, Naranon, or Alateen (see Chapter 14) represents one possible initial intervention which could prove effective in helping family members cope with the problem. Another option may be referral to a local treatment unit.

The chemically dependent individual elicits responses from the spouse and children, and within a disturbed family, each member feels tension and anxiety and grapples with facing the reality of a chemical dependency problem. Initially, this reality may be resisted and the problem denied and concealed from social contacts, relatives, and friends. As the problem progresses, subtle changes occur and the problem escalates. Friends no longer want to visit and there is concern about family reputation. There is a great deal of concern about the affected individual's drinking or drug-taking and its effects become the focus of anxiety. For family members who fail to protect this individual, there is retribution in the form of accusations of ungratefulness and disloyalty. Remissions, where substance abuse is controlled or absent, become infrequent or totally absent. Husband and wife become polarized, and distrust and resentment surfaces. At this stage, children may become behavioral problems in school and often tell their home-life problems to their teachers, e.g., the sixth-grader who tells the teacher about the yelling and fighting that occurs at home. The chemically dependent individual is often convinced that his or her children are unaware of the problem. The spouse begins to feel hopeless and blames self for the problem. Communication diminishes or becomes nonexistent, violent arguments may ensue, and financial instability and insecurity may follow. Sexual contact may be avoided. The spouse may try to compensate for the sick partner by becoming the decision-maker and assuming the role of both husband and wife (see Chapter 13). It is at this time that threats of divorce or separation may be made. The intensity of the problem has reached such a significant point that some type of intervention becomes necessary. Making excuses for the chemically dependent individual is no longer acceptable to the spouse, e.g., calling into work with a false medical excuse when the person is actually hung over, carrying the passed-out spouse into the bedroom and putting the person to bed. Scapegoats such as the accusatory boss, shrewish wife, or irresponsible children, are no longer justifiable. An ultimatum that such behaviors will no longer be tolerated may be issued. The crisis that is precipitated may convince the chemically dependent individual to seek help. However, it must be remembered that the chemically dependent individual may choose his or her chemical over the family. If the chemically dependent individual chooses to seek help, the potential for recovery may be increased. In either situation, family members may independently choose to participate in self-help groups (e.g., Alanon, Naranon [see Chapter 14]) or other, more intensive, forms of therapy. As the spouse understands his or her involvement in the illness, consideration may be given to reconciliation. The recollection of past disappointments may subside over time and there may be a gradual relinquishment of former roles. Channels of communication may reopen and both husband and wife may strive to develop social contacts and mutual interests.

The nurse must be objective, aware of the extreme sensitivity of the family situation, and must always refrain from being judgmental during the interview process. Failure to do this may precipitate a situation where the nurse is integrated into this sick system. The nurse must be open and honest with the family and direct them to appropriate resources to assist them in adapting to the problems of chemical dependency. For nurses who are not directly involved in family therapy, providing support and information for the family are critical factors in the recovery process.

As with physiological dysfunctions the nurse must always ask the question, "Is what I'm seeing due to alcohol or other drug abuse or is there some other etiology?" Ongoing monitoring of family recovery is necessary and in many cases after the chemically dependent individual has become drug-free, psychopathology that previously might have been masked, begins to surface. In such cases, psychotherapy (individual, couples, family) may be beneficial on a long-term basis through an independent practitioner or mental health clinic.

The crucial need for family involvement and the need to promote optimal functioning of each family member must be paramount in the nurse's mind when completing the assessment and planning nursing intervention for the family.

Employment

To assess the impact of chemical dependency on employment, the nurse will need to evaluate the effects within the workplace. The nurse will need to elicit responses for the following questions from the individual and/or family members: Is the individual's job secure or is it in jeopardy as a result of absenteeism or poor work performance? Are these problems related to chemical use and misuse? Job problems may precipitate financial difficulties. An already delicate marital relationship may be made even more tenuous by financial problems that stem from alcoholism or other drug-abuse problems. If hospitalization for treatment of chemical dependency would be recommended, it needs to be determined whether the individual's job will be secure during treatment. Some employers who do not understand the dynamics of chemical dependency may be reluctant to provide a medical leave of absence. Another vocational aspect may be the loss of a job(s) and a need to attain new job skills. With no period of sustained sobriety or abstinence, the prospect of vocational training or retraining may not be realistic. Strategies must be planned that assist the individual to adapt to his or her own unique situation.

NURSING AND THE RECOVERY PROCESS

The recovery process is a difficult concept to grasp due to the lack of a consistent, universally accepted definition (see Chapter 8). Some authorities suggest that the process begins when the individual accepts the fact that he or she can no longer control the intake of alcohol and/or other mood-altering chemicals and is able to associate this with the fact that as a result, certain areas of their lives have become unmanageable. A frequent basic assumption regarding recovery is that total abstinence from alcohol and other non-prescribed mood-altering drugs is mandatory. Return to a lifestyle that includes social or recreational use of drugs is unrealistic. The data that define which segment of the chemically dependent population could resume such a lifestyle are inconclusive.

Sobriety is a comprehensive term that includes abstinence as well as the expectation that other areas of a person's life will need to be changed, including stabilization of marital and family relationships; rectification of job-related difficulties such as absenteeism or poor work performance; avoidance of involvement with the criminal justice system such as disorderly conduct or drunken driving charges; improvement of one's self-image; and relationships with others. As can be surmised, the changes expected of the individual are extensive. To accomplish a change of such magnitude often requires a minimum of two to three years.

The chemically dependent individual may have difficulty imagining a lifestyle that is free of chemicals. To appreciate the dilemma, reflect on your own personal life. What is the first question you ask friends or relatives who visit your home? "Can I get you something to drink?" The good cheer and conviviality associated with drinking is perceived by some segments of society as positive. The chemically dependent individual must now develop a new lifestyle that does not involve mood-altering chemicals. Leisure activities may prove especially difficult and must be altered and restructured. In many instances, the individual may have had no previous outlets. When new options are recommended, there is a possibility that the individual may not be comfortable participating. Many communities have developed social clubs available for those individuals who must remain chemically free (e.g., Alano Clubs). To attain such goals requires a great deal of effort and support from family and friends.

Relapse may also be part of the recovery process. The duration of such an episode and its consequences must be dealt with swiftly and decisively. Modification of the treatment plan is critical. If relapse is identified quickly, it may be possible to minimize difficulties. The nurse must keep in mind that the chemically dependent individual is at risk for the redevelopment of a serious chemical dependency problem including all its ramifications, should he or she resume using non-prescribed mood-altering drugs.

Although great emphasis is placed on the individual's recovery, the family and each of its members must also be considered when evaluating the recovery process. In those cases where pathology surfaces, individuals must be provided with alternatives. Recovery includes the entire family system. With these basic concepts in mind, the nurse is able to assist the individual and his or her family in devising a recovery program.

COMMUNITY HEALTH SYSTEMS

The community health approach to chemical dependency looks beyond the impact of the disease on individual and family, and assesses the effect on the community. Community problems that may stem directly or indirectly from chemical dependency are traffic fatalities, venereal disease, and crime. In evaluating the community, the nurse completes a community diagnosis. In completing a community assessment, the nurse examines what segment of the population is at risk for developing chemical dependency problems as well as the current health and disease status of the population. The nurse must then identify or develop a network that responds to the actual or potential problems encountered by the chemically dependent population.

In developing strategies that promote health and reduce the vulnerability of the at-risk population, emphasis is placed on primary prevention. By definition, primary prevention might call for removal of the agent (e.g., alcohol) or decreasing the susceptability of the host (man and woman). Removal of the agent is unrealistic without major modifications in the present laws governing the sale of substances of abuse. In retrospect, it is well known that during the prohibition era and temperance movements there was a dramatic decline in the incidence of alcoholic cirrhosis. However, socially it proved ineffective as a deterent to the consumption of alcoholic beverages. To decrease the susceptability of the host, several approaches may be considered. For example, some states are giving strong consideration to raising the drinking age. While raising the drinking age may decrease traffic fatalities, there is also a need to increase the awareness of the general public to the hazards of drinking.

The nurse may develop informative programs for the general public. These can assist them in making a decision to drink or not to drink. Similarly, the nurse may work with special populations such as the elderly. Information provided could focus on issues that relate to drinking and the aging process such as the effect of loneliness, isolation, depression, retirement, or bereavement on drinking habits and patterns, as well as problems associated with simultaneous intake of alcohol and other drugs.

Secondary prevention emphasizes intervention and treatment. By being aware of actual or potential problems, the nurse can respond to the individual and family. The nurse in the community must be capable of making a decision whether an individual needs immediate medical attention (emergent state), can attain assistance within 24-72 hours (urgent state), or encourages the individual to seek services when motivated to do so (elective state). The nurse must be aware of community resources and how the network can be utilized. In some cases, the nurse may function as case manager, while in other instances the nurse monitors the patient's post-treatment. In either situation, the nurse evaluates the patient's compliance with recommended regimes and monitors progress in recovery. If the individual is having difficulty or has relapsed, the regime must be modified. The responsibility for recovery and decision-making rests with the individual, and the nurse is an adjunct to him or her.

For those individuals who are impaired by the chronic residual effects of alcoholism or other drug abuse (e.g., Wernicke-Korsakoff Syndrome, polyneuropathy), emphasis is placed on maintaining an optimal level of functioning within the limitations imposed by deteriorating health. Once again, the nurse must incorporate the available services in the community into the treatment process. Without linkages to community-based programs the patient may receive inadequate or marginal care. In some instances, the nurse may determine that available services are absent or insufficient. If this is the case, the nurse must function as a change agent. Therefore, the nurse must be aware of the political and economic realities of the community and must be able to identify the systems that meet the population's needs and are cost-effective. Dialogue must be initiated with community leaders and elected officials to apprise them of the problems encountered by the chemically dependent population, and alternatives to cope with the problem may be recommended. In order to effect change, the nurse must be more than just vocal or the system will remain unchanged. The nurse in the community functions within a comprehensive community-based system that is designed to respond to the needs of the general public. The nurse must make a personal decision and decide what level of involvement he or she is willing to undertake in order to improve the level of service for the population effected by alcohol or other drug abuse problems.

SUMMARY

Nurses may utilize different approaches when evaluating the problems of chemical abuse and dependency. This chapter has examined two of those approaches. The first, an individualized approach, relies heavily on the nursing process and assesses the impact of chemical dependency on the individual and his or her family. The second approach focuses on the community and identifies the health status of the community including which populations would be at risk for developing substance-use disorders.

When evaluating the chemically dependent patient, either in an acute care setting or in the community, the initial assessment concentrates on ascertaining the degree of intoxication or determining whether the patient is experiencing or has the potential to experience withdrawal problems (abstinence syndrome). Intoxication is a toxic brain syndrome that results from the consumption of a variety of drugs. With ethanol, a breath or serum blood alcohol test may be performed to obtain an objective measure of the level of intoxication. Other drugs may be qualitatively identified by obtaining a urine specimen for a toxicology screen. Narcan®, a narcotic antagonist, may be used to reverse the depressant effect of narcotics. Withdrawal problems may begin to occur when consumption of the mood-altering chemical ceases. The effects of chemical dependency are physiological and psychological depending on the chemical that is misused. The progression of withdrawal problems can be plotted and several evaluation tools (e.g., Selective Severity Assessment, Narcotic Withdrawal Worksheet) are available to monitor the progression. Prudent administration of sedative medication during withdrawal as well as a nonjudgmental supportive environment are important factors in assisting the patient during the acute phase. In addition, the nurse must be aware of the devastating psychosocial ramifications of the disease. The family sometimes must be treated concurrently. Job problems as well as involvement with the criminal justice system must be addressed. Recovery from substance-use disorders may require a minimum of two to three years.

Nurses, as a result of their diverse clinical and educational backgrounds, function in many different roles. For nurses who practice in the community, emphasis is placed on completion of a community assessment and the formulation of services that respond to identified needs. This process may include prevention programs. Primary prevention looks at decreasing the susceptability of the host or the removal of the agent. Secondary prevention focuses on intervention and treatment. In some cases, this process may mean referral to community resources. To accomplish this goal, nurses will need to be aware of the network of services that exist in their community.

Nurses, as members of the health care team, can and do provide services for the chemically dependent population. As the knowledge base regarding chemical dependence continues to expand, nurses face the challenge to remain current.

Nurses, as change agents, will be in an excellent position to effect the future directions of health care. Such a commitment will insure the continuation of services for individuals, families, and communities who are affected by chemical dependency problems.

REFERENCES

1. American Nurses Association: *Nursing: A Social Policy Statement.* Kansas City, 1980.

2. Victor, M.: Alcoholism. In: *Clinical Neurology, Vol. 2,* Second Edition, Baker, A.B. (Ed.). New York: Harper Brothers, p. 8, 1962.

3. Gross, M.H.; Lewis, E., and Hastey, J.: Acute alcohol withdrawal syndrome. In: *The Biology of Alcoholism, Vol. 3, Clinical Pathology,* Kissin, B. and Begleiter, H. (Eds.). New York: Plenum Press, pp. 191-263, 1974.

Chapter 13

Intervention and Recovery: a Family Focus

Rita Wisniewski, B.A., C.A.C.

OVERVIEW

This well-developed explication of the role of the family in the etiology and treatment of substance use disorders will be of great value to Allied Health Professionals whose work brings them into contact with spouses, parents, siblings, and children of alcoholics and other drug abusers. In a pleasant and informative style the author provides a wider view of the forces and dynamics with which substance abusers are often involved. In her brief introduction she vigorously affirms her faith in the family as the fundamental unit of society, the individual emphasis of the narcissistic "Me Generation" notwithstanding.

Then, in the bulk of her text she describes the nature and functioning of homeostatic processes within the family as an integrated organic unit. Ms. Wisniewski then fully explains how the progressive deterioration of the individual substance abuser is reflected in a parallel deteriorative process within the family as it struggles to establish a new level of equilibrium. She examines not only the ways in which addicts destroy their families, but ways in which family members may contribute to the destruction of their addict.

The author strongly advocates the values and benefits of an integrated treatment of the entire family, and the special ways in which such treatment combats the loneliness, isolation, withdrawal, and shame of families. She recommends special ways of dealing with the identified problems of families in turmoil, and health professionals will find ample suggestions for ways in which they can aid these families back to recovery.

A summary and references conclude the chapter.

INTRODUCTION

Chemical dependency is viewed as a family illness, and recovery is a family process. Clinical observation reveals that for each alcohol- or drug-dependent person there are at least four other people whose lives and well-being are significantly impaired due to their relationship with the abuser. This illness has many victims who are not chemically dependent, who are caught in the slow progression of symptoms and often more in need of help than the chemical abuser. In the past, most of the emphasis has been on the identified patient, the chemically dependent person, resulting in an overwhelming failure to cope with the needs of affected family members.

This country was founded on the notion of individual freedom. Particularly during the past two decades the sometimes subtle, sometimes blatant message has been that everyone should be doing "their own thing" in their own way. Novak (1) stated in 1976 that 10% of the nation's people were acting and speaking as if the family no longer was the basic unit of society. He concluded that this attitude has not proven to be a healthy focus for the individual, for the family, nor for the country.

A refocus for the 1980s appears to be developing as foreshadowed in the 1980 White House Conference on Families. Jim Bay Tucker, Chairperson of the conference stated, "We believe that the family unit is the foundation of our society . . . we believe that the well-being of the individual person and of human society at large is intimately linked with the family" (2, p. 1). In preparation for this conference, state meetings were held throughout the country. In Wisconsin, the Governor added that the family can be the one stable point in an increasingly flux-filled environment. The conference was seen as an overdue assessment of how actions by government and private institutions sometimes help or sometimes hinder the best interests of family structure. Relatedly, the final report indicated one of the top three issues repeated throughout the country was prevention and treatment of drug abuse. This clearly identified family problem demands our attention.

Chemical dependency is a complex problem that is not confined to a single person but is instead a complex relationship among the drug, the user, and other persons. Traditionally, some therapists had assumed that alcohol problems were primarily in the body, mind, or behavior of the user and consequently therapy was directed towards the individual. In recent years, with more rigorous application of social science concepts to sociobehavioral therapies, these assumptions are being challenged. A contemporary view of alcohol problems requires a consideration of the interacting biological, intrapersonal, and social systems that extend beyond the self. Hence, this chapter emphasizes chemical dependency and the recovery from it as a multifaceted illness with specific focus on family systems.

HOMEOSTASIS IN THE FAMILY
OF THE CHEMICALLY DEPENDENT

The definition of a family and its relationships to the concept of homeostasis has been an issue of discussion in recent years. A foremost task of the 1980 White House Conference on Families was to define the present-day family. Although thousands of participants acknowledged that the family still remains the basic unit of society, its form and roles have been rapidly changing. Based on this information as well as clinical experience, the word *family* as used in this chapter refers to the chemically dependent person and those individuals who are intimately linked with him or her in a lifestyle repeatedly affected by the drug-using and drinking behavior. These individuals, therefore, may not only be members of a traditional nuclear and extended family but also other significant persons such as partners, friends, co-workers, and employers. In a sense this system or group of people can be described as a *chemically dependent family*. Some theorists infer that inevitably the drug becomes the central life focus for each family member, since their behavior and emotions are primarily influenced by the alcohol or drug consumption and resulting behavior of the abuser. This approach will be better understood as we briefly discuss the concept of family homeostasis.

Initially the concept of homeostasis referred to the tendency of an organism to maintain internal balance or equilibrium of temperature, fluid content, and other functions by regulation of its bodily processes. This idea has also been used to describe human social interactions. It has been suggested that within the family system there is a tendency to maintain an internal equilibrium which minimally allows all members to function, and maximally affords the opportunity for growth. This equilibrium is maintained primarily by regulation of behavioral or reaction processes developed by each family member. Homeostasis then is a tendency of a social system to achieve balance among the various forces operating within and upon it. It is vital that the family maintains an emotional balance in order to sustain itself.

Certain roles and patterns constitute family equilibrium. Within the family system roles are sometimes assigned by a more dominating member, for example, a father with his children. Roles may also be assumed by assertive persons as in the case of the eldest child who becomes a controller, or a wife who is feeling powerless and takes on the role of a placater. The cultural and social impact on the family also incorporates subtle regulations to govern the roles members are to assume and the ways they are to relate to each other. Common examples in the history of family life can be found in messages like "wives obey your husbands" and "children should be seen and not heard."

Already present then, in every family system, is a balance structured to minimize the threats of pain and disruption. However, people in a chemically dependent family are involved in a series of cumulative crises and even though they behave in a manner which they feel will resolve the crises and permit a return to stability, this stability is not possible for any length of time due to the progressive symptoms of the addictive illness.

It is important for allied health professionals to be aware that initially, resistance is evoked from the family seeking to maintain equilibrium if any shift from within occurs; for example, a change in a member's usual response patterns. An even stronger resistance may occur when an attempt is made from outside the family to intervene in the system. Any suggested behavior that deviates from the patterned role of expectations may be perceived as threatening and disruptive to the established order. To avoid this family disruption the members may act in contrary ways in order to force behavior back to the direction of the familiar homeostasis. This tendency can become frustrating and confusing to the health care provider, and often leads to the unwillingness of professionals to confront directly the problem of alcohol or other drug dependency.

The impact of the abuser's behavior is experienced repeatedly by all those closely associated with him or her, including friends, family, employers, and partners. However, the nuclear family may be most harassed by the effects of the dependency's progression and bear the heaviest load in the recovery process, because some of the key elements in the maintenance of an operational family system either never existed or slowly erode and disappear. It is important that a family have meaningful purposes and goals. One of the chemically dependent family's chief purposes becomes the monitoring or control of the drug. The development of other goals gets lost in the unpredictability of the user's behavior, e.g., a wife who gives up all evening plans so that she is home to regulate her husband's alcohol consumption, or a family summer vacation never pursued because of one child's erratic drug behavior.

It is also important that a healthy family have a degree of order, which is fostered by effective rule-making. Because of the discord experienced in many chemically dependent families, rules are not viewed as meaningful or significant, especially by children. Effective communication is another key element of a vigorous family. Lack of self-esteem hinders the development of assertiveness and communication. Research repeatedly reveals low self-esteem among substance abusers as well as their family members. It follows then, that the communication styles for this population are not generally constructive. For some families even the basics of food, shelter, and activity are nonexistent or meager. It is of little surprise that spouses, children, and parents exhibit symptoms of physical and mental deterioration in the chemically dependent family.

Although the preceding theoretical background on the dysfunctional aspects of the chemically dependent family can be a helpful aid to allied health professionals, it is also important to appreciate the individuality of each person encountered and the uniqueness of each family that is presenting its symptoms. The distinctiveness of each case is influenced to a significant degree by the individual's cultural experiences. Ethnic and racial groups often have strong traditions promulgated by the family unit. To be effective, understanding and respect must be given to the cultural definitions of alcohol and other drug use, to the culture's prescriptions for the roles of family members, and to the cultural values of family solidarity, sanctity, and self-sufficiency.

In summary, the family system functions with roots, rules, roles, responses, reactions, and resistance to change. Within its scope of awareness and experience, it has developed its own unique homeostasis to enable nurturing at its optimum and survival at its minimum. These are the elements of family dynamics that become impaired in the development of alcohol and other drug dependency. These are the same elements that need to be considered in a holistic approach to the treatment of this illness.

PROGRESSIVE EFFECTS OF CHEMICAL DEPENDENCY ON THE FAMILY

The chemically dependent person has been identified by Catanzaro (3) as sometimes exhibiting characteristics of excessive dependency, emotional immaturity, low frustration tolerance, inability to express emotions, high level of anxiety in interpersonal relationships, perfectionism, compulsiveness, grandiosity, and sex role confusion. These personality traits, along with the deteriorating mind and body, seem to elicit from family members a vicious cycle of responses which, for the most part, impair their healthy functioning and do little to the dependency's progression. Indeed there are indications that the reactive behaviors are conducive to continued drinking or drug use.

Drug abuse is a realistic threat which often consumes the dependent person, and can be the cause of a variety of personal and family tragedies. Some of the following consequences can be readily assessed by a skillful observer: 1) The family member may be emotionally overwhelmed at the discovery that one of its members is a drug abuser; 2) the abuser as well as the family often become social outcasts, due to the fear and misunderstanding others have of this widespread community problem; 3) there may be medical needs and costs, as well as legal fees and fines, which place heavy financial demands on the family; 4) relationships with lawyers, judges, social workers, psychologists, clinics, and hospitals must be developed; 5) the family must often readjust its way of life to accommodate the impact of the drug abuse of one of its members, and begin to expend all of its resources to cope with the problem; and 6) the strain of drug abuse may cause the emergence of psychological problems in various family members. In attempting to cope with these realities, families are faced with the task of self-examination, self-exploration, and often self-incrimination as they attempt to define their roles as a causal or contributing factor in the process.

Jackson's (4) research focused on the adjustment of the family to the crisis of alcoholism and laid the foundation for more careful study and treatment of the family members and the family system. It is now possible to identify the developing symptomatic behaviors related to the family aspects of the illness on a time continuum, keeping in mind that the unique quality of each person's life and experience, as well as the individualized patterns of the family unit, will have a significant bearing on the progressive effects of alcohol and other drug dependency in the family. Nevertheless, the patterns presented below have been observed with enough consistency to warrant their study and use in a family assessment.

STAGES OF PROGRESSION IN THE FAMILY

OF THE CHEMICAL DEPENDENT

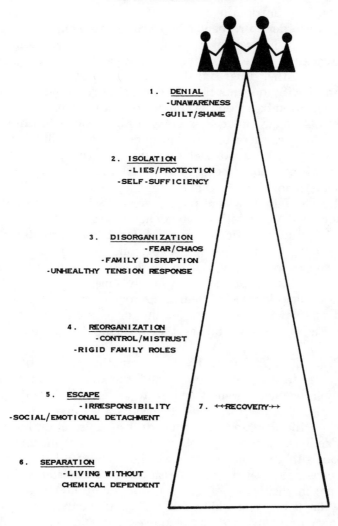

1 .   DENIAL
-UNAWARENESS
-GUILT/SHAME

2 . ISOLATION
-LIES/PROTECTION
-SELF-SUFFICIENCY

3 .   DISORGANIZATION
-FEAR/CHAOS
-FAMILY DISRUPTION
-UNHEALTHY TENSION RESPONSE

4 .   REORGANIZATION
-CONTROL/MISTRUST
-RIGID FAMILY ROLES

5 .   ESCAPE
-IRRESPONSIBILITY   7 . ←←RECOVERY→→
-SOCIAL/EMOTIONAL DETACHMENT

6 .   SEPARATION
-LIVING WITHOUT
CHEMICAL DEPENDENT

Figure 1

Stages of Progression

Stage 1 — Denial. The symptom of denial, which is the unconsciously motivated refusal to acknowledge the relatedness of alcohol or drug abuse with developing problems, is exhibited by family members as well as the drug abuser, in the early stages. In a strong denial system often the members can be deluded into not recognizing any existing problems. There appears to be three major factors contributing to this state.

1. In order to recognize any health problem, particularly in early stages, it is essential to be able to identify symptoms. Most people lack adequate education concerning the interaction among alcohol and other drugs and the body, mind, social, and spiritual relationships. Statements that chemical abuse does not exist in the family are often based on the absence of knowledge.

2. Although progress is being made through education and media coverage, there remains an aura of fear, guilt, and shame surrounding the illness of alcohol and other drug dependency syndromes. These feelings become overwhelming for family members and hinder recognition of the developing problem.

3. The family system itself is generally highly invested in its own survival. Along with this tendency is a strong degree of confidentiality around difficult issues leading to an unspoken rule of not revealing uneasy feelings to persons outside of the family circle, and in some cases, not to those inside the intimate sphere. Often the need to preserve the family image is a high priority. Therefore, at this stage of denial, approaches made by health care providers, which attempt to define or express concern about observable symptoms, will meet with strong resistance by family members.

Stage 2 — Isolation. By this time the periods of socially acceptable drinking are shorter, and the drug use patterns are becoming regular. Friends and relatives extend invitations less frequently, due to disruptive behaviors they have observed as related to the drinking and other drug use. Isolation has begun.

Family members themselves will withdraw from social participation with the goal of reducing the visibility of the unacceptable behavior and thereby the threat to the family status. Isolation is further intensified by the response to a cultural mandate which states that families should be self-sufficient and manage to resolve their own problems without recourse to outside aid. Employers get excuses for absences, relatives get rationalizations for behavior, neighbors are blamed or ignored, and community helpers are rejected.

There is little doubt, based on clinical experience, that children become intimately involved in this progression from a very early age. At the isolation stage, questions from the children are evaded by parents and there are strict rules not to talk about family issues with teachers. Physical violence sometimes occurs. Contacting social or law enforcement agencies mean a loss of status. What results then is physical or sometimes sexual abuse of children. In some cases the violence is projected only at the spouse, with the children attempting to be referees.

Without the advice of others, the family begins to search for the reason leading to the increase of chemical use. Family members feel strongly that if a rationale for using the drug can be identified, their behaviors can be modified to decrease the intake of the chemical by the abuser. The focus of attention for all members becomes the alcohol or drug. Discussions become increasingly unproductive. Each feels resentment of others' behaviors, and the expression of the resentment often leads to escalating discord and further drug use.

Periods of sobriety or promises of abstinence inhibit the family's acceptance of the seriousness of this illness and thwarts attempts to make appropriate adjustments. These short-lived assurances offer just enough respite to gather forces necessary to continue this destructive progression. Long-term goals recede into the background. Children experience increasingly frequent episodes of inconsistent behavior of parents. Spouses begin to be immersed in self-pity. It is at this time that many homemade remedies are used and as each fails, the anxiety and hopelessness mount. The family feels inadequate, different from others, and alone with its shameful secret.

Stage 3 — Disorganization. Thrown into closer contact with one another as outside interactions diminish, the behavior of each family member assumes exaggerated importance. The reality is that all members will find methods to deal with their mounting anxiety and frustration, and generally speaking, this stress-relieving behavior is not conducive to nurturing a healthy family structure.

The tension-relieving responses in spouses may include quarreling, nagging, berating, or retreating into silence. Among the children, they may include hyperactivity, learning difficulties, or behavior problems. Serious depression, high anxiety levels, and emotional and physical violence can evolve. Some family members develop somatic symptoms such as headaches, stomachaches, and dizziness. If a doctor is consulted, physical causes often can not be found. It is difficult sometimes for family members to see a connection between the abuser's drinking or the drug use and their own physical problems. As a result, the subject will often not be discussed with a doctor. At this stage the health care provider's awareness of family symptoms could lead to a more complete assessment. With adequate support, intervention may be possible.

Some specific responses of children at the disorganization stage are described by Cork (5). Interviews with 115 children of alcoholic parents indicate that tension and competition are high among siblings. There were significant findings of hostility and depression, with no child describing their family as normal. Some of the responses are a result of inconsistencies in parental behavior. Children are often used as tools in the struggle between mother and father. Youngsters are bewildered, yet questioning brings no satisfactory answers, as parents themselves do not know what is happening. Family members begin to worry about their own normality and inability to take constructive action of any kind.

Fear is one of the major characteristics at this stage. The paradoxical worry that relatives will interfere or will not help in an emergency, concern that employers may recognize symptoms and job loss will occur, thoughts of possible violence, car accident, legal problems, or personal destruction, permeate each day. Compounding this problem is the family's self-imposed isolation, making them alone and helpless in the world. All is chaos, and some family members feel trapped in an intolerable, unstructured system which offers no way out.

The Alanon Family Group has traditionally offered support to these family members. In the helpful literature distributed by this group, denial, isolation, and disorganization can all be found in the accounts related by family members of an addicted person.

> "After the first shock at the realization that one of my children was an alcoholic, I went through all the well-worn and useless attempts tried by those with an alcoholic in the family. I wept, I scolded, I tried to reason with her. I tried to bribe her. I withheld favors, and I even slapped her."

"By nature a husband feels the welfare of his family is his responsibility and when something arises that he cannot control, he rejects strongly. I blamed my wife's alcoholic problem for almost everything that I didn't like. Eventually I withdrew from family, friends, associates, and became very selfish. I was on a lonesome road, almost a complete stranger to my family and worst of all, I was fast losing the ability to communicate with others."

"When I started Alanon I was ill physically and mentally. My life was a mad obsession with my husband's alcoholism. The neglect of the children and myself was a frightening thing. Fear is contagious and our home was full of fear" (6, p. 7).

A word of caution to allied health professionals: At Stage 3 family members may also begin their own use of alcohol or other drugs. For example, the wife of an active alcoholic may decide it is better to join him than fight him. It is not unusual in studying case histories to see the rapid progression of the abusively drinking female bring her to treatment while her male partner slowly deteriorates from his addictive illness. Chemically dependent adolescents often have histories that reveal a lifetime of exposure to parental drinking behavior. The young peoples' method of coping is alcohol and drugs. Another frequent occurrence is that mood–altering drugs are often prescribed when family members present the aforementioned symptoms to their physicians. Unfortunately, due to the increasing stress, prescriptions are frequently abused. The risk of other family members becoming chemically dependent is thus heightened, and with more than one addicted member the family's problems are compounded.

Stage 4 — Reorganization. If the family remains together it will discover roles, rules, and reactions to maintain a homeostasis that incorporates the drinking or other drug use. Precipitating such a change may be a crisis like the loss of a job or a violent episode. It may simply be that the level of disorganization becomes intolerable.

Someone in the system will generally take control or command. An analogy made by the father of a drug addict was that of being commander of a ship. He described the slowly sinking ship as being analogous to the family system and the vicious progression of addiction likened to a storm–ravaged sea. The commander, even though he had concern for all the crew, refused to leave his post. This role of attempting to control the addictive process is a frustrating and ineffective one.

In marital relationships, as irresponsibility of the addict continues, spouses slowly ease their mates out of previous roles. There is slow withdrawal of respect and affection. The family learns to respond to the control of the non-using parent, and the chemical abuser becomes less necessary for the ongoing activity of the family. The addicted person may attempt to rejoin the family, or make alternate attacks at destroying the newly created homeostasis. He or she may at this time make statements about inability to control drug use as well as feelings of desperation. There may be some attempts to get the addict to Alcoholics Anonymous, Narcotics Anonymous, or treatment centers. However, if failure occurs, discouragement is deeper and another wedge has been inserted into the self-sufficiency of the family.

The children of the addict become more settled in their behavior during this stage. They no longer blame themselves, and accept the unpredictability of drug use. As one six-year-old stated in a counseling session: "Well, I'll just have to get used to it. I have a drunken father." At this time when conflict occurs between the addicted parent and the children, the other parent will generally decide in favor of the latter.

Some relief is also experienced if the non-using family members begin to make contact with agencies and self-help groups. They discover they are not alone, and experience a reduction of anxiety with the opportunity to discuss the problem openly for the first time. There appears to be a return to more consistent and productive thinking. The experience of taking over the situation and making it more manageable adds to the self-confidence of the non-using member. In contrast, the chemically dependent individual becomes less able to care for self and family. Without the controller, now desperately needed by the system, family life would be destroyed. Few families live out their lifespans remaining at this stage.

Steinglass (7) presents a life-history model of such an alcoholic family. In his research, he suggests that some families choose a solution to the alcoholic problem in the late family-resolution stage that he describes as the "stable wet alcohol family." Perhaps because the family's life has been relatively aproblematic (especially when external stressor events have not occurred), or perhaps as a result of the extreme effectiveness by which the family life has become organized around alcohol, these families have continued year after year with remarkably little change either with regard to alcohol use or the consequence of alcoholism for family life. They remain alcoholic systems; they remain remarkably stable; but they also have an unchanging quality, a sense of being "locked in concrete" (7).

Stage 5 — Escape. The progression of chemical dependency has now reached a catastrophic stage. Family members ultimately find ways to separate and protect themselves from the continual infliction of pain, either physical or emotional and sometimes both. Even though families may remain together in the same household, they develop methods of physical and psychological separation. For example, there are little or no shared responsibilities, minimal communication, no mutual support or social activities and, for many partners, no sexual contact. The walls of defense are strongly built.

Wegscheider (8) suggests that each family member finds a survival role through a self-deluding process, which assists him or her in growing more out of touch with reality and the disease's progression, thus allowing escape from pain. She specifically identifies and characterizes the survival roles:

> The "chief enabler" is generally the spouse or parent of the abuser. This person was earlier described as the controller or protector and takes on increasing responsibility thus enabling the addicted person to continue drug use without experiencing the resulting behavior.
> The "family hero" is often the eldest child who provides self-worth to the system. His or her achievement level is outstanding and often assists or replaces the enabler in the caretaking of the family.
> The "family scapegoat" is the child who is continually involved in trouble and presents a center of focus for the family. The blame of the addicted parent and family dysfunction is often placed here.
> The "lost child" is the very quiet, and withdrawn member who offers tremendous relief to the tension-ridden family.
> The "family mascot" is likely to be the youngest child with high energy sometimes diagnosed as hyperactivity. This behavior provides distraction and humor (8, p. 7).

Each specific role is theorized to be compulsive in nature. It not only allows survival in the chemically dependent family, but studies indicate that this role behavior of family members is taken into every other relationship they encounter. As a result, spouses may divorce and move from one marriage to another, each presenting a pattern of dependency. Children are unable to relinquish their roles, and often cross the threshold to adulthood with a definite handicap. Without professional help the defense systems and repressed feelings may become a primary problem for each family member. Using alcohol or drugs to escape the problem is sometimes the choice, based on family modeling.

Stage 6 — Separation. For some marriages this stage is the terminal one. The non-using spouse may have a history of short, repeated periods of separation. The problems involved in coming to the decision to terminate the marriage cannot be underestimated, as they involve 1) emotional conflicts, 2) practical circumstances, and 3) often conflicting advice from outsiders. At this stage, the chemically dependent person may no longer be able to tolerate the lack of status or rewarding role in the family, and chooses to desert or divorce.

When there is a divorce, remaining family members will reorganize at this time. In addition to the process experienced by other families where no drug problem exists, there are other issues that often develop. The drug-dependent person may make attempts to come back, or there may be attempts at violence. There are strong efforts on the part of both parents to gain the loyalty of the children. Often there are guilt feelings at deserting a sick person. Family members are often unable to break through the roles previously identified, and find difficulty in developing new nurturing relationships and their own healthy self-identity.

When the addicted person in the family is an adolescent or adult child, the separation stage can be most difficult. A divorce from the offspring is not an option. However, the stresses put on the marital relationship of the parents inevitably leads to the drug-abusing child leaving home either by choice, or upon demand of the parents. Requests to return are many, and sometimes stealing and violence follow. The young person is without bed and board and the parents choose to become providers again. Legal problems evoke concern. Feelings of strong conflict arise around parental responsibility.

Stage 7 — Recovery. Recovery is necessary for every family member to become a healthy, functioning person again. This recovery is *not* dependent on the decision of the abuser, but rather, is a choice of each individual. For many, treatment is experienced within the complete family system, offering the unit an opportunity to heal and rejoin in a nurturing relationship. For some, recovery is experienced with only part of the family. For others, it may be an individual treatment experience due to the loss of family, or refusal of other members to accept the health problem and pursue its recovery process.

Knowledge of the progression should be of assistance to all health care providers in viewing chemical dependency as a family illness. A more complete and knowledgeable assessment of the family system will also be an asset in offering appropriate recommendations to any family member.

FAMILY INTERVENTION

Because of the principle of homeostasis, a chemically dependent family tends to resist change over long periods of time. Any effort by one person to alter the established role behaviors threatens the family equilibrium. The basic purpose of intervention is to assist family and other significant persons in the life of the addicted person to understand the progression and to motivate a change in their ineffective response patterns.

Faced with the crises of most serious illnesses, a family can draw on cultural definitions for appropriate behavior and for procedures to terminate the crisis. However, that had not been so with chemical dependency, since only recently has there been information to guide the family. Without knowledge, understanding, and an established program, the family facilitates the progression, and only when the discomfort of the overfunctioning or enabling family members gets too painful do they reach out for help. Health professionals are often in a position to offer the needed help earlier, and assist the family in diminishing its suffering.

In the situation where the substance abuser is unwilling to recognize the alcohol or other drug problem, the health care provider can be most effective by focusing on the family member or members who are presenting the problem. The first phase of intervention responds to the progressive stages of denial, isolation, and disorganization. To combat these family responses, it is imperative to lay a solid foundation of education. Without accurate information about, and understanding of, alcohol or other drug dependency syndromes, a treatment regimen is difficult for the abuser or family to accept. Denial and minimizing may continue. It is also important that the family learns some basic concepts about family dynamics, so that any decisions to change homeostatic mechanisms are carefully preplanned and followed through to completion. Suggestions for the family at this intervention may include removal of ignorance by learning all the facts about the disease, its etiology, symptoms, and recovery process. In some cases, the health care provider may be qualified to offer this education. As a community service many hospitals, clinics, and agencies offer specifically designed programs. They often supply educational literature for participants and interested professionals. This first step of education seems to assist family members in counteracting denial with new information that dispels guilt and shame.

A second step may involve counterbalancing isolation and suppression, helping the family to deal with the reality of chemical dependency, and encouraging the members to share this reality with others outside the family circle. Involvement with a counselor who has experience in the field of alcohol and other drug abuse is most helpful. A sense of strength and direction is experienced when the family develops broader community support in self-help groups such as Alanon, Alateen, Naranon, and Families Anonymous.

Acquiring a healthy attitude based on knowledge, and developing the courage to practice new principles when dealing with the abuser, are the next steps in a family recovery. The disorganization patterns of Stage 3 are replaced by more effective responses. When family members get help they may improve in their ability to function as human beings, which often has a tremendous impact on the chemically dependent person. For example, in a demonstration project in the St. Louis Post Office, spouses of alcoholics were discovered to be failing in their jobs because of their inability to cope with their partner's alcoholism. With counseling and assistance these employee/spouses improved their job performance dramatically. As a by-product, 54% of the alcoholics stopped drinking and are recovering (9). In another study (10), a doctor worked with 32 wives of alcoholic men, and had no contact with their spouses during the project. One-half of the husbands gave up drinking and began the recovery process, and all the wives reported an improvement in the quality of their lives.

In working with alcohol and other drug dependency syndromes, it is important to identify complicating factors sometimes involved in family situations. There are spouses who need dependent partners to gratify their own misdirected needs; this may be true of parents and siblings as well. Masochism is defined as any enjoyment derived from being dominated or made to suffer. Some spouses or parents of drug abusers depend on this means of suffering to satisfy their own emotional needs. Some persons are sadistic and must have someone to punish, and a drug abuser serves the purpose well. There are other individuals who need to dominate and control. If any of these conditions exist, the non-user may have a more serious illness. It may have to be treated and arrested before it is possible for this family member to do anything other than contribute to the progression of the drug dependency.

After the family members have gained strength, they are ready to assess the appropriateness of staging a formal intervention. One intervention plan gained nationwide attention in an article describing the successful method used at Johnston Institute to interrupt the family progression and motivate the alcoholic into treatment (11).

The intervention team itself is described as two or more persons who are concerned and affected by the chemical abuser, such as parents, in-laws, esteemed friends, co-workers, and employers. Children need not be excluded as they are usually well aware of the problems, and their understanding of the illness can actually strengthen the relationship between them and the victim. In some treatment centers and agencies, an intervention counselor will assist the team members in preparation, and if appropriate, will join them in facilitating the encounter.

The procedure as defined by the Johnston model begins by each intervener listing the particulars about the abuser's behavior. Reading from a list sustains objectivity and curbs destructive emotion. Scheduling preparation sessions with a counselor also allows the family to vent feelings of anger and resentment. The lists are verbally presented by all interveners at a time when the abuser is completely sober, aware of the event, and conscious of the concern of those confronting him or her. This process is followed by outlining the proposal for family treatment and recovery. It is imperative that the intervention team be prepared to offer significant consequences if the chemically dependent person refuses to respond to the proposed treatment plan. Eighty percent of substance abusers who are exposed to this intervention strategy enter treatment, according to Johnston Institute statistics (11). If it fails, the approach can be used again. It is important to never stop presenting reality to the addicted person.

FAMILY TREATMENT

Phase I

Treatment of a family with a substance-abusing member is a complicated process, with therapy occurring simultaneously on many levels. In addition to responding to the needs of the family, treatment must also address the needs of each individual member.

Although Allied Health Professionals may not meet the family until the chemical abuser enters a treatment program, a complete family assessment should be done as soon as possible, to ensure that too much time in treatment is not spent in continual denial or minimizing by any family members, and to ascertain the symptom experiences not only of the abuser, but of the family as well. Any Allied Health Professional should be aware that in some cases the abuser enters treatment with little knowledge or encouragement from family members; it may be the family that rationalizes and resists therapeutic interventions. Early involvement of family members enables the family unit to focus away from the addict and direct some energy to evaluate dysfunctional behaviors they may have been using.

The first phase of family treatment, dealing with the stages of denial, isolation, and disorganization (see Figure 2) lays a solid foundation of education to replace the lack of knowledge and understanding of the progressive symptoms affecting family members. Families begin the treatment program at varying levels of awareness, depending on their previous experiences and involvements. The treatment staff needs to respond by developing an individualized care plan for each family. Even though some families may have had education and counseling during an intervention period, deepening their awareness of chemical dependency and healthier responses to stressors can be helpful.

During this early phase of treatment most programs offer treatment groups made up of family members. In addition to receiving information about the medical aspects of the disease, participants may increase their understanding of the family illness progression. The intrusive role of drug abuse should not be ignored, but put into perspective with other behaviors. Individual responses or roles that reinforce family problems should be described and explored. At this point it is advisable to work from a non-blaming stance. Confrontive techniques effective in group therapy with the abuser generally do not work with families, and tend to foster resistance and counterattack.

FAMILY TREATMENT OF CHEMICAL DEPENDENCY

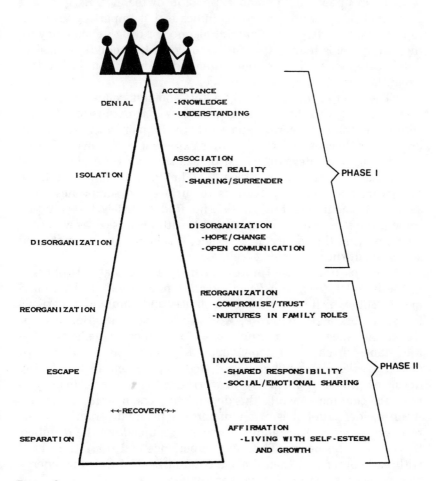

Figure 2

When the addict is admitted as a patient most treatment facilities will expect family members to participate in a family program. Topics for group education during this phase of treatment may include Illness of Chemical Dependency, Progressive Effects on the Family, Roles and Recovery, Self-Help, and Self-Care. Specialized group sessions are sometimes available for the families' children between the ages of six and twelve. The children's counselor focuses on the same instructional topics defined for the adults, using games, art forms, and peer interaction to assist in understanding and expression of feelings. Early results from such new family programs indicate that imparting information about the effects of parental alcohol or drug dependency on the family helps reduce the burden of guilt that children of alcoholics often carry. It also helps them adapt to change in lifestyle when the parent achieves abstinence.

The group process for both adults and children is an effective way of structuring an environment where it is permissible to talk about the "family secret" and to share the pain with others who understand because of their similar experiences. A sense of community begins to develop which breaks through the isolation and suppression described in Stage 2. The insight gained in these groups may allow many feelings to surface and sometimes erupt among its members. For those who find themselves facilitating these groups, as well as those Allied Health Professionals who may be supporting the family at this time, it is helpful to be aware and accepting of these emerging feelings.

Perhaps one of the more worthwhile guides at this phase is in the booklet, *Grief — A Basic Reaction to Alcoholism*, by Kellerman (12) in which he describes the abuser and family as experiencing great loss and, therefore, working through the grief process. Kellerman suggests that the same four steps precede the full acceptance of chemical dependency as precede the acceptance of death: denial, bargaining, anger, and depression. If the family does not get an opportunity to work through these feelings, particularly the anger, while the dependent person is in treatment, when it does erupt it is often inappropriate and destructive to the recovery process. The family treatment group allows the members to vent and be heard. They can experience and share their grief with each other and then make a commitment of time and energy to a recovery program or treatment experience.

Further emergence from isolation occurs through involvement in self-help groups (see Chapter 14) which are available throughout the country, some having affiliates around the world. Many treatment programs expect ongoing participation in a community group such as Alanon Family Groups, Alateen, and Naranon which has been organized as a companion family program for Narcotics Anonymous. A similar group, Families Anonymous, focuses on the parents of young people who are having problems, including drug dependency. All the family groups have an operational philosophy based on the Twelve Steps adapted from AA.

Basic to participating meaningfully in the groups is the acceptance of the disease concept, and a focus on developing a caring detachment from the dependent person. The reestablishment of self-esteem and reliance on a "Higher Power" is strongly incorporated in the steps. Self-care is also stressed. When family members are simultaneously involved in a self-help group with the dependent individual, there is a mutual goal of developing a lifestyle reflecting the Twelve Steps (see Chapter 14). The family is no longer alone and may more freely deal with the reality of the disease with understanding and supportive people. Fear begins to diminish as knowledge increases. Hope is rekindled as a return to mental stability is experienced.

As family members begin to experience change in themselves they discover that the old rules and reactions that had operated in the family prior to treatment no longer are effective, and a sense of disorganization as in Stage 3 is once again created. This disorganization can sometimes cause dismay for the recovering chemically dependent person, as well as those around him or her. Health care providers may have difficulty understanding why all things are not better since the alcohol or other drug use has ceased. However, in some family systems the pre-existing problems become more severe as they are no longer disguised by the drug. At such times open and skillful communication within the family is necessary to continue the growth and recovery. Although it is true that a small number of recovering people are able to develop or restructure a nurturing interaction pattern by themselves, for most some outside direction is necessary. Additional support and counseling diminishes the anxiety level and risk of relapse.

For people committed to a relationship or a family, a second phase of family treatment is appropriate. Maintaining the entire family unit in the recovery process is ideal and every effort should be made to do so. However, the reality of the disease is that often not all family members, including the abuser, are willing to accept treatment at the same time. The family may no longer be a viable unit. It is, therefore, important that assistance is available to whomever is seeking help. A knowledgeable counselor can help the family member, young or old, through the first phase and then support the development of communication skills and a strong sense of self-esteem and identity. Once again, this process is a step in intervention and prevention. Treatment for any family member can prevent the progressive effects that hinder his or her healthy growth and also affect the next generation.

A family's experiences with chemical dependency bring much pain and anger to the system, and a brief period in a treatment program does not immediately resolve years of anguish. For some adults, the hurt goes back to their family of origin where they themselves experienced a parental drinking or drug abuse problem. Statistics reveal that over 75% of the children raised in an alcoholic family will either themselves develop a chemical dependency problem or marry an abuser (13). At any stage it is very important that forgiveness take place within the family lest further recovery is hindered by continual resentment. The Twelve Steps of the self-help groups again offer guidance and support to allow this spiritual healing.

New and healthier family roles must be developed in a lifestyle free of chemical effects and chemical focus. Frequently families are not prepared for the shifts in equilibrium around dependence, dominance, support, and withdrawal. Periodically these shifts need to be reviewed and new sources of gratification discovered. The enrichment phase of the family treatment program moves to focus on reorganization, involvement, and affirmation. A family counselor or therapist also trained in chemical dependency is probably best qualified to assist the family to shift focus away from the identified patient and toward a review of mutual problems in living together. It is now suggested that the family as a unit, 1) overcome fears born of frequent past disappointment, 2) discuss problems not related to drinking or drug use, 3) develop trust, and 4) realize all are part of the problem and part of the solution.

There is no better way to understand the unique phenomena of role assignments or assumptions than to observe a system as it functions in therapy. Here a skilled therapist can evaluate 1) the varying levels of emotional strength in family members, 2) the psychological sensitivities in each member, 3) their intellectual capacity as well as physical stamina, 4) emotional chain reactions, 5) power exchanges, 6) communication patterns, 7) repetitive and predictable patterns, 8) functional behaviors which nurture development, and 9) dysfunctional patterns which retard growth.

The family therapist, then, becomes a student of the family's normative rules, affective and instrumental roles, verbal and non-verbal communication, and ways of dealing with pressures from within and outside the family. He or she provides feedback regarding the observed behavior, with a goal of improving techniques in problem–solving. The family can begin to reorganize with stronger commitments to roles and responsibilities, and the skills to resolve conflict.

Styles of family therapists differ greatly. The two main divisions are between those who are conductors (organizes, orchestrates, leads) and those who are reactors (less controlling, less structured). Clinical observations suggest that a more effective approach with dependent families is that of active conducting (14). This approach counterbalances the ambivalence, denial, and avoidance frequently present in dependent families. Setting definite specific goals early appears to have a more successful outcome. The "identified patient" effect is overcome more easily with the active approach.

Another suggestion for family counselors or therapists is the use of a time limit to maintain focus and motivation. It also helps identification of specific goals and forces a family to confront issues. Time limitation offers reassurances to those who fear that therapy will be interminable. It also encourages resistant members, by giving an expression of confidence that meaningful change really can occur during a short period of time, and breaks through the myth of mutual hopelessness which surrounds a long-standing drug-abuse problem.

Mutually satisfying social, emotional, and physical involvement with each other become the rewards experienced by a recovering family. This can be enhanced when multi-family therapy is appropriate. The isolation of a family is put into context with the interaction with other families who are attempting to meet the challenge of drug dependency syndromes and recovery. Multi-family therapy is a vehicle by which behavior change can occur, and basic coping skills can be developed through incidental learning and role modeling. Competition and group interaction can often speed up the change process, as families mutually enrich each other. Learning to express love or anger directly for the first time and be accepted happens in this extended family environment. Emotional isolation is replaced by mutual exchange of physical affection. The joy of a healthy, functioning family becomes a realistic expectation and experience.

According to a survey by Steinglass (15), no single technique has gained a dominant position or documented superior credentials regarding treatment of families experiencing an alcohol or other drug problem. In summary, the possibilities for a family program include, 1) pure family therapy, based on family systems' theoretical formulation of drug dependency, 2) group or individual approaches designed specifically to fulfill the criteria suggested by a family theory of drug dependency, 3) techniques involving concurrent work with other family members in addition to the identified patient, using a more traditional, individually oriented, psychodynamic base, 4) specialized techniques developed for working with spouses of drug dependents, and 5) supportive approaches geared to assist parents, spouses, and children of a dependent family member in dealing with common difficulties they face.

An individualized program which respects the uniqueness of each person and each family system, as well as their progression in the illness, is most effective. No matter which approach is used, however, the final stage of affirmation is a lifetime goal of all families, and certainly within reach of those recovering from alcohol and other drug dependency. Recovery is a process whereby all family members are nurturing each other in self-esteem and growth. Also, as their own family life is enriched, they reach out to share with others in the wider community. It is important that all Allied Health Professionals understand and support this complex long-term recovery process because often, misdirection and inappropriate focal points account for meager returns on large investments in the area of rehabilitation. The family and its resources represent a potential foundation from which the significant problems related to alcohol and other drug abuse can not only be defined but also resolved. The family still remains the pulse of life. Ignoring this fact is a form of societal regression. The family is a most potent rehabilitation force. The challenge now is to actualize its potential to the fullest.

SUMMARY

Alcoholism and drug abuse have detrimental effects on not only addicted persons but also on those who are significantly involved in their lives. Identified in this chapter are patterns followed by family, friends, and significant others, which run parallel to the progressive symptoms of chemical dependency. The recognition by health professionals of these patterns — denial, isolation, disorganization, reorganization, escape, separation, and recovery — can be helpful in procuring or providing appropriate assistance to individuals and be possible for caring persons to motivate the abuser into treatment through formal intervention methods discussed in this chapter.

Once the abuser has begun treatment, it is necessary to include the family and/or other significant persons in some form of treatment to insure the recovery of the family system. A number of techniques are explored including education, supportive counseling, and family therapy. As the family is a most potent force in intervention or rehabilitation it is an essential element in effective treatment for chemical dependency.

REFERENCES

1. Novak, J.: The family out of favor. *Harpers, 252:*37, 1976.

2. Tucker, J.B.: Keynote address, *The Governor's Conference on Children and Family,* Final Report, Wisconsin Department of Health and Social Services, p. 1, 1980.

3. Catanzaro, R.: *Alcoholism - The Total Treatment Approach,* Springfield, Illinois: Charles Thomas, 1968.

4. Jackson, J.: *The Adjustment of the Family to the Crisis of Alcoholism,* New Brunswick, New Jersey: Rutgers Center of Alcohol Studies, 1954.

5. Cork, R.M.: *The Forgotten Children,* Toronto, Ontario, Canada: General Publishing, Co., 1964.

6. Alanon. *Alcoholism - The Family Disease.* New York, New York: Alanon Family Group Headquarters, Inc., p. 10, 1972.

7. Steinglass, P.: A life history model of the alcoholic family. *Family Process, 19:*211-226, 1980.

8. Wegschieder, S.: *The Family Trap.* Minneapolis, Minnesota: Nurturing Networks, 1976, p. 7.

9. Mansell, M.: *Impact of Alcoholism on the Family.* New York, New York: National Council on Alcoholism, 1979.

10. Ewing, J.; Long, V., and Wenzel, G.: Concurrent group psychotherapy of alcoholic patients and their wives. *International Journal of Psychotherapy, 11:*329, 1961.

11. Hubbell, J.: A dynamic new approach to the alcoholic. *Reader's Digest, 108:*173-177, 1976.

12. Kellerman, J.: *Grief - A Basic Reaction to Alcoholism.* Center City, Minnesota: Hazelden, 1977.

13. Sauer, J.: *The Neglected Majority.* Milwaukee, Wisconsin: De Paul Rehabilitation Hospital, 1976.

14. Meeks, D.: Family therapy. In: *Alcoholism - Interdisciplinary Approaches to an Enduring Problem,* Tarter, E. and Sugarman, A. (Eds.). Reading, Massachusetts: Addison Wesley Publishing Co., 1976, pp. 835-852.

15. Steinglass, P.: Family therapy with alcoholics. In: *Family Therapy of Drug and Alcohol Abuse,* Kaufman, E. and Kaufman, P. (Eds.). New York, New York: Gardner Press, 1979, pp. 147-186.

Chapter 14

Self-Help Groups

Donald Busboom, B.A., M.Div.

OVERVIEW

In his chapter on self-help groups, Rev. Busboom focuses his attention primarily on Alcoholics Anonymous (AA), which celebrated its fiftieth anniversary in 1985. He provides a brief history of this paradigmatic group, and then provides specific information which will be extremely useful for the uninitiated: How to make a referral, the services provided, how meetings are conducted, and how the movement has burgeoned to become national and international in scope. Of special interest to Allied Health Professionals who are not themselves members of the AA Fellowship, the author provides explanatory comments on each of the Twelve Steps* that form the basis for individual recovery, and the corresponding Twelve Traditions* that govern the AA movement.

To conclude the chapter the author briefly discusses some derivative self-help groups: Alanon and Alateen for the families of alcoholics, Narcotics Anonymous for persons abusing drugs other than alcohol, and Overeaters Anonymous for persons with eating disorders.

A summary and references appear at the end of the chapter.

INTRODUCTION AND HISTORIC BACKGROUND

Most Allied Health Professionals have heard of Alcoholics Anonymous (AA); many have heard about Alanon, some have heard also of Alateen, and a few, no doubt, have heard of Narcotics Anonymous (NA). However, not many understand how

---

*The author's explanations and interpretations of the Twelve Steps and Twelve Traditions are solely his responsibility and should not be construed as necessarily representative of the philosophy of A.A.

these groups function, how to go about making referrals to them, or how these groups can be of help.

This lack of understanding is very unfortunate because these self–help groups are effective resources available to people suffering from addiction to alcohol and/or other drugs. They are also valuable resources for the families of addicted persons. For these reasons, this chapter provides information and interpretations of these groups for the Allied Health Professional, and makes suggestions regarding referrals.

Because it was one of the first major self–help groups in the U.S., and has subsequently been used as a model for the development of other similar groups, some information about the formation of AA may be useful. The fellowship of AA arose out of one man's desperate and seemingly futile desire to stay sober. Referred to as Bill W. by AA, Bill Wilson was a stockbroker from New York. He discovered liquor during World War I and fought what appeared to be a losing battle against it for some 20 years. In and out of treatment hospitals several times, it seemed Bill could not stay sober. His physician, Dr. William Silkworth, a specialist in treating alcoholics, wrote of Bill, "In late 1934 I attended a patient who, though he had been a competent businessman of good earning capacity, as an alcoholic of a type I had come to regard as hopeless" (1, p. xxxiii).

However, something happened to Bill, as a result of the intervention of a friend, Ebby, who, much like Bill, had also been unable to maintain sobriety. When Ebby came to him (two months sober!), Bill was impressed. Of that moment, Bill wrote, "I was shocked, but interested. Certainly I was interested. I had to be, for I was hopeless" (1, p. 10). Bill was convinced by his friend to give up fighting, to stop trying to do it by himself, and to surrender to help from outside himself. Soon after this encounter, Bill entered treatment for the last time. That was in November 1934; he never had another drink in his life — he was not, however, without a close call!

In June 1935, Bill was in Akron, Ohio on a business trip. While in a hotel lobby, he was gripped with the urge to drink. One of the principles of maintaining sobriety he had learned from his friend Ebby, was to help other alcoholics. In desperation, then, Bill sought out an alcoholic that he might help. As he talked to Dr. Bob, an Akron surgeon and a hopeless drunk, the first AA group was born, and with it, the fellowship of Alcoholics Anonymous. Dr. Bob soon became sober, never to drink again. A second

AA group was soon founded in New York City, and then another in Cleveland. The fellowship grew so that today there is scarcely a community in the United States or country in the world where AA is not present.

PURPOSE AND FUNCTION OF ALCOHOLICS ANONYMOUS: A NATIONAL MODEL

Allied Health Professionals not familiar with AA and its associated and derivative groups may derive some understanding from its Preamble.

> "Alcoholics Anonymous is a fellowship of men and women who share their experience, strength and hope with each other, that they may solve their common problem and help others to recover from alcoholism. The only requirement for membership is a desire to stop drinking. There are no dues or fees for AA membership; we are self-supporting through our own contribution. AA is not allied with any sect, denomination, politics, organization, or institution; does not wish to engage in any controversy; neither endorses nor opposes any causes. Our primary purpose is to stay sober and help other alcoholics to achieve sobriety" (2, p. 1). (Reprinted by permission of the *A.A. Grapevine.*)

It is for these reasons stated in the preamble that the health professional can find real friends in AA. Both share a common purpose: to help people. As stated, the only requirement for membership in AA, and thus for a referral to AA, is a desire to stop drinking. AA is open to anyone and everyone. It presents no barrier to any creed, color, or sex; there are no imposed costs for membership. AA does not ally with viewpoints, nor affiliate with organizations external to itself. It has no ambition to interfere with the health professional's goal of helping the alcoholic achieve sobriety (3). Since its purpose is to help other alcoholics, AA is a friend to Allied Health Professionals and is willing to cooperate with you (4). For the AA member it is a matter of self-preservation: "Practical experience shows that nothing will so much insure immunity from drinking as intensive work with other alcoholics. It works when other activities fail" (1, p. 89).

The Referral Process

Thus, AA is an excellent referral resource for alcoholics. But how does one go about making referrals? Alcoholics Anonymous is listed in virtually every telephone book in sizeable communities, and in many small, isolated communities, allowing one to make initial contact with AA in the community via the telephone. In most urban areas AA has established an "intergroup" or "central" office. Consequently, a telephone contact may either be with an individual AA member willing to cooperate, or with the office which cooperates by making the referral for you or providing suggestions about making more-specific contact (5). A special service often provided by the central AA office is a local AA directory which lists places, times, and meeting type by day of the week.

In the event that AA is not listed in your telephone directory, then a letter to the General Service Office, P.O. Box 459, Grand Central Station, New York, NY 10163, should bring assistance. The General Service Office Board has a special Committee on Cooperation with the Professional Community, whose goal is to provide Allied Health Professionals the best AA cooperation possible (6).

Some professionals encourage continuing contact with former patients staying sober in AA, and also develop a phone list of these persons (3), thus formulating their own referral system. This system has the double effect of supporting both present and former patients by involving them in helping "other alcoholics to achieve sobriety" (1, p. 1). Further AA contacts can often be obtained by contacting other professionals, doctors, lawyers, clergy, judges, nurses, or police. These persons frequently have knowledge of specific AA meeting dates, times, and locations (7).

Other Services Provided

What are the specific services your local AA office might offer in your work with patients? The pamphlet, *AA in Treatment Centers* (8), is a helpful resource. Local customs and policies may vary. However, in large measure, specific services depend on the resourcefulness of those involved. Some AA groups will supply health professionals with some basic AA literature packets or pamphlets, or subscriptions to *Grapevine* (the AA fellowship international journal). There is also available a hospital package of AA literature, obtained from the General Service Office, with specifically selected pamphlets relevant to patients in treatment (9). These may be furnished by the health professional as part of the basic literature package.

Another specific service often found helpful is having individual AA members come into the hospital, clinic, or office at appropriate times to perform a variety of functions. For example, AA members may meet individual patients on a one-to-one basis to offer support and encouragement. It is frequently helpful for a patient to talk with someone who is actually succeeding in a chemically-free lifestyle on the outside. The AA member may even serve as a temporary sponsor to the patient. Through the AA member, it may be possible to provide supportive community contacts, such as Alanon and/or Alateen, for the patient's family members. AA members may provide a lecture or series of lectures for patients focused on orientation to the AA program.

AA members are frequently willing to assist with arranging or providing transportation for patients. Many treatment staff persons find the practice useful as it gives a patient a personal introduction to AA outside the health care facility. The usefulness of this practice is often heightened if the AA meeting is easily accessible to the hospitalized patient for continued attendance after discharge. The ultimate choice of continued attendance is, of course, the patient's.

AA Meetings

What goes on at an AA meeting? In the first place, there are two basic types of meetings: closed and open (10). An open meeting, at which everyone is welcome, frequently has a speaker, or a panel. Who and what is decided by the host AA group or squad, but the topic focuses on the disease of alcoholism and recovery by the AA Twelve Step Program (discussed below). Because this type of occasional or periodic meeting (frequently monthly) is open to the public, it offers an opportunity to family and friends for education concerning alcoholism and recovery in AA. Also, many an individual, curious about his or her own drinking, began their own self-diagnostic process by first attending an open meeting and hearing a speaker tell his or her own story, which provides a non-threatening opportunity for such a curious person to identify with another's story without fear of judgment.

Closed meetings are more common. Quite simply this type is open to anyone who has a *desire* to stop drinking, and closed to all other people. Usually members share their personal experience with each other. Very often, the Twelve Steps provide the structure for the meeting. The group may decide to focus on a particular step, or a combination. The members may then relate the ways in which these have been of help and strength to them in their recovery. Groups may also choose to focus on the Twelve Traditions, a portion of the "Big Book," *Alcoholics Anonymous* (1), or on the "12 x 12," *Twelve Steps and Twelve Traditions* (11). They may choose to use a *Grapevine* article as a topic for the meeting. An individual member may choose a personal topic such as humility, anonymity, intolerance, how to handle holiday parties, continuing compulsion to drink, or others. Each AA group is autonomous and therefore determines its format democratically within its own membership.

Each AA group also determines its own leadership style. A group may elect certain members to serve in a variety of capacities, such as chairpersons, secretary, treasurer, publicity, literature, general service representative (GSR), and others of the group's own choosing. The GSR represents the local group at regional meetings. These leaders do not govern, but are rather called "trusted servants" (1, p. 564) who perform tasks on behalf of the group as assigned by the group. Officers are most usually changed regularly, e.g., semi-annually or annually.

AA Organization

Because there are tasks to be done on a larger level as well (10), AA is loosely organized nationally, and beyond, since it does perform services internationally. Some of the important services performed concern the preparing, printing, and distributing of official AA literature. The organization, called the General Service Office (GSO), handles questions from existing groups, aspiring groups, institutions (such as treatment centers, prisons, and industries), and helping professionals. AA has policies concerning public relations and the GSO assists in administering and interpreting these policies.

AA has entrusted the management of these functions of GSO to a custodial board, called the General Service Board of Alcoholics Anonymous. It has three specific functions or responsibilities: It provides oversight to the GSO, it is the respository of the Twelve Traditions (the suggested principles for relationships both within the Fellowship of AA and between the Fellowship and the larger community — public relations), and it is concerned with overall service provided by AA at all levels, i.e., from the local group to GSO. Twenty-one persons serve as trustees on this Board.

The AA General Service Conference is the connection between the Board and the local AA groups of both the United States and Canada. The Conference is made up of the 21 trustees of the Board, the GSO staff members, and 90 delegates from AA areas. The delegates are elected from the GSRs chosen by the local groups. This Conference has no authority to regulate or govern, but rather provides a consultative service only (10).

The Twelve Steps

The Fellowship of Alcoholics Anonymous has a list of official literature, which can be obtained from the New York office. The most basic text is called *Alcoholics Anonymous* (1), affectionately named by AA members as the "Big Book" or the "AA Bible." This helpful volume provides an introduction to AA via a brief history of its birth and development. It provides many recovery stories in which readers may see themselves, and thus further break down the denial that sometimes accompanies the disease of alcoholism. It includes special information for persons having particular problems: It has a chapter for wives, for the family, and another for employees. It has opinions on the AA recovery program by physicians and clergy.

By far the most popular and well-known portion of the Big Book, at least to many alcoholics, is Chapter 5, "How It Works." This chapter is closely followed in familiarity among AA members by both Chapters 6 and 7, "Into Action," and "Working With Others." These three chapters expound on the Twelve Steps which constitute the heart of the AA recovery program. Many alcoholism treatment facilities and therapeutic approaches choose the Twelve Steps as a basic guideline for directing and evaluating treatment and progress in recovery. This selection has at least a two-fold rationale. In the first place, it seems to have the value of time-tested experience. When in the past it seemed that nothing else worked to help the alcoholic recover, the Twelve Steps did work. This is the shared experience of thousands of recovering alcoholics.

Secondly, and equally important, many health professionals reason that if the Twelve Steps of AA serve as part of aftercare or follow-up recommendations, then it is a good and efficient use of time to provide introduction to these steps in a personal way. That it serves the sake of continuity is clear. It effectively removes an obstacle (unfamiliarity with the Twelve Steps) for a patient attending a first AA meeting (see Appendix 9).

In commenting about the Twelve Steps, one preliminary point must be made, and, perhaps, cannot be over-emphasized: "AA is not allied with any sect, denomination . . ." (2, p. 1). Strictly speaking, AA is a spiritual program, in the sense that every human being is a spiritual being, has morals and/or values that influence choices, decisions, relationships, perception of reality, and behavior. These values are shaped by beliefs held by the individual and vice versa. AA is not interested in prescribing or modifying values or beliefs, but instead is interested in suggesting how an alcoholic may use his or her existing values and beliefs to make recovery from alcoholism possible. Thus, Alcoholics Anonymous offers twelve suggestions (Twelve Steps) that can aid in making an alcoholic's values and beliefs effective in his or her own recovery when in the past these have been counter-productive to recovery. The AA Big Book has a helpful section titled "Spiritual Experience," which elaborates more on the specific nature of spiritual recovery (1, pp. 569-570).

Step One has a critical dynamic in the word "admitted," specifically related to two areas: Irretrievable loss of control over alcohol, and behavior which is unmanageable (i.e., behavior inconsistent with rational faculties, beliefs, or values, occurring specifically under the influence of, or preoccupation with, alcohol). Step One needs to be the primary focus in the beginning because it begins to soften and, ultimately, dispatch the denial which sometimes accompanies alcoholism.

Some alcoholism treatment facilities have a special treatment component called, specifically, "Step One Group." Patients are assigned to this group relatively early in their treatment. This process provides an opportunity to focus intensely in a personal way on powerlessness and unmanageability. Frequently a staff person has the responsibility of facilitating this experience.

Once a patient appears to give authentic acceptance to his or her "powerlessness over alcohol" and a life that has become "unmanageable," i.e., has personalized Step One, then he or she is ready to move on. A one-word summary of Step One is *honesty*. The need for help having been established, the patient is prepared to begin receiving help.

Step Two is the process of becoming open-minded and giving consideration to the help that is available. For our purposes, the most immediate help available is present right within the therapeutic setting. One way of paraphrasing Step Two is: I came to believe that there is help available to help me do what I cannot do for myself. Many patients, perhaps most, have little trouble admitting the treatment facility or health professional into that category. But few patients appear to make Step Two personal by relating it to their presence in treatment without some direction by staff, or by AA guidance. Without this assistance, Step Two remains for them a mysterious and abstract concept. This process has a spiritual dimension to it because it guides the patient to view relationships in a new way. The patient begins to see that it is not disgraceful to be dependent for help from others; rather it may be a mark of strength, especially if it comes from a new-found honesty. In Step Two, the patient begins becoming open-minded concerning the specific help available. A short summary word for Step Two can be *openness*.

Being willing to consider help is one thing; making a commitment to it is another. Step Three involves the matter of, "Made a decision . . ." This step also introduces a new concept, *God*. It is important to emphasize once again the statement of the AA Preamble, that AA is not allied with any sect or denomination. Step Three is not a religious function. Its focus is not on the intellectual, theological conceptualization of God; that is best left to those whose business it is. The focus is strictly spiritual. It is simply confined to surrendering that which is powerless and unmanageable; the will is powerless over alcohol, and the life is unmanageable. Therefore, these are surrendered, turned over as the patient conceptualizes this.

There is also another spiritual concept introduced in this step, related to the God-concept, but lifted apart: the word *care*. The patient is introduced to the idea of being cared for, of being taken care of. This concept cannot be taken for granted. Patients whose lifestyle has been characterized by the denial of the need for help continue to have struggles with allowing themselves to be taken care of. Frequently, this need is outside their trust level, and therefore requires patient but special attention. Also, the low self-image usually characteristic of the patient tends to prompt him or her to reject care. They perceive it as inconsistent with their self-image, since they do not see themselves as worthy of care. These feelings seem to persist even after patients give verbal assent to Step Three. Consequently, it is important to be aware that patients actually may be verbally complying but interiorly denying.

Step Three can be summarized as *willingness*. Thus, the first steps can each be summarized with a word, which spells out in a simple manner *how* the AA program works: *honesty, openness, willingness*. However, notice, for example, that the first three steps are but personal preparation for taking some action steps.

Step Four states: "Made a searching and fearless moral inventory of ourselves." Now that the effort is being made to set aside the denial sometimes characteristic of alcoholism, there is a growing open-mindedness, and a decision has been made to change, it is appropriate to recovery to begin examining more closely and honestly precisely what it is that has been denied for so long. Step Four suggests a self-inventory of behavior, especially related to drinking. Actually the patient may be encouraged to inventory whatever may be detrimental to recovery: Behavior which happened both long before the loss of control over alcohol took place, and during the alcoholism.

Many treatment facilities provide a Step Four orientation group for patients, which provides the opportunity to give more specific instructions concerning the mechanics. Another helpful aid is a Fourth Step guide. There are various guides available. The local central AA offices frequently have these available as part of their literature supply.

The Fifth Step, "Admitted to God, to ourselves, and to another human being the exact nature of our wrongs," suggests taking further spiritual action in regard to the inventory. It is important to distinguish this step from confession as it is understood by various religious denominations. Step Five is strictly an AA function, even though on the surface the mechanics may appear similar to confession. The primary concern of Step Five is to verbally relate the inventory of Step Four to drinking behavior, i.e., actual drinking, blackouts, hangovers, or preoccupation with drinking. People are then able to see more clearly the relationship between much of their behavior and their disease.

Many people in AA talk about the Fifth Step as an opportunity "to dump personal garbage," or to get things off one's chest. In addition to this relief effect, there is the happy fringe benefit of gaining a fuller realization of the destructive power and control the disease of alcoholism exercised over their lives and the lives of their loved ones. This realization is the "exact nature" of the inventory. Admitting verbally in the presence of another human being excludes the self-delusion which is sometimes a persistent characteristic of alcoholism. Alcoholic people come face-to-face with the reality of their disease, especially since this admitting is being done against the standard of their own personal moral code or value system, and, thus, many people fully realize for the first time how awesomely destructive this disease has been to their life.

During therapy, personal issues surface that relate to such things as fear, resentment, self-pity, intolerance, shame, and guilt. Good care includes providing patients the opportunity to process these issues spiritually via Steps Four and Five prior to discharge. It is another aid to recovery and may well reduce the possibility of relapse. It is the opinion of many practitioners in the field of alcoholism that a smaller ratio of patients relapse who have taken a Fifth Step than those who did not.

Who should hear the Fifth Step? Someone who understands alcoholism and who has good insight into such things as resentment, fear, guilt, and shame. This person can, perhaps, more fully understand the patient. It is also helpful, but not necessary, if it be someone who has some prior understandings of the particular person in his or her unique world situation. A clergy person is trained to listen to the type of material presented in the Fifth Step. Many have received special training by alcoholism treatment centers to do this type of work with clinical understanding. If they are also on the treatment staff, then the added dimension of teamwork is present and people benefit. Some treatment staff utilize community clergy to hear Fifth Steps, and often pay them a consultant fee for doing so.

One final comment about the Fifth Step needs to be made, regarding confidentiality. It is extremely important that the Fifth Step material revealed in private be treated with the strictest confidentiality. It is helpful to inform the patients of that fact, for example, during the orientation session for Step Four. That is also a good time to say some preliminary things about the Fifth Step. Many treatment modalities based on the Twelve Step model encourage patients to continue this program in conjunction with community AA. However, the health professional may occasionally find it helpful for a person to suggest doing a Step out of the apparent sequence. For example, a person might be encouraged to do an early Fourth and Fifth Step as a way of removing a shame or guilt obstacle to successful treatment. A patient might be encouraged to make an amend if a broken relationship is detrimental to the treatment process.

A remark concerning the wisdom of the structure of the Twelve Steps seems in order. One characteristic of the alcoholic seems to be well-intentioned impulsiveness. The Twelve Steps appear to count on that because they take pains to take a more deliberate approach to the various actions called for. For example, Step Two seems to be a preparation, a thinking through preliminary to the decision-making suggested in Step Three. Step Four, likewise, is an obvious preparation for the action suggested in the next one. This sequence of preparation and action is repeated also in Steps Six, Seven, Eight, and Nine. This approach is very careful to lead the recovering alcoholic beyond grandiose impulsiveness by breaking actions down into realistic, accomplishable tasks.

In any event, this program continues with Steps Six and Seven. Step Six suggests a growing willingness to change: "Were entirely ready to have God remove these defects of character." Actually, this step strengthens the second pillar of the AA program, the pillar of humility, the first one being honesty. Humility is, among other things, teachability. Step Six expresses the desire and willingness to be taught a new way of life necessary for sobriety.

Step Seven is the spiritual action step which follows on the heels of willingness. Being open for growth and maturity is absolutely essential for a contented sobriety. Another characteristic often besetting some alcoholics is perfectionism. The alcoholic is reminded by the Big Book: "We claim spiritual progress rather than spiritual perfection" (1, p. 60). Steps Six and Seven ensure progress as it is given to the alcoholic, and are also part of the flow of the mainstream initiated by Step Four and continued by Step Five. The change is from the negative to the positive. The emphasis shifts from guilt and shame over indiscretion and failure, to growth and accomplishments, from low self-esteem to a growing sense of self-worth. The alcoholic is truly being restored at this point.

Steps Eight and Nine present a shift in focus. The spotlight has been primarily on the recovering alcoholic up to this point. Step Eight now suggests taking a look at the other people with whom the alcoholic has been in relationships. The alcoholic is asked to take an inventory of those relationships, and to make a list of the people who were hurt or harmed by the alcoholic's behavior. Again, this step is preparatory to Step Nine. These steps lead the alcoholic through some sensitive and painful actions leading to healing and reconciliation. Many relapses seem to be the result of the failure to do Steps Eight and Nine.

Step Nine suggests that the recovering alcoholic "made direct amends to such people wherever possible, except when to do so would injure them or others." This step assumes a growing sensitivity on the part of the recovering person, a sensitivity to the hurt done to others. It demonstrates a growing willingness to make amends to them. Step Nine assumes a growing sensitivity to the feelings of others so as to avoid provoking further unnecessary pain, and requires a decreasing self-centeredness. The recovering alcoholic is willing to forego making the amend out of consideration for others. In some instances, making the amend might cause more harm than not making it. There may be some behavior committed by the practicing alcoholic that others would be better off not knowing. In these cases, the alcoholic can be contented to have dealt honestly with them in Steps Four and Five, to desire and ask for change in Steps Six and Seven, and to be *willing* to complete Steps Eight and Nine were it not for the potential injury caused to others by making the amend.

Step Ten is a maintenance step: "Continued to take personal inventory and when we were wrong promptly admitted it." This step is clearly in the spirit of Steps Four and Five. While in treatment, the alcoholic may learn about triggering behaviors, those that might lead to a relapse or at least, contribute to one. Step Ten is a way of monitoring behavior on a regular basis. Thus, the alcoholic has a tool which may be used to check behavior lapses which often precede relapses in drinking. This statement is often true: "Stinking thinking leads to drinking thinking leads to thinking drinking leads to drinking." Step Ten is a way of intervening in that chain, and is also a helpful tool for perpetuating growth. So much of the alcoholic's drinking life was taken up with negative thinking. Step Ten is helpful discipline to keep the growth going in the positive direction. By doing an honest inventory regularly, the recovering alcoholic has a tool by which to see growth, and thus to be grateful for a new life.

A variety of daily moral inventory devices in the form of folded wallet cards are available at many central offices. A sample, created and used by one recovering alcoholic, is shown below.

Step Eleven, also a maintenance step, picks up on the theme of Steps Two and Three and reinforces and enriches the spiritual surrender. How this spirituality is accomplished is really to be determined by the individual recovering alcoholic; alcoholics can be encouraged to be creative and personal in their individual working of Step Eleven. There are many helps available that appeal to the variety of people found among the Fellowship. A list is included here, and these are usually available through the Central Office. *The Little Red Book* (12) provides an opportunity for meditation on one's personal program. It provides a discussion of the Twelve Steps and touches on subjects such as sponsorship.

TABLE 1

LIABILITIES					ASSETS				
Change from	NEVER	SELDOM	SOMETIMES	OFTEN	Growth toward	NEVER	SELDOM	SOMETIMES	OFTEN
Resentment					Forgiveness				
Perfectionism					Self–Acceptance				
Condemning Self					Valuing Self				
False Pride					Humility				
Denial					Honesty				
Self-Pity					Gratitude				
Impatience					Patience				
Intolerance					Acceptance				
Compulsiveness					Delayed Gratification				
Inconsiderateness					Kindness				
Controlling Fear, Worry					Faith, Trust				
Negative Thinking					Looking for the Good				
Vulgar, Immoral Thinking					Spiritual, Moral Thinking				

(*Editor's Note:* This sample of a "daily moral inventory" is the author's interpretation and should not be construed as necessarily representative of the philosophy of A.A.)

Also, some questions and subjects for meditation are indexed in the Appendix. *Stools and Bottles* (13) provides some meditative thoughts on the first four steps, some critical character defects, and "31 Daily Reminders," which can be correlated to the days of the month. Another helpful tool with a strong spiritual emphasis is called *Twenty-Four Hours A Day* (14). This one and the next two to be mentioned all have daily meditations for a full year. Many treatment staff members provide this book to patients as part of the basic literature package. Another book frequently chosen by staff for patients is *A Day at a Time* (15), which has a helpful subject index following the December 31 reading. This index is helpful for finding a reading appropriate to a particular problem an alcoholic may be experiencing in recovery, such as resentments. A final book to be listed, and an important one, is *Day by Day* (16), authored by The Young People's Group in Denver, Colorado, Consequently, the book is frequently the choice to provide to young alcoholics. It speaks quite directly to them. This book contains a table of contents which assists in locating an appropriate reading for a personal struggle in recovery.

The Twelfth Step assumes that the recovering alcoholic is working the first eleven steps and thus has had a spiritual experience. Consequently, the shift is from self to others, especially to other alcoholics. The most basic way to do Step Twelve is to regularly attend AA meetings, where the recovering alcoholic finds other alcoholics. No matter the style or format of a particular AA group, the core of the meeting is the same, i.e., "to carry this message to alcoholics." The primary purposes of the Fellowship of AA are "to stay sober and help other alcoholics to achieve sobriety" (2, p. 1), and at the AA meeting, both are achieved. Step Twelve also reaches out to those still suffering and not yet in AA. In talking with and helping another suffering alcoholic, the recovering alcoholic forgets self and grows in service and love. Sharing what one has been given is an act of gratitude.

A further note for health professionals is in order in this discussion of the Twelfth Step. Earlier in this chapter, the potential helping role of the recovering alcoholic in the health care system was discussed. Mention was made of visits by the AA member, lectures, in-house AA meetings, transportation to AA meetings, etc. These all may be understood in the scope of the Twelfth Step, "to carry the message" which includes sponsorship (9, p. 5), the mutual relationship between a newer recovering alcoholic and a more mature recovering alcoholic. This relationship is ordinarily initiated by the newer AA seeking someone with more sobriety and growth to be available in a helping relationship. Many treatment staff members discover it to be helpful to encourage people to obtain at least a temporary sponsor prior to termination.

Finally, Step Twelve places the entire life of the AA under the wings of the spiritual program of the Twelve Steps which include life at home, at work, and at play, and attitudes and behavior. The closing words of the Twelve Steps state, "to practice these principles in all of our affairs."

The Twelve Traditions

Mention has been made of the Twelve Traditions of AA. Essentially, as the Twelve Steps relate to the individual, so the Traditions relate to the AA Group by describing the public relations policy of AA (see Appendix 10).

FOR THE FAMILY

Alcoholism is said to be a family disease. It is a disease that includes an alcoholic, but is not limited to the alcoholic. Consequently, successful treatment requires a recovery program for the entire family. Just as the recovering alcoholic has a support program via the AA program and meetings, so family members benefit from similar support.

Alanon

The family members of the alcoholic frequently find a common bond in their experiences. By attenting Alanon meetings, family members discover they are not alone, and find strength and hope for their own personal recovery and growth (17). Like AA, Alanon also uses a Twelve Step program for personal recovery and Twelve Traditions for group unity. These steps and traditions are derived from the program of Alcoholics Anonymous. Some members have loved ones recovering in AA. However, other members have loved ones who are still drinking (18). Frequently, the family members are the first to seek help. Therefore, Alanon is often the first referral that is made. Family members begin to learn the nature of alcoholism, especially as it afflicts family members. Thus, their recovery commences while, perhaps, the alcoholic is still drinking.

The World Services Office is the central office for all Alanon groups in the world. More information can be obtained by contacting this office at P.O. Box 182, Madison Square Station, New York, NY 10010.

Alateen

The World Services Office also provides information on Alateen, an association for the children of alcoholics (18). Inquiries concerning appropriate ages for referral may be directed to local groups. Through Alateen, young people find they are not alone nor at fault. They gain healthy self-concepts. They detach emotionally from the alcohol problem and acquire healthy ways of dealing with reality (19).

As with AA, most communities have a central office for Alanon. This office is frequently listed under the name, "Alanon Family Group." This office usually orders appropriate Alanon literature, also Alateen literature. It usually publishes a directory of meetings for both Alanon and Alateen.

SELF-HELP GROUPS
FOR OTHER SUBSTANCE-USE DISORDERS

Many alcoholics who also abuse or have an addiction to mood-altering drugs other than alcohol (20) may be referred by the health professional to attend Narcotics Anonymous (NA) in addition to AA. Some patients have had no active addiction to alcohol; their addiction has been strictly to other chemicals. NA offers to them the same caring support that AA offers to the alcoholic; in fact, NA uses "a program borrowed from Alcoholics Anonymous" (21, p. 3). NA meetings are the same type as AA meetings, and follow similar formats chosen by the group.

When referring a non-institutionalized person to NA for help with drug addiction, the book *Narcotics Anonymous* (21, p. 6) offers some important guidance and encouragement. "If you are an addict, you too can find a new way of life through the NA program . . . . We have become very grateful in the course of our recovery. Our lives have become useful, through abstinence and by working the Twelve Steps of Narcotics Anonymous" (21, p. x). NA meetings are devoted to members helping each other stay free of drugs. This is accomplished by "identification, hope, and sharing" (21, p. 9). "All we need are two addicts, caring and sharing, to have a meeting" (21, p. 10). Compared to AA, NA is newer. However, in many communities it is experiencing steady growth and is helping many addicts to maintain happy, chemically-free lifestyles. NA was started in 1953 in California and has expanded to practically all of the states, and also to several foreign countries. NA welcomes all addicts no matter the chemical; they also welcome "food addicts."

Some AA groups are willing to offer support to all addicts regardless of the chemical, be it alcohol or otherwise. This needs to be checked out with each local group, and the decision of each group needs to be respected since each is an autonomous group governed by "group conscience" and thus, entitled to make its own decision.

Nar-Anon and Families Anonymous are non-addict friends or relatives of the addict. "Very often the non-addict friend or relative finds he has much more trouble with his emotions and thinking than the addict . . . . We also need some kind of recovery program for ourselves, a place where we can find the personal identification that leads to emotional sobriety. Nar-Anon and Families Anonymous are two such programs" (22, p. 1).

For more information about NA, contact: NA World Services Office, Inc., P.O. Box 622, Sun Valley, California 91352.

Another important self-help group is Overeaters Anonymous (OA). OA is a support group for persons who have a desire "to abstain from compulsive overeating" (23, front flap). The structure of OA is very similar to that of AA. The Twelve Steps of AA have been modified by OA so references to alcohol and alcoholics are replaced by food and compulsive overeaters. OA has published helpful pamphlets for the professional such as *Introducing OA to the Clergy* (24), and *OA As Seen by a Doctor: The Doctor Lindner Report About OA* (25).

SUMMARY

When persons who are harmfully abusing mood-altering chemicals or are experiencing compulsive overeating attend self-help group meetings, they hear the experiences of others who have dependencies. By the process of identification the new member may begin to see his or her own addiction. The new member also hears stories that give hope and a way toward making hope a reality. The hope is to maintain abstinence and the program of the group is the means by which it may be achieved and maintained.

Allied Health Professionals may avail themselves of the many self-help groups available in most communities. These groups, such as Alcoholics Anonymous, Alanon, Narcotics Anonymous, Nar-Anon, Alateen, Families Anonymous, and Overeaters Anonymous are usually listed in the phone directory of communities where such groups are present. These self-help groups are concerned about helping others achieve and maintain chemically-free lifestyles. To that end, they are most cooperative.

Frequently, other community professionals can be of assistance by putting the Allied Health Professional in contact with members of these groups who are successfully abstinent.

Central offices for many self-help groups exist in many communities. They can often be of service by providing a variety of aid, e.g., literature, speakers, and directories of local meetings.

REFERENCES

1.   Alcoholics Anonymous World Services, Inc.: *Alcoholics Anonymous*, Third Edition of the Big Book. New York: AA Publications.

2.   The International Monthly Journal of Alcoholics Anonymous: *AA Grapevine, Inc.*, New York: The Alcoholics Anonymous Grapevine, Inc., March, 1983.

3.   Alcoholics Anonymous World Services, Inc.: *AA In Treatment Centers.* New York: AA Publications, 1979.

4.   Alcoholics Anonymous World Services, Inc.: *How AA Members Cooperate.* New York: AA Publications, 1974.

5.   Alcoholics Anonymous World Services, Inc.: *Alcoholics Anonymous in Your Community.* New York: AA Publications, 1966.

6.   Alcoholics Anonymous World Services, Inc.: *If You Are a Professional AA Wants to Work With You.* New York: AA Publications, 1972.

7.   Alcoholics Anonymous World Services, Inc.: *This is AA.* New York: AA Publications, p. 19, 1953.

8.   Alcoholics Anonymous World Services, Inc.: *AA in Treatment Centers.* New York: AA Publications, 1979.

9.   Alcoholics Anonymous World Services, Inc.: *Questions and Answers on Sponsorship.* New York: AA Publications, p. 19, 1958.

10.   Alcoholics Anonymous World Services, Inc.: *44 Questions.* New York: AA Publications, p. 18, 1952.

11.   Alcoholics Anonymous World Services, Inc.: *Twelve Steps and Twelve Traditions.* New York: AA Publications, 1957.

12.   *The Little Red Book.* Center City, Minnesota: Coll-Webb Company, Hazelden Publications, 1957.

13.   *Stools and Bottles.* Center City, Minnesota: Coll-Webb Company, Hazelden Publications, 1980.

14.   *Twenty-Four Hours a Day.* Center City, Minnesota: Coll-Webb Company, Hazelden Publications, 1954.

15.   *A Day at a Time.* Minneapolis, Minnesota: Compcare Publications, 1976.

16.   *Day by Day.* Center City, Minnesota: The Young People's Group in Denver, Colorado, Hazelden Publications, 1974.

17.   *Alcoholism, The Family Disease.* New York: Alanon Family Group Headquarters, Inc., 1972.

18.   *Living With an Alcoholic.* New York: Alanon Family Group Headquarters, Inc., 1976.

19.   *Alateen — Hope for Children of Alcoholics.* New York: Alanon Family Headquarters, Inc., 1982.

20.   Alcoholics Anonymous World Services: *The AA Member and Drug Abuse.* New York: AA Publications, p. 7, 1964.

21.   NA World Service Office, Inc.: *Narcotics Anonymous.* Sun Valley, California: C.A.R.E.N.A. Publishing Company, 1982.

22.   NA World Service Office, Inc.: *Narcotics Anonymous - For Those We Love and Others.* Sun Valley, California: C.A.R.E.N.A. Publishing Company, 1976.

23.   Overeaters Anonymous, Inc.: *Overeaters Anonymous.* Torrance, California: World Service Office, 1980.

24.   Overeaters Anonymous, Inc.: *Introducing OA to the Clergy.* Torrance, California: World Service Office, (no date given).

25.   Overeaters Anonymous, Inc.: *OA As Seen by a Doctor: The Doctor Lindner Report about OA.* Torrance, California: World Service Office, 1974.

Chapter 15

Development of Community Alcohol and Drug Treatment Systems

Bela Maroti, B.A., M.B.A.

OVERVIEW

This chapter focuses on the actual and potential value of applying community-organization and community-systems approaches to the development of prevention, intervention, and treatment services for substance abusers and their families. The author first provides a brief historic summary of the confluence of events and circumstances occurring during the first thirty years of this century through the repeal of Prohibition. Then he highlights the growth of public and private efforts at constructing new perceptions of the nature and treatment of alcoholism which emerged during the subsequent three decades. The bulk of the chapter focuses on the reasons and means for eliciting the broadest range of commitment, support, and cooperation from all segments of the community. The role of public and private financial support is explained, and the need for expanded employee health benefits and realistic insurance coverage is emphatically conveyed. The importance of citizens' planning groups and the necessity for coordination of disparate efforts into a consolidated continuum is particularly emphasized. A brief summary concludes this chapter.

INTRODUCTION AND HISTORIC BACKGROUND

Because alcoholism and other drug abuse is an enormous and still growing health problem affecting all segments of society, a wide array of services is required to deal with it effectively. The development of a community-based comprehensive treatment system is a complex process which is not possible without the support and involvement of the public and its leadership. Before examining the community organization process, and the planning and development of a community-based treatment system, a brief historical review and perspective of society's response to the problem of alcoholism may be useful.

Our society has responded differently at different times to the problems of alcoholism. From the first decade of this century until the 1930s, the perspective of alcoholism was moralistic, condemning the alcoholic as a weak and deviant individual. There was a growing sentiment among many people to condemn alcohol itself as an evil substance. This attitude culminated in the temperance movement which, for a number of years, affected our policies toward drinking. As a result, in part, of the influence of this movement, the yoke of the 18th Amendment was imposed upon the citizens of this country. This attempt at prohibition was not only unrealistic and unpopular, it was also disastrous to many people. The drinking pattern of society was substantially changed from a socially and legally acceptable pattern to an illegal and covert activity. The problem drinker not only had an unlimited supply of alcohol but there was a permissive social structure and tacit approval for his or her excessive behavior. Prohibition was unsuccessful at curtailing alcohol consumption and excessive drinking. Indeed, because of illegal manufacture and sales, it led to increased criminal activity while society continued to condemn the alcoholic as a morally weak individual.

Even the repeal of prohibition did not change this situation immediately. The beginning of a real change in public attitude came with the appearance of Alcoholics Anonymous in 1934, and the establishment of the National Council on Alcoholism in 1938. The emergence of these groups initiated a large-scale movement toward the recognition of the disease concept of alcoholism. Ms. Marty Mann, the founder of the National Council on Alcoholism, established the first nationwide, voluntary movement to develop a better understanding, deeper concern, and more realistic response to the problems of alcoholism. The establishment of local affiliate alcoholism Councils and their education efforts, both on a national and community level, greatly enhanced the change in public attitude toward this problem. This movement resulted in programs of early intervention, referral, and more humane treatment of this disease throughout the United States.

An early organized attempt on the community level to provide treatment resources for the alcoholic occurred in the 1960s.
The primary focus was the most visible group of alcoholics, the
indigent and homeless men on the Skid Rows of our major cities.
These were isolated attempts without adequate financial support,
maintained primarily through charitable contributions and the
personal sacrifice of individuals, most of whom were members of
Alcoholics Anonymous.

During the 1970s there emerged a vigorous nationwide movement toward the development of more comprehensive and integrated community-based service delivery systems for alcoholics
and other drug abusers. A principal impetus for this development
arose out of the establishment of a National Institute on Alcohol
Abuse and Alcoholism (NIAAA) and a National Institute on Drug
Abuse (NIDA) within the U.S. Department of Health, Education
and Welfare. Since 1970, NIAAA has provided direct funding
assistance to more than 850 treatment programs. In spite of all of
these developments, however, it is believed that less than 10% of
alcoholics today receive treatment.

The Uniform Alcoholism and Intoxication Treatment Act of
1974 provided a national model for approaching alcoholism as a
health problem rather than a legal/judicial or moral problem. The
Act decriminalized public drunkenness and established State man-
dates to foster and plan for comprehensive programming for
alcoholism. Federal funding incentives through NIAAA encouraged States to develop this legislation. Two Federal Courts of
Appeal agreed that alcoholism is an illness or a disease and held
that a chronic alcoholic could not be held criminally responsible
for public intoxication (Easter v. District of Columbia, 361 F.2d
50 [D.C. Cir. 1966]; Driver v. Hinnant, 356 F.2d 761 [4th Cir.
1966]). The U.S. Supreme Court, in Powell v. Texas, 392 U.S.
514 (1968), refused to reverse a conviction for public intoxication
because the record failed to show that the defendant could not
avoid being intoxicated in public. In addition to extending federal
assistance for programs, amendments provided for grants to States
which adopted the Uniform Alcoholism and Intoxication Treatment Act, and for the establishment of the Alcohol, Drug Abuse,
and Mental Health Administration. The legislation was further
amended with the enactment of the Comprehensive Alcohol
Abuse and Alcoholism Prevention, Treatment, and Rehabilitation
Amendments of 1976.

In spite of the substantial increase in treatment resources on the local community level during the last ten years, a large portion of the alcoholic population still receives minimal and inadequate treatment. To a great extent, this problem is due to the reluctance of health insurance programs to provide adequate coverage for the earlier treatment of alcoholics. Some States, to correct this situation, require insurance companies to provide coverage for the inpatient and outpatient treatment of alcoholism through legislative mandate. A properly structured community treatment system, in order to provide adeuqate treatment to the alcoholic and his or her family, should be eligible for third party support from both the public and private sector such as private insurance as well as Medicare and Medicaid for the indigent.

DEVELOPING COMMUNITY SYSTEMS

To develop such a coordinated community treatment system, one has to understand the recovery process (see Chapter 8), and must be able to establish the major programs necessary for successful intervention and treatment. A community treatment system should include early identification and referral services; emergency care and detoxification (see Chapters 7 and 12); inpatient and outpatient treatment services (see Chapter 11); long-term care in half-way houses and residential or extended-care facilities; vocational rehabilitation; and aftercare and follow-up services. One has to enlist the cooperation of all existing specialized and general health and social service resources. A successful community treatment system also needs the full backing of Alcoholics Anonymous, Alanon, and other self-help groups (see Chapter 14), without whose help and cooperation no treatment system can be adequate.

Because alcoholism and other drug abuse affects all levels and areas of society, including the workplace, both labor and industry have a big stake in solving the problem. Their participation in the planning process, as well as the development of early identification programs at the workplace, are essential requirements for the successful development of a coordinated treatment system.

Another important aspect of a community treatment system involves the strong consensus among health-care professionals that alcoholism is a family disease, and that the recovery process must necessarily include the whole family (see Chapter 13). The Alcoholics Anonymous movement recognizes this view by urging the spouse of the recovering person to join Alanon, but this concern for the family still requires greater commitment to the family-oriented treatment approach on the part of the community representatitves, as well as the treatment personnel, in the development of a comprehensive community treatment system.

The health insurance industry also needs to give further recognition to several aspects of prevention, intervention, and treatment. The funding of a comprehensive community treatment system is a very complex issue due to several factors, such as the present failure of our health insurance system to provide adequate coverage for the treatment of alcoholism. Because a comprehensive system will have to carry out activities such as outreach, information and referral services, and prevention activities, which are not now covered by insurance, it cannot exist without additional community support, such as government and private charitable dollars. Due to the economic hardship of some alcoholics, and the lack of a reimbursement mechanism for prevention and referral services, there is a need to combine the efforts of the governmental and private sectors. On the other hand, the community response to alcoholism does not have to be totally tax-supported. The existing private health insurance system must accept its share of financial responsibility. A number of states have mandated coverage under some group health policies for the inpatient and outpatient treatment of alcohol and other drug abuse. There is a great deal more effort needed on the part of insurance companies and some employers to provide the necessary coverage for the treatment of alcohol and other drug abuse.

The development of a truly comprehensive treatment system is not possible without the involvement of the community. This involvement may be accomplished through a representative citizens' planning group. The basic role of such a group is initiating the planning and development of a full range of services to meet the needs of the alcohol- and other drug-abusing person as close to home as possible. Such a group need not incorporate, have a large budget, or hire permanent staff, since its role is usually temporary, and for planning purposes. Once the initial planning has been accomplished, the role of the group can be changed or expanded to become a permanent board to sponsor some of the services or to oversee the operation of the system.

One specific task of the community planning group is to document the extent of alcohol- and other drug-abuse problems in the community. Services needed to effectively deal with the problems must be identified, particularly those of special populations such as women, youth, minorities, and others. The roles and responsibilities of existing agencies must be analyzed, including their capacity, utilization pattern, and service areas. Gaps in the system must be identified, and short- and long-range action plans must be developed to implement a coordinated treatment system.

Mobilization of all of these community resources is not a simple task and no ideal pattern exists. Each planning-organization effort must fit the needs and circumstances of the local community. The establishment of goals and objectives, the assignment of priority to programs, and the provision of services must be accomplished in an atmosphere of cooperation, coordination, and understanding. Since the planning group should represent the total community, the majority of members should be citizens interested in alcohol and other drug abuse, and, for the purpose of providing technical expertise to the committee, professionals representing major prevention, intervention, and treatment resources must also be included. A citizen action committee should include representatives of business and government, Alcoholics Anonymous, medical and allied health professions, and other health and welfare agencies, including the local Health Departments, general hospitals, social service agencies, and vocational rehabilitation agencies.

The goal of the planning effort should be to develop continuity of services for the alcoholic and other drug abusers through the establishment of a complete range of functions necessary for the best possible outcomes. It is also important that the programs of comprehensive and coordinated services be geographically accessible to patients, and sufficiently flexible in their organization to permit adaptation to individual needs. A citizen action committee should encourage cooperation and coordination between various public and private organizations to provide continuity of care for the patients, and a movement between services as his or her needs dictate. And, finally, there should be an agreement on cooperative funding by the public and private sectors, including grants-in-aid, private insurance, and voluntary contributions such as United Way.

The most critical factor in a community treatment system is the issue of coordination. An integrated community effort will measurably affect the quality and quantity of activities dealing with alcohol and other drug abuse. Coordination of the system requires not only commitment on the part of all the participating agencies, but it also requires a coordinator with well-defined responsibilities and authority. This individual must be knowledge-able about alcohol and other drug abuse, must have experience in community organization, and possess leadership abilities in order to gain the respect and acceptance of the participating organiza-tions.

In the past, alcoholism and other drug abuse programs depended very heavily upon the leadership of highly motivated recovering persons because there was a lack of commitment and training in the allied health professions. However, today, there are increasing numbers of professionals trained in alcoholism and other drug abuse treatment, and community organizations pre-pared to provide the leadership necessary to manage and coordi-nate a community treatment system.

SUMMARY

There is a need for ongoing community and citizen support for activities to ameliorate any major health and social problems. The effective voluntary involvement at the local, state, and national level must be an outgrowth of grass-root level under-standing and an urgency to deal with those problems as they are presently occurring throughout the country in the area of alcohol and drug abuse. In the next decade, the development and coordi-nation of treatment and intervention programs will depend much more heavily on the local initiative than they have in the past and community-based citizen advocacy will be critical to its success.

The comprehensive treatment system approach to substance use disorders presented here is but one method by which a com-munity can respond to the needs of its chemically dependent citizens. It is an approach that has been successfully used by this author over a number of years in many areas of Wisconsin and elsewhere in the United States.

PART 3

SPECIAL PROBLEMS

Chapter 16

Alcoholism, Drug Abuse, and Other Psychiatric Disorders

Ashok Bedi, M.D.

OVERVIEW

Based on his own research and clinical experience the author has prepared a chapter documenting the appearance, diagnosis, and treatment of psychiatric disorders most likely to occur *in conjunction* with substance use disorders. Although no causal relationships have yet been firmly established, it has frequently been observed — and often ignored — that alcohol and drug problems usually do not occur in isolation: As many as one-half to two-thirds of all treated substance abuse patients do have one or more diagnosable and treatable psychiatric problems. If these problems are not recognized and treated, it is often likely that such patients will relapse into abusive drinking and/or other drug abuse.

It is with these ideas in mind that the author introduces his topics and then proceeds to his discussions of common concomitant psychiatric disorders. Grouping these psychiatric problems as Adjustment Disorders, Personality Disorders, Conduct Disorders, Functional Disorders, and Organic Mental Disorders, he describes the clinical picture of each of the subcategories within the larger groupings, detailing the current psychiatric criteria of diagnoses, providing recommendations for treatment, suggesting when to call in specialized consultants, and related practical matters. Using case examples from his own clinical practice, Dr. Bedi amply illustrates the principles and purposes of appropriate diagnosis and treatment.

Allied Health Professionals troubled by the arcana of psychiatry will find this chapter quite useful. Written in a clear and straightforward style and without the usual abundance of jargon,

it clarifies and explains the nature of principal psychiatric problems so often found in our substance-abusing patients.

A summary and references conclude the chapter.

INTRODUCTION

Alcoholism is usually referred to as our country's third most
serious health problem, following cardiovascular disease and
cancer. According to a recent National Institute on Mental Health
(NIMH) epidemiological survey (1), the six-month prevalence of
alcoholism is 6.4% (afflicting 10 million Americans) and the six-
month prevalence of drug abuse and dependence is 2% (affecting
an estimated 3.1 million Americans). The lifetime prevalence of
these disorders is higher.

The precise causes of alcoholism remain moot. The presence
of a wide range of psychopathology, with varying degrees of
severity, in alcoholic populations has resulted in a number of
theories suggesting psychological causes. Alcoholic populations do
display significantly more depression, paranoid thinking trends,
aggressive feelings and acts, and significantly lower self-esteem
than non-alcoholic populations (2, 3). Ultimately, researchers may
discover that from a causative viewpoint, alcoholism is not a
unitary illness. Rather, it may prove to be a group of disorders
with a small common pathway manifested by an inability to
refrain from drinking and/or drink in a controlled manner.

This chapter is not an exhaustive review of the psychiatric
disorders often seen in association with substance use disorders. It
is an anecdotal account of the author's several years of experience
as a psychiatric consultant in a multidisciplinary setting in which
the primary treatment responsibility was the domain of an addictionologist, a newly emerging medical subspecialty, with its own
Board certification in a developmental stage. In such a setting, the
psychiatric consultant is usually invited to participate in individual
patient management after the detoxification process is complete,
usually during the second week of treatment, unless an emergency
warrants an earlier intervention (e.g., suicidal acts, acute manic
disorder, or psychotic state). The psychiatrist may play a useful
role in several aspects of the treatment process: differential diagnosis of associated psychiatric disorders and further investigation
if needed, appropriate psychopharmacologic and psychothera-

peutic interventions, ongoing liaison with the addictionologist and the multidisciplinary treatment team, participation in the acute care and the aftercare phases of the treatment, and as an educator, researcher, and student of the interface between chemical dependency and psychiatry.

Some of the common psychiatric disorders encountered in substance abuse populations include Adjustment Disorders, Personality Disorders (borderline, paranoid, antisocial, and mixed personality disorders), and Conduct Disorders. Functional Disorders (dysthymic and cyclothymic, affective, and anxiety, especially agoraphobia and panic attacks, and panic disorder) are also frequently seen. Schizophrenias, especially paranoid schizophrenia, and Eating Disorders, especially bulimia, are becoming more common. Organic Mental Disorders, including delirium, dementia, amnestic syndrome, organic delusional syndrome, organic hallucinosis, organic affective syndrome, organic personality syndrome, and intoxication and withdrawal are also frequently diagnosed in this population.

While these disorders do not represent an exhaustive list of the psychiatric syndromes encountered among substance abuse patients, they do account for the most frequently diagnosed problem likely to be seen in such populations. Therefore, the remainder of this chapter focuses on an explication of each of these psychiatric disorders as they are likely to manifest themselves, to enable Allied Health Professionals (AHPs) to more fully understand and participate in the full range of treatments now available.

In preparing this chapter the author examined the records of 100 consecutive inpatient admissions to the substance abuse treatment unit of a private psychiatric hospital in Milwaukee, Wisconsin, between December 1984 and August 1985. All patients underwent thorough evaluation by qualified psychiatrists, and diagnoses were made on the basis of criteria according to the *Diagnostic and Statistical Manual of Mental Disorders, Third Edition (DSM-III)* (4) as shown in Appendix 1. By definition all patients were diagnosed as having one or more substance use disorders, and 66% also had one or more additional psychiatric disorders on *DSM-III* Axis I or II. The frequency of such diagnosis are indicated in Table 1.

These systematic observations shed light on psychiatric morbidity among a substance use disorder population, but may not necessarily be representative of the universe of such populations. Certain diagnostic groups may be underrepresented because of the small size of the sample, and because diagnoses were made at the

TABLE 1
FREQUENCY OF PSYCHIATRIC DISORDERS
AMONG 100 HOSPITALIZED
SUBSTANCE ABUSE/DEPENDENCY PATIENTS

Psychiatric Diagnosis	Number and % of Patients
Adjustment Disorders	13
Dysthymic Disorders	7
Major Depression	6
Bipolar Disorders	2
Conduct Disorders	6
Anxiety Disorders	4
Schizo–affective Disorders	1
Personality Disorders	27
TOTAL	66

time of discharge rather than at admission. Relatedly, the private-hospital setting may have precluded certain diagnostic categories, such as organic mental disorders (q.v. below), who are more likely to be admitted to psychiatric units of general hospitals.

Nevertheless, the data shown in Table 1 do indicate that as many as two-thirds of substance abusers needing hospitalization do have one or more concurrent psychiatric disorders. It is suspected that further research may show different patterns of psychiatric disorders among alcoholics and other drug abusers if, 1) larger patient samples are studied; 2) more diverse samples are collected, e.g., public hospitals, outpatient clinics, general hospitals, and other facilities; 3) separate studies of special populations are done, such as adolescents, geriatrics, women, and others.

However, it is believed that knowledge of the probable presence of psychiatric disorders among substance abuse patients can be useful to all Allied Health Professionals dealing with such patients. Awareness of patient profiles and associated risk factors can be very helpful in prevention and treatment of substance use disorders, and the purpose of this chapter is to increase that awareness.

ADJUSTMENT DISORDERS

In our treatment center study, 13% of inpatients had a concurrent diagnosis of Adjustment Disorder, defined as a maladaptive reaction to an identifiable psychological stressor, that occurs within three months of the onset of the stressor. The maladaptive nature of the reaction is indicated by either 1) impairment in social or occupational functioning, and/or 2) symptoms that are in excess of a normal and expectable reaction to the stressor. In the *DSM-III* multiaxial system of diagnosis, Axis IV records the psychosocial stressors within a year prior to the current disorder. The severity of the stressor is rated on a scale of 1 (none) to 7 (catastrophic). It is assumed that the disturbance will eventually remit after the stressor ceases or, if the stressor persists, when a new level of adaptation is achieved. Adjustment Disorder is further specified according to the predominant presenting symptoms as Adjustment Disorder with depressed mood, anxious mood, mixed emtional factors, with disturbance of conduct, with mixed disturbance of emotions and conduct, with work or academic inhibition, with withdrawal, or with atypical features when the predominant manifestations involve symptoms that cannot be coded in any of the specific categories.

In the inpatient alcohol or chemically dependent population, the most common presentations are of individuals who may have a chronic history of alcoholism or other substance abuse, where a psychosocial stressor may further exacerbate their substance abuse, causing impairment in their job, marriage, or other relationships, legal difficulties, or a combination thereof, associated with depressed or anxious mood and social withdrawal, and a constellation of symptoms along the spectrum may bring them to clinical attention. Rarely would a psychosocial stressor invoke alcoholism or substance abuse in an individual with no prior history of such abuse, especially in women and adolescents, in this author's experience.

Individuals with Adjustment Disorders often consult their family physicians with symptoms of depression, anxiety, and other difficulties mentioned above, and it is not uncommon for well-meaning physicians to prescribe minor tranquilizers for these patients. This further compounds their problems of chemical dependency, since these individuals are vulnerable to abusing these medications by taking them in doses higher than prescribed, or mixing medications with alcohol or other drugs of abuse. Prevention of their particular complication may involve education of internists, and general and family practitioners about the abuse potential of prescriptions of minor tranquilizers to patients who may have problems with alcoholism and chemical dependency or abuse. A more appropriate intervention with such patients when they present to the physician may by for doctors to, 1) inquire about any stress factors within the last few months, 2) inquire routinely about their pattern of alcohol and substance use or abuse, 3) either offer these individuals supportive psychotherapy (if their training and schedule permits), or 4) refer them to their psychiatric consultant for further assessment and intervention.

When these patients are first seen by a psychiatric consultant in a chemical dependency treatment setting, his or her role includes, 1) ascertaining the nature and maladaptive impact of the psychosocial stressor in the patient; 2) offering individual supportive short-term psychotherapy to the patient while continuing with his or her chemical dependency treatment program (this usually involves 8-12 sessions over a 2-3 month period); and 3) serving as a liaison with the chemical dependency treatment staff so that they may be made aware of the psychosocial stressors compounding the patient's chemical dependency, thereby enabling them to provide additional individual, marital, familial, and employee-assistance interventions as indicated.

Case Example

Patient 1 was a married, white male, in his late 20s, admitted to an inpatient alcoholism treatment unit with a history of alcoholism and polydrug abuse of about ten years duration. He was seen in psychiatric consultation with a history of a schizophreniform episode eight years ago while in military service, associated with drug abuse, but without symptoms presently. Within the last few months, his father had died of cancer and a maternal uncle and cousin were killed in an accident. He was close to all these individuals. He complained of crying spells, anxiety, and guilt feelings. There were no acute medical problems. Patient was diagnosed as Alcohol Dependence Syndrome-Continuous, Mixed Drug Abuse, and Adjustment Disorder with Mixed Emotional Features. While he continued within the mainstream of the alcohol treatment program, he was seen for several sessions of supportive psychotherapy to work through the unresolved guilt. Other staff were also alerted to the issue and they provided further assistance. Patient responded well with remission of his symptoms of anxiety and depression. No medications were used.

PERSONALITY DISORDERS

Borderline Personality Disorder

This disorder is now being increasingly recognized and diagnosed among psychiatric patient populations in general, and among chemically dependent populations in particular. According to *DSM-III*, the essential feature is a personality disorder in which there is instability in a variety of areas including interpersonal behavior, mood, and self-image.

Interpersonal relations are often intense and unstable, with marked shifts of attitude over time. Frequently, there is impulsive and unpredictable behavior that is potentially physically self-damaging. Mood is often unstable, with marked shifts from a normal mood to a dysphoric mood or with inappropriate, intense anger or lack of control of anger. A profound identity disturbance may be manifested by uncertainty about several issues relating to identity, such as self-image, gender identity, or long-term goals or values. There may be problems tolerating being alone, and chronic feelings of emptiness or boredom. No single feature is invariably present. This disorder provides a fertile ground for substance abuse. The individual may use alcohol or other drugs as an impulsive, unpredictable, or self-damaging act, or to deal with their intense affect or affective instability, or in a frantic effort to deal with loneliness, depression, boredom, or as a suicidal effort. Mood-altering drugs, especially sedative-hypnotics, stimulants such as amphetamines and cocaine, and minor tranquilizers, may be used by them to deal with their affective shifts. They may use stimulants and hallucinogens to deal with their chronic feelings of boredom. Since these individuals are struggling with issues of identity and lack of long-term goals, identification with the substance-abusing subculture may provide them with a sense of pseudo-identity which may be more important to them than the pharmacokinetic properties of the drugs themselves. This idea may be well worth bearing in mind in the rehabilitation phase of treatment.

While detoxification and disruption of the substance-abuse cycle may only be the first step, addiction to the identification with a substance-abusing subculture, with its trappings of rituals and sense of belonging, needs to be replaced by the therapeutic subculture, for a long enough period of time, usually two years or more, during which time the identity disorder, including issues of self-image and long-term goals and values should be explored in a supportive, structured, psychotherapeutic aftercare program. Some or most of this time may have to be spent in a residential setting, perhaps in a transitional living unit in a halfway house where the staff is aware of the complexity of this disorder.

Case Example

Patient 2, a single white female in her 20s, a health profession trainee, was admitted to the inpatient impaired professional's program and was seen in psychiatric consultation with complaints of episodic depression for the last several years, but moreso in the last two years. During these episodes, she experienced terminal insomnia (i.e., early morning awakening and inability to return to sleep), crying spells, low energy, and inability to cope with her job. She attempted to deal with her symptoms by using alcohol and self-medication with antidepressants, minor tranquilizers, and other miscellaneous drugs. When feeling depressed and lonely, she would contemplate suicide by various methods including lethal overdose of medications, and had made several suicide attempts including wrist-cutting. She had consulted several psychiatrists but would drop out of treatment after a few sessions and resume control of her own treatment by self-prescription of the medications, mixing those with alcohol.

The patient had been admitted to the unit with overwhelming suicidal feelings and inability to cope with her job and daily life. Three days after admission, she claimed to be feeling considerably better and wanted to be discharged to return to work. There was considerable denial of her problems with depression, drug abuse, and her inability to cope outside the structure of the treatment program. She stayed on in the program when her work supervisors refused her permission to return to work without completing her treatment program. This assisted the treatment team considerably in setting appropriate limits to her behavior, e.g., sabotaging her own treatment and signing out prematurely from the program.

In the program, the patient behaved seductively and compliantly to the point where limits had to be set, e.g., requesting a two-day overnight pass to travel to another state, when she was not eligible even for a day pass. When this request was denied, the patient, who was thus far seductively compliant, reacted with anger and rage at not being granted a special pass, and the next day superficially lacerated her wrist. She also requested special arrangements to see the author for psychotherapy sessions several times a week, but would devalue the rest of the staff, particularly the nurses, and not take the opportunity to reach out to the rest of the staff. This overevaulation of the author's role and devaluing of some other staff, and splitting behavior, was confronted. She was not offered the special arrangement compared to the other patients, but was seen for weekly sessions. She gradually started to reach out to the other staff, reacting with less anger, rage, and acting out (e.g., suicidal gestures), and with more insight and constructive behaviors. It is planned that once this patient has better impulse control and insight, she will be transferred to the recovery home for several months, followed by up to two years of aftercare programing and weekly psychotherapy sessions.

This is only the tip of the iceberg from the case of a Borderline Personality Disordered individual with periodic depressive episodes, suicide attempts and associated problems with alcohol and drug abuse. In such cases, it is imperative that all staff involved in their management meet regularly to avoid the splitting behavior of the patient and minimize the patient's using the split to act out his or her wish to be special and gain control of the treatment process and thus sabotage any effective treatment. Also, long-term inpatient and extended-care treatment may be necessary.

Paranoid Personality Disorder

These individuals present with a pervasive, unwarranted suspiciousness and mistrust of people, as indicated by their expectation of trickery or harm; hypervigilance, manifested by continual scanning of the environment for signs of threat, or taking unneeded precautions, guardedness, or secretiveness; avoidance of accepting blame when warranted; questioning the loyalty of others; intense, narrowly focused searching for biases, with loss of appreciation of total context; overconcern with hidden motives and special meanings; and pathological jealousy. They seem to be hypersensitive with a tendency to be easily slighted, exaggerate their difficulties, ready to counterattack when perceiving any real or imagined threat, and unable to relax. They display restricted affectivity as evidenced by cold and unemotional appearance; pride in being objective, rational, and unemotional; lack of sense of humor; and absence of tender, sentimental feelings. These traits characterize the individual's current and long-term functioning and are not limited to episodes of illness.

The relationship of this disorder to Paranoid Disorders and Paranoid Schizophrenia is not clear, but it may predispose one to the later development of those other disorders. These features of Paranoid Disorders cause significant impairment in social, marital, and occupational functioning, or subjective distress. Such a patient may start using alcohol or other chemicals to deal with these intra-psychic and interpersonal difficulties. However, substance abuse further exacerbates their paranoid symptoms and their interpersonal difficulties and functioning, compounding the vicious cycle.

In the author's experience, these individuals are best treated in the mainstream of alcoholism and chemical dependency treatment programs, with opportunities for peer support and confrontation of their defenses. Psychiatric input is helpful in establishing a baseline of their personality organization, monitoring them monthly for 12-18 months to rule out underlying Paranoid or Schizophrenic Disorder which may need further intervention, and providing additional individual support during their recovery program.

Antisocial Personality Disorder

The essential feature is a personality disorder in which there is a history of continuous and chronic antisocial behavior in which the rights of others are violated, persistence into adult life of a pattern of antisocial behavior that began before the age of fifteen, and failure to sustain good job performance over a period of several years.

Lying, stealing, fighting, truancy and resisting authority are early childhood signs of the disorder. In adolescence, unusually early or aggressive sexual behavior, excessive drinking, and use of illicit drugs are frequent. In adulthood, these kinds of behavior continue, with the addition of an inability to sustain consistent work performance, or to function as a responsible parent, and failure to accept social norms with respect to lawful behavior.

When substance abuse and antisocial behavior begin in childhood, and continue into adulthood, both Substance Use Disorder and Antisocial Personality Disorder should be diagnosed if the criteria for each disorder are met, regardless of the extent to which some of the antisocial behavior may be a consequence of the Substance Use Disorder (for example, illegal selling of drugs, or the assaultive behavior associated with alcohol intoxication). When antisocial behavior in an adult is associated with Substance Use Disorder, the diagnosis of Antisocial Personality Disorder is not made unless the childhood signs were also present and continued without a remission of five years of more between age fifteen and adult life.

These individuals are more likely to be encountered in penal institutions than treatment settings. After detoxification and initial phases of treatment, rehabilitation is more likely to succeed in a supportive but confrontive, peer-pressured, long-term therapeutic community setting. The legal mandate to complete such a treatment may be useful in the early phases of the treatment to engage these individuals. In the later stages of treatment, patients may start exploring signs of personal distress, complaints of tension, inability to tolerate boredom, depression, and the conviction (often correct) that others are hostile towards them. They may start exploring their interpersonal difficulties, and the role that their behavior plays in initiating and perpetuating these problems. It is important for the staff to offer a blend of firmness, consistency, and limit-setting, with feelings and a sense of hope.

Mixed Personality Disorder

This diagnosis should be considered when the individual has a personality disorder that involves features from several of the specific personality disorders but does not meet the criteria for any one such disorder. However, if an individual qualifies for any of the specific personality disorders, that category should be noted even if some features from other categories are present. For example, an individual who fits the description of Compulsive Personality Disorder should be given that diagnosis even if some mild dependent or paranoid features are present. In a Mixed Personality Disorder, for instance, the patient may show features of an antisocial personality, e.g., lack of ability to function as a responsible parent, or failure to accept social norms with respect to lawful behavior; additional features of an histrionic disorder, e.g., self-dramatization, incessant drawing of attention to oneself; further features of a narcisstic disorder, e.g., grandiose sense of self-importance or uniqueness, cool indifference, or marked features of rage, inferiority, shame, humiliation, or emptiness in response to criticism, indifference of others, or defeat, a sense of entitlement, i.e., expectations of special favors from others without assuming reciprocal responsibilities. One frequently encounters individuals with such a constellation of personality traits among chemically dependent patient populations. Addressing the impact of this is usually very important in treatment planning.

Case Example

Patient 3 was a middle-aged, professionally successful business executive who was admitted for inpatient treatment for alcoholism in an impaired professional program. He was seen in psychiatric consultation for associated symptoms of chronic depression. This patient presented with a Mixed Personality Disorder including borderline, narcississtic, and antisocial traits, leading to interpersonal difficulties and chronic depression. There was a gambling quality in his business dealings, interpersonal relationships, and in his manner of seeking treatment. He had a wife and an extramarital relationship with a much younger woman. He was unable to decide about the future of his marriage or the other relationship. After entering treatment, the patient continued to direct his own program, and did not comply with team recommendations. If he dropped out of the program, his wife threatened to leave him, and in that event, he would decide to move in with his girlfriend. If he successfully pursued the treatment, his marriage could be repaired, in which event his girlfriend would leave him. In either case, he stood to gain in one or the other of the two relationships. This strategy had served him well in his business dealings. Now he was using this gamble in his intimate interpersonal relationships and in his dealing with the treatment process. He stood to win the battle but lose the war. The staff was made aware of the dynamics of the patient's personality structure and politics of his interpersonal dealings, so that they could confront his self-destructive behavior, and get his treatment back on course toward recovery, and enhance his integrity in his interpersonal dealings.

CONDUCT DISORDERS

In our clinical study, 6% of the patients presented with a diagnosis of Conduct Disorder. These disorders are usually evident in childhood or adolescence. The essential feature is a repetitive and persistent pattern of conduct in which either the basic rights of others or major age-appropriate societal norms or rules are violated. Further subclassification of these disorders is based on the degree of socialization (attachment to others) and the presence of aggressiveness. Onset is usually prepubertal for the under-socialized type and pubertal or post-pubertal for the socialized type.

The course of the disorder is variable. Mild forms frequently show improvement over time, while severe forms tend to be chronic. Some individuals may continue their antisocial behavior and generally poor social functioning into adulthood, particularly the undersocialized aggressive type, and thus later qualify for the diagnosis of Antisocial Personality Disorder.

Complications include school suspension, legal difficulties, Substance Use Disorders, venereal diseases, unwanted pregnancy, high rate of physical injuries from accidents and fights, and suicidal behavior.

In our current model for treatment of Substance Abuse Disorders in adolescents with concurrent psychiatric disorders, including Conduct Disorders, our inpatient adolescent program is an eight-bed unit established at a psychiatric hospital where we treat chemically dependent youngsters between the ages of 12 and 18. The treatment program was designed with a "dual diagnosis capacity." That is, the program not only provides for the diagnosis and treatment of adolescent chemical dependency, but also for the diagnosis and treatment of coexisting emotional and behavioral disorders. The unit staff comprises a multidisciplinary treatment team including the medical director who is a child and adolescent psychiatrist, a pediatrician, a clinical psychologist, alcohol and other drug abuse counselors, nurses, social workers, teachers, activity therapists, a student assistant liaison worker, and a chaplain. Because the unit is part of a general psychiatric hospital, the program has access to several other child and adolescent psychiatrists who provide individual psychotherapy for patients when indicated. The hospital also provides our adolescent patients an opportunity to attend a local high school. An ongoing evaluation is conducted by the multidisciplinary team following admission, to determine whether or not there are significant coexisting emotional problems that need to be addressed in treatment.

Treatment begins immediately following the patient's admission to the inpatient unit. The program is conceptualized as consisting of three components or phases. Phase I is an intensive inpatient program aimed specifically at treating chemical dependency problems. This does not mean that coexisting emotional problems are ignored, but merely that the emphasis is on the treatment of chemical dependency during this phase. Phase II provides a bridge between traditional psychiatric services and traditional chemical dependency services. In this part of the program there is a shift in emphasis from the treatment of chemical dependency to the treatment of emotional and behavioral problems of those youngsters who have diagnosable psychiatric illness. The shift in emphasis occurs without losing sight of the 12 Steps of Alcoholics Anonymous. Phase III of the treatment program is aftercare. The adolescents begin to participate in the aftercare program just prior to their discharge from the hospital and continue to participate for a period of six months following discharge.

Conduct Disorders are the most prevalent disturbance diagnosed, but Major Depressions, Dysthymic Disorders, Attention Deficit Disorders, Eating Disorders, Personality Disorders including Narcissistic and Borderline Personality Disorders, and psychotic illnesses have been diagnosed. As these patients complete their Fifth Step of the AA-oriented program, the focus begins to shift to addressing their emotional problems. Individual psychotherapy is initiated and, for these youngsters, group therapy takes on a more psychodynamic orientation. Psychotropic medications are utilized if they are deemed to be a necessary adjunct to the treatment program. So as not to lose sight of the chemical dependency problems, these youngsters continue in AA Step groups, the educational series, and individual drug counseling. The family system is evaluated at the time of admission, and this evaluation process continues after admission to the family therapy sessions. Not commonly, other family members are found to have chemical abuse problems or psychiatric illness, and in these cases family members are often referred for individual drug counseling and rehabilitation, individual psychotherapy, or couples therapy.

When treatment goals have been sufficiently achieved, a discharge date is set by the multidisciplinary team. At this point the patient is instructed to obtain a sponsor for continued participation in AA/NA meetings following discharge. The student assistant liaison worker conducts return-to-school meetings with the patient and the school personnel. The patient then participates in aftercare group meetings prior to discharge to facilitate transition in the aftercare program.

FUNCTIONAL DISORDERS

Dysthymic Disorder

Also included in this category are Cyclothymic Disorders. According to the recent NIMH Survey (1) of the three Epidemiologic Catchment Area (ECA) sites using the diagnostic interview survey (5, 6) and the *DSM-III* (4) criteria, a total of 1.2%-2.6% of males, 2.9%-5.4% of females, and a total of 2.1%-3.8% of the total population, are suffering from Dysthymic Disorders, estimated for a six-month prevalence rate. Lifetime prevalence rates are higher. Clinical experience bears out that the prevalence of Dysthymic Disorders among the substance-abuse population is at least equal to the general population prevalence rates and probably much higher. Patients with Dysthymic Disorder usually present with symptoms characteristic of depression, but not of sufficient severity and duration to meet the criteria of Major Depression. Symptoms may be persistent or separated by periods of normal mood lasting days to weeks but not months. If the pattern of symptoms continues for two years or more in adults and one year for children and adolescents, a Dysthymic Disorder is diagnosed.

Dysthymic Disorder may provide a substrate for the development of alcoholism or other Substance Abuse Disorders. Oftentimes, upon careful assessment, it becomes apparent that the patient had a Dysthymic Disorder in childhood or early adolescence, providing a nucleus for the onset of alcoholism or other Substance Abuse Disorder. This drug use helps cover over the depressed mood and the low self-esteem. Such issues reappear during the course of rehabilitation and need to be addressed for a successful outcome. A number of aspects of treatment are important to consider. First, it is important to have a baseline psychiatric evaluation during the early phase of treatment, usually during the first two weeks, although the first week is generally avoided to allow for detoxification and rule out alcohol- and other substance-induced depression. Second, the patient should have a periodic — usually monthly — reassessment. These monthly meetings also provide an opportunity for supportive psychotherapy and a chance to integrate the patient's participation in the program from a psychodynamic viewpoint. Third, for dysthymic patients it is necessary to extend their aftercare program for 18-24 months to provide a sufficient length of time in a supportive and holding environment to work through the issues of self-esteem and interpersonal relationships. Fourth, antidepressant medications are generally not beneficial in this group. A very small subgroup may benefit from the monoamine oxidase (MAO) inhibitor group of antidepressant drugs, especially when the dysthymia is impairing effective participation in the aftercare treatment, and blocked productivity at school, work, or home, and in interpersonal relationships and leisure-time planning. Other symptoms necessitating antidepressant drug therapy are pessimistic attitudes about the future, brooding about past events, feeling sorry for oneself, insomnia or hypersomnia, low energy level or chronic tiredness, tearfulness, and recurrent thoughts of death and suicide. Some of the common MAO inhibitor group of antidepressant medication available and used in the United States are isocarboxazid (Marplan®), phenelzine (Nardil®), and tranylcypromine (Parnate®). These are potent medications and require close monitoring, including evaluation of hepatic and hemopoetic symptoms, special dietary precautions (i.e., avoidance of tyramine-containing foods, such as certain cheeses, yogurt, alcohol, sour cream, chocolate, soy sauce, yeast extracts, coffee, etc.), and avoidance of certain over-the-counter medications (e.g., cold and sinus medications and decongestant inhalers, etc.). These medications must be prescribed under psychiatric supervision. Usually they are used from 9-12 months, long enough to disrupt the maladaptive patterns of the Dysthymic Disorder and alcoholism and substance abuse, and to permit the evolution of more adaptive strategies to deal with their lives with the help of the structure and support of the treatment program.

Case Example

Patient 4 was a female health professional in her mid-30s, admitted with complaints of alcohol abuse episodically since age 15, depression since age 15, feeling unliked, unable to feel good about herself, excessive dependence on the opinions of others to define herself, and episodes of depressive mood swings during which she would tend to eat more. She felt anxious, depressed, and suicidal, with sleep pattern changes, usually hypersomnia, and crying spells. These symptoms had exacerbated considerably prior to admission, following an abortive attempt at a major reshuffle in lifestyle including a relocation abroad. In spite of a warm personality and good physical appearance, the patient had had only one, short-lived, close relationship. The patient's father was a warm, supportive individual, while the patient had identified with her mother who had a history of psychiatric hospitalization following two losses: a stillborn baby and losing another child following Rh incompatibility by age six months. An older sister had had two psychiatric hospitalizations for depression and was treated with antidepressant medications. There was a family history of alcoholism in the maternal grandmother and a paternal uncle. The patient's routine laboratory investigations, including a thyroid evaluation, were within normal limits. The patient was seen in psychiatric consultation because of an inadequate response to the alcoholism treatment program and continuing feelings of depression. She was diagnosed as Alcohol Dependence Syndrome-Continuous, and Dysthymic Disorder. It was recommended that the psychiatrist follow up the patient for individual, supportive psychotherapy during her treatment program and aftercare, with a trial of MAO inhibitor antidepressant medication, if there continued to be an impasse in her treatment process.

Cyclothymic Disorder

The essential feature is a chronic mood disturbance of at least two years duration, involving numerous periods of depression and hypomania, but not of sufficient severity and duration to meet the criteria for a Major Depressive or Manic episode. The depressive periods and hypomanic periods may be interspersed with periods of normal mood lastings as long as several months at a time. In other cases the two types of periods are intermixed or alternate. During depressive periods there is depressed mood or loss of interest or pleasure in all or almost all usual activities and pasttimes, and additionally, some other symptoms, such as insomnia or hypersomnia, feelings of inadequacy, social withdrawal, loss of interest in or enjoyment of sex, etc. During hypomanic periods there is an elevated, expansive, or irritable mood and additional symptoms, such as decreased need for sleep, more energy than usual, inflated self-esteem, increased productivity, hypersexuality, talkativeness etc. Substance abuse is particularly common as a result of self-treatment with sedatives and alcohol during the depressed periods, and the self-indulgent use of stimulants and psychedelics during the hypomanic periods, which further exacerbates and complicates the underlying disorder. This disorder is apparently more common in females.

When Cyclothymic Disorder presents concomitantly with alcoholism or substance abuse, a useful clinical strategy is to continue the patient's treatment in the mainstream of a chemical dependency treatment program for up to two years. This provides needed structure for these patients to maintain their sobriety for a long enough period to experience themselves and their relationships unaltered by chemicals, and use of a treatment program and individual supportive psychotherapy to evolve more adaptive methods to deal with their mood swings. The author generally recommends individual supportive psychotherapy sessions at least on a monthly basis for up to two years. Those individuals who are unable to cope with their daily lives, jobs, and relationships because of their mood swings, and in spite of the structure of the program and individual psychotherapy, may benefit from the use of lithium therapy. Lithium is generally required in lower than conventional doses in Cyclothymic Disorders. Others may need more intensive individual psychotherapy, i.e., weekly sessions for one to two years, especially if the patient has adequate motivation and ego strength to make optimal use of psychotherapeutic intervention.

Affective Disorders

The first results of the largest and the most comprehensive survey of mental disorders (1) ever conducted in the U.S. show that over a six-month period, 6% of the adult population suffer from Affective Disorders including Major Depression, Manic-Depression, and Dysthymia. Of these, 0.7% have Manic episodes, 3.1% have a Major Depressive episode, and 3.2% have Dysthymia. Based on the 1980 U.S. census these proportions translate into 9.4 million adult Americans suffering from Affective Disorders over a six-month period. Of these, 1 million have Manic episodes, 4.9 million have Major Depressive episodes, and 5.1 million have Dysthymia. The lifetime prevalence rates are obviously higher. Further findings indicate that the prevalence rates were almost twice as high for women (8.2%) as for men (up to 4.6%). The rates were highest in women ages 25 through 44 (up to 11.4%).

Reports of the prevalence of Affective Disorders in alcoholics vary from 3% to 98%. Some have attributed this wide range of estimates to use of different diagnostic instruments, e.g., the Hamilton Depression Rating Scale, the Zung Self-Rating Depression Scale, or the Minnesota Multiphasic Personality Inventory. These studies (7, 8) used varied patient selection criteria and widely different criteria for diagnosing Affective Disorder. To further examine the correlation between alcoholism and Affective Disorders, we conducted a study of 421 consecutive admissions to an alcoholism and drug rehabilitation hospital (9). Patients were screened for alcoholism using National Council on Alcoholism criteria and were diagnosed as Affective Disorders, using a modification of the Research Diagnostic Criteria (5, 6). The study found that about 33% of the alcoholic inpatients were diagnosed as having had Affective Disorder in their lifetime. Forty-three percent of the females were diagnosed as affectively disordered, compared with 29% of males. Grouping by age and sex showed that females ages 20 through 30 had a 60% prevalence of Affective Disorder, which was statistically significant. When this subgroup was compared with all males, all other females, and the rest of the patients as a group, there was still a significantly higher prevalence.

A literature review (10-13) and the NIMH epidemiological study (1) indicated that females have a higher prevalence of Affective Disorder than males. Hence, in the context of this variable, affectively disordered alcoholics followed a pattern more closely resembling Affective Disorder than alcoholism alone. Marital status also was shown to be a significant variable in predicting Affective Disorder among alcoholic inpatients, with a 36% prevalence rate among those not presently married versus 26% in married alcoholics. A literature review (14-16) indicated that the rates of depression tend to be lower in married males, but there was some evidence for higher rates among married women.

Case Example

Patient 5 was a married white male in his mid-30s, in public service, admitted to an inpatient program with a history of alcoholism of several years' duration, which had increased considerably in severity over the last two years. He was seen in psychiatric consultation for additional problems of loss of impulse control several days prior to admission when he was verbally and physically belligerent with his spouse and fellow workers. On psychiatric examination he reported a history of mood swings for the last two years, during which he would become easily irritable, angry, and belligerent, with increased pressure of speech, yelling on the telephone, and sleeping only 3-4 hours. During these upswings he would over-commit himself by volunteering for numerous committee responsibilities, but was unable to sustain these when not manic. On mental status evaluation, patient presented with increased psychomotor activity and pressure of speech, mood was anxious, agitated, and euphoric. Thought pressure was increased with flight of ideas. He tended to be grandiose but had no formed delusions. He was diagnosed as Alcohol Dependence Syndrome-Continuous, and Bipolar Affective Disorder-Manic, and was treated with lithium therapy and regular psychiatric follow up with bimonthly meetings.

Case Example

Patient 6 was an executive in his mid-40s, a married white male, admitted to an inpatient program with a history of alcohol abuse since his teens, with episodic exacerbation when in his 30s and again a few months prior to admission. Upon psychiatric consultation, patient reported several months' history of feeling depressed, with crying spells, low spirits, insomnia, feelings that if he died his family members would be better off with his insurance money, and suicidal ideation. He attempted to deal with his depressive symptoms by increasing his alcohol consumption. Consequently, he lost his job, and his marital and familial relationships were strained. Patient 6 was diagnosed as Alcohol Dependency Syndrome-Continuous, and severe Agitated Depression, and was treated with antidepressant medication, regular psychiatric follow-up, and participation in the alcoholism treatment and rehabilitation program. He now has a new job and his marital, familial, and overall life adjustment is gradually improving.

These case examples and information typify some of the treatment guidelines in dealing with patients with alcoholism and Affective Disorders. For example, Allied Health Professionals must be aware that alcoholism, drug dependence, and Affective Disorders effect 6-7% of the population in each category over a six-month prevalence period, and that up to 33% of alcoholics and other substance abusers suffer from concurrent Affective Disorder during their lifetime. Relatedly, special subgroups of inpatient alcoholic populations (i.e., women ages 20-30) have a lifetime prevalence of Affective Disorder of up to 60%. Although the frequent concurrence of these two classes of disorders do not necessarily allow the prediction of one based on the presence of the other, Allied Health Professionals are well advised to be aware of the need for recognition, assessment, and treatment of both disorders when present in the same patient. Treatment of one without adequate attention to the other invites relapse and failure.

Assessment of concurrent Affective Disorders includes careful history of the evolution of alcoholism and Affective Disorder in the patient's lifetime; the temporal connections, if any, of the two disorders; family history, if any, of alcoholism or Affective Disorder; ruling out any medical disease contributor to the Affective Disorder, e.g., thyroid dysfunction, especially in young women; medication history with special attention to certain antihypertensive medications such as Aldomet® and beta blockers, which are known to cause depression in a proportion of patients; and a detailed present mental status evaluation to assess the type and severity of the Affective Disorder (e.g., mild, moderate, or severe; Manic-Depressive or Mixed Affective Disorder, or a Dysthymic Disorder).

Treatment interventions include regular psychiatric followup, supportive individual psychotherapy, consultation liaison with the alcoholism treatment team to coordinate treatment effort, use or appropriate antidepressant and anti-manic medication (e.g., lithium therapy, major tranquilizers, or others). The medications should be used in minimum effective doses. As clinical conditions permit, an attempt is made to wean the patient off the medication while the psychiatric follow-up is continued, so that the patient's Affective Disorder may be monitored and medications reinstituted if there is any symptom of relapse.

Once the patient's liver functions have normalized, the Dexamethasone Suppression Test (DMST) (17) may provide a useful baseline to monitor the presence of depression. This blood test is relatively inexpensive, and possible to administer on an outpatient basis. It may be repeated every few months, to monitor the remission status. In patients who are able to maintain remission of alcoholism and Affective Disorders without use of any medications, psychiatric follow-up of up to two years is generally helpful, at decreasing frequency of contact. Those who need more intensive psychiatric treatment or medication may need a longer period of follow-up as clinical conditions warrant.

The DMST is advocated as a specific laboratory test for the diagnosis of depression (17). In the recommended procedure, the patient takes a 1 mg tablet of dexamethasone at 2300 hours (11:00 p.m.). The next day, blood samples for determination of plasma cortisol are drawn at 1600 and 2300 hours. The plasma cortisol level in either sample, above which a DMST may be considered abnormal, is $5\mu g/dl$. This version of the DMST identifies melancholic (depressed) patients with a sensitivity of 67% and specificity of 96%. The test has certain medical and drug exclusion criteria which invalidate the test (e.g., alcoholism, especially 10-21 days after withdrawal, marijuana use, hepatic disease). In the author's experience, if the DMST is performed in the alcoholic and substance-abuse population in the third week of hospitalization and after liver enzyme elevation has subsided, it is generally a useful aid in assisting with the diagnosis of depression.

Case Example

Patient 7 was a retired executive in his 60s, a widowed white male, who was admitted to an inpatient alcoholism treatment program and seen in psychiatric consultation with complaints of depression, intermittent insomnia, agitation, racing and "bad" thoughts in his head, and a suicide attempt with carbon monoxide poisoning in his garage prior to admission. This depression was of several years' duration after his wife's death and as all of his adult children gradually left home. Patient 7 also had a history of abuse of minor tranquilizers and alcohol of several years' duration, ostensibly to help him deal with depression by self-medication. There was also considerable secondary gain from his symptoms (e.g., enmeshing his children in his life as he avoided other relationships). An attempt was made to treat him without any medication at first to control the issues of secondary gain. Patient 7 also abused his antidepressant medication, e.g., taking it inconsistently and at times at doses higher than prescribed, and sometimes making suicidal gestures with overdose. Physical exam and laboratory tests including liver enzymes were normal. Without antidepressant medication however, his symptoms worsened as he experienced insomnia with only 1-2 hours of sleep while frequently pacing the unit floor. A DMST was performed and was positive with serum cortisol levels of $5\mu g/dl$ and $8\mu g/dl$. Antidepressant medication was reinstituted in appropriate doses, under close supervision, with good response in controlling depressive symptoms. Issues of dependency are now being worked through in the treatment program.

Anxiety Disorders

The NIMH survey (1) found that Anxiety Disorders, which include Phobias, Panic Disorder, and Obsessive-Compulsive Disorders, are among the most common psychiatric illnesses within the study population. Approximately 8% of the people surveyed suffered from an Anxiety Disorder over a six-month period. Although some of these disorders are relatively mild, others are so severe that the afflicted individuals have been afraid for years of venturing outside their homes.

Anxiety Disorders in general may predispose an individual to abuse alcohol, sedatives (especially minor tranquilizers), or other drugs to cope with the anxiety states. Sometimes, well-meaning physicians may prescribe minor tranquilizers, or other sedatives, for symptom relief in these patients. However, some of these patients may stay on these medications for years, obtained legally or illegally. They trade the problems of drug dependence for their anxiety states, as the price of remaining functional in their lives.

The most common of these disorders is Agoraphobia with or without Panic Disorder. These individuals present with a history of marked fear of public places from which escape might be difficult, e.g., crowds or public transportation. This leads to increasing constriction of normal activity. Agoraphobia may be associated with Panic Disorder, in which the patient has at least three panic attacks within a three-week period. Panic attacks are manifested by discrete periods of apprehension or fear and associated symptoms such as difficulty breathing, palpitations, chest pain or discomfort, choking or smothering sensations, dizziness, trembling, shaking, tingling in hands or feet, hot and cold flashes, fear of dying, going crazy, or doing something uncontrolled during the attack.

A common complication of Panic Disorder is the development of an anticipatory fear of helplessness, or loss of control of one's mind during a panic attack, so that the individual becomes reluctant to be alone or in public places away from home. When many situations of this kind are avoided, the diagnosis of Agoraphobia with Panic Attacks should be made rather than Panic Disorder. The individual often develops varying degrees of nervousness and apprehension between attacks, leading to a generalized state of anxiety. In advanced cases, the panic attacks, anticipatory fear, and generalized anxiety state form a continuum which may lead to severe incapacitation and social withdrawal, and forms a ripe substrate for alcohol and other substance abuse.

Case Example

Patient 8 was a married white female in her late 20s, a health professional seen in consultation with a history of panic attacks which started about two years ago, following the sudden death of one of her parents of cardiac disease. She was the first to arrive at the scene and administered CPR, but the parent never regained consciousness, and died shortly thereafter. The patient started abusing alcohol to ward off the resulting panic attacks. Later, her physician prescribed minor tranquilizers to deal with the panic attacks. In the current treatment program, she had to be detoxified from alcohol use, then gradually weaned off the minor tranquilizers over a period of two weeks. The patient's medical checkup, including the thyroid assessment, was within normal limits. In psychotherapy sessions, the patient started to explore issues of unresolved grief. She was also referred to a biofeedback and relaxation-training program to assist her in dealing with panic attacks and anticipatory fear without use of alcohol or drugs.

The key principals of the treatment of Agoraphobia with Panic Attacks in patients with alcoholism and other Substance Abuse Disorders include, initally, treatment of their alcoholism and other substance abuse, including detoxification. Some of the patients may be addicted to high doses of sedatives and minor tranquilizers, and it may be safer to do a sedative tolerance test (18), establish the level of tolerance, calculate the phenobarbitone dose equivalent, and wean them over the next ten days (see Chapters 5 and 11).

During a sedative tolerance test a patient is given 200 mg of pentobarbitol and changes in the neurologic exam are assessed after one hour (18). If the patient is asleep but arousable an hour after the test dose, the degree of tolerance is none or minimal, and estimated 24-hour pentobarbitol requirement is none; if the patient is drowsy, with slurred speech, coarse nystagmus, ataxia, and marked intoxication, there is definite tolerance and estimated 24-hour pentobarbitol requirement is 400 to 600 mg; if the patient is comfortable with a fine lateral nystagmus as the only sign of intoxication, the degree of tolerance is marked, and the estimated 24-hour pentobarbitol requirement is 800 mg; if there are no signs of drug effects, perhaps persisting signs of abstinence and no intoxication, the degree of tolerance is extreme, with an estimated 24-hour pentobarbitol requirement of 1000 to 1200 mg or more. The test is then repeated 3 to 4 hours later using a dose of 300 mg of pentobarbitol. No response to the 300 mg dose suggests a habit above 160 mg per day. Either pentobarbitol or phenobarbitol may be used with withdrawal. Phenobarbitol has a longer duration of action and hence requires one third the amount of pentobarbitol. Phenobarbitol is given in equally divided amounts orally every 8 hours. Both the pentobarbitol and phenobarbitol can be reduced at a rate of one-tenth the starting dose per day, with the patient to be weaned off over 10 days.

A psychiatric evaluation should include assessment of bio-, psycho- and social factors contributing to the symptoms; for example, medical problems such as thyroid disorders or cardiac conditions like mitral valve prolapse syndrome, which are not uncommon and may masquerade as Panic Disorders. Psychological factors such as unresolved grief, other major stressful life events, job changes, relocation, and other variables may contribute to these disorders. Social factors such as change of life stage may also make a contribution. The adult life may be divided into four stages: child-bearing, child-rearing, child-launching, and post-child-launching. Women are most susceptible to Agoraphobia with Panic Disorders at the change-over points of these stages, particularly if there has not been much preparation and if there is a paucity of external and internal resources to deal with the changes.

After careful evaluation and treatment of any underlying medical contributors to the disorders, the patient is treated with individual supportive psychotherapy to deal with the psychosocial aspects of the disorder. Biofeedback and relaxation-training also may offer useful adjuncts for treatment of Anxiety Disorders.

Biofeedback is a treatment modality that educates the patient to relax by altering his or her level of awareness, for example, to an "alpha state" of consciousness, thereby learning to control and/or manage symptoms of pain and anxiety. The alpha state can be measured by an electroencephalogram (EEG), signifying that the body and brain are in a state of relaxation, with the parasympathetic nervous system predominant. It teaches the patient to be in touch with body changes which signal the movement between the parasympathetic and sympathetic nervous system (frequently called the stress response). When the patient perceives the shift of the stress response, the patient is able to consciously return his or her body to the physiologically more relaxed state associated with the brain's alpha wave pattern (approximately 3-7.5 cycles per second).

Other biofeedback modalities frequently utilized are the electromyograph (EMG), measuring muscle tension changes, and thermal biofeedback, measuring vasoconstriction/vasodilation in the extremities. They are utilized 1-2 times per week for 8-16 weeks, to promote and facilitate the achievement of relaxation by allowing the body to associate the relaxed feeling with visual and/ or auditory cues from the biofeedback machine. Each patient is also given a programed relaxation tape-recording to practice with three times a day. Such tapes often include instructions for deap breathing, progressive muscle relaxation, and guided imagery exercises.

The biofeedback program is structured to provide both concrete and abstract approaches to assist in promoting a new, balanced harmony of the body and mind. The tapes and equipment used provide concrete and objective data, as does the daily log in which the patient records symptom occurrence and intensity, hours of sleep, prescribed medications taken, food eaten, recommended physical exercise (30 minutes daily), number of times the tape was used, and events of the day. Also reinforced is the elimination of chemicals identified as stressors to the body: caffeine, salt, sugar, alcohol, and chocolate. In the treatment sessions, the patient is assisted in the process of identifying physiologic responses to physical and interpersonal events that have occurred to him or her. In addition, most patients are helped to understand normal physiologic responses to emotions.

Many patients who have abused chemicals have lost their ability to be in touch with normal and natural physiologic patterns of emotions. Their only indicator of feelings has been the anxiety which they learned to eliminate, albeit increasingly unsuccessfully, with chemicals. Those patients who began to abuse chemicals to control their underlying Anxiety Disorders (Agoraphobia, panic attacks, or other phobias) as well as those who began to abuse to avoid emotional pain (i.e., loneliness, isolation, grief, depression), or ease interpersonal conflict in relationships at home or at work, or because they are copying a response learned from parents, spouse, or siblings, all finally abuse whenever anxiety is experienced. Thus, learning how to experience anxiety as normal, natural, time-limited, and controllable, is an integral part of recovery.

In selected patients who do not respond adequately to the structure of the alcoholism and chemical dependency treatment program, individual supportive psychotherapy, and other adjuncts to treatment, like biofeedback and relaxation training, use of specific panic-blocking medications should be considered. These are safe, non-addictive medications, but should be used only under proper medical supervision. Medications include Imipramine®; Doxepin®; the MAO-inhibiting group of antidepressants, such as Nardil®, Parnate®, and others; or beta-blockers, such as Inderal®. Medications are only used as adjuncts and not as the mainstay of the treatment effort. Patients must continue with their recovery program, psychiatric follow-up, and other modalities such as biofeedback or relaxation training. After six months, an attempt is made to wean the patient off the medication or reduce the dosage. Once the medication has been discontinued and the patient is symptom-free, he or she should have psychiatric consultation available, should there be any exacerbation of symptoms.

Schizophrenic Disorders

In this section a group of schizophrenic-like psychoses resulting from alcoholism and substance abuse are described and discussed. At times, the presenting symptoms are indistinguishable from Schizophrenia and may actually result in a full-fledged acute or chronic Schizophrenic illness. At other times, there are significant differences in the presenting symptomatology and the course of the illness. These aspects are discussed with emphasis on recognition, treatment, and follow-up. This differentiation between Schizophrenia and drug-induced psychotic reactions is of considerable clinical significance if misdiagnosis is to be prevented. Treatment instituted for misdiagnosed Schizophrenia could subject the patient to the unnecessary hazards of long-term major tranquilizer use, such as tardive dyskinesia, a potentially irreversible neurological disorder resulting in involuntary movements of body. Identification and treatment of acute drug abuse problems are also discussed in Chapter 7 of this handbook.

Perhaps the best established of the schizophrenic-like psychoses of known pathology are the psychotic states accompanying *acute amphetamine intoxication*, first described in some detail by Connell (19), and later discussed by Bell (20). The illness usually takes the form of acute hallucinosis, perhaps with a delirious overlay (clouding of consciousness), and may arise after taking a single large dose of amphetamines. The state of consciousness may be completely lucid, and the resemblance to a typical Schizophrenic psychosis may be extremely close.

Resemblance to a chronic Schizophrenic illness is even closer in the psychoses which arise on the basis of *chronic* amphetamine intoxication. The patient becomes depressed, tense, and anxious, and begins to feel that something strange is going on, then he or she may feel that he or she is being pursued by a gang, and that people are talking about him or her. Auditory hallucinations, especially of a persecutory kind, hearing one's thoughts being spoken aloud, feeling one's thoughts are being interfered with, are also present. While the psychosis may be indistinguishable from a Schizophrenic one, in a majority of cases there may be exogenous features, such as visual illusions and hallucinations intermittently.

The subjective experience has a dream-like quality. There may be a degree of confusion or some impairment of memory for recent events, although this is rarely severe or sustained. In contrast to Schizophrenia, the patient's affective reaction is brisk and adequate. Differential diagnosis is established by the presence of amphetamines in the urine specimen, rapid onset, and rapid recovery once the drug is withdrawn.

Alcoholic Hallucinosis is characterized by auditory hallucinations occurring in the absence of clouding of consciousness; and confusion, or disorientation, after long-continued abuse of alcohol. Visual, olfactory, and tactile hallucinations, tremulousness, and epileptic fits sometimes occur, and the condition may develop into typical *delirium tremens* (21-25). In the majority of cases the onset of the illness is in the period immediately following cessation of drinking, most frequently after 12-48 hours of complete abstinence.

The phenomenology of alcoholic hallucinosis has been studied by several researchers (22-27), who report that the most common experience is of hallucinatory voices. The patient shows an appropriate emotional response to the voices and if they are threatening he or she may try to escape or even attempt suicide. The voices are usually recognized as belonging to the patient's friends or family, but sometimes they are not familiar, and rarely are they attributed to the devil or God. In this respect they resemble the auditory hallucinations of Schizophrenia. Visual hallucinations, when they occur in alcoholic hallucinoses, are similar in character to those of delirium tremens (25).

Alcoholic hallucinosis is generally a benign transient illness lasting a few days, but rarely some weeks and months, and ending with acquisition of insight and no permanent sequelae. If the drinking is resumed the hallucinosis sometimes persists indefinitely (22). Occasionally, as in four patients observed by Victor and Hope (22), the hallucinations continue even though the patient does not drink, and a picture clinically indistinguishable from Schizophrenia emerges.

The relationship between alcoholism and Schizophrenia is complex and has a number of components, according to Freed's (28) formulation. First, both conditions could conceivably arise from a shared inherited predisposition, although Rimmer and Jacobson (29) disputed this notion when they found that rates of alcoholism in Schizophrenics and their relatives were no higher than in the general population. Second, Alcohol Dependence could occur in those who had already developed a Schizophrenic illness; this idea is quite reasonable and is in line with the current emphasis on the multifactoral etiology of Alcohol Dependence. The third possibility is that prolonged and heavy alcohol consumption increases the likelihood of development of a Schizophrenic illness, with or without genetic or other predisposition, as maintained by Davison (30). Disagreement about the diagnostic criteria for Schizophrenia, and about the distinction, if any, between Schizophrenia (nuclear schizophrenia) and Schizophrenic Psychoses (reactive schizophrenia, schizophreniform psychoses) makes this issue however, a complex one.

Reports of *acute psychoses* among chronic users of cannabis without previous history of psychiatric distrubance, usually occurring after a short period during which the drug has been taken in much more than customary amounts, commonly appear in the psychiatric literature (31-35).

Thacore (31) described four cases in East Indians, arising after the use of "bhang." Prominent symptoms included anxiety, apprehension, suspiciousness, paranoid ideas (with ideas of reference and persecutory delusions) and auditory hallucinations, and the condition cleared within ten days. In another study, Thacore (32) compared 25 consecutive cases of schizophrenia-like conditions attributable to cannabis seen in his practice, with 25 consecutive patients with Paranoid Schizophrenia. Patients with cannabis psychosis differed from the cases of Schizophrenia in that the former tended to display bizarre and violent behavior, to be anxious, to have insight, and to show little in the way of thought disorder.

Negrete (33) asserts that such cases arise after chronic heavy use of the drug and that the condition is characterized by impairment of the sensorium, poverty of thought, impairment of intellectual function, and paranoid ideation. Knight (34) has described chronic schizophreniform psychoses among Jamaicans in which cannabis use seems to have been at least a contributory factor in the cause. Spencer (35) has reported, from the Bahamas, a number of cases of subacute schizophrenia-like psychoses, apparently precipitated by excessive use of cannabis, and lasting for a few weeks, although some disturbances such as flattening of affect, amnesia for the onset of the illness, and a minor degree of thought disorder, may persist for much longer.

Cocaine Psychoses have been reported (36) by physicians in attendance at rock concerts and elsewhere. They observed acute anxiety reaction, with symptoms including high blood pressure, racing heart, anxiety, and paranoia. More severe effects, such as tactile and other hallucinations and delusions, are uncommon but do occur, mainly in habitual intravenous abusers. Cocaine psychosis is qualitatively similar to an amphetamine psychosis but lasts a shorter time.

Although there is no physical dependence on cocaine, sometimes psychological withdrawal symptoms such as anxiety and depression arise. Perceptual disturbances, paranoid thinking, and, rarely, psychoses occur in chronic cases. The treatment is symptomatic.

Psychedelics Psychoses have also been reported among drug abusers (36). There are many psychedelics or hallucinogenic drugs, some natural and some synthetic (see Chapter 4). The best known are mescaline, psilocybin, and the synthetic drug Lysergic Acid Diethylamide (LSD). The most common adverse effect of LSD and related drugs is the "bad trip," which resembles the acute panic reaction to cannabis, but can be more severe and occasionally produces true psychotic symptoms. The "bad trip" ends when the immediate effects of the drugs wear off (in the case of LSD, 8-12 hours).

Prolonged adverse reactions to LSD present the same variety of symptoms as "bad trips" and "flashbacks." They have been classified as Anxiety Disorders, Depressive Disorders, and psychoses. Most of these adverse reactions end after 24-48 hours, but sometimes they may last weeks or even months. The most likely candidates for adverse reactions are schizoid and pre-psychotic personalities. The treatment for prolonged reactions to psychedelic drugs is symptomatic including appropriate psychotherapy, and if necessary, tranquilizers, antipsychotic, and antidepressant medications. See Chapter 4 for full discussion.

Eating Disorders

This class of disorders is characterized by gross disturbance in eating behavior, and includes Anorexia Nervosa, Bulimia, Pica, Rumination Disorder of Infancy, and Atypical Eating Disorder. The most common of these are Anorexia Nervosa and Bulimia. Recent studies (37) agree that the prevalence of these disorders has been increasing in the last decade, and females outnumber males, usually 10:1.

Patients with Anorexia Nervosa present with an intense fear of becoming obese, which does not diminish as weight loss progresses. They claim to feel fat even when emaciated. To be diagnosed as Anorexia Nervosa, the weight loss must be at least 25% of the original body weight. If under 18 years of age, weight loss from original body weight plus projected weight gain expected from growth charts may be combined to make the 25%.

Bulimic patients present with recurrent episodes of binge eating. During these binges, there is a rapid consumption of a large amount of food in a discrete period of time, usually less than two hours. Such foods are usually high in calories, easily ingested, and inconspicuously eaten, and the binge is terminated by abdominal pain, sleep, self-induced vomiting, or purging by use of laxatives or diuretics. These individuals have frequent weight fluctuations of greater than ten pounds due to alternating binges and fasts. They often have depressed mood and self-deprecating thoughts following eating binges.

Eating disorders interface with alcoholism and other drug abuse in a number of ways. Anorexics may abuse diet pills to control their appetite and reduce their weight. They may use stimulants to fuel their obsessive need for exercise. The use of these drugs leads to excessive stimulation and often mimics an anxiety state with insomnia. To counteract these symptoms these individuals may further abuse minor tranquilizers and sedatives, leading to a vicious cycle of stimulant/sedative dependence.

Bulimics often abuse laxatives, diuretics, and cathartics to counteract the bloated feelings caused by their eating patterns. Bulimic women who seek treatment have a high prevalence of Affective Disorder and alcohol and/or other drug abuse, and they also frequently attempt suicide (37). In a study (37) of 108 normal-weight bulimic women who were evaluated using *DSM-III* criteria, 43% had a history of Affective Disorder and 18% had a history of alcohol and/or other drug abuse.

In the author's experience, when individuals are treated for alcohol and/or other drug abuse, the associated Eating Disorder often becomes more apparent and at times even exacerbated, substituting food addiction for drug addiction, thus sustaining addictive behavior. Additional intervention and treatment in a program specializing in treatment of Eating Disorders may be necessary for successful rehabilitation.

Eating Disorders programs are usually a multimodal intervention with several components. Patients initially see a psychiatrist for an evaluation. He or she may additionally assess the patient's height, weight, and laboratory work-up to assess the impact of the Eating Disorder on the body chemistry. In severely medically ill patients a further consultation with an internist or an endocrinologist may be necessary. While this medical evaluation is proceeding, the patient consults with the nutritionist or dietician in the program to re-establish healthy eating habits. It is recommended that initially a minimum of five family sessions be held to assess and intervene if necessary in the family dyanmics. The centerpiece of the program is the weekly Eating Disorders psychotherapy group with participation in at least 20 sessions. Peer support and confrontation by individuals struggling with similar problems is very beneficial to confront a patient and then educate him or her to identify and eliminate maladaptive behaviors and expose new and healthier strategies which deal with the vicissitudes of adulthood. Patients continue with additional individual psychotherapy as deemed necessary. Multiple treatment components of the program are established to deal with biopsychosocial aspects of the Eating Disorders. The goal of the program is to medically stabilize these patients, treat associated psychiatric disturbances (e.g., depression) as indicated, re-establish healthy eating habits, improve interpersonal communication and relationships within the family system, enhance self-esteem, and consolidate the fragile sense of identity of these patients.

Case Example

Patient 9 was a single white female in her mid-30s, who was admitted to an inpatient impaired professional's program with a history of amphetamine abuse and laxative abuse of several years' duration. For the last several years, she used alcohol especially on evenings and weekends. She was chronically depressed for the last several years and had an eating problem. She would fast, diet to control her weight, and then binge and purge. She was afraid of intimate relationships with men and women and had confusion about issues of identity and sexuality. She had separate dietary and psychiatric consultations to deal with her issues of identity, sexuality, and Eating Disorder. She participated in an Eating Disorders program for a few weeks, and then the treatment team decided that she could continue in the mainstream of the chemical dependency program with additional support and participation in the Eating Disorders program as needed.

ORGANIC MENTAL DISORDERS

In *DSM-III* a distinction is made between *Organic Brain Syndromes* and *Organic Mental Disorders*. The former refers to a constellation of psychological or behavioral signs and symptoms without reference to etiology (e.g., Delirium, Dementia); the latter designates a particular organic brain syndrome in which the etiology is known or presumed (e.g., Alcohol Withdrawal Delirium, Multi-Infarct Dementia).

By tradition, disorders that are related either to aging of the brain or to the ingestion of a substance are classified as mental disorders. For purposes of our discussion we will use the terms *Organic Brain Syndrome* and *Organic Mental Disorder* interchangeably. The *DSM-III* Organic Brain Syndromes include nine categories: delirium, dementia, amnestic syndrome, organic delusional syndrome, organic hallucinosis, organic affective disorders, organic personality syndrome, intoxication, and withdrawal. When evidence from the history, physical examination, or laboratory tests, of a specific organic factor is found, and is judged to be etiologically-related to the disturbance, a diagnosis of Organic Mental Disorder is made. Readers are referred to *DSM-III* (4) for details of diagnostic criteria of these mental disorders. Following is a summary of the core features of the nine categories of the Organic Brain Syndromes.

Delirium

The core features are the disturbances of memory and orientation, developing over a short period of time and fluctuating over time.

Dementia

Characterized by deterioration of previously acquired intellectual abilities, of sufficient severity to interfere with social and/ or occupational functioning.

Amnestic Syndrome

Short- and long-term memory disturbance is the predominant feature.

Organic Delusional Syndrome

Here, delusions are the predominant clinical feature.

Organic Hallucinosis

Hallucinations are the predominant feature.

Organic Affective Syndrome

Characterized by disturbance in mood closely resembling those in Manic or Major Depressive episodes.

Organic Personality Syndrome

Marked change in personality involving either emotional lability, impaired impulse control or social judgment, marked apathy and indifference, or suspiciousness.

Intoxication

Maladaptive behavior during the waking state due to the recent ingestion and presence in the body of a toxic substance.

Withdrawal

Development of a substance-specific syndrome that follows the cessation of or reduction in intake of a toxic substance that was previously regularly used by the individual to induce a state of intoxication.

Substance-induced Organic Mental Disorders are presumed to be caused by the direct effects of substances on the central nervous system. Ten classes of substances that can be taken non-medically to alter mood or behavior are listed below for greater diagnostic specificity. For each class of substance, a category corresponds to each of the Organic Brain Syndromes that have been frequently reported to be associated with the substance. The number of possible syndromes vary from substance to substance.

Alcohol. Intoxication, withdrawal, withdrawal delirium, hallucinosis, amnestic disorder, dementia.

Barbiturate or Similarly Acting Sedative or Hypnotic. Intoxication, withdrawal, withdrawal delirium, amnestic disorder.

Opioid. Intoxication, withdrawal.

Cocaine. Intoxication.

Amphetamine or Similarly Acting Sympathomimetic. Intoxication, delirium, delusional disorder, withdrawal.

Phencyclidine (PCP) or Similarly Acting Arylcyclohexylamine. Intoxication, delirium, mixed.

Hallucinogen. Hallucinations, delusional disorder, affective disorder.

Cannabis. Intoxication, delusional disorder.
Tobacco. Withdrawal.
Caffeine. Intoxication.

These disorders represent a significant area of diagnosis in psychiatry. Twenty percent of the hospital first-admissions in the U.S. are due to a diagnosable Organic Mental Disorder. One quarter of the total psychiatric hospital inpatient population in the U.S. is occupied by these patients. Fifty-two percent of inpatients and 15% of the outpatients diagnosed in public institutions were drug- and alcohol-induced Organic Brain Syndromes.

Case Example

Patient 10 was a married, white male in his 40s, admitted to an inpatient alcohol treatment unit with a 22-year history of Alcohol Dependence. He was seen in psychiatric consultation with complaints of depression, loss of interest in work, social withdrawal, crying spells, intermittent insomnia, anorexia, weight loss (15 pounds in one month), and thoughts of death and suicide. He also reported some ideas of reference (e.g., people were insinuating that he was homosexual). Physical exam and laboratory tests were normal. Patient was diagnosed as Alcohol Dependence Syndrome-Continuous and Organic Affective Syndrome, and was treated with a low dose of a major tranquilizer with good response in both his affective symptoms and ideas of reference. Antidepressant medication was considered, but has not been necessary yet because of gradual improvement with the low dose of the major tranquilizer alone, which is planned to be weaned over the next several months under psychiatric supervision.

There are two aspects of diagnostic work-up to be considered. First, is it important to establish the phenomenology of the presenting syndrome; for example, establish which of the nine organic mental disorders is present. This process is done by history and a mental status evaluation. Development of a substance-specific syndrome that follows the cessation of, or reduction in, intake of a substance that was previously regularly used by the individual to induce a state of intoxication establishes the presence of a withdrawal state. Maladaptive behavior due to recent ingestion of a substance establishes presence of intoxication. Marked change in personality, involving emotional lability, impaired impulse control or judgment, marked apathy or suspiciousness, are features of an Organic Syndrome. Mood disturbances resembling manic or depressive episodes in an individual with a history of substance abuse may point to an Organic Affective Syndrome. Hallucinations are predominant in Organic Hallucinosis, while delusions are predominant in Organic Delusional Syndrome. Memory defect is the hallmark of the Amnestic Syndrome. Dementia is characterized by impairment of previously acquired intellectual abilities, while disturbance of attention, memory, or orientation, developing over a short period of time, and fluctuating over time, should alert one to the possibility of Delirium. Second, one should establish the etiological agent by history, and screening of urine, blood, and/or Breathalyzer® as appropriate (see Chapter 6).

The salient treatment principles of dealing with Organic Mental Disorders include 1) establishing the identity of the etiological agents(s) by means of appropriate biochemical or other tests (see Chapter 6), and 2) initiating appropriate medical treatment(s) to address presenting problems, such as management of the intoxication or withdrawal state, correcting electrolyte disturbances, starting vitamin therapy, and so on. 3) Baseline neuropsychiatric functioning should be determined, by means of a mental status examination, neuropsychological testing, electroencephalogram (EEG), computerized tomography (CT scan), and other methods. Neurologic consultation may also be appropriate. 4) Appropriate symptomatic treatment for the presenting Organic Mental Disorder should also be initiated; for example, individual supportive psychotherapy, neuroleptic medications (for Organic Delusional Syndrome or Organic Hallucinosis), antidepressant medication and/or lithium therapy (for Organic Affective Syndrome), and so on. Medications should be used at the minimum effective dosage levels, and only for a limited period of time. At regular intervals — at least monthly — attempts should be made to wean the patient from the medications, which should then be discontinued if there is no recurrence of symptoms. 5) During this management period the patient's mental status should be monitored and re-evaluated on an ongoing basis to determine if the Organic Mental Disorder is receding. Serial EEGs may be particularly useful with patients having delirious states; serial neuropsychologic testing (every 6-12 months) may be particularly useful with patients having Amnestic Syndromes. 6) But among patients with more pervasive Organic Disorders, such as Dementias, extended-duration residential care may have to be considered. Such consideration is particularly necessary for patients with precarious or tenuous personal, family, or community support systems, and those with a history of relapses, to avoid further organic insult to the nervous system, and to provide a milieu most conducive to intensive treatment and rehabilitation while protecting the patient's abstinence and sobriety.

SUMMARY

About two-thirds of alcoholic or chemically dependent inpatients had concomitant psychiatric disorder in our clinical study. The most common psychiatric disorders seen in such clinical populations often included Adjustment Disorders, Conduct Disorders, Personality Disorders, Dysthymic and Cyclothymic Disorders, Affective Disorders, Anxiety and Eating Disorders, Schizophreniform Disorders, and Organic Mental Disorders. In an earlier study, 33% of alcoholic inpatients had concurrent lifetime prevalence of an Affective Disorder, while women alcoholic inpatients of 20–30 years of age had a 60% prevalence of Affective Disorders. The common modes of presentations of these disorders, their interaction with alcohol and other Substance Abuse Disorders, the resultant clinical picture and their recognition and treatment are discussed. The role of a psychiatric consultant in the management of these patients in a multidisciplinary treatment team setting is discussed. Judicious use of medications such as antidepressants or lithium, and other treatment modalities such as biofeedback, or Eating Disorders programs as appropriate, are emphasized. It was found that collaborative efforts among psychiatrists, addictionologists, and the entire multidisciplinary treatment team yielded optimal results in the holistic management of patients' chemical dependency, psychiatric disorder, and the vicissitudes of associated personality disorders. Case examples are presented where possible to elucidate some diagnostic and treatment principles.

REFERENCES

1. Myers, J.K.; Weissman, M.M.; Tischler, G.L.; Holzer, C.E.; Leaf, P.J.; Orvaschel, H.; Anthony, J.C.; Boyd, J.H.; Burke, J.B., Jr.; Kramer, M.; Stoltzman, R.: Six-month prevalence of psychiatric disorders in three communities. *Archives of General Psychiatry, 41:*959–967, 1984.

2. Selzer, M.L.; Winokur, A.; Wilson, T.: The drunken driver: psychosocial study. *Drug and Alcohol Dependence, 2:*239, 1977.

3. Selzer, M.L.; Winokur, A.; Wilson, T.: A psychosocial comparison of drunk drivers and alcoholics. *International Journal of Studies on Alcohol,* *38:*1286, 1977.

4. American Psychiatric Association. *Diagnostic and Statistical Manual of Mental Disorders, Third Edition.* Washington, DC: APA, 1980.

5. Robins, L.N.; Melzer, J.E.; Coroughan, J.; Ratcliff, K.: National Institute of Mental Health Diagnostic Interview Schedule: its history, characteristics, and validity. *Archives of General Psychiatry, 38:*381-389, 1981.

6. Robins, L.; Orvaschel, H.; Anthony, J.; Blazer, D.; Burman, M.A.; Burke, J.: The Diagnostic Interview Schedule. In *Epidemiologic Field Method in Psychiatry, The NIMH Epidemiologic Catchment Area Program.* Easton, W.W. and Kessler, L.G. (Eds.). New York: Academic Press Inc., (in press).

7. Keller, M.H.; Taylor, C.I.; Miller, W.C.: Are all recently detoxified alcoholics depressed? *American Journal of Psychiatry, 136:*586-588, 1979.

8. Hamm, J.E.; Meyar, L.F.; Bowron, G.: The quantitative measurements of depression and anxiety in male alcoholics. *American Journal of Psychiatry, 136:*580-582, 1979.

9. Bedi, A.R.; Halikas, J.A.: Alcoholism and affective disorder. *Alcoholism: Clinical and Experimental Research, 9:*133-134, 1985.

10. Helgason, T.: Epidemiology of mental disorders in Iceland: a psychiatric and demographic investigation of 5,395 Icelanders. *Acta Psychiatrica Scandinavica, 40:* supplement 173, 1-258, 1964.

11. Stromgren, E.: Contribution to psychiatric epidemiology and genetics. *Acta Jutlandica Medicalsk Serie* (Medical Series), 16 (Vol. XI), 1-86, 1968.

12. Fromming, J.: The expectation of mental infirmity in a sample of Danish population. *Occasional Papers of Eugenics* No. 7, London: Cassell, 1951.

13. Winokur, A.; Clayton, P.J.; Reich, T.: *Manic Depressive Illness.* St. Louis, Missouri: C.V. Mosby, 1969.

14. Adelstein, A.M.; Downham, D.Y.; Stein, A.; Susser, M.W.: The epidemiology of mental illness in an English city. *Social Psychiatry, 3:*47-59, 1968.

15. Comstock, G.W.; Helsing, K.J.: Symptoms of depression in two communities. *Psychological Medicine 6:*531-563, 1976.

16. Grad de Alarcon, J.; Sainsbury, P.; Costqin, W.R.: Incidence of referred mental illness in Chichester and Salisbury. *Psychological Medicine, 5:* 32-54, 1975.

17. Bernard, J.; Carroll, M.B.; Greden, J.F.; Tarida, J.; Albala, A.A.; Haskett, J.F.; Norman, J.M.; Dronfol, Z.; Lohr, N.; Steiner, M.; de Vinge, J.P.; Young, E.: A specific laboratory test for the diagnosis of melancholia: standardization, validation, and clinical utility. *Archives of General Psychiatry, 38:*14-22, 1981.

18. Jackson, A.H.; Shader, R.I.: Guidelines for the withdrawal of narcotics and general depressant drugs. *Diseases of the Nervous System, 34:* 162, 1973.

19. Connell, P.H.: *Amphetamine Psychosis.* Maudsley Institute of Psychiatry, Monograph No. 5. London: Chapman, 1958.

20. Bell, D.S.: Comparison of amphetamine psychosis and schizophrenia. *British Journal of Psychiatry, 111:*701, 1965.

21. Victor, M.; Adams, R.D.: The effect of alcohol on the nervous system. *Research Publication Association for Research in Nervous and Mental Diseases, 32:*526-573, 1953.

22. Victor, M.; Hope, J.M.: The phenomenon of auditory hallucinations in chronic alcoholism: a critical evaluation of the status of alcoholic hallucinosis. *Journal of Nervous and Mental Disorders, 126:*451-481, 1958.

23. Gross, M.M.; Halpert, E.; Sabot, L.; Polizos, P.: Hearing disturbances and auditory hallucinations in the acute alcoholic psychoses. I. Tinnitus: incidence and significance. *Journal of Nervous and Mental Disorder 137:* 455-465, 1963.

24. Scott, D.F.: Alcoholic hallucinosis: an etiological study. *British Journal of Addictions, 62:*113-125, 1967.

25. Sabot, L.M.; Gross, M.M.; Halpert, E.: A study of acute alcoholic psychoses in women. *British Journal of Addictions, 63:*29-49, 1968.

26. Sarvay, S.M.; Pardes, H.: Auditory elementary hallucination in alcohol withdrawal psychosis. *Archives of General Psychiatry, 16:*652-658, 1967.

27. Scott, D.F.; Davies, D.L.; Malherbe, M.E.L.: Alcoholic hallucinosis. *International Journal of Addictions 4:*319-330, 1969.

28. Freed E.X.: Alcoholism and schizophrenia: the search for perspectives. *Journal of Studies on Alcohol, 36:*853-881, 1975.

29. Rimmer, J.; Jacobson, B.: Alcoholism in schizophrenics and their relatives. *Journal of Studies on Alcohol, 38:*1781-1784, 1977.

30. Davison, K.: Drug-induced psychoses and their relationship to schizophrenia. In *Schizophrenia Today,* Kemali, D., Bartholoni, G. and Richter, D. (Eds.). Oxford: Pergamon Press, 1976.

31. Thacore, V.R.: Bhang psychoses. *British Journal of Psychiatry, 123:* 225-229, 1973.

32. Thacore, V.R.: Cannabis psychoses and paranoid schizophrenia. *Archives of General Psychiatry, 33:*383-386, 1976.

33. Negrete, J.C.: Psychological adverse effects of cannabis smoking: a tentative classification. *Canadian Medical Association Journal 108:*195-202, 1973.

34. Knight, R.: Role of cannabis in psychiatric disturbance. *Annals of the New York Academy of Sciences, 282:*64-71, 1976.

35. Spencer, D.J.: Cannabis induced psychoses. *International Journal of the Addictions, 6:*322-326, 1971.

36. Freedman, A.M.: Drug dependence. *Comprehensive Text Book of Psychiatry* 3rd Edition, Kaplan, H.I., Freeman, A.M., and Sadock, B.J. (Eds.). Baltimore, Maryland: Williams & Wilkins Company, 1980.

37. Hatsukami, D.; Eckert, E.; Mitchell, J.E.; Pyle, R.: Affective disorder and substance abuse in women with bulimia. *Psychological Medicine, 14:* 701-704, 1984.

Chapter 17

Alcohol and Drug Dependency Problems in Special Populations: Women

George Jacobson, Ph.D.

OVERVIEW

In the past five years there has been a virtual eruption of interest in and attention to the problems and needs of special populations, with a strong emphasis on women. This chapter focuses on this particular group by first reviewing and summarizing some of the new information available regarding emerging issues and problems, and then critically examining attitudes of society toward women and their substance abuse. We move to a detailed examination of how groups of women in treatment view themselves, how they perceive themselves as individuals and in the context of the environment within which they live. That discussion is followed by in-depth analysis of self-concept, personality, perception, and other aspects of individual psychology which describe women in the treatment setting. This information is used to provide special insights and understandings regarding possible etiologies of substance abuse disorders, consequences of chemical dependency, and, most importantly, cues to Allied Health Professionals relevant to their roles in treatment and rehabilitation settings.

Although some of our inferences and conclusions regarding this particular population are tentative — and, when noted, outright speculative — the breadth and depth of empirical information provided can be immediately applicable by a wide range of health-care providers in a variety of clinical environments.

A summary and references conclude the chapter.

INTRODUCTION

Although they are not a miniroty group in this country, much current popular literature implies that women are viewed as long-term victims of oppression and male domination and have only recently begun to express their awareness of their unfortunate and negelcted status. Certainly in terms of political power, occupational opportunity, economic and financial independence, legal status, and other aspects of adult living which most men tend to take for granted, women do indeed appear to have received less than fair and equal treatment.

Whereas their general situation is gradually improving, progress is painfully slow in the recognition of special problems and needs of addicted women. That is, chemically dependent and substance-abusing women seem to be targets of discrimination, for both society at large and the substance-abuse establishment. While the former may probably be intentional, the latter is usually inadvertent and may be attributable to ignorance and neglect. That is, much of what is currently known or believed to be true about substance abuse and chemical dependency is based primarily on observations of, and research with, men. Some of that information may be erroneously generalized to women. Moreover, policy-making bodies, hospital and clinic administrations, the treatment community, and the alcoholism and drug dependency establishment in general (with some notable exceptions, such as Alanon) have traditionally been dominated by men. A largely middle-class white male bias pervades the field, often to the detriment of women. With the exception of the late Ms. Marty Mann, founder of the National Council on Alcoholism, and a few courageous women of public stature (e.g., Ms. Betty Ford, Ms. Mercedes McCambridge) who have rejected the convention of anonymity, women have played only a small and peripheral role in the development of current prevention, treatment, research, and educational policies and practices. Perhaps in the future women will cease to tolerate their status as members of the neglected majority.

Regardless of the reasons for such neglect, as benign as they may be, increasingly greater numbers of chemically dependent women are making known their special problems and needs, both real and apparent. It is those problems and needs which occupy the focus of this chapter.

SPECIAL PROBLEMS:
PSYCHOLOGICAL AND PHYSIOLOGICAL

Predisposing and Precipitating Factors

Recent research has identified some gender-related variables — some only superficial and others of greater significance — which may play an important role in the etiology of chemical dependencies among women, and which may influence the direction and outcome of treatment. One psychologist has reported that alcoholic women tend to express problems involving incomplete or inadequate feminine identification, and so may use alcohol because it helps them to feel "more like women" (1). Other studies suggest that women are more likely than men to begin using alcohol to excess during periods of significant life crises, such as divorce or death of a spouse. This type of "reactive" alcoholism differs in many ways from the "essential" or lifestyle alcoholism which is more often typical of men. Relatedly, some research indicates that periods of significant depression more frequently precede the development of an addictive disorder among women than among men (2). Thus there is a greater likelihood that women's alcoholism may be "secondary" rather than "primary." These two distinctions, essential-reactive and primary-secondary, are important dimensions to keep in mind for purposes of diagnosis, evaluation, and treatment-planning, as recent research suggests that differential rehabilitation approaches are needed. It should be emphasized, of course, that men too may be reactive rather than essential alcoholics, or secondary rather than primary alcoholics, or experience significant depressive episodes which antedate the onset of abusive drinking, but the probability is greater among women.

Biological and Psychosexual Factors

Other empirical evidence suggests that biological and psychosexual characteristics of women may be relevant to chemical dependency problems. For example, given proportionately equivalent doses of alcohol calculated on the basis of body weight, a woman's body will absorb and metabolize the drug differently than a man's. She will show a higher blood alcohol level (BAL, or concentration of alcohol circulating in the bloodstream), which is attributed to the higher ratio of fat to muscle in the composition of the female body (3). Body fluids and hormonal balance also play an influential role in the absorption and metabolism of alcohol among women, depending on complex changes which occur before, during, and after menstruation. Some researchers have speculated that "premenstrual tension," which approximately 60% of all women interviewed reported experiencing to some degree, may be only one aspect of a more complex premenstrual syndrome (PMS) which is associated with physical and emotional changes that are often related to increased drinking (3). Although PMS has been shown to have a powerful psychological basis, apparently dependent on the individual's feelings and attitudes regarding menstruation (or, perhaps, womanhood and feminity more generally), it can nonetheless influence a woman's drinking behavior and the effects of alcohol. Relatedly, irregular menstruation is another frequently reported problem among drug-abusing women, although we do not know if menstruation is disrupted or suppressed by the chemicals *per se*, or by the stress which is associated with addictive diseases and chemical dependency.

Alcoholic women also report a disproportionately high rate of other gynecologic problems and sexual dysfunctions. Although we are uncertain as to whether these problems are causes or effects of substance abuse, they are nonetheless significant matters which require special attention. For example, one group of specialists reported that approximately 19% of the alcoholic women they interviewed had never experienced orgasm, versus only 8–10% of mature women in the general population (4). And because alcoholic women frequently (46% in one sample studied) marry or otherwise become sexually involved with alcoholic men, they very often report sexual problems attributable to their partners (4). More than one-third of a group of alcoholic women recently surveyed acknowledged that they had been raped (at an average age of approximately 20), and 40% reported having been involved in incestous relationships (4). Since both of these events often have unfortunate consequences for subsequent sexual adjustment, special counseling for sexual problems appears to be a particular need in women's treatment programs. That this is indeed the case is indicated in the fact that 56% of the women treated in one clinic expressed a definite need for a variety of sex-therapy services (5). Relatedly, miscarriages, abortions, and infertility were reported by 25–40% of women studied at the same clinic, again indicating a need for obstetric and gynecologic attention among chemically dependent women (4).

Because men are often more reticent regarding sexual concerns we do not know the extent to which they may experience sexual dysfunctions and reproductive abnormalities (see Chapters 8 and 10 for information regarding sexual functioning during recovery). Nevertheless, it is quite evident that psychosexual and reproductive problems deserve special focus as part of the overall rehabilitative efforts for women.

Drinking Patterns

The concept of "telescoping" which is applied to the development of alcoholism among women implies that the progression of the illness occurs more rapidly for them than it does for men. Indeed this appears to be the case, as it is consistently reported that women present themselves for treatment approximately six to eight years after the onset of heavy or problem drinking, whereas among men an average of eleven to fifteen years elapse between onset of alcohol abuse and first treatment (5). Alcoholic women tend also to be older at the time of onset of problem drinking, although because of the telescoping effect (which may turn out to be more apparent than real) they are not necessarily older than men at time of first treatment. One can only speculate about possible causes of the telescoping of the so-called progression of alcoholism, such as sex-related differences in physiological responsiveness to the effects of alcohol, lower tolerance levels, the greater psychological suggestibility and emotional dependency which women have been traditionally taught to expect of themselves, and other complex interactions of biological, psychological, and social factors. This pattern may change in the future, however, since recent surveys of school-age children indicate that girls now begin drinking at an earlier age than was the norm fifteen or twenty years ago (6).

In addition, women's drinking patterns seem to differ from those of men. Males will more often drink in groups, with companions, in taverns or other public places, or as part of some social occasion. By contrast, women are more often cited as being solitary drinkers or "closet alcoholics," drinking alone and usually at home. This difference suggests that alcohol may serve a different purpose for women, facilitating social withdrawal rather than making social interaction more comfortable. It also implies that female alcoholics are more likely to feel isolated, withdrawn, and cut off from a meaningful social milieu. As a result of this drinking pattern, women are less likely to be observed publicly intoxicated and, therefore, less likely to experience serious troubles due to drinking. Consequently, because much of a woman's drinking tends to be unobserved — or ignored and covered up for as long as possible — the notion of telescoping may be more apparent than real. However, as "double standards" dissolve and public drinking becomes more socially acceptable for women, we may begin to see these patterns changing and male and female alcoholics becoming more alike. In the meantime, allied health practitioners may be well-advised to recognize and appreciate these differences.

SPECIAL PROBLEMS: SOCIAL AND ATTITUDINAL

In addition to the psychological, physiological, and other factors discussed above, women are also faced with a variety of other special conditions resulting from the imposition of certain social sanctions and expectations (including those which women place on themselves), public attitudes and values, prejudices, and widespread discrimination. A reflection of these special conditions may be seen in the increasingly higher estimates of alcoholism among women which have been published periodically since the end of World War II. Between 1948-1950 prevalence figures suggested that women represented 10-14% of adult alcoholics in the United States (5, 7). During the next decade, 15-20% was a frequently cited figure, followed by 20-25% during the next decade (5, 7). By the end of the 1970s the prevalence estimates had risen to 28-30%, and the notion of a one-to-one ratio of male and female alcoholics has been occasionally mentioned (5, 7). This gradual increase may be attributed to improvements in society, more women in the work force, more women as heads of household, changing sex-roles for women, or some combination of all such variables. The general impression derived from these data is one of gradual change, growing pressure for continued change, and, ultimately, the development of a greater demand for change in the status quo of the male-dominated establishment.

One such area of change is seen in the results of a recent survey (8) which indicated that the absence of child-care services and facilities is a major deterrent to some women entering treatment. The traditional sex role of women as mothers is a biologically fixed one, of course, but the absence of adequate child-care assistance seems to be discriminatory and implies a social prejudice against women/mothers as patients. Whereas the situation may be somewhat eased for women whose husbands (or other family members) can fill the child-care role, single, divorced, or separated mothers have special difficulties. The situation is dramatically complicated for women who must spend thirty days in an in-patient treatment program or three to six months at a halfway house. Health-care providers, and their institutional employers, may be called upon to provide innovative residential arrangements for women with young children, or to shift to greater utilization of outpatient and partial hospitalization programs with day-care services within the facility. Such arrangements represent no more than a recognition of current reality.

Innovative child-care and residential arrangements must also be accompanied by changes in traditional prevention, identification, and intervention programs which will be responsive to other problems attritutable to, or at least related to, social and attitudinal issues. It should be recognized at the outset that women tend to be protected against the consequences of their own deviant drinking and are thereby prevented from entering the treatment continuum at the earliest — and presumably the most treatable — point. For example, husbands and other family members often report covering up, ignoring, or rationalizing the woman's drinking problems until they become manifestly undeniable, and, by then, require more-radical treatment. (Paradoxically, however, men are later more likely to divorce an alcoholic spouse than are women.) Relatedly, police are less likely to apprehend, and then more reluctant to issue citations to, women who are driving while intoxicated, and that closes another avenue of entry into the intervention system. Publicly intoxicated women are also more likely to be escorted home by police than transported to a hospital or other treatment facility, and another treatment opportunity is again denied or at least postponed. And although more women are participating in the work force they seem not to be participating in the increasing number of union- and/or employer-sponsored occupational alcoholism programs, for a variety of reasons. Erratic attendance, declining work performance, or other signs of problem-drinking may be overlooked or attributed to other causes (e.g., the euphemistic "time of the month"), by male supervisors who may also be reluctant to confront women regarding their behavior at work. The use of typically male-oriented identification criteria (e.g., public intoxication, fights and arrests while intoxicated) also militates against early identification and intervention. Also, because of the nature of employment opportunities available to women, and because women are more likely to be part-time workers, they may not have access to some of the health-care and sick-leave benefits available to males. And when medical and other health care is sought, physicians and other allied health practitioners are unlikely to recognize, diagnose, and treat alcohol abuse or alcohol dependence as such. These diagnoses are often overlooked or intentionally avoided in the misguided effort to not offend the patient. "Situational" or "adjustment" reactions, anxiety states, neurotic depression, or other diagnostic entities which are more discreet or less socially unacceptable are likely to be offered, and too often some mild tranquilizer or other addicting drug will be prescribed. Our experience suggests that women in treatment are likely to be abusing one or more prescribed medications rather than, or in addition to, alcohol (9). Such abuse or addiction may occasionally be iatrogenic. There is an associated notion that it is somehow more socially acceptable for women to abuse or be addicted to pharmacologic/psychotropic medications than to alcohol.

Paradoxically, as women gain greater equality of employment opportunities, equality of treatment in the workplace, and increased upward mobility in professional stature and public and private job hierarchies, they come under closer scrutiny and, simultaneously, more peer pressure to drink socially. The stress and tension associated with some professions or careers also increases the probability of using alcohol to cope with job-related difficulties. And women who are out-of-role in their employment (i.e., have jobs other than the traditional one of secretary, nurse, or teacher), are more likely to be heavy- or problem-drinkers, as are unmarried women, childless women, and women who are heads of household. Thus, there are both advantages and disadvantages to a liberalization of conventional norms and attitudes.

In the meantime, however, conventional norms and attitudes being what they are, women are placed under additional burdens which are not generally applicable to men. For instance, guilt and loss of self-esteem may be special problems which society creates and maintains for women. A female alcoholic is more strongly censured and stigmatized by society, and women who drink alone in bars or other public places are viewed as being "loose," "cheap," or "available" for sexual encounters. A woman who drinks heavily during pregnancy and gives birth to a child with a fetal alcohol syndrome (see Chapter 10) may experience an even greater burden of guilt, and an alcoholic woman who disappoints, neglects, or deserts her family is more harshly judged than her male counter-parts who may more freely do the same.

All of these social and attitudinal biases must be taken into consideration by health-care professionals in all aspects of provid-ing education, prevention, diagnosis, intervention, or treatment services for women with substance abuse or chemical dependency problems. As society evolves in its views of women, one may remain hopeful about the alleviation and remediation of these particular concerns.

TREATMENT-RELATED DIFFERENCES BETWEEN MALES AND FEMALES, AND TREATMENT OUTCOME

Although a great many studies have attempted to describe the nature and characteristics of alcoholic patient populations, and to relate those characteristics to treatment outcomes, less than 10% of the published research included separate results for men and women. Consequently, we do not have a meaningful picture of the female populations of alcoholism-treatment units (ATUs) nor do we know how treatment affects women, nor the charac-teristics of the efficacious ATU programs.

One group of researchers (10) has tried to correct this situa-tin by doing comprehensive outcome studies of nearly all patients admitted to seventeen state-funded ATUs between April and September 1977. The results of their work is summarized here because it represents a large-scale attempt to discover some of the basic distinctions between male and female alcoholics, as well as demonstrating some of the characteristics of good treatment utilization studies through which the rehabilitation of female alcoholics may be improved.

In the interest of brevity many details must be omitted, but their study population was composed of 83% men and 17% women (229 of 1,340 patients), which is fairly typical of the sex ratio in publicly funded ATUs. Twenty-seven percent of the women were thirty years old and younger, 57% were between 31-50 years of age, and 16% were 51 years old and older. Approxi-mately one-fourth of the women were never married, one-fourth were currently married, 10% failed to report their marital status, and the remaining 40% were separated, divorced, or widowed. Seventy-eight percent of the women were white; 42% had less than a high school education, 35% were high school graduates, and 23% had gone beyond high school. Approximately one-quarter of the women were "homemakers," 48% were unemployed, 16% worked full-time, and 10% part-time, outside the home, and 2% were retired. Inaptient treatment programs ranged in duration from 30 days to 90 days. At the time of the three-month post-hospitalization follow-up, 81% of the women were available for inerview, and 73% were contacted for eight-month follow-up (versus 70% and 66%, respectively, for men, indicating a greater social and geographic stability among women). Follow-up interviews were conducted in person when possible, or by telephone or mail if necessary.

ATUs in which these patients were treated were classified as having either a primarily medical orientation (a high concentration of physicians, psychiatrists, RNs and LPNs, and relatively frequent use of Antabuse and major and minor tranquilizers), a peer group orientation (a high concentration of alcoholism rehabilitation counselors and trainees, emphasis on alcohol-education seminars, Alcoholics Anonymous and Alanon), or a rehabilitation-professional orientation (higher concentration of psychologists, social workers, rehabilitation counselors, occupational and recreational therapists, and emphasis on family therapy, occupational, vocational, and relaxation therapies). The orientation of the ATU and the sex of the client interacted to produce some significant differences in treatment outcome. For example, women treated at ATUs with a strong medical orientation were less likely to be drinking at the time of follow-up (31%) than were women treated at ATUs with low medical orientation (54%). But women from ATUs with a strong peer-group orientation were more likely to be drinking at follow-up (46%) than were women from ATUs lower on this orientation (39%). By contrast, 38% of the men treated at high medical-orientation units, and 42% from the low medical-orientation units, were drinking at follow-up. From the high and low peer-orientation ATUs, 34% and 43% of the men were drinking at follow-up. The implications of these data are fairly clear: Female alcoholics are likely to respond more favorably (i.e., more likely to be abstinent at follow-up) to medically oriented treatment, while male alcoholics tend to respond better to a peer-treatment approach.

The sex of the individual patient, and the sex ratio at the treatment facility, also interact to affect rehabilitation outcome. One researcher reported that completion of treatment rose from an average of 35% to a mean of 59% when women were treated in sexually homogeneous groups. The group (10) studying the 17 state-funded ATUs found that the average percentage of female alcoholics still drinking at follow-up was higher (49%) among women who had been at units which had higher than average proportions of men in treatment, compared to women treated on units with lower than average male:female ratios (only 35% still drinking at follow-up). An opposite effect obtained for men, however. When treated at ATUs with a higher male:female ratio, 38% of the men were drinking at follow-up, but when the male: female ratio was lower, 42% of the treated men were still drinking at follow-up.

From these studies we can make reasonable inferences about treatment-related sex differences and treatment outcomes. First, more men than women are likely to enter inpatient treatment. Second, women are most likely to be between the ages of 31-50, white, unmarried, not employed outside the home, and with less than a high school education. Third, women are more likely to remain abstinent after treatment in a facility with a more dominant medical orientation and a lesser emphasis on peer orientation. Fourth, completion of treatment may be increased if sexually homogeneous therapy groups are available. And fifth, a lower male:female patient ratio in the treatment facility is related to an increased probability of abstinence among women at three- and eight-month follow-up intervals.

Characteristics of Women in Treatment

A relatively vast literature is available describing the characteristics of males in treatment for a variety of substance-abuse and chemical-dependency problems. Comparable information for women, however, is sparse and scattered throughout dozens of professional publications. To remedy this situation and to provide Allied Health Professionals a unified picture of women in treatment, all of the information presented in this section is derived from a recently completed in-depth study (9) of a group of 43 adult females treated for alcohol abuse, alcohol dependence, and other forms of substance use disorders. Because the treatment facility, rehabilitation programs, and patient populations discussed herein are believed to be representative and typical, allied health practitioners will have a reasonable basis for appreciating much that may be useful in their own clinical approaches to women in treatment.

Sociodemographic description. The average age of our sample (N = 43) was 35 years, and ages ranged between 18-69 years. On the average, the women were high school graduates, and none reported less than an eighth-grade education. Thirty percent of the women were married, 33% were single, 23% were divorced, 9% were separated, and 5% were widowed. The mean number of children per patient was 1.4, but 40% of the women had none, 19% had one, 17% had two, 12% had three, and the remainder had 4-6 children each. The patients had been hospitalized for a mean of twelve days at the time we initiated our interviewing and testing battery.

Brain dysfunction and cognitive performance. Because it is virtually a universally reported phenomenon that heavy drinking results in some degree of impairment of brain functions necessary to a variety of human behaviors, we routinely used a three-test battery to assess the level of functioning in three important spheres. One of the tests, the Shipley Institute of Living Scale (SILS) assesses one aspect of langauge skills — vocabulary — and provides information about the ability to perform abstract-thinking processes. The differences between the two sets of functions is presumed to indicate a cognitive deficit; although this "conceptual quotient" (CQ) says nothing about the permanence of any such dysfunction, it is useful for deciding if the patient is likely to profit from educational seminars, counseling, the "talk treatment" of traditional group therapy, and related aspects of rehabilitation. For our sample the mean "vocabulary age" was 16.4 years (i.e., performance was equivalent to that of a 16.4-year-old "normal" individual; vocabulary age ranges between 9.5 and 21 years for normals, 11.9-20.2 for our sample) and the mean "abstraction age" was 14.12 years (normal range = 7.8-20.5 years, range = 8.4-19.7 years for our sample). The overall "mental age" of our female patients was an average of 15.3 years, (normal range = 8.4-20.8 years, 10.2-18.4 for our sample), and the mean CQ was 85.7. Overall the Shipley data indicate that approximately half (48.8%) of our female patients are within the "normal" part of the distribution. Of the remainder, however, 21% must be considered "probably pathological" according to the norms, and another 31% are "slightly," "moderately," "quite," or "very" likely to be experiencing some degree of cognitive dysfunction which may affect their response to treatment.

A related tool, the Bender Visual Motor Gestalt test, indicates a relatively mild to moderate level of impairment in visuomotor performance among the majority of the women tested. While this measure does provide signs of brain dysfunction, it is of a nonverbal intellectual nature. The information is nonetheless valuable, however, as we can infer from it the extent to which patients may profit from, or be frustrated by, various types of occupational, recreational, and activity therapy.

The third related measure, the Graham–Kendall Memory for Design test (MFD), also assesses brain dysfunction, from which we can infer certain conclusions about short-term memory and new learning experiences. None of our patients showed any unequivocal signs of dysfunction in these activities, but 13.5% were in the "borderline" category. The remainder (86.5%) scored within the "normal" range.

Personality. A number of different measures were used to directly and indirectly assess various aspects of what is loosely referred to as personality variables. One such measure, the Eysenck Personality Inventory (EPI), places our patients in a two-dimensional matrix labeled "introversion-extraversion" in one plane and "stability-neuroticism" in the other plane. Results indicate that our sample of substance abusers are only slightly less "extraverted" than average American college students, but quite a bit more "neurotic." In practical terms these data imply that female patients are relatively emotionally labile, unstable, or overreactive, likely to express a number of physical and psychosomatic complaints, and prone to feelings of worry, tension, and anxiety. At the same time they are likely to be somewhat outgoing, sociable, and gregarious, somewhat impulsive and unreliable, perhaps optimistic, somewhat aggressive or prone to outbursts of anger, and unlikely to plan for or anticipate the future.

To a great extent these somewhat simplistic interpretations are supported and amplified by a more comprehensive and sophisticated personality measure called the Sixteen Personality Factors questionnaire (16-PF). This test indicates the patient's position on sixteen pairs of bipolar scales (e.g., reserved-outgoing, trusting-suspicious) which are descriptive of a variety of personality dimensions. Because separate norms are available, we can compare our women's responses with those of adult females in the general population. For explanatory purposes, all of the inferences presented below are based on modal responses (i.e., the most-frequently appearing scores), and it must be kept in mind that all descriptive terms are relative and comparative, rather than absolute.

Thus, we find that, in support of the EPI inferences, the average or typical female respondent tends to have a relatively low level of frustration tolerance, to be easily annoyed and emotionally unstable, or emotionally immature, is changeable, may prefer to avoid some of the demands of reality, and may express physical and/or psychosomatic complaints, feelings of tiredness and fatigue, etc. At the same time they may have a need to exercise control of their emotions and so may not be very open or expressive, and may appear to be somewhat compulsive, controlled, and concerned about social appearances and personal reputation. Such women may also be tense, restless, impatient, and frustrated. Characteristically they seem to be shrewd, unsentimental, and perhaps manipulative of others. To a certain extent they are also unconcerned about practical, "down to earth" matters, probably cheerful and noncompetitive, often somewhat passive and dependent, and perhaps somewhat willing to disregard society's norms or become engaged in antisocial behavior. None of these characteristics or traits are expressed to a pathological extent, and women in treatment appear to be close to the average for women in general.

Self-concept. The ways in which women in treatment perceive, interpret, and evaluate themselves as individuals, family members, and social beings suggest that they deviate from a "normal" group to a considerable extent, but do not differ markedly from a group of psychiatric patients. Based on the results from administering the standardized Tennessee Self-Concept Scale (TSCS) to our group of female substance abusers, some useful inferences can be made. Again, this description of our patient group's self-concept is based on relative rather than absolute values.

We find first of all, and probably somewhat contrary to expectation, that on the average these women are honestly self-critical and do not appear to be making a deliberate effort to present themselves in a fictitiously favorable light. We find also that they tend to define their self-concept more by affirming what they are than by rejecting what they are not. Accompanying this tendency is a moderate degree of conflict, confusion, or contradiction over what elements actually comprise their notion of self, an uncertainty or indecisiveness over who or what they are. Not unexpectedly, overall level of self-esteem is below average, compared to scores of "normal" groups. Female substance abusers have doubts about their value and worth as individuals, may perceive themselves as undesirable, have little self-confidence, and may experience feelings of anxiety or depression. They express a weak sense of personal identity, an unformed or uncertain notion of who or what they are as individuals. They also have a slight problem with self-acceptance or self-satisfaction, and a similar degree of difficulty in defining or identifying their own actions and behaviors as a basis of self-awareness.

The TSCS identifies five aspects of self-concept, all but one of which — social self — is problematic for this group of chemically dependent women. Social-self perception is essentially within the average range, implying a sense of adequacy and worth in social interactions with other people in general. Although this perception is not an especially strong one, it does represent the most favorable attribute the women perceive in themselves. On the other hand, they hold a relatively dim view of their physical self, encompassing notions of physical appearance, health, skills, and sexuality. There is a similarly low appreciation of the moral-ethical self, suggesting a feeling of being a "bad" person, with little moral worth, dissatisfaction with religion (or lack of religion) or conventional moral and ethical values. Their sense of personal worth, adequacy as a person, or self-evaluation of their own personality, is equally low. Feelings of adequacy in terms of relationships with family and/or intimate friends are also relatively low, from which we infer a sense of isolation, loneliness, or alienation.

Although not a test of psychopathology *per se*, other portions of the TSCS allow us to make inferences about ways in which our patients resemble other patient-groups in terms of similarity of response patterns. Thus, we note that substance-abusing women in treatment bear a very close resemblance to psychiatric patients in general, and particularly those who were diagnosed as personality disorders and those classified as neurotics. There was far less similarity between our patients and other groups diagnosed as psychotic.

While we do not represent our self-concept data as being definitive of all alcohol- and drug-abusing women, health-care professionals can certainly use this information as a guide to the nature and extent of problems which they may encounter among their own chemically dependent female patients. These data can also provide clues to the structure and direction of treatment appropriate for such patients. For example, attention to physical fitness, diet, and exercise may be useful for improving physical self-concept; family therapy may be valuable for improving one's sense of integration and value within the family unit.

Patterns of alcohol and drug use. Individual administration of a sophisticated and complex differential diagnostic instrument, the Alcohol Use Inventory (AUI), provides us a basis for describing the patterns, purposes, and consequences of self-reported alcohol and drug use among our sample of hospitalized women (11). Analyses of results indicate three identifiable characteristics. To a moderately high degree the women tend to be continuous, sustained drinkers, rather than obsessive-compulsive, or binge drinkers. We infer regular, perhaps daily, alcohol use for six months or more, possibly for the purpose of coping with the stresses and anxieties of living. These inferences suggest that prolonged treatment and support may be necessary because drinking has become an important coping mechanism. Relatedly, we observed a moderately high frequency of unsuccessful prior attempts to use accepted facilities and procedures to stop drinking, such as attending AA, turning to religion, visits to physicians, or the use of medications, especially sedatives and tranquilizers. The third characteristic is a relative absence of marked deterioration or skid-row sequelae of abusive drinking: few instances of frequent job loss, public drunkenness, geographic movement, use of non-beverage alcohol ("products"), morning drinking, and related behaviors.

At a more moderate level, it is typical of our female patients to report that alcohol helps them to relax socially and facilitates social interaction, and that it allows them to feel as though their intellectual functioning were improved. Alcohol tends to facilitate withdrawal or isolation, since the women appear to be relatively more solitary than convivial drinkers. There are also indications that, to a moderate extent, drinking tends to cause fear, worry, anxiety, depression, and avoidance of other people, while to the same extent the women also report using alcohol as a mood-altering drug to help them cope with tension, anxiety, worry, or depression. Hence, we see the potential for the development of an escalating spiral, in which the drug causes an exacerbation of the very symptoms it is being used to treat.

It is relatively common for these patients to report moderate loss of control over their own behaviors while drinking (*not* loss of control over consumption), perhaps in the form of some deficits in perceptual-motor integration, minor accidents, passing out, and related experiences. Moderately frequent reports of some physical and psychological withdrawal symptoms were also typical, but rarely severe. The use of drugs other than, or in addition to, alcohol was also reported by many of the women, but not on a distinctly regular or addictive basis. The quantity of alcohol ingested on a daily basis averaged approximately 6-8 ounces of absolute ethanol — the equivalent of a half pint of distilled spirits, or 1½ pints of wine, or a quart of beer.

Contrary to expectations, marital problems were not as frequently reported, nor as severe, as one might think. This observation was confounded, however, because the AUI administration procedures instruct respondents to ignore a portion of the questionnaire if they have not been living in a marriage or "marriage-type" relationship within the past six months. Consequently we do not know the extent to which alcohol or other drugs may have been implicated among the 32% of women who were divorced or separated. For the 30% who were currently married, however, there were moderate indications that marital problems (e.g., jealousy, suspected or actual infidelity) preceded or provoked the drinking. Equally frequent, however, were the indications that the women's drinking contributed to or caused the marital discord. In either event, these data have obvious implications for the use of marital or couples' therapy in the overall rehabilitation plan.

Perceptual, cognitive, and behavioral characteristics. Although a number of other tests and measurements were administered to our sample of hospitalized women, only a few of them will be relevant to clinical concerns. We found, for example, that there were no strong tendencies for patients to be "sensation seekers." That is, their substance use or abuse seemed unrelated to thrill- or adventure-seeking, a search for new experiences, release from inhibitions, or escape from boredom. If anything, the opposite appears to be true, contrary to the popular belief that substance-abusers need some non-chemical alternative means of getting "high." We would recommend instead that perhaps more attention ought to be paid to helping women learn to cope with their current experiences.

Another of our measures allows us to infer that our female moreso than our male patients tend to express an external "locus of control." That is, they are apt to view themselves as being relatively passive victims of external events and circumstances, rather than active participants in the shaping of their own destinies. They are more likely to believe in luck or fate than their own personal responsibility for individual behavior. These characteristics are associated with what appears to be an inability to profit from one's own mistakes, difficulty in taking active steps to improve their circumstances, little emphasis on personal skills or achievements. Relatedly, most of our women, were, on the average, relatively "field dependent," or reliant on external sources of information in particular perceptual and problem-solving tasks. This observation has several significant correlates, further suggesting some difficulties in resisting external environmental pressures, a relative inability to approach problems in an analytic fashion, perhaps some lack of insight or self-awareness, and a more global or undifferentiated level of cognitive functioning.

An intensive personal interview revealed other characteristics which may define special needs of women in treatment. For example, economic dependence on current or former spouse, parents, or others was expressed by many of our patients, and perhaps financial counseling or preparation for a greater degree of independence ought to be part of any comprehensive rehabilitation program. Some measure of difficulty in establishing and maintaining meaningful long-term interpersonal relationships was another frequently expressed problem, indicating that perhaps therapies which are built on that foundation may not be appropriate for many female substance-abusers. Further research is needed to clarify this issue, but in the meantime this observation further indicates a sense of isolation or alienation among many of our respondents. A related inability to establish and maintain long-term goals, perhaps not unique to women or substance-abusers, forms a basis for the inference that future objectives requiring extended commitments may be inappropriate for many women in treatment, and perhaps efficacy of rehabilitation is more closely tied to resolution of present, immediate issues and problems.

SUMMARY

Readers ought not to conclude that the observations and interpretations presented in this chapter represent an exhaustive or comprehensive statement about what is known regarding the special population discussed. Far from it — in fact, we are just beginning to scratch the surface of a need for more, and more-definitive, knowledge. Nor do we intend to convey the notion that few exceptions to our findings will be encountered by other health-care professionals. One of the unfortunate by-products of attempting to develop useful generalizations is the inadvertent formation of stereotypes and the necessity for focusing on similarities within the populations, at the expense of the array of individual differences. There will be — there are! — exceptions when one speaks in terms of trends, tendencies, averages, and related phrases. Therefore, readers should be cautious about inferring that materials discussed in this chapter can necessarily be generalized to the special populations with whom they are working. Much of the information herein was derived from an all-volunteer sample of hospitalized patients, and it is known that persons who volunteer for participation in research projects often differ in significant ways from the general population from which they were selected. Along similar lines, it is not necessarily true that the descriptive data are uniquely characteristic of the special populations. It is not our intent to imply that observations about the behavior of women are inapplicable to men, since our studies are primarily descriptive rather than comparative. We believe that all of these *caveats* are reasonable and warrant consideration, but they do not vitiate the potential applications of our observations by astute, careful, and thoughtful health-care practitioners.

ACKNOWLEDGMENTS

The author is grateful to Ms. Sandy Ryba and Mr. James Riedel for their invaluable assistance in collecting much of the information on which this chapter is based. Several students from the University of Wisconsin (Milwaukee) also assisted in working with our female patients, and the author acknowledges the contributions of Beth Michelac, Martha Davis, and Michael Schubilske.

Much of the research on which this chapter is based was supported by grant funds from the Scientific Advisory Council of the Distilled Spirits Council of the United States (DISCUS).

Preparation of this chapter was supported in part, by funds donated by the Hospital Auxiliary, Friends of De Paul, to the Research Department.

The opinions, conclusions, and interpretations expressed are solely the responsibility of the author and are not necessarily reflective of those of the funding organizations or any institution with which the author is affiliated.

REFERENCES

1. Wilsnack, S.C.: The needs of the female drinker: dependency, power, or what? *Proceedings of the Second Annual Alcoholism Conference of the National Institute of Alcohol Abuse and Alcoholism.* Washington, D.C.: National Institute on Alcohol Abuse and Alcoholism, (U.S. DHEW Pub. No. [NIH] 74-676), pp. 65-83, 1973.

2. Schuckit, M.A.; Pitts, F.N.; Reich, J.; King, L.F., and Winokur, G.: Alcoholism. I. Two types of alcoholism in women. *Archives of General Psychiatry, 20:*301-306, 1969.

3. Lein, A.: *The Cycling Female: Her Menstrual Rhythm.* San Francisco: W.H. Freeman & Co., 1979.

4. "Sexual Medicine for Alcoholics." *Sexual Medicine Today, 5:*26-27, (6, June), 1981.

5. *Alcohol Abuse Among Women: Special Problems and Unmet Needs, 1976.* Hearing from the Subcommittee on Alcoholism and Narcotics of the Committee on Labor and Public Welfare, 94th Congress, Second Session, on Examination of the Special Problems and Unmet Needs of Women Who Abuse Alcohol, September 29, 1976.

6. O'Gorman, P.A., and Lacks, H.: *Aspects of Youthful Drinking.* New York: National Council on Alcoholism, 1979.

7. *Alcohol and Health. Third Special Report to the U.S. Congress.* Washington, D.C.: National Institute on Alcohol Abuse and Alcoholism, (U.S. DHEW Pub. No. [ADM] 79-832), 1978.

8. Jacobson, G.R.: Women and Alcoholism. In: *There is a Morning After.* Task Force on Women and Alcohol, Milwaukee Council on Alcoholism, 1978-1979.

9. Jacobson, G.R.: Diagnosis, assessment, and levels of care: special issues in the treatment of women. *Proceedings of the Hazelden Information Exchange* (Minneapolis, Minnesota: September 15, 1982). Center City, Minnesota: Hazelden, 1983.

10. Sokolow, L.; Welte, J.; Hynes, G., and Lyons, J.: Treatment-related differences between female and male alcoholics. *Focus on Women: Journal of Addictions and Health, 1:*42-56, 1980.

11. Horn, J.L. and Wanberg, K.W.: Females are different: on the diagnosis of alcoholism in women. *Proceedings of the First Annual Alcoholism Conference of the National Institute on Alcohol Abuse and Alcoholism.* Washington, D.C.: National Institute on Alcohol Abuse and Alcoholism (U.S. DHEW Publ. No. [NIH] 74-675), pp. 332-354, 1973.

Chapter 18

Alcohol and Drug Dependency Problems in Special Populations: Children and Adolescents

George Jacobson, Ph.D.

OVERVIEW

Because some degree of drug use appears to be the norm among the youth of this country, the author begins this chapter with selected details of the results of major nation-wide surveys of high school students, demonstrating the extent to which alcohol, cannabis, cocaine, opiates, and other mood- and mind-altering chemicals are being used. This epidemiologic information is followed by detailed descriptions of children and adolescents in treatment for a variety of substance use disorders. Based entirely on the author's several years of research and clinical experience with children and adolescents, the descriptive materials are primarily empirical and pragmatic, aimed at communicating to other Allied Health Professionals, in a direct and straightforward manner, information which says "This is the nature of the kids we've worked with, this is what they were like, these are the problems they were experiencing, and here are some ideas about clinical treatment that you may find useful." In the final major section of this chapter, the author describes the outcomes of treatment over several short- and long-term intervals, not in terms of conventional indicators of "success" or "failure," but in terms of particular behaviors, feelings, attitudes, and other variables more appropriate to children and adolescents. He identifies common treatment mistakes and clinically inappropriate strategies when he recognizes them, and recommends reasonable alternatives where possible.

A summary and references conclude the chapter.

INTRODUCTION

Media attention to the problems of adolescent substance abuse over the past five years or so has created the impression of an epidemic of drug abuse sweeping rampantly among the youth of this country. It would seem that a generation of American teenagers are sniffing, snorting, popping, and shooting their way through their developmental years at an unprecedented rate. While valid epidemiologic data are scarce, it would seem that anecdotal accounts of the continuing rise in the incidence of teenage drug abuse may be somewhat exaggerated.

Recent epidemiologic research suggests that, with the exception of cocaine abuse, which does appear to be increasing, the use of alcohol and other drugs has leveled off and may actually be declining among teenagers. On the other hand, there are some data which suggest that age of initial use of various drugs may also be declining: Children may be younger when they first try a drug. It is too early to tell if these results actually represent meaningful trends, but these issues are dealt with at some length in the section on Epidemiology below. And what of the adolescents whose drug use is so serious as to bring them to the attention of treatment professionals? What sorts of characteristics and behaviors do they bring with them into the treatment setting? Based on the clinical and experimental work of the author and his colleagues, discussed in detail in the section on Patient Characteristics below, it would appear that teens in treatment are not the egregiously pathological persons one might expect.

Generally speaking, they are about 15–16 years old, about half of them are still in school, and boys outnumber girls at a ratio of better than 2:1. Most frequently they are abusing alcohol and at least one other drug concurrently. They tend to be of approximately average intelligence, have suffered little or no measurable organic brain damage, and very often have a low opinion of themselves. They appear to be outside the mainstream of contemporary adolescence, but whether this is a cause or an effect of the substance abuse remains to be determined.

A number of other clinically relevant data, and their implications for treatment, are described at length below. Allied Health Professionals (AHPs), forearmed with this information, should have a much better understanding of the nature of these children and the problems they face, thereby being able to provide the quality of care needed to habilitate and rehabilitate young lives.

The issues of treatment outcome are more difficult to discuss, and few clear and unambiguous conclusions can be presented, because criteria of "success," "recovery," or "rehabilitation" are themselves unclear and ambiguous. Perhaps our expectations for the effectiveness of treatment are unrealistic and need to be modified. What we see in our treatment of substance-abusing adolescents parallels the experience of health-care professionals everywhere: The "best" patients have the "best" outcomes. Adolescents from supportive, intact families who participate in their child's treatment; adolescents who remain active and cooperative throughout the treatment continuum and follow our treatment recommendations; these are the teens whose post-hospitalization behaviors and adjustments are most likely to be positive.

But even with our imperfect treatments and our ambiguous and inconsistent criteria of recovery, we do have many encouraging observations to present, again based on our own clinical experience and research data. A large majority of teenage patients do remain engaged in their inpatient programs for the prescribed length of stay; many return to school; most show a decline in the frequency of involvement with law enforcement authorities. Depending on the length of follow-up intervals, from one-quarter to two-thirds of treated adolescents report decreases in their alcohol and drug use, and a surprisingly large proportion represent themselves as having been abstinent.

While an expanded discussion of treatment outcomes, presented later in this chapter, may appear to be too academic in a handbook of this nature, think again. If we don't know about the effectiveness of our therapeutic work, should we nevertheless continue doing it? Certainly we can learn as much from our mistakes as we do from our successes, and therefore we owe it to our patients and to ourselves to examine, confront, and correct our treatment goals and methods where warranted. It is in the Treatment Outcome section of this chapter that we attempt to do so.

EPIDEMIOLOGY OF SUBSTANCE USE

Among the publications (1-8) reporting epidemiologic surveys of substance use among children and adolescents during the past ten years or so there appears to be a consensus, if not unanimity, that what was believed to be a growing epidemic probably peaked at some time in the late 1970s or early 1980s.

One can infer from the data that the period between 1979-1982 represents the point at which growth in the incidence and prevalence of substance use reached a more-or-less recognizable plateau. Since then the percentage of children reporting substance use seems to have held at a relatively steady level in general, with some actual declines for a few specific drugs, and some increases for others (especially cocaine).

A look at some of these data in detail will provide allied health and social service workers a better idea of what the current generation of children is using. It must be kept in mind, however, that these data were based on self-reports, and some degree of under-reporting is suspected. Relatedly, most of the surveys involved only those children and adolescents who were still in school, and therefore we should not assume that the data are representative of all substance-abusing and/or chemical dependent kids. (The author uses the term "kids" intentionally and without disrespect; he has met very few children and adolescents who do not refer to themselves and their peers as kids.) The information will be useful nonetheless, perhaps moreso for AHPs and other personnel working outside the hospital or clinic setting.

Because the surveys reported by Johnston and his colleagues (6) are the most thorough and comprehenseive, most of the data reported below are derived from their reports. They contacted 16,947 students in 112 public and 22 private schools throughout the country for their latest survey and found that by the time American teenagers are seniors in high school 93% of them have used alcohol, 71% have used tobacco, 57% have used marijuana or hashish, 27% have used stimulants, 19% have used inhalants, 16% have used cocaine, 15% have used hallucinogens, 14% have used sedatives, 13% have used tranquilizers, 9% have used opioids other than heroin, and 1.2% have used heroin. These data represent *lifetime prevalence* figures, i.e., responses to questions such as "Have you *ever* tried [name of each specific drug or class of drugs] . . . ."

Recency data (i.e., "In the past month have you used. . .") for that same group of high school seniors reveal the following figures for use of each of the specific drugs or classes of drugs named: alcohol, 69%; tobacco, 30%; marijuana or hashish, 27%; stimulants, 9%; inhalants, 3%; cocaine, 0.2%; hallucinogens, 4%; sedatives, 3%; tranquilizers, 2.5%; opioids other than heroin, 2%; and heroin, 0.2%.

Their data on thirty-day *prevalence of daily use* (i.e., "Have you used. . . on 20 or more occasions during the past 30 days") reveal the following patterns: alcohol, 5.5%; tobacco, 21.2%; marijuana or hashish, 5.5%; stimulants, 0.8%; inhalants, 0.2%; cocaine, 0.2%; hallucinogens, 0.2%; sedatives, 0.2%; tranquilizers, 0.1%; opioids other than heroin, 0.1%; and heroin, 0.1%. It is this group of adolescents — those reporting virtually daily use of the specified drug — that should be of greatest concern to us. Of equal concern are some related observations reported in the survey, e.g., nearly 14% of the daily smokers indicated that they smoke half a pack of cigarettes or more per day, and 41% of the daily drinkers stated that on at least one occasion during the past two weeks they had "five or more drinks in a row."

The bit of good news that emerges from these statistics is this: For almost every class of drug and every prevalence-period (lifetime/ever, past year, past month, and daily use during the past month) declines in useage can be seen over the nine years that the annual surveys have been done. Some selected examples will illustrate this point. Beginning with thirty-day prevalence of daily use noted in the immediately preceding paragraph, the use of alcohol is down from its 1979 peak of 6.9%, tobacco use dropped from its 1976–1977 high of 28.8%, marijuana and hashish use has dropped from its 1978 peak of 10.7%, while all other daily drug use shows either no change or some slight increases. Lifetime/ever data are similar, but stimulant use and cocaine use were at their peaks shortly before or at the time of the most-recent survey.

The authors state it best when they point out that

"This year's findings suggest that the decline in overall *illicit drug use*, which began a couple of years ago, is real and continuing. Current use of an illicit drug (that is, some use in the past 30 days of one or more illicit drugs) is down to 32% in 1983 from a peak level of 39% in 1979. . .

"Annual prevalence (the proportion reporting any use in the prior year) dropped from 54% to 49% over the same four-year interval. Lifetime prevalence is down less over the interval, suggesting that an increased rate of quitting [drug use] is in part responsible for the decline.

"Much of the decline is attributable to an ongoing drop in the use of the most popular of the illicit drugs, *marijuana*, for which current use has dropped from 37% in 1979 to 27% in 1983 and annual prevalence has dropped from 51% to 42% over the same interval" (6, p. 11).

The bad news, however, is that

"Another drug of great concern at present is *cocaine.* . . The annual prevalence of cocaine more than doubled between 1975 and 1979 and then leveled off in 1980 and 1981 at 12%. The prevalence rates in 1982 and 1983 were both 11%, suggesting that the period of dramatic increase is over. However, other statistics on drug-related medical emergencies and treatment demand suggest that the 'casualties' from the earlier period of very rapid increase are *still* rising. We interpret this in part to be due to the time lag between initiation and the development of a pattern of use, and resulting experiences, which give rise to events discernible in such social agency statistics.

"Findings. . . from. . . follow–ups of past graduating classes in this study show that the incidence of cocaine use in these recent classes continued to rise sharply in the years after high school, giving this drug the latest age–of–onset pattern of any studied here" (6, p. 12).

And the worst news is that

". . . it would be a disservice to leave the impression that the drug abuse problem among American youth is anywhere close to being solved. . .

"[The current statistics represent] truly alarming levels of substance use and abuse, whether by historical standards or in comparison with other countries. In fact, they still probably reflect the highest levels of *illicit* drug use to be found in any industrialized nation in the world" (6, p. 14).

CHARACTERISTICS OF CHILDREN AND ADOLESCENTS IN TREATMENT

It is strikingly clear from the foregoing epidemiologic data that some degree of drug use is the norm for children and adolescents in America today. Of every 100 adolescents who finish high school, only 7 will not have used alcohol, only 29 will not have smoked cigarettes, and only 43 will not have used cannabis in some form. How different from these kids are those who present themselves for treatment at our hospitals and clinics? It is toward answering this question that this section is directed.

All of the information and observations presented below are drawn from three major clinical research and evaluation studies (9-12) conducted by the author and his colleagues between 1980-1986, and the data therefore are quite current and up to date. During those years a total of 341 young patients were observed, studied, and treated; while these patients may differ in some specific details from those being treated by readers of this handbook, it is nonetheless reasonable to assume that some useful generalizations can be made from one population to another.

Sociodemographic Characteristics

Over the years some fluctuations — but few consistent or clinically important changes — in sociodemographic characteristics have been noted. In some cases changes are more apparent than real, attributable to changes in the way we asked our questions, or the introduction of new questions which perhaps we should have been asking all along.

Age is one of those variables that has remained constant over the years, varying between 15.61 and 15.79 years as the mean. The youngest patients were 12 years old (less than 2% or our population); the oldest were 19 (less than 1% of our adolescents), since the notion of adolescence is frequently defined by chronology rather than by those transitional tasks and conflicts representative of this stage of human development. Hence patients over the age of 18 or 19 may be automatically assigned to an adult unit.

The sex ratio of our treatment population has been only somewhat more variable, ranging between 61%-69% male and 31%-39% female. Among those patients who were asked, 100% reported being single and none had children. AHPs are reminded, however, that questions about marital status, parenthood, and pregnancy should be dealt with directly, as such facts would have a significant bearing on treatment. In such cases not only would conventional family therapy be indicated, but special attention would be needed to deal with the particular problems of teenage marriages and premature parenthood.

Racial and ethnic composition of our patient populations has been more variable but always predominantly white (85%-93%). Blacks have never exceeded 3%-8%, Hispanics have ranged between 3%-6%, and Native Americans have never exceeded 1%-2%. Religious preference, when asked, was most likely to be Catholic (55%-64%), with Protestant a distant second (25%-32%).

It is in the area of educational attainment and school attendance that these clinical groups will appear to differ from general populations. On the average these patients had attained 8.75-9.3 years of education, but 29%-38% were no longer in school, for a variety of reasons; 57% had dropped out, 4% had been expelled, 4% had been suspended, and the remainder reported "other" reasons or did not respond to the question. This high rate of noncompletion (approximately twice the national average high school dropout rate) could represent an important issue in treatment, as one may need to direct attention to motivating patients for returning to school, enrolling in GED programs or other alternatives to a conventional educational setting, vocational training, job-seeking skills, and related matters. Many inpatient or residential long-term treatment programs will, of course, need to provide special educational activities and/or personnel on site, and most AHPs can expect to work with public and private educational/vocational agencies. For most families of these young patients, completing one's education in one way or another will be a focal issue in treatment, and often an area of very strong conflict. For others, however, the issues are those of finding a job and preparing for adulthood and independence.

Most of these young patients (92% in one sample, 86% in another) were still living at home with their parents, but approximately 8% were group-home residents. Another 2% each reported living with friends, living alone, and "other" arrangements. Parents' marital status was evenly divided between married (48%) and divorced (47%), while 2% each reported their parents as separated or widowed.

Legal problems were quite common among our patients: 67% in one sample and 83% in another reported "trouble with law enforcement agencies," and they had an average of four arrests each. The average age of first arrest was 12 for one group, 15 for another. Consequently, 14% of the youthful patients had been referred to treatment by law enforcement agencies, and 42% were referred by other health and social service agencies. Hence, AHPs can reasonably expect to have to perform a good deal of liaison work with police and courts, perhaps probation and parole agents, and children and family services personnel.

The foregoing sociodemographic data will be most valuable for AHPs who have little experience in working with children and adolescents, as an indication of the patterns and characteristics one might expect to encounter. More-experienced personnel will find the information useful for comparative purposes, particularly when trying to match patient-characteristics to clinical components in order to maximize treatment efficacy.

Patterns of Alcohol and Drug Use

The importance of accurately documenting family and peer group patterns of alcohol and other drug use cannot be over-emphasized in working with children and adolescents. Peer pressure is an extraordinarily salient force at this time of life, and the single most consistent reason given by these youthful patients for their own substance use is their perception that "all the other kids are doing it," or "most of my friends are dopers," or "I hang out with the druggies." Certainly the earlier-cited epidemiologic data support this perception, at least regarding alcohol, cannabis, and tobacco. Consequently, it is often a therapeutic necessity to remove the young person from his or her drug-using peer group and substitute an affiliation with drug-free peers who can promote and support a lifestyle of abstinence and sobriety.

Knowledge of parental and familial substance-use patterns is no less crucial, particularly since some alcoholism syndromes seem to be familial. That is not to say that alcoholism — or any other substance-use disorder — is inherited or genetically transmitted, but all evidence certainly indicates that it tends to run in families. Consequently, it is sometimes in the child's best interest to remove him or her from a destructively alcoholic family environment. Obviously such a move cannot alter one's biopsychosocial history, but at the very least it can provide a respite from a hostile or unhealthy environment. However, because of the radical nature of such an option it is not one that should be recommended without due consideration and extreme caution.

The fact is, however, that the author and his colleagues have found a very consistent pattern of parental alcohol and other drug problems. In one sample of 80 adolescents, 32 of them reported that at least one member of their family had been formally diagnosed and/or treated for chemical dependency and/or emotional problems. In another of our study-groups 42% of 130 teenagers indicated that one or both of their parents had a history of alcohol and/or other drug abuse, and another 11% indicated similar problems among their siblings or other family members. Our third study-group of 108 adolescents was similar to the other two: 18% reported that both parents were substance abusers, 36% reported father only, 5% reported mother only, and 9% reported siblings or other family members.

Quite clearly, then, the old saw that "alcoholism is a family illness" has more than one meaning. Family therapy becomes an even more important element of treatment for these youthful patients, as AHPs can reasonably expect half or more of their young clients will come from alcohol- and/or other drug-abusing families.

As much as parents may influence their children (for better or for worse) during the early developmental years, at some point between ages 8-12 the importance of peers begins to assume ascendancy and remains powerfully influential throughout adolescence and often into young adulthood and beyond. Not surprisingly, then, we found that fewer than 4% of all our adolescent patients belonged to peer groups in which abstinence was the norm. In one of our study-groups a strikingly high proportion (84%) of the teenagers said they had no "straight" (i.e., nondrug-users) friends at all. The accompanying tables illustrate the nature of peer group involvement with alcohol (Table 1) and other drugs (Table 2), and further emphasize the importance of directing treatment toward formation of new and positive peer-group affiliations. Of course one does not know if our adolescent patients became drug abusers because of their peer group's attitudes and behaviors, but one can be sure that the probability of a drug-free lifestyle is markedly reduced by a return to the drug-abusing adolescent subculture.

The patterns of substance use found by the author and his colleagues among their study-group patients may prove instructive to AHPs now working with children and adolescents. Looking first at alcohol we found 3% of our patients were abstainers, 16% light drinkers, 32% moderate drinkers, and 49% heavy drinkers according to a widely used quantity/frequency criterion (overall average consumption was in excess of two ounces of ethanol per day). According to another popular set of criteria those same patients were classified as non-drinkers = 1%, non-problem drinkers = 9%, alcohol misusers = 47%, and alcoholic-like drinkers = 43%. Correspondingly, the average age of first alcohol use was 10.5 years. The

TABLE 1
ALCOHOL USE AMONG PEERS

Do your friends. . .	Frequency	Percent	Adjusted Percent
Abstain	3	3.8	5
Drink 1-2 timer per week, fewer than 5 drinks at a time	9	11.3	15
Drink heavily once in a while — not more than twice a week — 5 drinks or more at a time	18	22.5	30
Drink regularly — more than twice a week — but fewer than 5 drinks at a time	6	7.5	10
Drink heavily on a regular basis — 5 or more drinks at a time, three or more times a week	24	30.0	40
No response	20	25.0	

From Zupek *et al.* (11); reprinted by permission of authors.

TABLE 2
OTHER DRUG USE AMONG PEERS

Do your friends use (all other drugs except alcohol)	Frequency	Percent	Adjusted Percent
Never	1	1.3	1.6
Several times a year	2	2.5	3.3
Several times a month	3	3.8	4.8
Weekends	3	3.8	4.8
Several times a week	18	22.5	29.0
Daily	18	22.5	29.0
Several times a day	17	21.3	27.4
No response	18	22.5	

From Zupek *et al.* (11); reprinted by permission of authors.

most common setting in which alcohol use occurred was at parties, but a wide range of other circumstances was reported (see Table 3). The significance of Table 3 lies in its treatment–related implications for the need for greater parental/adult supervision, the importance of peers, and the need for social and recreational activities that do not involve alcohol. (The need for more-stringent attention to local laws governing underage drinkers is a related social-action issue worthy of our attention as AHPs, as well as a responsibility as concerned adults and conscientious parents.)

Patterns of other drug use among our three major study-groups are shown in Tables 4 and 5. Quite obviously, alcohol and cannabis were the most widely used and abused drugs, coinciding with the epidemiologic data from the nation-wide high school surveys. Looking at study-groups I and II (Table 4) we see that 88.5%-90% of the patients were regular weekly users of alcohol, and 36%-50% were regular daily drinkers; 80%-96% were using cannabis on a regular weekly basis, and 57%-75% were daily users. Table 4 also shows that 65%-91% were using the two drugs in combination on a weekly basis, and 17%-37% were using the alcohol-cannabis combination daily. In study-group III (Table 5), 40% of the respondents were using cannabis "several times a week," and 100% of the respondents had used marijuana and/or hashish at least once. Two-thirds of this group reported having used cocaine, and two-thirds had used tranquilizers.

Polydrug use, abuse, and dependence was quite common among our child and adolescent groups, with the alcohol-cannabis combination most prevalent. In talking with our patients,

---

TABLE 3
USUAL ALCOHOL USE ENVIRONMENTS

When you're having alcohol, where do you usually drink?	Frequency	Percent*
At home, with parents	10	13
At home, without parents	31	39
In cars	43	54
Parks, other public places	50	63
Friends' homes, without parents	52	65
At parties	56	70
In bars	33	41
Sports events, concerts	33	41

*Exceeds 100% because respondents could check all applicable circumstances.

From Zupek, *et al.* (11); reprinted by permission of authors.

TABLE 4
PATTERNS OF REGULAR WEEKLY AND DAILY USE OF ALCOHOL AND OTHER DRUGS AMONG TWO GROUPS OF HOSPITALIZED PATIENTS (N = 238)

| | STUDY GROUP I (N = 130) | | | | | | STUDY GROUP II (N = 108) | | | | | |
| | Weekly | | | Daily | | | Weekly | | | Daily | | |
SUBSTANCES	Male	Female	Total	Male	Female	Total	Male	Female	Total	Male	Female	Total
Alcohol	87	88	88.5	33	41	36	87	95	90	45	59	50
Cannabis	75	88	80	47	73	57	96	97	96	72	81	75
Tranquilizers	15	16	15	4	6	5	10	11	10	1	11	4
Amphetamines	7.5	18	11.5	—	10	4	8.5	16	11	7	8	7
Sedatives/hypnotics	6	4	5	—	2	1	3	—	2	3	—	2
Hallucinogens	1	2	1.5	—	—	—	6	8	6.5	3	—	2
Narcotics (opiates)	—	4	1.5	—	—	—	4	16	7	—	3	1
Cocaine	—	—	—	1	—	1	6	8	6.5	4	3	4
Alcohol and cannabis	66	63	65	13	24	17	87	97	91	30	51	37

All figures shown are percentages; percentages may vary from 100 due to rounding.
From Herrington, *et al.* (9); reprinted by permission of authors.

TABLE 5
PATTERNS OF DRUG USE AMONG HOSPITALIZED PATIENTS
STUDY-GROUP III (N = 68)

SUBSTANCES	Never Used	Used & Quit	Using Several Times Per Year	Using Several Times Per Month	Using Regularly on Weekends	Using Regularly Several Times Per Week	Using Daily	Using Several Times Per Day	No Response
Cannabis	—	12	3	7	3	40	10	25	—
Tranquilizers	31	32	21	4	3	3	—	—	6
Amphetamines	12	26	18	18	1	15	4	3	3
Sedatives/hypnotics	46	32	10	4	—	—	1	—	6
Hallucinogens	31	43	13	7	—	—	1	—	4
Narcotics (opiates)	47	26	18	3	—	1	—	—	4
Heroin	82	7	1	—	—	—	—	—	9
Cocaine	29	40	12	6	1	6	—	—	6
PCP	68	22	1	—	—	—	—	—	9
Other Drugs	22	18	1	—	—	4	3	3	49

All figures shown are percentages; percentages may vary from 100 due to rounding.
From Zupek et al. (11); reprinted by permission of authors.

however, we found that on the average they had been using 5-6 different chemicals in combination at some point during their drug-use history. On a regular weekly basis, 2-3 drugs used in combination was the average. Overall, then, AHPs working with children and adolescents can reasonably anticipate very high rates of dual- and multiple-drug problems.

Some rather specialized psychometric procedures with a small subgroup (N=30) of juvenile inpatients revealed some diagnostically and therapeutically useful information about these substance-abusers. To a consistently high degree the kids indicated that they used alcohol to help them feel better about themselves — smarter, wittier, more attractive, more relaxed — and to facilitate their social interactions. There was very little solitary drinking, almost no obsessive-compulsive drinking, and a relatively high level of sustained (regular) drinking. To a lesser degree these patients indicated that they did sometimes use alcohol as a mood-elevator, but also experienced some feelings of worry, guilt, or fear about their drinking. Most of these youthful drinkers had already experienced some symptoms of withdrawal, and most recognized some degree of loss of control over their own behavior while drinking. (This latter characteristic should not be confused with so-called loss of control over drinking. Rather, it may represent a lowering of normal inhibitions, thereby allowing them to behave in ways they could not or would not while sober.)

Readers will recognize in this pattern some very important clues to the development of appropriate treatment goals and methods. For example, increased self-awareness and self-esteem; group therapy and social-skills training to enhance interpersonal relationship abilities; recognition of the need for normal inhibitions, and help in overcoming those that are not personally or socially useful.

Concurrent Psychiatric Problems

Although discussed at length in Chapter 16, it is worthy of note here to indicate that psychiatric interviews and psychological testing with our juvenile patients revealed a consistent prevalence of concomitnat disorders in approximately 20% of the cases. In descending order of frequency, diagnoses included a variety of adjustment disorders, borderline personality disorder, antisocial personality disorder, depression (referred to as dysthymic and affective disorders in Chapter 16), toxic psychosis (see Organic Mental Disorders in Chapter 16), and one case each of phobic disorder and conversion disorder. Although our prevalence estimates are quite conservative, AHPs should be aware of the at least one in five probability of concurrent psychopathology among youthful substance abusers.

Personality Characteristics

Assessment of personality characteristics by means of widely used and standardized psychometric techniques revealed a pattern that included a relatively lower level of what may be called ego strength. In practical terms "low ego strength" refers to traits such as emotional instability, being easily frustrated and annoyed, feeling dissatisfied with one's family and the restrictions of life, feeling unable to cope with life, evading responsibilities, and giving up easily. These traits were more characteristic of the girls than the boys in our study-group. Also more marked among the girls than the boys was a tendency to be aggressive, perhaps hostile, unconventional and rebellious, demanding of attention and admiration.

The girls also showed a tendency to be more emotional and impulsive, undependable, careless of interpersonal and social obligations, willing to disregard the rules of society in meeting their own needs or fulfilling their own desires. The girls were also more likely than the boys to be characterized by jealousy and suspicion, perhaps wary and cynical regarding the motives and intentions of others, demanding and irritable. (This cluster of feelings and behaviors certainly suggests that the traditional forms of therapy and counseling might be quite difficult for these girls.) At the same time, the girls tended to be worrying, insecure, and moody; perhaps experiencing some feelings of guilt and depression, and a sense of personal inadequacy. Contrary to popular opinion, it is obviously possible for these widely divergent and seemingly incompatible traits to coexist in persons whom at one time would have been labeled "sociopathic" or "delinquent." While one may not be able to refrain from behaving in a socially unacceptable way, one may certainly experience guilt afterwards.

On the other hand the boys appeared to be more realistic and tough-minded in a practical, no-nosense way, having no illusions about what life is likely to offer them. They were also more likely to be questioning or rejecting of traditional, conservative, ideas and expectations, perhaps more experimenting and risk-taking.

Finally, the girls expressed more feelings of tension and frustration, restlessness, and impatience, suggesting some difficulty in tolerating inactivity.

Readers must keep in mind that these personality characteristics are described in relative terms, and do not represent absolutes. It must also be pointed out that in none of these traits did our patients approach a point that may be considered extreme or overtly pathological, although they did deviate from statistical norms typical of males and females in this age group.

On another of our personality assessment measures this study-group of young substance-abusers differed markedly from criterion groups of normal adolescents and adult alcoholics. Our child and adolescent patients were more extroverted and emotionally unstable than both other groups. The terms used to describe the study-group included touchy, restless, aggressive, excitable, changeable, impulsive, and active. Thus, there was some reasonable degree of agreement between our sets of personality measurements. Again, these descriptors were more typical of the girls than the boys, but for neither should one necessarily infer marked pathology or extreme deviance.

Self-Concept

In assessing self-concept it appeared that for the most part the kids in the study-groups were reasonably honest and straightforward in describing how they perceived themselves, neither minimizing nor exaggerating their problems. They did not appear to be denying any of their difficulties, nor did they seem to be defensive. If anything, the opposite may be true: They seemed to lack those positive subtle defenses, assumedly unconscious in nature, necessary for establishing and maintaining even a minimally positive sense of self-esteem and personal worth. One must wonder, therefore, about the validity and value of those popularly held notions about "breaking down denial" and "breaking through defenses" as being crucial to successful treatment of chemically dependent patients. The author would suggest, in fact, that perhaps the treatment of child and adolescent substance-abusers should aim toward helping them develop some reasonable and appropriate sense of themselves as valued and worthwhile individuals.

In this context, then, it is necessary to note that overall self-concept and level of self-esteem was quite poor, weak, and generally negative. Sense of personal identity and evaluation of one's own behavior could also be called weak and/or negative, and level of self-acceptance was marginal at best. To at least a marginally positive extent the study-group patients expressed slightly favorable evaluations of "physical self," including one's body, health, physical appearance, sexuality, and functioning; "social self," how one thinks he or she is perceived by others in social interactions, the sense of adequacy and competence in interacting with others; and, to a lesser degree, "personal self," or feelings of adequacy or competence as a person, apart from one's body and one's social interactions. Clearly, treatment should, and can, attempt to build on these slightly positive aspects of self-concept and self-esteem.

More-negative aspects of self-concept, and perhaps more difficult to treat effectively, included the "moral-ethical self," the extent to which one sees oneself as a basically good or bad individual, perhaps in a religious or spiritual sense as well as a moral-ethical one; and the "family self," one's feelings of being a loved, valued, or worthwhile member of a family (or family-like group). To be sure, group therapy, family therapy, and some of the tenets of AA/NA may be efficacious in attempting to deal with these problems, but certain aspects of personality, discussed earlier in this chapter, seem to militate against these traditional approaches to treatment. These are difficult problems, and there are no simple solutions.

The picture is further complicated by the observation that the general pattern of responding to the self-concept questionnaire was similar to that of a mixed group of psychiatric patients, and more closely resembled that of personality disorder patients (see Chapter 16). Again, one ought not necessarily infer the presence of overt psychopathology, but these observations do coincide with aspects of personality discussed above

Another complicating factor, inferred from other components of our in-depth studies of hospitalized children and adolescents, is the extent to which they feel themselves to be victims. That is, they perceive little or no cause-and-effect relationship between their behavior and events in the external environment, implying a feeling of being a victim of circumstances, at the mercy of fate, luck, or chance, and therefore unable to change or improve their situations. Regardless of the reality of such an outlook — and who actually knows what external forces, if any, may rule our lives — people who feel helpless about influencing their environment, about directing their own lives, are likely to stop trying, to give up, to abdicate the responsibility for one's life, to develop (or maintain) a sense of "what's the use. . . nothing I do seems to make any difference anyway. . ." Indeed, it is not surprising that such an attitude or belief would be associated with drug use: If one cannot alter one's circumstances or improve one's life, then why not at least temporarily alter or improve, through chemicals, one's feelings, mood, and perceptions regarding life and the world in which we live. Again, difficult problems, and no simple solutions. One might apply the success-and-mastery techniques that have been evolving in the context of the newer cognitive therapies, with a corresponding emphasis on personal responsibility for one's life and, to paraphrase two popular treatment dicta, the courage to try to change those things that can be changed, and a de-emphasis on the inability to manage one's life.

Perceptual, Congitive, and Behavioral Characteristics

Administration of several related assessment techniques revealed no marked cognitive, perceptual, or intellectual deficits among children and adolescents tested. Abstract reasoning and concept formation was generally within the normal range, as was estimated general intelligence, and short- and longer-term memory. When pathology was detected it was generally mild and not of the sort likely to interfere with active involvement in treatment.

Related testing revealed, however, an unusually (but not unexpectedly) high number of symptoms believed to be diagnostic of one or more forms of attention deficit disorders. Such disorders, which used to be called "hyperactivity," "hyperkinetic child syndrome," or "minimal brain dysfunction," have recently been shown to occur much more frequently among the children of alcoholics, as well as among child and adolescent substance-abusers (10, 12, 13). It is the impression of the author and his colleagues (12, 13) that attention deficit disorders are too often overlooked by clinicians unaccustomed to working with children, and AHPs are strongly encouraged to include appropriate diagnostic methods routinely. Too often these children with attention deficit disorders are undiagnosed or misdiagnosed and may be rejected by traditional treatment programs for what is simply passed off as "disruptive behavior." Another frequently overlooked variable which may have significance for both diagnosis and treatment is sensation-seeking, also called need for stimulation, excitement, or risk-taking. Although we do not infer a causal relation between sensation-seeking and drug abuse, our study--groups did show what we believe to be a strong preference for high-stimulation behaviors. In descending order of quantitative values, the patients expressed an interest in thrill- and adventure-seeking (e.g., participating in exciting, risky, and potentially dangerous activities), disinhibition (e.g., a preference for persons and/or activities usually inaccessible to inhibited individuals, and a need for alcohol and/or other drugs for such purposes), experience-seeking (e.g., increased awareness of unusual or unique sensations, heightened self-awareness), and boredom susceptibility (e.g., an intolerance of sameness, familiarity, or predictability).

The last of these four traits, if they may be called such, appeared to be of less motivational importance, while the first two seemed to be more significant. While the meaning of this particular constellation of stated behavioral preferences remains unclear, some speculation may be worthwhile. From what is currently known about attention deficit disorders we may infer that these expressed needs or interests are related to the physiology and psychology of immature central nervous system processes, and this possibility may carry important implications for treatment. Certainly the need for alcohol and other drugs to overcome one's inhibitions, as discussed earlier in this chapter, is another possible interpretation of our observations. Another possibility is that danger, thrills, and risks may represent "tempting fate," or trying to exercise some personal effectance in an environment usually unresponsive to individual efforts.

Other possible explanations exist, of course, including a variety of physical, psychological, and sociocultural theories. Perhaps more to the point, however, is that it may be therapeutically useful to redirect these needs or interests into non-chemical, socially acceptable, and personally beneficial channels. If one knows, for example, that an adolescent has a need for adventure, why not channel that into an Outward Bound program? If another teenager has been using drugs "to get into myself," why not direct her toward meditation or autohypnosis? Why not use dance and movement therapy, aerobic and other vigorous physical activities; painting and other art therapies; all to make positive use of energy, activity, and creativity, in the service of self-exploration, self-expression, self-understanding, communication, integration, and health.

TREATMENT OUTCOMES

Because notions of "success" and "failure" are always subjective, often ambiguous, and sometimes idiosyncratic, those terms
are intentionally avoided in this discussion of treatment outcome.
Instead, the author simply and straightforwardly presents the data,
providing interpretations where they may be useful, but generally
allowing the information, observations, and self-reports to speak
for themselves.

The purpose of this section is primarily to inform AHPs of
the sorts of outcomes they might reasonably expect when working
with children and adolescents in a reasonably typical, traditional
intitutional setting. Some useful generalizations may be made
from the author's experiences to the reader's circumstances. For
example, children and adolescents are not simply miniature adults,
but have their own particular problems, needs, values, lifestyles,
world views, and so on. Therefore, programs and facilities specially
designed for children and teens, and specifically trained staff, are
more likely to have a favorable effect than adult-oriented programs and personnel that have been geared up (or down) and
transferred over to a younger patient population. Relatedly, AHPs
need to keep in mind that while rehabilitation may be an appropriate concept in working with adult patients, *habilitation* may be
the more relevant operational construct in dealing with children
and adolescents. More importantly, one must recognize and
respect the vast differences in world-view and time-perspective
that exists for different age groups. A 15-year-old girl and a
51-year-old married woman will have different understandings of,
and reactions to, the notion of, for example, "life-long abstinence," or "changing your lifestyle," or "take my advice," "learn
from my experience," and so on.

With these ideas in mind, then, we will look first at the
process of treatment as it occurred, then the patient's view of
treatment three months after discharge from an inpatient unit,
then behavioral and self-report outcomes at intervals of three
months to two years.

Average length of stay on the unit was 23 days, with most
(79%) discharges occurring in a planned and scheduled manner.
However, a small proportion (3%) of patients were discharged prematurely for a variety of disciplinary reasons, while 4% signed
themselves out of treatment against medical advice, and 14%

eloped from the program. During the residential period urine screens revealed that 14% of the patients had been using alcohol or other drugs while in treatment. On the average, patients participated in two family therapy sessions, but most (56%) of the kids did not take advantage of the alternative activities offered (e.g., movies, swimming, etc.). A majority (46%) of the patients participated in AA and/or NA meetings at least twice weekly, and another 33% attended weekly meetings. At the time of discharge, favorable prognoses were recorded for 40% of the patients.

When telephone surveys were conducted three months after discharge from the hospital, ex-patients were virtually unanimous in expressing favorable subjective evaluations of selected aspects of their treatment. Individual counseling and group counseling were perceived as having been equally valuable in their problem-solving functions, and the individual- and group-counselors were themselves equally valued for their assistance in the problem-solving process. It is instructive to note that attitude was more highly esteemed than ability. For example, whereas only 18% of the ex-patients pronounced themselves "very satisfied" with their group therapist's ability to help them solve their problems, 33% were "very satisfied" with the group therapist's attitude of respect and concern for them as persons. This finding suggests that the personality of the therapist may be more important than the ability of the therapist in helping to promote change, and that comes as no particular surprise.

When former patients from one study-group were contacted at three and six months after completion of treatment, 43% and 49%, respectively, reported abstinence from alcohol during the preceding 90-day period (compared to a 3% abstinence rate at the time of admission). At those same two follow-up intervals 44% and 61%, respectively, reported no drug use during the intervening three months. Among those persons who did report drug use since discharge, marijuana was most commonly named as the substance of choice, and drug use was most likely to occur during the first month after treatment. During the first three months after hospitalization two-thirds of the sample had received additional treatment for alcohol and/or other drug problems, and that proportion fell to 49% during the second three-month interval. During the same two intervals, 21% and 39%, respectively, reported no participation at all in AA, NA, or other self-help groups, but 55% and 47%, respectively, stated that they had been attending three or more meetings per month.

Very few (14%-16%) of the former patients had had any legal problems at all between discharge and follow-up, but among those who did, it was most often alcohol- or drug-related.

The pattern of school attendance fluctuated during the post-hospitalization follow-up intervals. Whereas 29% of the sample were not in school at the time of admission to treatment, that figure dropped to 20% at the three-month follow-up and rose to 24% at the six-month follow-up. School dropouts accounted for most of the non-attenders: 57% at the time of admission, 78% three months after treatment, and 75% three months later.

Another of our study-groups was divided in half and 50% were contacted at three months, and another 50% at six months, after completion of inpatient treatment, and in some important aspects their short-term outcomes differed from those reported above. In this second group we found 30% total abstinence from alcohol and other drugs at the three-month follow-up, and 35% at the six-month follow-up. Among those persons who had not abstained, 22% and 25% were using one or more chemicals only "occasionally" (i.e., less than weekly), and 44% and 45% were "regular" (once weekly or more) substance-users. These regular users favored an alcohol-cannabis combination (46% and 50%), while 25% and 30% preferred cannabis only, 13% used alcohol only (and only at three-month follow-up), and 17% and 20% used other combinations.

Looking at other post-hospitalization variables, 59% of the former patients said they had attended no AA or NA meetings during the past three months, and 57% reported no attendance during the entire six-month period. Among those who did attend, however, 34% and 35% had been participating in four or more meetings per month. Other forms of treatment (usually outpatient group therapy) were being used by 41% of the respondents on a regular and continuing basis at both follow-up intervals.

As with our other study-group, arrests had been relatively rare: 17% of those contacted at three months, and 13% of those contacted at six months, reported problems with law enforcement agencies. School attendance, however, appeared to be somewhat poorer: Among this study-group as a whole, 38% were dropouts at the time of treatment, but 42% of the three-month group, and 44% of the six-month group, had left school.

Other post-hospitalization indicators provided reason for guarded optimism about the present and future course of events for these kids. Among that half of the sample contacted at three months after hospitalization, 34% reported that their peer groups were comprised solely of non-users; among that half of the sample first contacted at six months after hospitalization, 52% reported only non-users as peers. Similarly, at the three-month follow-up 60% of the respondents self-reported improvement in overall quality of life, and 78% so reported at the six-month interval. Relatedly, 62% indicated improved family relations at three months, and 65% at six months, post-hospitalization.

What about long-term outcomes? Readers may benefit from the experience of the author and his colleagues when they followed another study-group of adolescents for up to three years after discharge from an inpatient unit (post-discharge follow-up interval ranged between 9-36 months, with a mean of 21 months).

Looking first at abstinence data, self-reported periods of non-use ranged from one day to two years, with an overall average of five months. More specifically, 31% of the former patients had remained abstinent for a week or less, 6% reported having been abstinent for more than a week but less than a month; and 63% said they had abstained for a month or longer, with an average of eight months of unbroken abstinence.

Among the 47% of adolescents reporting total abstinence from alcohol and other drugs at the time of follow-up, the mean duration of such abstinence had been 13 months. Among the 11% of the sample reporting "occasional" (less than weekly) current substance use, three months of post-discharge abstinence had been their average. The remaining 42% reported an average of approximately six weeks of abstinence before resuming "regular" (weekly or more often) use of chemicals. Most (50%) of these regular users preferred the alcohol-cannabis combination, while one-third used cannabis only, 8% used alcohol only, and the remainder were using other combinations.

Only 14% of the respondents indicated any AA or NA participation at all since discharge, and of those participants 60% were still attending meetings. But another 17% had sought and received other forms of treatment. Curiously, there were no differences in duration of initial period of abstinence (averaging eight months) between those who did and did not participate in post-discharge treatment, except when that treatment was AA and/or NA, in which case the average period of abstinence increased to twelve months.

Over the long haul, arrest rates remained encouragingly low (19%, versus 67% prior to treatment) while school dropout rates remained high (58%, versus 31% prior to treatment). However, 35% did return to school, and 6% had graduated since treatment. Overall quality of life had improved for 83% of the respondents (e.g., having a more-positive outlook on life, feeling better about themselves as individuals, having a stronger sense of self-confidence and an improved self-concept, getting along better in school, finding improved interpersonal and social relations, feeling more responsible for their own lives). Family relations had also improved for two-thirds of the respondents, in ways such as more open communication, more-understanding attitudes, less fighting within the family, and a greater feeling of closeness.

Although these treatment outcome findings are far from perfect, they are to a certain extent quite promising and provide reason for optimism. Some additional inferences from the author's experience may provide readers some useful clues to improving the efficacy of their own treatment for children and adolescents. For example, overall quality of treatment is improved by segregation: Kids feel better about, and become more involved in, programs that are solely theirs, facilities that are solely theirs (at least during specific hours or on particular days), and personnel who are solely theirs. (Adult patients also prefer being thus segregated from the children and adolescents.) As a related example, duration of initial abstinence can be prolonged by immediate post-hospitalization movement into an AA or NA group, but only if the group is composed entirely of peers — no adults — except for whatever administrative help the kids may request. As another guide to improving treatment, it is important to remember that even though chemical dependency is a serious problem, and therapy is a serious endeavor, we can be serious without being solemn, we can laugh at ourselves and laugh with one another, without detracting from the business at hand. If we can remember what it felt like to be a kid, and then apply those memories and feelings in a positive and empathic way, we can probably provide significantly improved clinical services to our child and adolescent patients.

SUMMARY

Annual epidemiologic surveys of thousands of high school students reveal a general pattern of gradually declining prevalence of drug use over the past few years. Nevertheless, nearly all students have used alcohol, and more than half have used cannabis, before high school graduation. Moreover, the prevalence of cocaine use appears to be increasing, and American youth has the highest levels of illicit drug use among all industrialized countries.

A sociodemographic composite of children and adolescents in treatment reveals a 15-16 year old white male, still in school and living in the parental home. He is likely to have been arrested at least once, and comes from a substance-abusing peer group. Regular weekly use of alcohol, cannabis, or both is the most common pattern of substance abuse, usually in a social rather than solitary setting, and often for purposes of self-enhancement.

Concurrent psychopathology may be diagnosed in at least one out of five patients. Feelings of frustration and dissatisfaction with life, inability to cope with problems, acts of rebelliousness and aggressiveness, and a tendency toward emotional instability and rejection of social obligations and traditional (middle-class) values seems more common, or more marked, among girls than among boys. Poor self-concept and low levels of self-esteem are the norm, and there are marked feelings of being unable to do anything to improve one's life, that one is simply at the mercy of chance or fate.

General intelligence, abstract thinking, concept formation, memory, and other cognitive/intellectual functioning seems generally unimpaired, but certain evidence suggests a high prevalence of undiagnosed — and probably untreated — attention deficit disorders. There is a concomitantly high level of expressed need for certain forms of sensation, stimulation, or excitement.

Treatment evaluation studies at three months post-hospitalization, and treatment outcome studies at 3-, 6-, and 21-month post-hospitalization are generally positive. Patients have an appreciation of the attitudes, abilities, and effects of therapists and therapy. Two typical indicators of what is commonly thought to be "successful" treatment, abstinence rates and ongoing AA/NA participation, may appear to be disappointing; but decreased rates of arrest, reports of improved family relations, and subjective impressions of improved quality of life, all suggest that there is reason to be optimistic about the present and future lives of these children and adolescents.

ACKNOWLEDGMENTS

Portions of the clinical and experimental studies reported in this chapter were supported by funds from Friends of De Paul

(De Paul Rehabilitation Hospital Auxiliary), and the author gratefully acknowledges that donation.

The author gratefully acknowledges the cooperation and contributions of Mr. James Riedel, Ms. Sandy Ryba, Mr. Michael Schubilske, and Ms. Martha Davis in collecting data on which portions of this chapter are based; Ms. Pat Johnson for preparation of tables and manuscripts; Mr. Bill Zupek and Mr. Al Gamroth for data analyses and computer-assisted information storage and retrieval; and Ms. Mary Venus for her dedicated hours of telephone interviewing.

The opinions and conclusions represented in this chapter are the sole responsibility of the author, and do not necessarily reflect the policies or procedures of any agency or institution with which the author is affiliated, nor those of any funding agency.

REFERENCES

1. U.S Department of Health, Education, and Welfare. *Second Annual Report to the President and Congress of the United States: Drug Abuse Prevention, Treatment, and Rehabilitation.* Washington, DC: U.S. DHEW, 1979.

2. U.S. Department of Health and Human Services. *Fourth Special Report to the U.S. Congress on Alcohol and Health.* Washington, DC: DHSS, 1981 (DHHS Pub. No. ADM 81-1080).

3. U.S. Department of Health and Human Services. *Fifth Special Report to the U.S. Congress on Alcohol and Health.* Washington, DC: U.S. DHHS, 1983 (DHHS Pub. No. ADM 84-1291).

4. O'Brien, R., and Cohen, S.: *The Encyclopedia of Drug Abuse.* New York: Facts on File, 1984.

5. O'Brien, R., and Chafetz, M.: *The Encyclopedia of Alcoholism.* New York: Facts on File, 1982.

6. Johnston, L.D.; O'Malley, P.M., and Bachman, J.G.: *Drugs and American High School Students, 1975-1983.* Washington, DC: U.S. Department of Health and Human Services, 1984 (DHHS Pub. No. ADM 85-1374).

7. Smart, R.G.; Goodstadt, M.S.; Adlaf, E.M.; Sheppard, M.A., and Godwin, C.C.: Trends in the prevalence of alcohol and other drug use among Ontario students, 1977-1983. *Canadian Journal of Public Health, 76:*157-162, 1985.

8. Benson, P.L.; Wood, P.K.; Johnson, A.L.; Eklin, C.H., and Mills, J.E.: *1983 Minnesota Survey on Drug Use and Drug-Related Attitudes.* Minneapolis, Minnesota: Search Institute, 1983.

9. Herrington, R.E.; Riordan, P.R., and Jacobson, G.R.: Alcohol and other drug dependence in adolescence: characteristics of those who seek treatment, and outcome of treatment. In *Currents in Alcoholism,* Vol VIII, Galanter, M. (Ed.). New York: Grune & Stratton, pp. 253-267, 1981.

10. Jacobson, G.R.: Adolescent substance abuse. Presented at De Paul Rehabilitation Hospital Training Seminar, Milwaukee, Wisconsin, May 1982.

11. Zupek, W.S.; Gamroth, A.J.; Rugg, C., and Moberg, D.P.: De Paul Rehabilitation Hospital inpatient adolescent population characteristics: an evaluation-research outcome study. Milwaukee, Wisconsin: De Paul Rehabilitation Hospital, Unpublished Report, 1986.

12. Jacobson, G.R.: *Alcoholism and Other Drug Abuse Problems Among Adolescents*. Boca Raton, Florida: CRC Press, Inc., 1987 (in press).

13. Jacobson, G.R.; Halikas, J.A.; Morse, C., and Lyttle, M.: Psychological characteristics of adolescent substance abusers referred by the juvenile courts. Presented at the Second Congress of the International Society for Biomedical Research/Annual Meeting of the Research Society on Alcoholism. Santa Fe, New Mexico; June 24-29, 1984.

PART 4

APPENDICES

Appendix 1

American Psychiatric Association Criteria for Diagnosis of Substance Use Disorders

In our society, use of certain substances to modify mood or behavior under certain circumstances is generally regarded as normal and appropriate. Such use includes recreational drinking of alcohol, in which a majority of adult Americans participate, and the use of caffeine as a stimulant in the form of coffee. On the other hand, there are wide subcultural variations. In some groups even the recreational use of alcohol is frowned upon, while in other groups the use of various illegal substances for recreational purposes is widely accepted. In addition, certain substances are used medically for the alleviation of pain, relief of tension, or to suppress appetite.

The diagnostic class deals with behavioral changes associated with more or less regular use of substances that affect the central nervous system. These behavioral changes in almost all subcultures would be viewed as extremely undesirable. Examples of such behavioral changes include impairment in social or occupational functioning as a consequence of substance use, inability to control use of or to stop taking the substance, and the development of serious withdrawal symptoms after cessation of or reduction in substance use. These conditions are here conceptualized as mental disorders and are, therefore, to be distinguished from nonpathological substance use for recreational or medical purposes.

The disorders classified in this section are to be distinguished from the corresponding portions of the Organic Mental Disorders section. Whereas, the Substance Use Disorders refer to the maladaptive behavior associated with more or less regular use of the substances, the Substance–induced Organic Mental Disorders describe the direct acute or chronic effects of these substances on the central nervous system. Almost invariably, individuals who have a Substance Use Disorder will also at various times have a Substance–induced Organic Mental Disorder, such as an Intoxication or Withdrawal.

For most classes of substances, pathological use is divided into Substance Abuse and Substance Dependence, defined below:

SUBSTANCE ABUSE
Pattern of pathological use

Impairment in social or occupational functioning due to substance use

SUBSTANCE DEPENDENCE
Tolerance or withdrawal

(For Alcohol Dependence and Cannabis Dependence a pattern of pathological use or impairment in social or

434

Minimal duration of disturbance of
at least one month

occupational functioning is also required. For the exception of Tobacco
Dependence, see p. 445.)

SUBSTANCE ABUSE

Three criteria distinguish nonpathological substance use from Substance
Abuse.

A pattern of pathological use. Depending upon the substance, this may
be manifested by: intoxication throughout the day, inability to cut down or
stop use, repeated efforts to control use through periods of temporary abstinence or restriction of use to certain times of the day, continuation of substance use despite a serious physical disorder that the individual knows is
exacerbated by use of the substance, need for daily use of the substance for
adequate functioning, and episodes of a complication of the substance intoxication (e.g., alcoholic blackouts, opioid overdose).

*Impairment in social or occupational functioning caused by the pattern
of pathological use.* Social relations can be disturbed by the individual's failure to meet important obligations to friends and family, by display of erratic
and impulsive behavior, and by inappropriate expression of aggressive feelings.
The individual may have legal difficulties because of complications of the
intoxicated state (e.g., car accidents) or because of criminal behavior to
obtain money to purchase the substance. (However, legal difficulties due to
possession, purchase, or sale of illegal substances are highly dependent on
local customs and laws, and change over time. For this reason, such legal
difficulty on a single occasion should not be considered in the evaluation of
impairment in social functioning for diagnostic purposes.)

Occupational functioning can deteriorate if the individual misses work
or school, or is unable to function effectively because of being intoxicated.
When impairment is severe, the individual's life can become totally dominated by use of the substance, with marked deterioration in physical and psychological functioning. Incapacitation is more frequently associated with
chronic Opioid and Alcohol Dependence than with dependence on other
substances.

Frequently individuals who develop Substance Use Disorders also have
preexisting Personality Disorders and Affective Disorders with concomitant
impairment in social and occupational functioning. It is therefore necessary
to determine that the social or occupational impairment associated with the
diagnosis of Substance Abuse or Dependence is actually due to the use of the
substance. The best clue is a change in functioning that accompanies the
onset of a pathological pattern of substance use, or the development of
physiological dependence.

Duration. Abuse as used in this manual requires that the disturbance
last at least *one month.* Signs of the disturbance need not be present continuously throughout the month, but should be sufficiently frequent for a
pattern of pathological use causing interference with social or occupational
functioning to be apparent. For example, several episodes of binge drinking
causing family arguments during a one-month period would be sufficient
even though between binges the individual's functioning was apparently not
impaired.

Isolated instances of pathological use of a substance can be adequately diagnosed by noting the specific Organic Brain Syndromes that were associated with this use. For example, a history of one or more instances of maladaptive use of alcohol over a three–week period may be noted as prior episodes of Alcohol Intoxication.

SUBSTANCE DEPENDENCE

Substance Dependence generally is a more severe form of Substance Use Disorder than Substance Abuse and requires physiological dependence, evidenced by either tolerance or withdrawal. Almost invariably there is also a pattern of pathological use that causes impairment in social or occupational functioning, although in rare cases the manifestations of the disorder are limited to physiological dependence. An example would be an individual's inadvertently becoming physiologically dependent on an analgesic opioid given to him by a physician for the relief of physical pain.

The diagnosis of all of the Substance Dependence categories requires only evidence of tolerance or withdrawal, except for Alcohol and Cannabis Dependence, which in addition require evidence of social or occupational impairment from use of the substance or a pattern of pathological substance use.

Tolerance. Tolerance means that markedly increased amounts of the substance are required to achieve the desired effect or there is a markedly diminished effect with regular use of the same dose. When the substance used is illegal and mixed with various diluents or with other substances, tolerance may be difficult to determine. In the case of alcohol, it should be noted that there are wide individual variations in the capacity to drink large quantities of alcohol without intoxication. Since some persons have the capacity to drink large amounts despite limited drinking experience, the distinguished feature of tolerance is that the individual reports that the amount of alcohol he or she can drink before showing signs of intoxication has increased markedly over time.

Withdrawal. In withdrawal, a substance–specific syndrome follows cessation of or reduction in intake of a substance that was previously regularly used by the individual to induce a physiological state of intoxication.

Many heavy coffee drinkers are physiologically dependent on caffeine and exhibit both tolerance and withdrawal. However, since such use generally does not cause distress or social or occupational impairment, and since few if any of these individuals have difficulty switching to decaffeinated coffee or coffee substitutes, the condition does not appear to be of clinical significance. Therefore, caffeine dependence is not included in this classification of mental disorders. In contrast, Caffeine Intoxication is often clinically significant and, therefore, is included.

CLASSES OF SUBSTANCES

Five classes of substances are associated with both abuse and dependence: alcohol, barbiturates or similarly acting sedatives or hypnotics, opioids, amphetamines or similarly acting sympathomimetics, and cannabis. Some of these substances are used medically, such as the amphetamines, barbiturates, and opioids. Three classes of substances are associated only with abuse because physiological dependence has not been demonstrated: cocaine, phencyclidine (PCP) or similarly acting arylcyclohexylamines, and hallucinogens. Finally, one substance, tobacco, is associated only with dependence, since heavy use of tobacco itself is not associated with impairment in social or occupational functioning (though the reaction of others to the tobacco use may cause difficulties).

USE OF MULTIPLE SUBSTANCES

Substance Abuse and Dependence frequently involve several substances. Individuals with Barbiturate or Similarly Acting Sedative or Hypnotic Abuse or Dependence often may also have problems with alcohol or, more rarely, use amphetamine to counter sedative effects. Individuals with Opioid or Cannabis Abuse or Dependence usually have several other Substance Use Disorders, particularly of barbiturates or similarly acting sedatives and hypnotics, amphetamines or similarly acting sympathomimetics, and cocaine.

When an individual's condition meets the criteria for more than one Substance Use Disorder, multiple diagnoses should generally be made. (The exception to this is when the abuse or dependence involves so many substances that the clinician prefers to indicate a combination of substances rather than list each specific substance. See pp. 447–448.)

RECORDING SPECIFIC DIAGNOSES

The clinician should record the name of the specific substance rather than of the entire class of substances, using the code number for the appropriate class. Examples: The clinician should write 305.73 Amphetamine Abuse, In Remission (rather than Amphetamine or Similarly Acting Sympathomimetic Abuse); 304.11 Valium Dependence, Continuous (rather than Barbiturate or Similarly Acting Sedative or Hypnotic Dependence); 305.91 Compazine Abuse, Continuous (rather than Other, Mixed, or Unspecified Substance Abuse).

SUBCLASSIFICATION OF COURSE

No entirely adequate method for subtyping the course of these disorders is available. However, the following guidelines should be used to indicate the course of the illness in the fifth digit.

Code	Course	Definition
1	Continuous	More or less regular maladaptive use for over six months.
2	Episodic	A fairly circumscribed period of maladaptive use, with one or more similar periods in the past.
3	In remission	Previous maladaptive use, but not using substance at present. The differentiation of this from no longer ill and from the other course categories requires consideration of the period of time since the last period of disturbance, the total duration of the disturbance, and the need for continued evaluation or prophylactic treatment.
0	Unspecified	Course unknown or first signs of illness with course uncertain.

OTHER FEATURES OF SUBSTANCE USE DISORDERS

Associated features. Personality disturbance and disturbance of mood are often present, and may be intensified by the Substance Use Disorder. For example, antisocial personality traits may be accentuated by the need to obtain money to purchase illegal substances. Anxiety or depression associated with Borderline Personality Disorder may be intensified as the individual uses a substance in an unsuccessful attempt to treat his or her mood disturbance.

Abuse of certain substances, particularly cocaine, hallucinogens, or cannabis, may be associated with identification with countercultural lifestyles or, more rarely, identification with non-traditional religious or mystical ideas.

In chronic Abuse and Dependence, mood lability and suspiciousness, both of which can contribute to violent behavior, are common.

Age at onset. Alcohol Abuse and Dependence usually appear in the 20s, 30s, and 40s. Opioid, Cocaine, Amphetamine or Similarly Acting Sympathomimetic, Hallucinogen, Cannabis, Cocaine, Phencyclidine (PCP) or Similarly Acting Arylcyclohexylamine, and Tobacco Use Disorders more commonly begin in the late teens and 20s. Two patterns of onset for Barbiturate or Similarly Acting Sedative or Hypnotic Abuse and Dependence have been identified (p. 441). When a Substance Use Disorder begins early in life, it is often associated with failure to complete school and a lifelong pattern of low occupational achievement.

Complications. The abuse or dependence associated with each class of substance may cause an Organic Brain Syndrome. For example, prolonged Alcohol Dependence may cause Alcohol Withdrawal Delirium, Alcohol Amnestic Disorder, or Alcohol Hallucinosis. Similarly, Hallucinogen Delusional Disorder may be a complication of chronic hallucinogen use. Complications of the specific intoxication states, such as traffic accidents and physical injury due to Alcohol Intoxication, have been noted in the Organic Mental Disorders section.

Frequently there is a deterioration in the general level of physical health. Malnutrition and a variety of other physical disorders may result from failure to maintain physical health by proper diet and adequate personal hygiene.

Use of contaminated needles for the intravenous administration of opioids, cocaine, and amphetamines can cause hepatitis, tetanus, vasculitis, septicemia, subacute bacterial endocarditis, embolic phenomena, or malaria. Materials used to "cut" the substances can cause toxic or allergic reactions. Use of cocaine by means of the intranasal route ("snorting") sometimes results in erosion of the nasal septum.

Physical complications of chronic Alcohol Dependence include hepatitis, cirrhosis, peripheral neuropathy, and gastritis. In addition, chronic Alcohol Dependence increases the risk and seriousness of heart disease, pneumonia, tuberculosis, and neurological disorders. The long-term potential for respiratory disorder in chronic cannabis use is controversial. The long-term physical complications of chronic and heavy tobacco use are discussed on pp. 445-446.

Depressive symptoms are a frequent complication of Substance Use Disorders, and partly account for the high rate of suicide by individuals with Substance Dependence. Suicide associated with alcohol and other substances can occur in both intoxicated and sober states.

Predisposing factors. Personality Disorders, particularly Antisocial Personality Disorder, predispose to the development of Substance Use Disorders.

Prevalence. Most of the Substance Use Disorders are common, especially those associated with alcohol and tobacco. Others, such as Opioid Abuse, are rare. For example, about 16% of the American public report *some* problem associated with alcohol within the past three years, and about 4% report more than trivial problems. In some economically deprived urban communities, Opioid Abuse and Dependence are widespread.

Sex ratio. Substance Use Disorders are diagnosed more commonly in men than in women.

Differential diagnosis. Nonpathological substance use for recreational or medical purposes is not associated with impairment in social or occupational functioning or a pathological pattern of use.

Repeated episodes of substance-induced intoxication are almost invariably present in Substance Abuse or Dependence, although for some substances it is possible to develop dependence without ever exhibiting frank intoxication (e.g., alcohol). Furthermore, substance-induced intoxication as an isolated episode not involving either abuse or dependence is common.

There are now methods to detect the presence of alcohol, barbiturates and similarly acting sedatives and hypnotics, opioids, cocaine, and amphetamines in serum or urine. In some cases the tests indicate that an individual who thinks he or she has been using one substance, such as cocaine, has in fact been taking something else, such as amphetamine crystals.

A test dose may be used to establish tolerance to barbiturates by administering 200 mg of a short-acting barbiturate (usually pentobarbital) hourly until early signs of intoxication appear. The total amount of barbiturate required to produce these signs of intoxication is multiplied by a factor of three, giving an approximation of the individual's daily tolerance level to barbiturates.

When Opioid Dependence is suspected, signs and symptoms of Opioid Withdrawal may be precipitated by the subcutaneous administration of 0.4 mg of naloxone, an opioid antagonist. (This should not be administered to individuals with a history of cardiac disease or coronary insufficiency.)

305.0x Alcohol Abuse

303.9x Alcohol Dependence

The essential feature of Alcohol Abuse is a pattern of pathological use for at least a month that causes impairment in social or occupational functioning.

The essential features of Alcohol Dependence are either a pattern of pathological alcohol use or impairment in social or occupational functioning due to alcohol, and either tolerance or withdrawal. Alcohol Dependence has also been called Alcoholism.

Course. When abuse or dependence develops, it is usually within the first five years after regular drinking is established. Heavy drinking in adolescence (before age 16) is particularly likely to be associated with later problems.

Although Alcohol Dependence and Abuse can continue into old age, they may remit with aging, sometimes in response to the development of physical complications. Occasional drinking with rare or no episodes of intoxication *does* occur in some persons with a clear prior history of Alcohol Dependence. Therefore, drinking that is currently moderate should not be considered evidence for the absence of Alcohol Dependence in the past.

There are three main patterns of chronic pathological alcohol use. The first is regular daily intake of large amounts; the second is regular heavy drinking limited to weekends. These two patterns are included in the fifth-digit subtype "Continuous." The third pattern is long periods of sobriety interspersed with binges of daily heavy drinking lasting for weeks to months. This pattern corresponds to the fifth-digit subtype "Episodic."

Familial pattern. Alcohol Abuse and Dependence are more common among family members than in the general population. Evidence of a genetic factor is the increased prevalence of Alcohol Dependence in the early-adopted offspring of parents with the disorder.

Diagnostic criteria for Alcohol Abuse

A. *Pattern of pathological alcohol use:* need for daily use of alcohol for adequate functioning; inability to cut down or stop drinking; repeated efforts to control or reduce excess drinking by "going on the wagon" (periods of temporary abstinence) or restricting drinking to certain times of the day; binges (remaining intoxicated throughout the day for at least two days); occasional consumption of a fifth of spirits (or its equivalent in wine or beer); amnesic periods for events occurring while intoxicated (blackouts); continuation of drinking despite a serious physical disorder that the individual knows is exacerbated by alcohol use; drinking of non-beverage alcohol.

B. *Impairment in social or occupational functioning due to alcohol use:* e.g., violence while intoxicated, absence from work, loss of job, legal difficulties (e.g., arrest for intoxicated behavior, traffic accidents while intoxicated), arguments or difficulties with family or friends because of excessive alcohol use.

C. Duration of disturbance of at least one month.

Diagnostic criteria for Alcohol Dependence

A. Either a pattern of pathological alcohol use or impairment in social or occupational functioning due to alcohol use:

Pattern of pathological alcohol use: need for daily use of alcohol for adequate functioning; inability to cut down or stop drinking; repeated efforts to control or reduce excess drinking by "going on the wagon" (periods of temporary abstinence) or restricting drinking to certain times of the day; binges (remaining intoxicated throughout the day for at least two days); occasional consumption of a fifth of spirits (or its equivalent in wine or beer); amnesic periods for events occurring while intoxicated (blackouts); continuation of drinking despite a serious physical disorder that the individual knows is exacerbated by alcohol use; drinking of non-beverage alcohol.

Impairment in social or occupational functioning due to alcohol use: e.g.,violence while intoxicated, absence from work, loss of job, legal difficulties (e.g., arrest for intoxicated behavior, traffic accidents while intoxicated), arguments or difficulties with family or friends because of excessive alcohol use.

B. Either tolerance or withdrawal:

Tolerance: need for markedly increased amounts of alcohol to achieve the desired effect, or markedly diminished effect with regular use of the same amount.

Withdrawal: development of Alcohol Withdrawal (e.g., morning "shakes" and malaise relieved by drinking) after cessation of or reduction in drinking.

305.4x   Barbiturate or Similarly Acting Sedative or Hypnotic Abuse

304.1x   Barbiturate or Similarly Acting Sedative or Hypnotic Dependence

The essential feature of Barbiturate or Simialrly Acting Sedative or Hypnotic Abuse is a pattern of pathological use for at least one month that causes impairment in social or occupational functioning. The essential feature of Barbiturate or Similarly Acting Sedative or Hypnotic Dependence is either tolerance or withdrawal.

There are two patterns of development of dependence and abuse. In one, the individual has originally obtained the substance by prescription from a physician for insomnia, but has gradually increased the dose and frequency of use on his or her own. At first this increase is intended for sleep, but the individual then discovers that adjusted doses of the substance during the day seem to help in coping with daily living problems through relief of tension and anxiety. Individuals with this pattern are more apt to be from a middle-class background, between ages 30–60, and female. The other pattern involves individuals who are apt to be males in their teens or early 20s who, with a group of peers, use substances obtained from illegal sources. The initial objective is to attain a "high" or euphoria, or to counteract the stimulant effects of amphetamines.

Course. The most common course is heavy daily use that results in dependence. A significant number of individuals with dependence eventually stop using the substance, and demonstrate a permanent recovery, even from the physical complications of the disorder.

Diagnostic criteria for Barbiturate or Similarly Acting Sedative or Hypnotic Abuse

A. *Pattern of pathological use:* inability to cut down or stop use; intoxication throughout the day; frequent use of the equivalent of 600 mg or more of secobarbital or 60 mg or more of diazepam, amnesic periods for events that occurred while intoxicated.

B. *Impairment in social or occupational functioning due to substance use:* e.g., fights, loss of friends, absence from work, loss of job, or legal difficulties (other than a single arrest due to possession, purchase, or sale of the substance).

C. Duration of disturbance of at least one month.

Diagnostic criteria for Barbiturate or Similarly Acting Sedative or Hypnotic Dependence

Either tolerance or withdrawal:

Tolerance: need for markedly increased amounts of the substance to achieve the desired effect, or markedly diminished effect with regular use of the same amount.

Withdrawal: development of Barbiturate or Similarly Acting Sedative or Hypnotic Withdrawal after cessation of or reduction in substance use.

305.5x   Opioid Abuse

304.0x   Opioid Dependence
The essential feature of Opioid Abuse is a pattern of pathological use for at least one month that causes impairment in social or occupational functioning.
The essential feature of Opioid Dependence is either tolerance or withdrawal.

Course. Opioid Abuse and Dependence are generally preceded by a period of "polydrug use," which may involve tobacco, alcohol, marijuana, sedative–hypnotics, prescription and nonprescription cough syrups, hallucinogens, or amphetamines. The use of these other substances usually continues after the use of opioids is established. Once a pattern of Opioid Dependence is established, substance procurement and use usually dominates the individual's live.

Approximately half of the individuals who engage in Opioid Abuse go on to develop Opioid Dependence. Once Opioid Dependence is established, the course is a function of the context of the addiction. For example, the vast majority of persons who became dependent on heroin in Vietnam did not return to their addiction when back in the United States. In contrast, it is believed that most individuals who become dependent on opioids in the United States become involved in a chronic behavioral disorder, marked by remissions while in treatment or prison or when the substance is scarce and relapses on returning to a familiar environment where these substances are available and friends or colleagues use these substances. In the United States, in this century, persons with Opioid Dependence have a high annual death rate (approximately 10 per 1,000) because of the physical complications of the disorder and a lifestyle often associated with violence. Among those who survive, increased abstinence is found with the passage of years, with final cessation of dependence an average of about nine years after its onset.

Diagnostic criteria for Opioid Abuse
A. *Pattern of pathological use:* inability to reduce or stop use; intoxication throughout the day; use of opioids nearly every day for at least a month; episodes of opioid overdose (intoxication so severe that respiration and consciousness are impaired).
B. *Impairment in social or occupational functioning due to opioid use:* e.g., fights, loss of friends, absence from work, loss of job, or legal difficulties (other than due to a single arrest for possession, purchase, or sale of the substance).
C. Duration of disturbance of at least one month.

Diagnostic criteria for Opioid Dependence
Either tolerance or withdrawal:
Tolerance: need for markedly increased amounts of opioid to achieve the desired effect, or markedly diminished effect with regular use of the same amount.
Withdrawal: development of Opioid Withdrawal after cessation of or reduction in substance use.

305.6x Cocaine Abuse

Since only transitory withdrawal symptoms occur after cessation of or reduction in prolonged use, a separate category of dependence is not included.

The essential feature of Cocaine Abuse is a pathological pattern of use for at least one month that causes impairment in social or occupational functioning.

Course. The development of Cocaine Abuse may take two to eight months of cocaine use. Paranoid ideation, suspiciousness, and ritualistic behavior generally occur late in the course of abuse. Although habitual use has lasted 10 to 15 years in some persons, Cocaine Abuse does not have as prolonged a course as is usually the case with Barbiturate and Opioid Abuse.

Diagnostic criteria for Cocaine Abuse

A. *Pattern of pathological use:* inability to reduce or stop use; intoxication throughout the day; episodes of cocaine overdose (intoxication so severe that hallucinations and delusions occur in a clear sensorium).

B. *Impairment in social or occupational functioning due to cocaine use:* e.g., fights, loss of friends, absence from work, loss of job, or legal difficulties (other than due to a single arrest for possession, purchase, or sale of the substance).

C. Duration of disturbance of at least one month.

305.7x Amphetamine or Similarly Acting Sympathomimetic Abuse

304.4x Amphetamine or Similarly Acting Sympathomimetic Dependence

The essential feature of Amphetamine or Similarly Acting Sympathomimetic Abuse is a pattern of pathological use for at least a month that causes impairment in social or occupational functioning. The usual pattern is "runs" of daily use for 10 to 14 days at a time. The essential feature of Amphetamine or Similarly Acting Sympathomimetic Dependence is either tolerance or withdrawal.

Course. See Cocaine Abuse above.

Diagnostic criteria for Amphetamine or Similarly Acting Sympathomimetic Abuse

A. *Pattern of pathological use:* inability to reduce or stop use; intoxication throughout the day; use of substance nearly every day for at least one month; episodes of either Amphetamine or Similarly Acting Sympathomimetic Delusional Disorder or Amphetamine or Similarly Acting Sympathomimetic Delirium.

B. *Impairment in social or occupational functioning due to amphetamine or similarly acting sympathomimetic use:* e.g., fights, loss of friends, absence from work, loss of job, or legal difficulties (other than due to a single arrest for possession, purchase, or sale of the substance).

C. Duration of disturbance of at least one month.

Diagnostic criteria for Amphetamine or Similarly Acting Sympathomimetic Dependence

Either tolerance or withdrawal:

Tolerance: need for markedly increased amounts of substance to achieve the desired effect, or markedly diminished effect with regular use of the same amount.

Withdrawal: development of Amphetamine or Similarly Acting Sympathomimetic Withdrawal after cessation of or reduction in substance use.

305.9x   Phencyclidine (PCP) or Similarly Acting Arylcyclohexylamine Abuse

The essential feature of Phencyclidine or Similarly Acting Arylcyclohexylamine Abuse is a pattern of pathological use for at least a month that causes impairment in social or occupational functioning.

Because no clear withdrawal syndrome or tolerance to this substance has been produced experimentally or observed clinically, a category for dependence is not included.

Course. See Cocaine Abuse, p. 443

Diagnostic criteria for Phencyclidine (PCP) or Similarly Acting Arylcyclohexylamine Abuse

A. *Pattern of pathological use:* intoxication throughout the day; episodes of Phencyclidine or Similarly Acting Arylcyclohexylamine Delirium or Mixed Organic Mental Disorder.

B. *Impairment in social or occupational functioning due to substance use:* e.g., fights, loss of friends, absence from work, loss of job, or legal difficulties (other than due to a single arrest for possession, purchase, or sale of the substance).

C. Duration of disturbance of at least one month.

305.3x   Hallucinogen Abuse

The essential feature of Hallucinogen Abuse is a pattern of pathological use for at least one month that causes impairment in social or occupational functioning.

Because no clear withdrawal syndrome has been produced experimentally or observed clinically, a category for dependence is not included.

Course. The course is unpredictable and is probably related to the nature of the underlying pathology that played a role in the onset of use. Most individuals rapidly resume their former lifestyle after only a brief period of abuse.

Diagnostic criteria for Hallucinogen Abuse

A. *Pattern of pathological use:* inability to reduce or stop use; intoxication throughout the day (possible only with some hallucinogens); episodes of Hallucinogen Delusional Disorder or Hallucinogen Affective Disorder.

B. *Impairment in social or occupational functioning due to hallucinogen use:* e.g., fights, loss of friends, absence from work, loss of job, or legal difficulties (other than due to a single arrest for possession, purchase, or sale of the illegal substance).

C. Duration of disturbance of at least one month.

305.2x   Cannabis Abuse

304.3x   Cannabis Dependence

The essential feature of Cannabis Abuse is a pattern of pathological use for at least a month that causes impairment in social or occupational functioning. The essential features of Cannabis Dependence are impairment in social or occupational functioning due to cannabis use, and tolerance (withdrawal has not been conclusively demonstrated). The existence and significance of tolerance (Cannabis Dependence) with regular heavy use of cannabis are controversial.

Course. Many users stop or decrease their use of cannabis spontaneously or when impairment in functioning develops.

Diagnostic criteria for Cannabis Abuse

A. *Pattern of pathological use:* intoxication throughout the day; use of cannabis nearly every day for at least a month; episodes of Cannabis Delusional Disorder.

B. *Impairment in social or occupational functioning due to cannabis use:* e.g., marked loss of interest in activities previously engaged in, loss of friends, absence from work, loss of job, or legal difficulties (other than due to a single arrest for possession, purchase, or sale of the substance).

C. Duration of disturbance of at least one month.

Diagnostic criteria for Cannabis Dependence

A. Either a pattern of pathological use or impairment in social or occupational functioning due to cannabis use.

Pattern of pathological use: intoxication throughout the day; use of cannabis nearly every day for at least a month; episodes of Cannabis Delusional Disorder.

Impairment in social or occupational functioning due to cannabis use: e.g., marked loss of interest in activities previously engaged in, loss of friends, absence from work, loss of job, or legal difficulties (other than a single arrest due to possession, purchase, or sale of an illegal substance).

B. *Tolerance:* need for markedly increased amounts of cannabis to achieve the desired effect or markedly diminished effect with regular use of the same amount.

305.1x Tobacco Dependence

The essential features are continuous use of tobacco for at least one month with either 1) unsuccessful attempts to stop or significantly reduce the amount of tobacco use on a permanent basis, 2) the development of Tobacco Withdrawal, or 3) the presence of a serious physical disorder (e.g., respiratory or cardiovascular disease) that the individual knows is exacerbated by tobacco use. In practice this diagnosis will be given only when either the individual is seeking professional help to stop smoking, or, in the judgment of the diagnostician, the use of tobacco is seriously affecting the individual's physical health. It should also be noted that a heavy smoker who has never tried to stop smoking, who has never developed Tobacco Withdrawal, and who has no tobacco–related serious physical disorder, according to the criteria in this manual, does not have the disorder of Tobacco Dependence, even though physiologically the individual is almost certainly dependent on tobacco.

At present, the most common form of Tobacco Dependence is associated with the inhalation of cigarette smoke. Pipe and cigar smoking, the use of snuff, and the chewing of tobacco are less likely to lead to Tobacco Dependence for several reasons. First of all, the probability of developing serious health complications is lower than with cigarette smoking, probably because relatively little smoke is inhaled; consequently, there is less distress arising from health concerns about the need to take the substance repeatedly. Second, the more rapid onset of nicotine effects with cigarette smoking leads to a more intensive habit pattern that is more difficult to give up owing to the frequency of reinforcement or the greater physical dependence on nicotine.

In recent years the evidence that tobacco use predisposes to a variety of serious physical disorders has led many individuals who are heavy smokers to attempt to give up the habit. However, many are unable to stop at all or, if they do, often resume tobacco use within a matter of months.

The difficulty in giving up tobacco use on a long-term basis, particularly with cigarettes, may be due to the unpleasant nature of the withdrawal syndrome, the highly overlearned nature of the habit that stems from the repeated effects of nicotine, which rapidly follow the inhalation of cigarette smoke (75,000 puffs per year for a pack-a-day smoker), and the likelihood that a desire to use tobacco is elicited by environmental cues, such as the ubiquitous presence of other smokers and the widespread availability of cigarettes.

When efforts to give up smoking are made, Tobacco Withdrawal may develop.

The most common tobacco-related serious physical disorders are bronchitis, emphysema, coronary artery disease, peripheral vascular disease, and a variety of cancers. The diagnostician must assess the role of tobacco use as an etiological or exacerbating factor for the particular individual after considering both individual circumstances and the latest available scientific information. If the individual with a serious case of one of the tobacco-related physical disorders continues to use tobacco, despite awareness of its harmful effects, a reasonable inference can be made that the individual is dependent on tobacco.

Associated features. Individuals with this disorder are frequently distressed at their inability to stop tobacco use, particularly when they have serious physical symptoms that are aggravated by tobacco use. Some individuals who are dependent on tobacco may have difficulty remaining in social or occupational situations that prohibit smoking.

Age at onset. Tobacco Dependence usually begins in late adolescence or early adult life.

Course. The course of Tobacco Dependence is variable. Some individuals repeatedly attempt to give up tobacco use without success. Others have a brief course, in that when they experience concern about tobacco use they make a prompt effort to stop and are successful in total cessation, although in many cases they may experience a period of Tobacco Withdrawal lasting from days to weeks. Studies of treatment outcome suggest that the relapse rate is greater than 50% in the first six months, and approximately 70% within the first twelve months. After a year's abstinence subsequent relapse is unlikely.

Impairment. Since tobacco use rarely causes any identifiable state of intoxication as does alcohol, there is no impairment in social or occupational functioning as an immediate and direct consequence of tobacco use.

Prevalence and sex ratio. A large proportion of the adult population of the United States uses tobacco, the prevalence among men being greater than that among women. Among teenage smokers, boys are affected approximately as often as girls. The prevalence of Tobacco Dependence as defined here is not known. Some individuals give up smoking as they grow older without ever meeting the criteria for the disorder. However, since surveys have shown that approximately 50% of smokers express a desire to be able to stop and are unable to do so, and since serious physical disorders that are aggravated by smoking are common, Tobacco Dependence is obviously widespread.

Familial pattern. Cigarette smoking among family members of individuals with Tobacco Dependence is more common than in the general population. However, the evidence for a genetic factor is extremely weak.

Differential diagnosis. The major differential diagnostic problems will be to determine whether or not a particular physical disorder, in an individual who is a heavy smoker, is exacerbated by tobacco use, and how long a period of abstinence from tobacco use justifies the judgment that the disorder is no longer present or is in a state of remission.

Diagnostic criteria for Tobacco Dependence

A. Continuous use of tobacco for at least one month.

B. At least one of the following:

1. serious attempts to stop or significantly reduce the amount of tobacco use on a permanent basis have been unsuccessful

2. attempts to stop smoking have led to the development of Tobacco Withdrawal

3. the individual continues to use tobacco despite a serious physical disorder (e.g., respiratory or cardiovascular disease) that he or she knows is exacerbated by tobacco use.

305.9x   Other, Mixed, or Unspecified Substance Abuse

Other Substance Abuse should be recorded if a substance abused cannot be classified in any of the categories noted above, e.g., glue (inhalants), amyl nitrite.

Mixed Substance Abuse should be noted when the substances abused are from more than one nonalcoholic substance category, e.g., amphetamines and barbiturates. This category should be used only when the specific substances cannot be identified or when the abuse involves so many substances that the clinician prefers to indicate a combination of substances rather than list each specific substance.

Unspecified Substance Abuse should be recorded when a substance abused is unknown.

304.6x   Other Specified Substance Dependence

This category should be used when the individual is dependent on a substance that cannot be classified in any of the previous categories, e.g., codeine or corticosteroids.

304.9x   Unspecified Substance Dependence

This diagnosis can be used as an initial diagnosis in cases in which the specific substance is not yet known.

304.7x   Dependence on a Combination of Opioid and Other Nonalcoholic Substances

This category should be used when the individual is dependent on both an opioid and a nonopioid nonalcoholic substance. An example might be dependence on both heroin and barbiturates. This category should be used only when the specific substances cannot be identified or when the dependence involves so many substances that the clinician prefers to indicate a combination of substances rather than list each specific substance.

304.8x Dependence on a Combination of Substances, Excluding Opioids and Alcohol

This category should be used when the individual is dependent on two or more nonopioid nonalcoholic substances. An example might be dependence on both amphetamines and barbiturates. This category should be used only when the specific substances cannot be identified or when the dependence involves so many substances that the clinician prefers to indicate a combination of substances rather than list each specific substance.

(American Psychiatric Association. *Diagnostic and Statistical Manual of Mental Disorders, Third Edition.* Washington, DC: APA, 1980. Reprinted by permission.)

Appendix 2

Michigan Alcoholism
Screening Test
(MAST)

Name_____   I.D. No._____

Yes	No		Question
☐	☐	**0**	1. Do you enjoy a drink now and then?
☐	■	**2**	2. Do you feel you are a normal drinker?
■	☐	**2**	3. Have you ever awakened the morning after some drinking the night before and found that you could not remember a part of the evening before?
■	☐	**1**	4. Does you wife (or parents) ever worry or complain about your drinking?
☐	■	**2**	5. Can you stop drinking without a struggle after one or two drinks?
■	☐	**1**	6. Do you ever feel guilty about your drinking?
☐	■	**2**	7. Do friends and relatives think you are a normal drinker?
☐	■	**2**	8. Are you always able to stop drinking when you want to?
■	☐	**5**	9. Have you ever attended a meeting of Alcoholics Anonymous (AA)?
■	☐	**1**	10. Have you gotten into fights when drinking?
■	☐	**2**	11. Has your drinking ever created problems with you and your wife?
■	☐	**2**	12. Has your wife (or other family member) ever gone to anyone for help about your drinking?
■	☐	**2**	13. Have you ever lost friends or girlfriends because of your drinking?
■	☐	**2**	14. Have you ever gotten into trouble at work because of drinking?
■	☐	**2**	15. Have you ever lost a job because of drinking?
■	☐	**2**	16. Have you ever neglected your obligations, your family, or your work for 2 or more days because you were drinking?
■	☐	**1**	17. Do you ever drink in the morning?
■	☐	**2**	18. Have you ever been told you have liver trouble? Cirrhosis?
■	☐	**2**	19. Have you ever had Delirium Tremens (D.T.s), severe shaking, heard voices or seen things that weren't there after heavy drinking?
■	☐	**5**	20. Have you ever gone to anyone for help about your drinking?
■	☐	**5**	21. Have you ever been in a hospital because of drinking?
☐	☐	**0**	22. Have you ever been a patient in a psychiatric hospital or on a psychiatric ward of a general hospital?
☐	☐	**0**	23. a. Have you even been seen at a psychiatric or mental health clinic, or gone to any doctor, social worker, or clergyman for help with an emotional problem?
■	☐	**2**	b. Was drinking part of the problem?

■ □ **2** 24. Have you ever been arrested, even for a few hours, because of drunk behavior?

■ □ **2** 25. Have you ever been arrested for drunk driving?

NOTE: Bold–face numerals represent scoring weights of individual items; blackened boxes indicate positive (alcoholic) responses.

From Selzer, M.L.: The Michigan Alcoholism Screening Test: the quest for a new diagnostic instrument. *American Journal of Psychiatry, 127:* 89–94, 1971. ©1971, American Psychiatric Association. Reprinted by permission.

Appendix 3

National Council on Alcoholism Criteria for the Diagnosis of Alcoholism (NCA CRIT)

MAJOR CRITERIA FOR THE DIAGNOSIS OF ALCOHOLISM	

Criterion	Diagnostic Level

TRACK I. PHYSIOLOGICAL AND CLINICAL

A. Physiological Dependency

    1. Physiological dependence as manifested by evidence of a *withdrawal syndrome* when the intake of alcohol is interrupted or decreased without substitution of other sedation. It must be remembered that overuse of other sedative drugs can produce a similar withdrawal state, which should be differentiated from withdrawal from alcohol.

a.	Gross tremor (differentiated from other causes of tremor)	1
b.	Hallucinosis (differentiated from schizophrenic hallucinations or other psychoses)	1
c.	Withdrawal seizures (differentiated from epilepsy and other seizure disorders)	1
d.	Delirium tremens. Usually starts between the first and third day after withdrawal and minimally includes tremors, disorientation, and hallucinations.	1

    2. Evidence of *tolerance* to the effects of alcohol. (There may be a decrease in previously high levels of tolerance late in the course). Although the degree of tolerance to alcohol in no way matches the degree of tolerance to other drugs, the behavioral effects of a given amount of alcohol vary greatly between alcoholic and nonalcoholic subjects.

a.	A blood alcohol level of more than 150 mg without gross evidence of intoxication	1
b.	The consumption of one–fifth of a gallon of whiskey or an equivalent amount of wine or beer daily, for more than one day, by a 180 lb. individual.	1

451

3. Alcoholic "blackout" periods. (Differential diagnosis from purely psychological fugue states and psychomotor seizures.)   2

B. Clinical Major Alcohol-Associated Illnesses. Alcoholism can be assumed to exist if major alcohol-associated illnesses develop in a person who drinks regularly. In such individuals, evidence of physiological and psychological dependence should be searched for:

Fatty degeneration in absence of other known cause	2
Alcoholic hepatitis	1
Laennec's cirrhosis	2
Pancreatitis in the absence of cholelithiasis	2
Chronic gastritis	3

Hematological disorders

    Anemia: hypochromic, normocytic, macrocytic, hemolytic with stomatocytosis, low folic acid   3

    Clotting disorders: prothrombin elevation, thrombocytopenia   3

Wernicke-Korsakoff syndrome	2
Alcoholic cerebellar degeneration	1

Cerebral degeneration in absence of Alzheimer's disease or arteriosclerosis   2

Central pontine myelinolysis ⎱	diagnosis only	2
Marchiafava-Bignami's disease ⎰	possible postmortem	2
Peripheral neuropathy (see also beriberi)		2
Toxic amblyopia		3
Alcohol myopathy		2
Alcoholic cardiomyopathy		2
Beriberi		3
Pellagra		3

TRACK II. BEHAVIORAL, PSYCHOLOGICAL, AND ATTITUDINAL

All chronic conditions of psychological dependence occur in dynamic equilibrium with intrapsychic and interpersonal consequences. In alcoholism, similarly, there are varied effects on character and family. Like other chronic relapsing diseases, alcoholism produces vocational, social, and physical impairments. Therefore, the implications of these disruptions must be evaluated and related to the individual and his pattern of alcoholism. The following behavior patterns show psychological dependence on alcohol in alcoholism:

1. Drinking despite strong medical contraindication known to patient.   1

2. Drinking despite strong, identified, social contraindication (job loss for intoxication, marriage disruption because of drinking, arrest for intoxication, driving while intoxicated).   1

3. Patient's subjective complaint of loss of control of alcohol consumption.   2

MINOR CRITERIA FOR THE DIAGNOSIS OF ALCOHOLISM

	Diagnostic
Criterion	*Level*

TRACK I. PHYSIOLOGICAL AND CLINICAL
A. Direct Effects (ascertained by examination)
   1. Early:

Odor of alcohol on breath at time of medical appointment	2

   2. Middle:

Alcoholic facies	2
Vascular engorgement of face	2
Toxic amblyopia	3
Increased incidence of infections	3
Cardiac arrhythmias	3
Peripheral neuropathy (see also Major Criteria, Track I, B)	2

   3. Late (see Major Criteria, Track I, B)
B. Indirect Effects
   1. Early:

Tachycardia	3
Flushed face	3
Nocturnal diaphoresis	3

   2. Middle:

Ecchymoses on lower extremities, arms, or chest	3
Cigarette or other burns on hands or chest	3
Hyperreflexia, or if drinking heavily, hyporeflexia (permanent hyporeflexia may be a residuum of alcoholic polyneuritis)	3

   3. Late:

Decreased tolerance	3

C. Laboratory Tests
   1. Major — Direct

Blood alcohol level at any time of more than 300 mg/100 ml	1
Level of more than 100 mg/100 ml in routine examination	1

   2. Major — Indirect

Serum osmolality (reflects blood alcohol levels): every 22.4 increase over 200 mOsm/liter reflects 50 mg/100 ml alcohol	2

   3. Minor — Indirect
   Results of alcohol ingestion

Hypoglycemia	3
Hypochloremic alkalosis	3
Low magnesium level	2
Lactic acid elevation	3
Transient uric acid elevation	3
Potassium depletion	3

   Indications of liver abnormality

SGPT elevation	2
SGOT elevation	3
BSP elevation	2

Bilirubin elevation	2
Urinary urobilinogen elevation	2
Serum A/G ratio reversal	2

Blood and blood clotting

Anemia hypochromic, normocytic, macrocytic, hemolytic with stomatocytosis, low folic acid	3
Clotting disorders prothrombin elevation, thrombocytopenia	3

ECG abnormalities

Cardiac arrhythmias, tachycardia, T waves dimpled, cloven, or spinous, atrial fibrillation, ventricular premature contractions, abnormal P waves	2

EEG abnormalities

Decreased or increased REM sleep, depending on phase	3
Loss of delta sleep	3
Other reported findings	3
Decreased immune response	3
Decreased response to Synacthen test	3
Chromosomal damage from alcoholism	3

TRACK II. BEHAVIORAL, PSYCHOLOGICAL, AND ATTITUDINAL

A. Behavioral

    1. Direct effects

        Early:

Gulping drinks	3
Surreptitious drinking	2
Morning drinking (assess nature of peer group behavior)	2

        Middle:

Repeated conscious attempts at abstinence	2

        Late:

Blatant indiscriminate use of alcohol	1
Skid row or equivalent social level	2

    2. Indirect effects

        Early:

Medical excuses from work for variety of reasons	2
Shifting from one alcoholic beverage to another	2
Preference for drinking companions, bars, and taverns	2
Loss of interest in activities not directly associated with drinking	2

        Late:

Chooses employment that facilitates drinking	3
Frequent automobile accidents	3
History of family members undergoing psychiatric treatment; school and behavioral problems in children	3
Frequent change of residence for poorly defined reasons	3
Anxiety–relieving mechanisms, such as telephone calls inappropriate in time, distance, person, or motive (telephonitis)	2
Outbursts of rage and suicidal gestures while drinking	2

B. Psychological and Attitudinal
    1. Direct Effects
        Early:
            When talking freely, makes frequent reference to drinking
            alcohol, people being "bombed," "stoned," etc., or ad-
            mits drinking more than peer group   2
        Middle:
            Drinking to relieve anger, insomnia, fatigue, depression,
            social discomfort   2
        Late:
            Psychological symptoms consistent with permanent
            organic brain syndrome (see also Major Criteria, Track
            I, B)   2
    2. Indirect effects
        Early:
            Unexplained changes in family, social, and business rela-
            tionships; complaints about wife, job and friends   3
            Spouse makes complaints about drinking behavior,
            reported by patient or spouse   2
            Major family disruptions; separation, divorce, threats of
            divorce   3
            Job loss (due to increasing interpersonal difficulties),
            frequent job changes, financial difficulties   3
        Late:
            Overt expression of more regressive defense mechanisms;
            denial, projection, etc.   3
            Resentment, jealousy, paranoid attitudes   3
            Symptoms of depression: isolation, crying, suicidal pre-
            occupation   3
            Feelings that he is "losing his mind"   2

Diagnostic Level 1. Classical, definite, obligatory: A person who fits this
    criterion must be diagnosed as being alcoholic.
Diagnostic Level 2. Probable, frequent, indicative: A person who satisfies this
    criterion is under strong suspision of alcohooism; other corroborative evi-
    dence should be obtained.
Diagnostic Level 3. Potential, possible, incidental: These manifestations are
    common in people with alcoholism, but do not by themselves give a
    strong indication of its existence. They may arouse suspicion, but signi-
    ficant other evidence is needed before the diagnosis is made.

From Criteria Committee, National Council on Alcoholism. Criteria for the
diagnosis of alcoholism. *Annals of Internal Medicine,* 77:249–258, 1972.
Reprinted by permission.

Modified NCA Criteria for the Detection of Alcoholism (MODCRIT)

This is a modified version of the original NCA Criteria for the diagnosis of alcoholism (NCA CRIT). This version has been field-tested during the past five years, and some minor modifications have been made.

Name_____   Date of Birth_____

Date_____   Date of Admission _____

Hosp. I.D. No. _____   Room Number_____

Years of Education_____   Sex _____

A. Psychological and Attitudinal Indicators (Track II) *Minor Criteria*

	Criterion	Diagnostic Level	Comments
	1. Direct Effects		
	Early:		
(1)	a. When talking freely, makes frequent reference to drinking alcohol, people being "bombed", "stoned," etc., or admits drinking more than peer group.	2	
	Middle:		
(2)	b. Drinking to relieve anger, insomnia, fatigue, depression, socal discomfort.	2	
	Late:		
(3)	c. Psychological symptoms consistent with permanent organic brain syndrome (see also Major Criteria, Track 1, B).	2	
	2. Indirect effects		
	Early:		
(4)	a. Unexplained changes in family, social and business relationships; complaints about wife, job and friends.	3	

	Criterion	Diagnostic Level	Comments
(5)	b. Spouse makes complaints about drinking behavior, reported by patient or spouse.	2	
(6)	c. Major family disruptions; separation; divorce, threats of divorce.	3	
(7)	d. Job loss (due to increasing interpersonal difficulties), frequent job changes, financial difficulties.	3	
	Late:		
(8)	e. Overt expression of more regressive defense mechanisms; denial, projection, etc.	3	
(9)	f. Resentment, jealousy, paranoid attitudes.	3	
(10)	g. Symptoms of depression: isolation, crying, suicidal preoccupation.	3	
(11)	h. Feelings that he is "losing his mind."	2	

B. Behavioral Indicators (Track II) *Minor Criteria*

	Criterion	Diagnostic Level	Comments
	1. Direct Effects		
	Early:		
(12)	a. Gulping drinks	3	
(13)	b. Surreptitious drinking	2	
(14)	c. Morning drinking (assess nature of peer group behavior)	2	
	Middle:		
(15)	d. Repeated conscious attempts at abstinence	2	
	Late:		
(16)	e. Blatant indiscriminate use of alcohol	1	
(17)	f. Skid Row or equivalent social level	2	
	2. Indirect Effects		
	Early:		
(18)	a. Medical excuses from work for variety of reasons.	2	
(19)	b. Shifting from one alcoholic beverage to another.	2	
(20)	c. Preference for drinking companions, bars and taverns.	2	
(21)	d. Loss of interest in activities not directly associated with drinking.	2	
	Late:		
(22)	e. Chooses employment that facilitates drinking	3	
(23)	f. Frequent automobile accidents	3	
(24)	g. History of family members undergoing psychiatric treatment; school and behavioral problems in children.	3	
(25)	h. Frequent change of residence for poorly defined reasons.	3	

		Criterion	Diagnostic Level	Comments
(26)	i.	Anxiety–relieving mechanisms, such as, telephone calls inappropriate in times, distance, person or motive (telephonitis)	2	
(27)	j.	Outbursts of rage and suicidal gestures while drinking	2	

C. Indicators of Psychological Dependency (Track II) *Major Criteria*

		Criterion	Diagnostic Level	Comments
(28)	1.	Drinking despite strong medical contradiction known to patient	1	
(29)	2.	Drinking despite strong, identified social contraindication (job loss for intoxication, marriage disruption because of drinking, arrest for intoxication, driving while intoxicated).	1	
(30)	3.	Patient's subjective complaint of loss of control of alcohol consumption.	2	

D. Indicators of Physiological Dependency (Track I) *Major Criteria*

		Criterion	Diagnostic Level	Comments
(31)	1.	Alcoholic "blackout" periods. (Differential diagnosis from purely psychological fugue states and psychomotor seizures.)	2	
	2.	Withdrawal syndrome: when the intake of alcohol is interrupted or decreased without substitution or other sedation.		
(32)	a.	Gross tremor (differentiated from other causes of tremor.	1	
(33)	b.	Hallucinosis (differentiated from schizophrenic hallucinations or other psychoses.)	1	
(34)	c.	Withdrawal seizures (differentiated from epilepsy and other seizure disorders.)	1	
(35)	d.	Delirium tremens. Usually starts between the first and third day after withdrawal and minimally includes tremors, disorientation and hallucinations.	1	

INTERVIEWERS COMMENTS

After Jacobson, G.R.; Niles, D.H.; Moberg, D.P.; Mandehr, E.; Dusso, L.: Identifying alcoholic and problem–drinking drivers: Wisconsin's field test of a modified NCA criteria for the diagnosis of alcoholism. In *Currents in Alcoholism, Vol. VI: Treatment, Rehabilitation, and Epidemiology*. Galanter, M. (Ed.). New York: Grune & Stratton, 1979.

Appendix 5

State Medical Society of Wisconsin, Guideline Admission Criteria for Chemical Dependency Treatment Services

GUIDELINE ADMISSION CRITERIA
FOR CHEMICAL DEPENDENCY TREATMENT SERVICES

The State Medical Society Committee on Alcoholism and Other Drug Abuse has developed with the approval of the SMS Board of Directors, guideline admission criteria for the following chemical dependency treatment services:
(1) Detoxification
(2) Inpatient Evaluation and Rehabilitation
(3) Outpatient Treatment

DETOXIFICATION
Admission to the hospital depends on the presence of one or more of the following:
1. Presence of a clustering of withdrawal symptoms (not all inclusive):
   a. tremulousness (inner/outer shakes)
   b. insomnia
   c. irritability/restlessness
   d. vague somatic complaints
   e. nausea, vomiting, diarrhea
   f. diaphoresis
   g. headaches
   h. abnormal vital signs
   i. mental confusion/fluctuating orientation
   j. hallucinations, hallucinosis
   k. psychoses
   l. seizures
   m. delirium tremens
   n. stupor
   o. rhinorrhea
2. Presence of associated medical problems.

3. Suspected alcohol and drug dependency.
4. History of withdrawal syndrome.
5. History of prolonged intoxication.
6. Signs and symptoms that may be due to specific chemical dependency, not listed above, but recognized by the physician.

INPATIENT EVALUATION AND REHABILITATION

Admission to the inpatient program depends on medical stability, the absence of acute withdrawal symptoms which may interfere with rehabilitation (and/or completion of detoxification), and the presence of one or more of the following:

1. Need for environmental control.
2. Need for 24-hour behavioral monitoring and confrontation.
3. Counterproductive medical or psychosocial situation.
4. Presence of a clustering of the following:
   a. Neurological psychological symptoms
      1) denial
      2) anguish
      3) mood fluctuations
      4) over-reaction to stress
      5) lowered stress tolerance
      6) impaired ability to concentrate
      7) limited attention span
      8) high level of distractability
      9) extreme negative emotions
      10) extreme anxiety
      11) extreme depression
   b. Reversible memory impairments
   c. Thought process impairment
      1) impairment in abstract thinking
      2) limitations in ability to conceptualize
      3) periodic episodes of mental confusion
5. Previous outpatient treatment has failed.
6. Multiple drug dependency.

OUTPATIENT TREATMENT

Admission to outpatient treatment depneds on one or more of the following:

1. Patient does not fit criteria for detoxification, specifically, patient does not present acute withdrawal symptoms (refer to detoxification criteria).
2. Patient does not fit criteria for inpatient evaluation and rehabilitation program.
3. Patient has ability to remain sober for at least five days.
4. Patient is willing to take Antabuse if medically recommended.
5. Patient is willing to attend AA.
6. Patient is willing to have family involvement.

From Wisconsin State Medical Society, Committee on Alcohol and Other Drug Abuse. Guideline admission criteria for chemical dependency treatment services. *Wisconsin Medical Journal, 80:*11, 5, 1981. Reprinted by permission.

Appendix 6
Nursing History Form for Use with Chemically Dependent Patients

NURSE'S ADMISSION SHEET

Time _____

Condition at admission _____
_____

Reason for Admission: _____
_____

Drug _____
Amount _____
Last Used _____
Drug _____
Amount _____
Last Used _____
Drug _____
Amount _____
Last Used _____
Drug _____
Amount _____
Last Used _____
Drug _____
Amount _____
Last Used _____
Special Diet _____
_____
Allergies: _____
_____
Medical Needs/Problems _____
_____
_____
_____
_____
_____
_____
_____
_____
_____

Withdrawal Symptoms:
A.M. Tremors _____ Black Out _____
Hall. _____ Conv. _____
_____
_____

FORM 726 REV. 5-81   OVER

Name

Age
Date
M.D._____ Room_____
Time of admission:_____ By _____
How _____ Accompanied By _____
                                TEMP _____
                                BAL _____
                                Ht. _____
                                Wt. _____

Eating	Tremor	Sleep	Sensor.	Halluc.	Contct.	Agitat.	Sweats	Temp	Pulse	Convul.	B/P	TOT.

Item ✓/0	Locked	cbpd	locker	transferred
Clothes				
Valise				
Purse				
Billfold				
Toilet Art.				

Toothbrush _____ Toothpaste _____ Comb _____
Medicine _____ If yes, refer to med sheet
Orientation: Family _____ Visiting Hrs _____
Restr/PJ's _____ Prosthesis_____
Your Room # _____ Call Bell _____
Ate Last _____ Meals-Times-Tray _____
Dining Rm_____ Smoking Allowed_____
Shower/Bath_____ Telephones_____Labwork_____
Car____License#_____Security Not._____

General Appearance   Key:
                                      1. Rash
                                      2. Scar
                                      3. Bruise
                                      4. Other

Signature _____ Signature _____

461

Admission Assessment _____   Psych History: _____
_____   _____
_____   Dx: _____
_____   Treatment _____
_____   _____
_____   Suicide Ideation _____
_____   Suicide Attempts _____
_____   _____
_____   Current Status:
_____   Alert_____ Agitated_____Eye Cont._____
_____   Depressed _____
_____   Feelings about admission _____
_____   _____
_____   _____
_____   Inappropriate Behavior (if any) _____
_____   _____
_____   _____
_____   Any drugs brought in?_____
_____   Drug Free Environment Explained_____
_____   Signature: _____
_____   Transfer to Rehab-Date _____ .
Morning Rounds_____   Treatments _____
Family _____   _____
                                        _____
Care of Children:_____   _____
                                        Scheduled Appts: _____
Job:_____Hours_____   _____
Voc. _____   _____
Legal _____   _____
Staff: Nursing_____   Current Meds _____
MD/PA_____Clergy_____   _____
Counselor_____Family_____   W/D Meds Start: _____
For summary of needs and proposed   Finished: _____
action plan, refer to Interim   General Comments: i.e., Program Involv,
Care Plan   _____
                                        _____
_____   _____
                                        _____
Signature   _____
                                        _____

                                                        Signature

Reprinted by courtesy of De Paul Rehabilitation Hospital, Inc.

Appendix 7

Selective Severity Assessment (SSA) in the Identification of Withdrawal Status

Signs and Symptoms		Present	Guidelines
1. Eating Disturbances		*Based on Meal Prior to Exam*	New admission by history. Substantial snack may be considered a meal. If patient does not eat — score it — don't interpret why.
	0	= Ate and enjoyed all of it.	
	3+-4+	= Ate about half of what was given.	
	7+	= Ate none at all.	
2. Tremor	1+	= Tremor not visibly apparent, but can be felt by the examiner placing his fingertips lightly against the patient's fingertips.	Automatic 7 for tongue tremor & NOTIFY PHYSICIAN immediately. Don't attempt to judge if tremor is from anxiety or withdrawal. Older patient with senile tremor — score it.
	3+-4+	= Tremor is moderate with arms extended.	
	7+	= Marked tremor even when arms are not extended.	
3. Sleep Disturbances	1+	= Patient gets up once.	New Patient by history. After 1st night by staff observation. Score — even if normally works nights and stays up. Weekends — score from scheduled light out time.
	4+	= Awake half the night.	
	7+	= Completely sleepless.	

SELECTIVE SEVERITY ASSESSMENT (SSA) (continued)

Signs and Symptoms	Present	De Paul Guidelines
4. Clouding of Sensorium	0 = No evidence of clouding of sensorium. 1+ = Cannot do serial 7 substractions or knows correct date but is uncertain. 2+ = Disoriented for time by no more than 2 calendar days. 3+ = Disoriented for time by more than 2 calendar days.	Not confusion — strictly orientation and serial 7's. Patient with obvious learning disability. Do not score failure on serial 7.
5. Hallucinations. Record frequency, content, intensity and if patient has insight into hallucination.	0 = No hallucinations. 1+ = Auditory hallucinations. 2+ = Visual hallucinations. 3+ = Non-fused auditory and visual. 4+ = Fused auditory and visual.	REPORT IMMEDIATELY TO PHYSICIAN. Since patient may be progressing to Stage II or III. Call on each individual episode. If no action taken, call MEDICAL DIRECTOR. Score based on time since last SSA.
6. Quality of Contact	*Awareness of examiner and people around him/her.* 1+ = Drifts off slightly. 2+ = Appears to be in contact with examiner, but is unaware of or oblivious to the surroundings or other people around him/her. 3+-4+ = Periodically appears to become detached. 7+ = Makes no contact with the examiner.	Critical in relation to progression of Stage I → II → III. Observe in period just prior to SSA.
7. Agitation	*Based on amount of movement (not anxiety or tremor).* 1+ = Somewhat more than normal activity. 3+-4+ = Moderately fidgety and restless. 7+ = Paces back and forth during most of the interview.	Not anxiety or tremor. Measure of movement or inability to be still.
8. Paroxysmal Sweats	1+ = Barely perceptible sweating. 3+-4+ = Beads of sweat obviously observable. 7+ = Drenching sweats.	Palms or forehead damp = 1

SELECTIVE SEVERITY ASSESSMENT (SSA) (continued)

Signs and Symptoms	Present	De Paul Guidelines
9. Temperature	1 99.5 or below 2 99.6 — 99.9 3 100 — 100.4 4 100.5 — 100.9 5 101 — 101.4 6 101.5 — 101.9 7 102 — 102.4 8 102.5 — 102.9 9 103 and over	If temperature is over 102, notify physician immediately.
10. Pulse	1 70 — 79 2 80 — 89 3 90 — 99 4 100 — 109 5 110 — 119 6 120 — 129 7 130 — 139 8 140 — 149 9 150 and over	
11. Convulsion	NOTIFY PHYSICIAN	

General Comments: May give 0 except with temperature and pulse. Be objective.
If score 〉20 — discuss with physician.
If lower and you are concerned on any specific mentioned above — CALL.

Modified after Gross, M.H.; Lewis, E.; Hastey, J.: Acute aclohol withdrawal syndrome. In *The Biology of Alcoholism*, *Vol. 3: Clinical Pathology.* Kissin, B. and Begleiter, H. (Eds.). New York: Plenum Press, 1974; and Gross, M.; Lewis, E.; Nagarajan, M.: An improved system for assessing the acute alcoholic psychosis and related states in alcohol intoxication and withdrawal: experimental studies. In *Advances in Experimental Medicine and Biology, Vol. 35.* Gross, M. (Ed.). New York: Plenum Press, 1973.

SSA SCORES

		Present	*Overall*	*Average*
1.	Eating Disturbance			
2.	Tremor			
3.	Sleep disturbance			
4.	Clouding of sensorium			
5.	Hallucinations			
6.	Quality of contact			
7.	Agitation			
8.	Paroxysmal sweats			
9.	Temperature			
10.	Pulse			
11.	Convulsions			
	TOTALS			

Admissions SSA Score _____

Day 1 SSA Score   _____

Day 2 SSA Score   _____

Day 3 SSA Score   _____

SCORING

0 − 19	Mild alcohol withdrawal
20 − 24	Moderate alcohol withdrawal
Over 25	Severe alcohol withdrawal

Narcotic Withdrawal Worksheet

ABSTINENCE SIGNS IN SEQUENTIAL APPEARANCE AFTER LAST DOSE OF NARCOTIC IN PATIENTS WITH WELL ESTABLISHED PARENTERAL HABITS															
Time and date															
Grade 0															
Craving															
Anxiety															
Grade 1															
Yawning															
Perspiration															
Lacrimation															
Rhinorrhea															
"Yen" sleep															
Grade 2 Increase in above signs plus:															
Mydriasis															
Gooseflesh (piloerection)															
Tremors (muscle twitches)															
Hot & Cold flashes															
Aching bones and muscles															
Anorexia															
Grade 3 Increased intensity of grade 2 plus:															
Insomnia															
Increased BP															
Increased temp.															
Increased resp. rate and depth															
Increased pulse															
Restlessness															
Nausea															
Grade 4 Increased intensity of above plus:															
Febrile facies															
Position-curled up on hard surface															
Vomiting															
Diarrhea															
Weight loss 5 lb. daily															
Spontaneous ejaculation or orgasm															
Hemoconcentration															
Blood pressure, pulse, temp.															

Reprinted by courtesy of De Paul Rehabilitation Hospital, Inc.

Appendix 9

The Twelve Steps
of Alcoholics Anonymous

THE TWELVE STEPS

1. We admitted we were powerless over alcohol — that our lives had become unmanageable.
2. Came to believe that a Power greater than ourselves could restore us to sanity.
3. Made a decision to turn our will and our lives over to the care of God as we understood Him.
4. Made a searching and fearless moral inventory of ourselves.
5. Admitted to God, to ourselves, and to another human being the exact nature of our wrongs.
6. Were entirely ready to have God remove all these defects of character.
7. Humbly asked Him to remove our shortcomings.
8. Made a list of all persons we had harmed, and became willing to make amends to them all.
9. Made direct amends to such people wherever possible, except when to do so would injure them or others.
10. Continued to take personal inventory and when we were wrong promptly admitted it.
11. Sought through prayer and meditation to improve our conscious contact with God as we understood Him, praying only for knowledge of His will for us and the power to carry that out.
12. Having had a spiritual awakening as the result of these Steps, we tried to carry this message to alcoholics, and to practice these principles in all our affairs.

Appendix 10

The Twelve Traditions
of Alcoholics Anonymous

THE TWELVE TRADITIONS

1. Our common welfare should come first; personal recovery depends upon AA unity.
2. For our group purpose there is but one ultimate authority — a loving God as He may express Himself in our group conscience. Our leaders are but trusted servants; they do not govern.
3. The only requirement for AA membership is a desire to stop drinking.
4. Each group should be autonomous except in matters affecting other groups or AA as a whole.
5. Each group has but one primary purpose — to carry its message to the alcoholic who still suffers.
6. An AA group ought never endorse, finance, or lend the AA name to any related facility or outside enterprise, lest problems of money, property, and prestige divert us from our primary purpose.
7. Every AA group ought to be fully self-supporting, declining outside contributions.
8. Alcoholics Anonymous should remain forever nonprofessional, but our service centers may employ special workers.
9. AA, as such, ought never be organized; but we may create service boards or committees directly responsible to those they serve.
10. Alcoholics Anonymous has no opinion on outside issues; hence the AA name ought never be drawn into public controversy.
11. Our public relations policy is based on attraction rather than promotion; we need always maintain personal anonymity at the level of press, radio, and films.

12.   Anonymity is the spiritual foundation of all our Traditions, ever reminding us to place principles before personalities.

Reprinted by permission of A.A. World Services, Inc.

Index